DEFENCE DIPLOMACY
&
NATIONAL SECURITY STRATEGY

Views from the Global South

Editors

Ian Liebenberg
Dirk Kruijt
Shrikant Paranjpe

SUN PRESS

Defence Diplomacy and National Security Strategy: Views from the Global South

Published by African Sun Media under the SUN PReSS imprint

All rights reserved

Copyright © 2020 African Sun Media and the authors

This publication was subjected to an independent double-blind peer evaluation by the publisher.

The authors and the publisher have made every effort to obtain permission for and acknowledge the use of copyrighted material. Refer all enquiries to the publisher.

No part of this book may be reproduced or transmitted in any form or by any electronic, photographic or mechanical means, including photocopying and recording on record, tape or laser disk, on microfilm, via the Internet, by e-mail, or by any other information storage and retrieval system, without prior written permission by the publisher.

Views reflected in this publication are not necessarily those of the publisher.

First edition 2020

ISBN 978-1-928480-54-9
ISBN 978-1-928480-55-6 (e-book)
https://doi.org/10.18820/9781928480556

Set in Dante MT Std 12/15

Cover design, typesetting and production by African Sun Media

SUN PReSS is an imprint of African Sun Media. Scholarly, professional and reference works are published under this imprint in print and electronic formats.

This publication can be ordered from:
orders@africansunmedia.co.za
Takealot: bit.ly/2monsfl
Google Books: bit.ly/2k1Uilm
africansunmedia.store.it.si *(e-books)*
Amazon Kindle: amzn.to/2ktL.pkL

Visit africansunmedia.co.za for more information.

Contents

Acknowledgements vii

Introduction 1

1   Brazil's National Defence Strategy, Defence Diplomacy and Management of Strategic Resources 13
Adriana A. Marques and Jacintho Maia Neto

2   Chilean Defence Policy: Moving forward 33
Andrés Villar and Francisco Rojas

3   Colombia – Not So Unusual After All: A case study on the transnational making of the boundary between 'defence' and 'public security' 49
Manuela Trindade Viana

4   Cuba's Defence Diplomacy: Hard and soft power, 1959-2018 67
Dirk Kruijt

5   Venezuela's Defence Diplomacy under Chávez and Maduro (1999-2018) 87
Dirk Kruijt

6   South Africa's Defence Diplomacy in Africa 101
Ian Liebenberg and Raymond Steenkamp-Fonseca

7   National Security in Complex Times: The South African military dimension 127
Shadrack Ramokgadi, Tobie Beukes and Ian Liebenberg

8   Namibia's Defence Diplomacy: A first exploration 155
André du Pisani

9   The Trajectory of Zimbabwe's Foreign Policy and Defence Diplomacy 179
Torque Mude and Sadiki Maeresera

10	China in a Global World	189
	Ian Liebenberg and Justin van der Merwe	
11	India's Military Diplomacy	207
	Rahul Anand Maslekar	
12	Managing India's Strategic Resources and Reserves	221
	Ajey Lele	
13	India's Security Strategy: Beyond deliberate ambiguity?	239
	Shrikant Paranjpe	
	Epilogue	265
	Index	281
	Contributing Authors	287

Acknowledgements

The editors would like to acknowledge the financial and moral support of the Dean, Professor Sam Tshehla, Faculty of Military Science, and Stellenbosch University during the course of editing and in preparation of the final manuscript. Gratitude is also extended to the Deanery of the Faculty of Military Science, Stellenbosch, for providing seed funding for the publication of the first edition of this work in South Africa. This consistent support from the Office of the Dean is deeply appreciated as always.

We also express our appreciation for the professional services rendered by the staff at African Sun Media, especially Wikus van Zyl for his kind and enthusiastic support and most cordial assistance during the publication process, as well as Davida van Zyl for her careful, professional, kind, dedicated and always prompt assistance during the editing process.

We convey our gratitude for the always supportive attitude and splendid spirit by the team of researchers and assistants at the Centre of Military Studies, Faculty of Military Sciences of Stellenbosch University, housed at the South African Military Academy in Saldanha. Their support, critical input and at times taking over responsibilities of one of the resident editors provided space to spend quality time on this work. We wish to thank Jeanne Enslin for superb language editing and assistance with the source lists.

Likewise, many colleagues within the Faculty of Military Science, academics, theorists and expert practitioners in the broad national and international networks from which the editors could tap, should be recognised. In this case, especially colleagues and peers from Latin American countries, the continent of Africa (especially Southern Africa) and India are relevant. Inputs on drafts of our work by academicians from BRICS countries such as Russia need to be mentioned, especially Professor Emeritus Vladimir Shubin, former Deputy Director of the Institute for African Studies, Moscow.

Finally, our thanks are due to the panel of three anonymous peer reviewers (national and international) who, while very positive about the value of the work, provided constructive and meaningful criticism that added immense value to the end product. No one has exclusive control of, and command over, the heights of knowledge creation. The critique of these peers during the double-blind review process managed by African Sun Media ensured a creative soundboard and platform for dialogue between editors and contributors to enrich the work.

The support of the various universities, academic platforms, think tanks and dedicated research foundations with which we were and are in contact or associated with is highly appreciated.

THE EDITORS

Introduction

International relations have since the earliest of times reflected many dimensions. At some point, mostly due to Western academic influence, the term "international politics" dominated the scene and became the framework of analysis with the term "nation" as a core assumption. The term international politics brings to mind power to influence or coerce either through soft measures such as policy and dialogue (diplomacy) or hard measures such as the projection of military power. The notion of nation as broadly understood today is seen as having some classic roots. The notion of the Greek city states is frequently mentioned whether in terms of cooperation or war. The Greek city states Sparta and Athens went to war as an example of a power struggle, but also cooperated with other Greek city states when necessary to defend themselves against contending powers such as the Persian Empire.

In Europe, the feudal state and an era of monarchs and rule by the royalty were gradually replaced by the formation of the nation-state. The transition to the nation-state frequently took place through the mobilisation for and enactment of internal wars in Europe. Consider the rise of Prussia (later Germany), France and the torturous unification of Italy in the 19th century. Though conflict played an important role, attempts at some minimal consensus and mutual accommodation to minimise war and its negative consequences were also seen. In this regard, the Treaty of Westphalia (1648) as an early attempt to restrict war in Europe is notable. The treaty set about a process with long-term consequences. The notion of national sovereignty was born and this idea and practice were to spread far. The notion of nation-building and the use of military as instrument of the state is a close and traditional one, ever since the beginnings of the Greek city state. In different forms, even if they were ancient kingdoms, i.e. in Africa, the same applies. The holders of power, for example the King or Chieftains in order to maintain security for their own collective, and dominance over others if deemed necessary, are closely linked to military capacity either as a threat or direct tool. Ancient Egypt is one example.

Early attempts at nation-building were to spread the concept and its material outcomes outside Europe through (violent) colonisation and later empire-building by Western powers of large areas and communities outside Europe were to experience the results. To a large extent, the European outlook imposed on the former colonies an artificial nationhood, as previously colonised communities were grouped together mostly along the lines of the geographical territories as dominated by colonial powers such as The Netherlands, Portugal, Spain, Belgium, Germany, (then) Great Britain, France and Italy. The winds of change in Asia and Africa during the late 1950s and 1960s saw the Asian and African countries becoming independent. In the case of Africa, the newly independent states followed the previous borders as defined and decided on in Europe during the Berlin Conference (1884/1885) in which Bismarck played a leading role to formalise the colonisation of Africa by Western powers. In the case of Asia, the Dutch, French and the British withdrew in the face of independence movements and their own financial limitations of being able to hold on to the empires. In South Asia, the process began in the late 1940s with the British withdrawal from the Indian subcontinent followed by the Dutch and the French from Southeast Asia in the 1950s.

In the East, areas ruled by the Dutch were clustered together during colonial rule. India became independent in 1947 after years of struggle against British colonialism. Britain, as an alleged "Empire on which the sun never sets" dominated India from 1757 to 1947. Ever since the Indian Mutiny during 1857/1858 the Indian people fought for their independence; a struggle that succeeded in 1947 with the declaration of independence. India's struggle set a historic example. It was a struggle marked by the important role that mass passive resistance (under Mahatma Gandhi's influence) could play in achieving national liberation and establishing a democracy that still lasts. The former British India was to split into India and Pakistan, the latter a Muslim majority state which later was to see a military coup d'état. Since 1947, a long-lasting conflict over the Kashmir began which still lasts today and recently heated up again.

China after a period of relative disruptive Western colonial intervention returned to what perhaps can be called the geographical space of a perceived "greater" China as many ages before. While China became a republic in 1912 under Sun Yat-sen it was to experience a wide-ranging and destructive Japanese invasion before World War II and a civil war between communists and nationalists that was to end with the defeated nationalists establishing a nationalist government in exile in 1949 on the island of Taiwan (the latter seen by the Chinese government as an errant province). In a sense then, the European model of nationalism (or in cases a paradigm widely accepted in current discourse) had long-term consequences, some of which we still see today. Actions by major global actors involve elements of national interests and touches foreign policy conceptualisation, making and executing. In tandem, defence diplomacy as interconnected to foreign policy plays an important role. A broader look at this stands as one rationale of this edited work. In the case here, the cases under discussion were all earlier seen as the "Third World", with perhaps China more befitting the term "Second World".

International political frameworks or theories built around the nation as a central construct brought in theoretical approaches (or paradigms, if you wish) such as realism (later revised and refined to include neorealism), the liberal institutional approach, dependency theory and developmental theories (call it a critical sociological approach to world or global politics) and in later years, gender and environment orientated frameworks. In terms of international politics, a shift occurred from international relations or politics to what can best be described today as *global politics*. Numerous actors other than the state became part of the global socio-political and economic setting; a process partly facilitated by what some describe as globalisation. Much of this historical evolution – in cases even an evolution-revolution – to borrow a term from Thomas Hanna, made the study of global politics much more interesting, but also more complex (especially if one assumes that we live in a world that some observers choose to call a post-truth society). No single approach dominates any longer and many more actors than the state (or nation-state) have entered real developments and theoretical discourse. In the case of this work, the notion of the state or nation as entity remains part of our analysis.

Contemporary political and military developments are much more convoluted, consistently interactive and multilayered – in short – more complex. Due to globalisation and the spread of liberal capitalism, many more actors became involved such as civil-society groups, multinational companies, trans-national business interests, international organisations and non-governmental groups, global interactive networks united on an issue-related consensus (i.e. ecology, deep ecology, nature conservation, human rights, gender rights, climate change). Today, it makes more sense to talk about *global politics*, whatever one may wish to understand under the term in the context of both nation-state and non-state actors as participants in the world order – or perhaps more cynical, increasing global disorder.

Simultaneously, the idea of larger, medium and smaller national actors, including nation-states, has remained. We still see "national clashes" of interest. The cold war era debates revolved around issues of national interests, but are also closely coupled with different ideological angular optics and a social practice – i.e. capitalism versus communism or socialism (the latter broken up into many socialisms such as democratic socialism, socialist and communist parties that participated in national democratic politics, i.e. Euro-socialism). Or consider African socialism and other models of socialism, i.e. Marxism-Leninism, Mao Zedong or Giap's interpretation of communism in Vietnam that played a role, in many cases the ruling ideologies still vexed around national or geographical interests. In various countries communist parties still exist but now abide by the parliamentary rules of law. Think about India, South Africa, Russia, Italy, and Portugal in this regard. In others such as North Korea, the old approach still holds while China is evolving along the lines of what perhaps can be called socialism of a special type.

In Latin America, the Republic of Cuba stands between the choices of losing past gains in socialist terms in favour of (vulgar) capitalism or finding a pathway in between. In the case of Cuba – a country still faced by an aggressive neighbour that, since 1959, keeps its grudges against a smaller country that chose its own historical trajectory; and in doing so kicked far above its political weight in the Non-Aligned Movement (NAM) during the 1970/1980s and on the continent of Africa. Cuba's foreign policy and astute use of politico-military projection played an important role to bring about Namibian independence in 1990 and indirectly contributed to end apartheid, despite covert support from various Western states for the regime in Pretoria.

The Cold War (a term that originated in the West and is mostly used in the West and should perhaps be called the "Cold War syndrome") saw what was viewed as a bipolar world. Whether it was bipolar in the real sense of the word is a different question. At the time, China under Mao followed its own pathway to communism and the country having had numerous internal development challenges enacted through various plans and from time-to-time radically revised or streamlined plans, was somewhat less involved in international conflicts (there were exceptions such as brief support for liberation movements and the building of the railway line between Tanzania and Zambia during the late 1970s). Chinese involvement at the time did bother apartheid Pretoria's leaders as it was viewed as an additional "Red Threat" apart from Moscow's Marxism-Leninism (USSR).

India, the world's largest democracy established early during the decolonisation period is notable in the Global South. In many respects, India set an example of choosing its own international pathway while interacting with the Western economies, even cooperating with the former coloniser, Britain, within the framework of the Commonwealth of Nations; yet acted independently along with the other newly independent states. During the Cold War, India also chose to work closely with the Soviet Union in terms of economic deals, especially where the acquisition of arms was concerned and so maintained a balanced course between dependency on only one power block or another. As independent state, India's leadership in the Non-Aligned Movement (NAM) during the 1970s and 1980s is another example.

In China, the efforts put into the four modernisations project since the 1980s detracted from a unified international foreign policy and a unique defence diplomacy with the exception of some minimal military support for African countries' liberation movements during the 1970s, yet also entertaining exchanges with the USA during Mao's era of "ping-pong" diplomacy.

The Cold War had a wider influence. The Soviet Union and its allies supported liberation movements in their anti-colonial struggles. Africa is one example and so are various other so-called "Third World" countries. Africa was liberating itself and throwing off the shackles of colonialism. Given Africa's experience of colonialism and the effects of what Africans and others saw as neo-colonialism and neo-imperialism, namely a Western/USA-driven post-World War II world order of the "free market", the IMF and World Bank and GATT which kept the core states of the world (the USA and Western Europe) commanding the heights of the global economy, African states faced various choices, none of these easy. After World War II, the USSR, Eastern Europe and China followed a different model, namely various experiments with socialism. Within this complex international scene, African countries had to choose between economic pathways for the future and where they stood in the "East-West conflict".

Various experiments and approaches followed. These were based on the socio-political, developmental conditions, economic strengths or weaknesses, leadership styles and pragmatic ideological choices. This phase saw the growth of regionalism in Asia and Africa. India had hosted the first Asian Relations Conference in Delhi in 1947 to promote a sense of regionalism. The Asian Relations Conference brought together many leaders of the independence movements in Asia. This conference is looked at as the beginning of the attempt to create a sense of regionalism in Asia. This was followed by the Bandung conference of 1955 in Indonesia. This was the first Afro-Asian conference that sought to provide a broader base for the concept of regionalism to include the countries of Africa. The Bandung Conference was a historic event. It tried to spread the concept of regionalism to Asia and Africa. Unfortunately, Bandung was the first and the last Afro-Asian conference to take place.

The end of the Korean War saw the beginning of cold war alliances in Asia. The fundamentals of regionalism – independent understanding of world affairs and peace approaches came under stress due to the alliance system. Pakistan, Iran, Iraq, Turkey, Thailand, Taiwan, Japan, New Zealand and Australia became part of the American system of alliances, while China, Mongolia, the Indo-Chinese states and North Korea became pro-Soviet. Further, the countries of Asia were not able to overcome their intrastate conflicts despite the umbrella of regionalism. The period from Bandung of 1955 to Belgrade of 1961 was a period that saw a movement away from regionalism towards nonalignment.

The spirit of regionalism did, however, continue to grow in the Southeast Asian region. It saw the formulation of Malaysia-Philippines-Indonesia (*MAPHILINDO*) and the Association of Southeast Asia (ASA) that went on to merge in a successful regional organisation Association of Southeast Asian Nations (ASEAN).

The Middle East saw the continuing rivalry between the US and the Soviet Union play its part in the Arab-Israel dispute. African states, for example, had to choose whether to support the liberation struggles of the long-oppressed Palestinian people. In such conditions a choice for Palestinian liberation was bound to stir tensions – then and now. The majority of African states tried to steer clear (at least in policy-speak) from the Western-dominated capitalist pathway. One saw a focus in Africa on African socialism, mixed economies as elsewhere; a choice to steer between the West-East conflicts. These "Third World" countries, as they were pejoratively called in Western political and economic (as well as academic) circles, stood together as countries mostly from the southern hemisphere (today more accurately perhaps referred to as the Global South). They had to find a way in the middle. But most of them had fought or were fighting Western colonialism and its aftermath. The imposition of the Washington consensus and with it liberal capitalism brought deep divisions and kick-started a rich-poor gap that was to increase during the decades thereafter and up till today ensconced in the glib mantra of globalisation. Coupled with this, the much spoken about development theory and modernisation theory benefitted only some.

The "trickle-down" effect of modernisation and the spread of capitalism was not to benefit all. In Asia the Asian tigers rose and saw benefits. So did Japan during the Cold War. Today some would argue that Japan became a "silent giant". In Africa and Latin America, others struggled and were in fact on the receiving end of global capitalist exploitation which in cases bordered on economic destabilisation. In the case of Cuba, a long-term vendetta by the USA followed that still lasts. Non-core or peripheral economies found themselves bound into economic prisons from which escape seemed remote. Latin-America represents a different trajectory while some similarities to other developments on the globe can be discerned.

Latin American and Caribbean nations had become independent in the early 19th century. Only Cuba remained a Spanish colony until 1898 and was then "liberated" by American marines. European military missions (by Germany, France and Great Britain) had shaped and strongly influenced Latin-American armed forces. After World War II, US hegemony in political, financial and defence matters of Latin America and the Caribbean became clear, sometimes underlined by direct military interventions, the last one in Panama in 1989 (in 1903 the US had created the latter country, previously a part of Colombia). The Organization of American States and the Inter-American Defense Latin America structure were instruments of political and military control, reinforced by multiple dictatorships of the "National Security Governments". Following Brazil's coup in 1984, ten similar dictatorships emerged in the region. The only exceptions were the nationalist-progressive military governments in Peru and Panama in the 1970s. The Cuban Revolution (1959) favoured many efforts of establishing "socialist revolutions". With the exception of Nicaragua (1970), all efforts failed. Only between 2000 and 2015, did the major Latin American nations take their distance from their powerful northern neighbour, but at present (2019/2020), neoliberal presidents in the larger nations (Argentina, Brazil, Chile, Colombia, Peru) seek stronger political and military ties with the United States.

The phenomenon of security regimes (or rule by reactionary military juntas) during the Cold War had peculiar, though cynical outcomes. During the 1970s and even the 1980s, Latin American authoritarian regimes drifted closer together under the tutelage of the US. The case of Chile under Pinochet and Argentina under various juntas are examples. In following a zealous anti-communist war, these countries extensively oppressed their own civilian populations with a mass murder of perceived left-wingers – a common phenomenon (in Latin-American political literature, these internal war of state oppression (rather state terrorism) was frequently referred to as a *guerra sucia* or dirty war).

Elsewhere, the state of Israel cooperated with the apartheid regime in terms of offensive nuclear research as well as arms production. For strategic reasons, Israel even briefly cooperated with a brutal dictator on African soil, Idi Amin Dada of Uganda, before relationships soured. The Latin-American military regimes and Israel were not the only ones to cooperate with apartheid South Africa. The nationalist Chinese government on the island of Formosa (Taiwan) in turn also cooperated with South Africa in more than cordial ways. The Pretoria regime developed close relations with military regimes in Argentina and Chile and authoritarian states such as Uruguay and Paraguay, all of them with dismal human rights records. On African soil, South Africa, France and the USA worked with their favourite dictators such as Mobutu of Zaire and even Hastings Banda of Malawi, if needed, including military and arms exchanges. The exchange of arms and arms-related research frequently took place between these states. Uganda under Amin, mentioned above, was an interesting case of falling in and out of favour with the West and some Middle East countries, including Israel.

The end of the cold war brought in new challenges. It saw the rise of ethnic nationalism based right on self-determination. This concept was to give legitimacy to the newly created states of Europe and the newly emergent states such as East Timor, Eritrea, and South Sudan. It also saw the growth of asymmetric warfare in form of the events of 9/11 and its escalating aftermath where states that were seen as non-pliant to the West were toppled at will by the USA and its "coalition of the willing". While there was an apparent switch to a unipolar world order, the eventual emergence of China, resurgent Russia and the post-Maastricht European Union perhaps brought in a sense of multipolarity.

The hegemonic interests, especially of the United States, saw interference in the politics of other countries (as many times earlier on, during the Cold War). The Middle East became especially prone to military intervention by the US under the concept, "coalition of the willing". Compare interventions in Afghanistan and Iraq or take note of the role of the French, the UK and the USA in the intervention in Libya to topple and kill Gadaffi in 2011.

In the case of Libya, regime change was imposed under the guise of the Responsibility to Protect (R2P). Libya apparently was a different case to others in North Africa. In Tunisia, very little Western interference occurred – at least not in military terms. The Arab spring in Tunisia and Egypt brought "regime-change" (in fact only a change of the leader) and no fundamental transition. There was no military interference by a show of Western military force projection in the case of Egypt. In Egypt, regime change took place, but after elections the military returned to power (assuming that the military released the levers of power at all).

The fluidity of global politics can bring about rapid change with (unforeseen) outcomes. Karl Popper's notion of unintended consequences is relevant here. Libya was apparently an exceptional case. There was no inclination from France, the UK and the USA to solve the matter diplomatically or through a negotiated settlement, despite the fact that the African Union (AU), Turkey and Russia proposed a negotiated regime change. These initiatives were briskly sidelined. We will not discuss it for long but an independent Libya, economically stable and growing in stature in Africa and its eccentric leader became an increasing irritant as a pivot of influence. Gadaffi had to be toppled and the demonstrations against the Gadaffi regime provided a perfect pretext for intervention and the killing of Gadaffi. Libya was not a pliant state in terms of US/Western hegemony. It was a stable state and not in debt with the World Bank. Moreover, Libya's international profile and economic influence was on the rise in Africa and southern Europe. All this played a role to enforce regime change. Today Libya is a failed state in all respects with consequences still felt in northern Africa (SAHEL), Europe and the Middle East – a situation unlikely to be resolved or turning for the better in the decade to come. Whether it was intended to create a failed state by those that intervened is a moot point. Anyone with some political-military foresight could have predicted the future of a failed state in Northern Africa. Exactly for this reason the African Union, Turkey and Russia proposed a different approach.

The death of Gadaffi did not bring more peace and stability; not in North or West Africa, not in the Middle East and not more political-economic certainty in Europe. On the contrary, conflict (potential) increased sharply. This all to serve as demonstration that international relations (or in its broader sense, global politics) did not become less complicated. In fact, it may have become cloudier if not outright stormy. The war against terror that is waged by the US (with France and the UK and to an extent The Netherlands as loyal junior followers) is pestered by stereotypes; much like under apartheid, all resistors to the system are labelled terrorists. Violent actions are countered by state action. Some may say terrorist actions are countered by the state-terror of strong (self-perceived) hegemons.

There is little to be seen about defence diplomacy derived from a peace-driven foreign policy approach by the USA and its coalition of the willing. This spells no good for the future. Asymmetric warfare (though different in content from context to context) arises and may increase. Notions of specific communities' aspirations (i.e. the Kurdish question) and their contextual struggles, but also contestation for scarce resources on the globe and wars of greed play an important role. In cases, major powers exploit age old conflicts and grudges as proxy forces, reminding one about old-style divide and rule or divide and gain political leverage for own interest. Again the situation of the Kurds in the Middle East comes to mind. Globalisation has a down-side, another face of Janus. With greater integration, implosion of time and space and international flow of goods and capital comes a greater rich-poor gap, fragmentation, alienation and conflict, the latter frequently transformed into violence on multilayered levels; violence best to be analysed without falling for glib mantras and stereotypes, not to mention the pragmatic fabrication of "facts" to justify military intervention. In this regard, the recent killing of a senior military leader of Iran by a US drone attack is one example of how conflict can be escalated virtually overnight. There seems to be little of an understanding that all conflicts are not "terrorist" or religiously inspired. Too little analysis is taking place of conflicts that arise because of greed, control over scarce resources, intervention by states outside relevant regions, water security or the maintenance of trade routes (especially in northern Africa) and grudges held by minorities over years, if not centuries. Likewise, the role of increasing poverty within and between states and its violent side effects are massively under-researched and deserve much more attention by theorists and policymakers.

Against the above complex global collage, this edited volume looks at the defence diplomacy of various countries in the Global South on a *capita selecta* basis. The work is compiled in times when global politics are cloudy, if not warped; one sees permanent flux with new crises arising with a context of revolutions in warfare and the countering of resistance by the aggressive projection/export of state terror. State terror or foreign military intervention even in cases not announced or not on the radar of Western media, such as French actions in West Africa and regular drone attacks by the USA in East-Africa spring to mind here.

A note of caution is perhaps necessary here. This edited work does not explicitly address religious conflict or conflict around scarce resources under the cloak of religious justification. The fog and dust of regionalised war and the stereotyping of enemies under one class, namely that of Political Islamic terrorists is but one complicating factor. Another complicating factor is the salient but persistent role of Political Christianity that is driving the so-called war against terror making for a seemingly self-fulfilling prophecy as end game. The term Political Christianity is seldom discussed or analysed. Is it not recognised due to ignorance, manipulative politics or through strategic silence? The latter questions are important and necessary – if not crucial – debates and strongly advisable for future research. While this point is not addressed by our contributors in this work, we suggest that the link between Political Christianity and the legacy thereof with the aggressive projection of military power by hegemonic states be analysed.

The term Political Christianity certainly deserves to be brought into the political discourse and thoroughly analysed in terms of its ongoing contribution to current global conflict, its effect on foreign policy and projection of power and in turn its effect on defence diplomacy in a global political-military context in permanent flux.

This project started during 2017 as result of an exchange of ideas between the editors that are from different continents but with an interest in the global history of conflict, defence, national security strategies and defence diplomacy or lack of it. In our case Asia, Africa and Latin-America became of particular interest. Contributors were identified and approached. The contributors are from countries that we here broadly call the "Global South". Theorists, analysts and expert practitioners that contributed are all well versed in their fields of interest. The work recognises a need for a clearer analysis of global politics, specifically through a focused discussion on the defence diplomacy of various countries in the South, from the large to the small. The context differs from country to country and from continent to continent as well as political system to political system against the background of sometimes a shared collective historical experience and memory, in other cases some contrasting experiences. It speaks for itself that not all countries could be included. In some cases, expert potential participants that were approached could not contribute. The nature of the work also does not allow for a wide-ranging case-to-case and inter-case comparative perspectives between the continents of the Global South. Both time and funding were limitations here and such research will have to remain for the future. Hence, the extent to which this specific study represents *broader casing* as known in qualitative research is limited.

The aim here is to contribute to the ongoing dialogue on global politics, especially as they relate to defence diplomacies of countries in the Global South on various continents. While the contributors are not addressing foreign policy per se, the reader will be able to deduct a lot around this from the readings here as foreign policy and defence policies including defence diplomacy have a lot in common. In other cases, some enlightening notes are made around strategic resource management and national security strategies and the evolvement of such strategies.

In terms of the structuring of the work, the reader will see three parts. The first part is dedicated to Latin-America, the second part to cases on the African continent, more particularly southern Africa, and the last part to China and India (the "Far East"). In the case of Africa, originally six potential contributors including two countries from Western Africa were approached. However, only three chapters were finally included. In the case of larger and potentially more influential actors such as India more than one chapter is included. As editors, we decided to include three chapters on India as experts were available to contribute. South Africa, despite numerous internal challenges and economic woes, for the moment is a large and relatively influential state on the African continent, the only African state to form part of BRICS – at least until overtaken by Nigeria or other contenders such as Angola. In the case of South Africa, experts were also available with an interest in related but different areas and two chapters on South Africa are included.

The perspectives brought together in this volume are shared with the reader at a time in history where there is clearly no end of history in sight. The notion of a so-called *clash of civilisations* vested in vast generalisations mostly based on the lack of knowledge and emotional intelligence about intricate global socio-political dynamics, cultural specifics and the effect of deepening poverty and a struggle for scarce resources undermines current analytical thinking and problem-solving approaches rather than contribute to them. The quasi-ideology of *civilisations in conflict* is followed by many political scientists with a north-bound gaze. On the converse, others argue that there is an urgent need for a critical and constructive dialogue between "civilisations" (historical communities and social identity groups), "nations" and within nations or communities of self-chosen citizens. Instead of a much debated "clash of civilisations" – to such an extent that the term *clash between civilisations* has become a near mantra – what is needed globally, is a dialogue between civilisations and nations. Should such a dialogue not be prioritised, it would be for the worse.

The work appears at a time where some argue that we see the decline of a hegemonic power (the US) which will for the most part lead to less predictable and likely more aggressive responses by the declining power. With reference to the US, such a decline is taking place on a historical continuum that slides on a scale from a global policeman mentality to a dangerous international rogue as Gwynne Dyer argues. Others suggest that we are about to enter the change from one hegemony to be replaced by another, in this case China taking the place of the US.

Simultaneously, other large powers are rising. In the case of India, a strong international actor is rising and holds international sway and significant military power. India seems to be an apologetic hegemon, or at least has no pronounced wish to project military power aggressively outside its immediate interests, though relations with Pakistan remain a thorny issue, perhaps likely to become thornier. Japan is a silent giant. Brazil prepares to sway significant political-military power by deploying soft power. What will happen in the future? Russia, after having been pushed back by an encroaching European Union (EU) and North Atlantic Treaty Organization (NATO) since the 1990s, is returning to the international arena. For Russia, feeling more and more beleaguered since 1993, such a "return" is both logic and necessary – understandably so. Some theorists foresee a return to multipolarity and perhaps with good outcomes for a relatively more peaceful globe. Others see new hegemonies arising. There are more such as the academician Vladimir Shubin, who asks: Hegemony? Which hegemony? Which hegemon? Whose hegemony? Hegemony so perceived by whom for what purposes?

The work cannot provide all answers. And it raises many questions. It can contribute however, we trust as editors, to a better understanding of the current state of defence diplomacies (and within a broader collage perhaps foreign policy and the national security strategies – the latter coupled to "national" interests). In this sense, the work aims to assist in clarifying some issues and we trust will encourage a more open and deeper dialogue about the multilayered complexities of international politics, defence, "national security" and defence diplomacy within an ever changing – and perhaps less predictable – framework of global politics.

In cases, more questions are raised than answered by this edited volume. This is a good thing because such questions call for more RE-search, RE-flection and new searches for clarity and solutions and serious dialogue based on solving or preventing localised and global conflict. Are we into hegemonic struggles? Is so-called "terrorism" the only danger to the global community? Can one define terrorism at all without keeping numerous other variables in mind? What are the consequences of a hegemonic state or state-centred terrorism and the export or maintenance of state terror? Think about (apartheid) Israel or the USA. And, if so, of what nature are these terrorisms and can they be solved or countered? What role for defence diplomacy, if any? What are the links between national security strategy and defence policy? What do the management of strategic resources and the writing of national security strategies have in common in the South? Can national security strategies in tandem with well thought-through defence diplomacies break the increasing rich-poor gap, state abuse and the common development problems of smaller and marginalised communities within states that hold conflict potential? Are defence policies supplementary or contrary to national foreign policy? Against which background is defence diplomacy changing? Is it changing against a background of national interests or the flexibilities and complexities of global politics, rather than just international relations between states but also influenced by other major non-state actors, movements and organisations? Are we going to experience another era of one-sided hegemony and the decline of it? If we are, where are we going? Are the power infused clandestine and military interventions by the US and European states that play along as the coalition of the willing, giving rise to new alienation, fragmentation, struggles in the Middle East and Africa? What can the Global South do about it? Can all terrorists be glibly classified as one and the same? In fact, what is terrorism and what not? What exactly constitutes resistance – on various levels and within geospatial territories – to the negative effects of globalisation? Can all such resistance be discredited by using the term terrorist as bogeyman?

It is the view of the editors that this volume may become one building block for fruitful future discussion. As editors, we trust that such dialogue on defence diplomacy will facilitate more peace and less violence on a globe desperately in need of human security, development, growth and the closing of the rich-poor gap and racial tensions on multiple layers of society.

Ian Liebenberg
Dirk Kruijt
Shrikant Paranjpe

01

Brazil's National Defence Strategy, Defence Diplomacy and Management of Strategic Resources

Adriana A. Marques and Jacintho Maia Neto

Abstract

This chapter examines Brazil's policies for the protection of its strategic resources. The new agenda on security and defence is reshaping the Armed Forces missions at the domestic level (which includes support for natural disasters and constabulary missions), and at international level, characterised by asymmetric conflicts and non-traditional threats, such as international terrorism, and arms, human and drug trafficking. The transnational character of these threats has been boosting the countries to search for shared resolutions. In this context, the process of horizontalisation of diplomacy and the increasing involvement of the military in non-coercive activities has raised questions regarding the limits placed on the armed forces in the international arena, and has shed light on the prospect of using the military apparatus as a peaceful instrument of foreign policy. Discussing how these issues materialised in Brazilian defence policies, and how the defence sector is acting to provide national development and protection to the national strategic resources through deterrence and cooperation, are the central themes of this chapter. The chapter is divided into three sections: the first session present Brazil's defence documents and show the country's main objectives in this field, as well as the role of defence diplomacy in achieving them. The second section describes the main defence diplomacy activities developed by Brazil in South America, while the third section details the strategic projects that the country has been developing in order to guarantee its sovereignty, national treasures and territorial integrity. For this chapter, we consulted academic literature on Brazilian defence policy and the governmental documents related to the subject.

Introduction

The complementary relationship between diplomacy and war, as described from a realist point of view by Aron (1962), has returned to the centre of academic debate in recent decades. The horizontalisation of diplomacy and the increasing involvement of the military in non-coercive activities has raised questions about the limits placed on the armed forces in the international arena, while also shedding light on the use of military apparatus as a peaceful instrument of foreign policy.

Parag Khanna (2011) postulates that diplomacy has never been more important, yet its scope, agents and modus operandi differ greatly from those advocated by the authors of classical realism during the Cold War. Ministries of foreign affairs no longer have the monopoly on diplomatic activities, as members of other ministries and representatives of subnational governments, as well as organised sectors of civil society, develop and negotiate their agendas in the international arena without interfering with states' foreign policy. The systematisation of this practice has minimised the negative image that the concept of paradiplomacy inspired.

The end of the East-West conflict also had significant consequences for the military apparatus. Since the 1990s, there has been an increase in participation by the armed forces in cooperative activities (humanitarian aid, natural disaster support, exchanges in teaching and technical-professional areas, support for security and development activities, etc.) at both the international and regional level, and as part of bilateral agreements. The process of diplomatic decentralisation, coupled with the expansion of the military's non-coercive activities, has ignited the debate on diplomatic actions carried out by the defence sector.

Some authors frame this phenomenon in the context of the transformations that the United States (US) and Western European armed forces underwent after the end of the Cold War. Farrell, Rynning, and Teriff (2013) show that the armies of the US, the United Kingdom (UK), and France were generally restructured as expeditionary forces between the early 1990s and the late 2000s. In the case of the UK and France, this restructuring involved the development of a new doctrine that would enable forces to operate in a more dispersed and holistic, and less lethal way to achieve strategic objectives. Meanwhile, Cottey and Forster (2004) note that since the 1990s, NATO countries have conducted military exercises with their former enemies, and the US has established bilateral military cooperation relations with China and India, and initiated understandings in the defence field with the Association of Southeast Asian Nations (ASEAN), the Organization of American States (OAS), the African Union (AU), and the Southern African Development Community (SADC).

According to the constructivist perspective on international relations, defence diplomacy seeks to mitigate the behaviour of the state through a focus on conflict and war. The main difference between this perspective and the realist view is the use of cooperation, or cooperative and non-coercive military power. In this way, defence diplomacy is part of a wider diplomatic context, related to the construction of the image of both the Armed Forces and of the country itself, and can be considered an extension of the country's public diplomacy. It is essentially a set of activities and initiatives that are followed by the armed forces, in conjunction with regular diplomacy, particularly with reference to the foreign armed forces in peacetime (Singh, 2011).

According to the constructivist view, the objective of defence diplomacy is the achievement of security and external defence. In the context of global and regional strategic engagement, this creates sustainable cooperative relationships by building trust and facilitating conflict prevention, introducing transparency in defence relations, reinforcing perceptions of common interest, changing the fixed mindset of partners, and improving cooperation in other areas (Muthana, 2011:3).

As will be shown in this chapter, Brazil fits into the constructivist perspective, as its defence diplomacy seeks cooperation as a means of creating trust and integration. This position was made explicit in the documents produced by the Defence sector from the 1990s and constitutes a central part of the objectives set out in the National Defence Policy (PND). In its turn, the National Defence Strategy (END) states that Brazil will promote neither hegemony nor domination, as the Brazilian people are not willing to exert their power on other nations, preferring to grow without coercing others (Brazil, 2008).

This statement, besides reinforcing the Brazilian tradition of peaceful coexistence with its neighbours, makes explicit another fundamental principle of Brazil's foreign policy, which is its desire to become a major power. The military have played an important role in this, and since the founding of the Superior War College (ESG in Portuguese) in 1949, they have supported the idea that the Brazilian government needs to articulate the political, economic, social and military sectors in order to guarantee the security and development of the country.

Golbery do Couto e Silva, one of the main exponents of Brazilian geopolitical thought and founder of ESG, saw Brazil as an underdeveloped country, incapable of achieving the same level of technology as developed countries. In order to overcome this, the author suggested that Brazil accept the tutelage of a great power that could give it the technology and capital necessary to develop economically. Couto e Silva believed that Brazil should become the "privileged satellite" of the US in Latin America which, in the author's view, would bring mutual benefits: the US would receive raw materials, while Brazil would gain technology and the know-how to generate a robust production system to enable it to export to other underdeveloped countries. Since then, the idea that security and development are linked has crystallised in the imagination of Brazil's foreign and defence policymakers.

Since the 1970s, Brazil has abandoned the idea that automatic alignment with the US is the best way to become a power, and instead has sought strategic autonomy in concert with other developing countries. After the redemocratisation of the country in the 1980s, the process of Brazilian approximation with other South American countries in the political and military fields intensified (Marques, 2003). Along with this, the idea that Brazil would grow without using coercion over others arose in its defence diplomacy in a more articulated way during the Fernando Henrique Cardoso presidency (1994-2002).

This chapter will discuss Brazil's policies of deterrence and cooperation for the protection of its strategic resources, and is divided into three sections: the first section discusses Brazil's defence documents, showing the country's main objectives in this field, as well as the role of defence diplomacy in achieving these goals. The second section describes the main defence diplomacy activities developed by Brazil in South America, while the third section details the country's strategies for guaranteeing its sovereignty, national treasures and territorial integrity.

Brazil's defence documents

Although Brazil does not have a National Security Strategy, it does have documents in the Defence sector that guide policy and strategy in this area, namely: the National Defence Policy, the National Defence Strategy, and the White Paper on National Defence. In 1996, during Cardoso's presidency, the first Brazilian defence document was enacted to provide a conceptual and normative description of Brazil's place in the international system (Cepik & Bertol, 2016).

The National Defence Policy (PDN), 'which is aimed at threats from abroad, has as its primary purpose to establish the objectives for the defence of the Nation's capabilities at every level and every sphere of power, with the involvement of the military and the civilian sectors' (Brazil, 1998:5). In addition, the PDN follows the principles of Brazilian foreign policy in the search for a 'peaceful resolution of disputes, with the resort to the use of force only for self-defence' (Brazil, 1998:9). As we can see, the main legal framework for national defence focuses on external threats, respecting the sovereignty of other peoples, and using force only as a last resort for self-defence.

In 1999, the organisational structure of the Armed Forces was modified (Brazil, 1999). Prior to this, the Armed Forces were headed by the Ministers of State of the Navy, the Army, the Air Force, and the General Staff of the Armed Forces. On 10 June 1999, with the creation of the Ministry of Defence (MOD), a new architecture for the national defence sector was established.[1] The MOD is a key institution for consolidating the political direction of the military (Oliveira, 2005), and its creation meant it was necessary to reformulate the National Defence Policy; however, this would only happen in 2005.

The new version of the PND maintained its main purpose, with a slight difference, that the National Defence Policy 'aimed mainly towards external threats is the conditioning document of the highest level of defense planning' (Brazil, 2005:2). By stating that the PND was aimed mainly towards external threats, the Brazilian government sought to align its defence policy with the United Nation's (UN) extended concept of security, and to regulate the traditional internal role of the Brazilian Armed Forces in reducing internal vulnerabilities. Because the PND is the highest level of defence planning, the MOD was able to review and prioritise the documents being formulated by the three branches of the Brazilian Armed Forces.

Another important milestone was the first National Defence Strategy (END in Portuguese), published in 2008 (Brazil, 2008). The END was designed by an inter-ministerial committee chaired by the MOD and coordinated by the Minister-in-Chief of the Secretary for Strategic Affairs, and consisting of the Minister of Planning, Budget and Management; the Minister of Finance; and the Minister of Science and Technology, assisted by the Navy, Army and Air Force Commanders.

Despite the absence of the Ministry of Foreign Affairs in the committee that prepared the END, and some discrepancies between their normative propositions, pointed out by analysts, the PND and the END can be seen as related stages in the evolution of Brazilian defence policy (Oliveira, 2007; Cepik & Bertol, 2016). The END focuses on middle- and long-term strategic actions, and aims to modernise the national defence structure through three primary processes: reorganisation of the Armed Forces, the restructuring of the Brazilian defence industry, and the troop requirements policy for the Armed Forces (Brazil, 2008). As one aspect of the END, each of the Armed Forces were responsible for drawing up their Equipment and Deployment Plans, redefining their territorial structures, and developing new procurement programmes for materials, equipment and armaments (Brazil, 2008).

In 2010, Complementary Law 136 (Brazil, 2010) was passed, resulting in the restructuring of the MOD with the creation of the Armed Forces Joint Staff. Its primary mission is to promote the concept of unity amongst the service branches in order to optimise military resources for national defence and border security, as well as rescue and humanitarian operations. The creation of this new structure within the MOD placed the Chief of the Joint Staff at the same hierarchical level as the Commanders of the three branches of the Armed Forces (Navy, Army and Air Force), all of whom, together with the MOD, comprise the Military Defence Council, the highest level adviser to the President of the Republic regarding the use of military resources (Brazil, 2012b).

The new legislation extended policing power to the Navy and the Air Force (Brazil, 2010), enabling the three branches of the Armed Forces to act in support of the Public Security Forces and in the frontier areas. Another important factor defined in Complementary Law 136 was the determination that, from 2012 onwards, the three main documents of the Defence sector would be reviewed and approved by the National Congress every four years.

Complementary Law 136 also stipulated that the PND and END be updated in 2012 (Brazil 2008, 2012c), the year in which the National Defence White Paper (LBDN in Portuguese) was drawn up, a document about defence-related activities in Brazil. In addition to providing internal and external transparency on how the Brazilian Armed Forces are used, the LBDN helped deepen society's pool of knowledge on the military field (Brazil, 2012b).

According to this new legal framework, the strategic projects of the three branches of the Armed Forces had a new impetus, along with the defence industry, which received fiscal incentives through the new legislation that defined terms such as 'Defence Material, Strategic Material, Defence System and Strategic Defence Company',[2] enabling a resurgence of the defence industrial base (Brazil, 2012a, 2013a, 2013b).

In 2016, 20 years after the first Brazilian defence document, the PND, END and LBDN were updated and forwarded to the National Congress for consideration. The National Defence Objectives (ODN in Portuguese) have remained relatively stable in all PND versions, regardless of the political party spectrum of the Brazilian government, and the constant ministerial changes. It is worth noting that Brazil had 11 Defence Ministers during the 19 years of existence of the Ministry.[3] The stability of NDOs over the years can be observed in Table 1.1.

TABLE 1.1 Comparison of national defence objectives in PND

1996	2005	2012	2016
Guarantee sovereignty, preserve territorial integrity, heritage, interests	Guarantee sovereignty, national treasures, territorial integrity	Guarantee sovereignty, national treasures, territorial integrity	Guarantee sovereignty, national treasures, territorial integrity
Guarantee rule of law and democratic institutions			
Maintain national cohesion and unity	Contribute to preservation of cohesion and national unity	Contribute to preservation of cohesion and national unity	Contribute to preservation of cohesion and national unity
	Promote regional stability	Contribute to regional stability	Contribute to regional stability, international peace and security
Contribute to maintenance of international peace and security	Contribute to maintenance of peace and international security	Contribute to international peace and security	
Protect individuals, goods, resources that are Brazilian/under Brazilian jurisdiction	Defend national interests, Brazilian citizens' assets and resources abroad	Defend national interests, Brazilian citizens' assets and resources abroad	Protect individuals, goods, resources and national interests abroad
Achieve and maintain Brazilian interests abroad			
Give Brazil significant role in international affairs, greater role in international decision-making process	Participation of Brazil in community of nations, and broader role in international decision-making processes	Intensify Brazil's participation in community of nations, and international decisions	Increase Brazil's participation in community of nations and role in international decision-making processes

1996	2005	2012	2016
		Maintain Armed Forces that are modern, joint, well-trained, balanced, professional, adequately deployed throughout the national territory	Assure the capability of defence for accomplishment of the Armed Forces constitutional missions
		Structure Armed Forces around capabilities, provide personnel and material in accordance with strategic and operational planning	
		Develop Defence Industrial Base to ensure autonomy in vital technologies	Promote productive and technological autonomy in Defence area
		Develop potential for defence logistics and national mobilisation	
		Raise awareness amongst Brazilian people about the importance of defence matters for the country	Expand involvement of Brazilian society in National Defence matters

SOURCE: Adapted by Marques and Maia Neto, from: Brazil (1998), (2005), (2012c), (2016b)

The slight changes in the ODN reflect the domestic and international political context in which the different versions of the PND were drafted. In the 1996 version, there was explicit reference to the commitment of the Brazilian Armed Forces to the maintenance of democratic institutions. This objective is not included in later versions of the PND and has been replaced by the promotion of regional stability and commitment to international peace and security.

In the 2012 version, one objective was removed and five were added to the PND, raising the total ODN to eleven. Elaborated after the publication of the first END (2008), and concurrent with the public debate that guided the preparation of the LBDN, the 2012 PND explained in more detail all the contexts in which the need to structure the defence sector was conceived.

In the 2016 version, the documents sought a more integrated vision with other sectors of government, and adopted a more simplified structure, as explained by ODN. In line with Chancellor Celso Amorim's thesis that Brazil should adopt a grand strategy combining foreign policy and defence policy (Amorim, 2015), the PND established national defence capabilities that should be sought by the various sectors of the government structure. These national capabilities will result in the military capabilities that will guide the processes of transformation of the Armed Forces, especially those processes directed to the strategic projects of each branch. The projection of national power is another point detailed in the 2014 PND, as for the first time the document highlights the need to set up expeditionary forces to support the country's commitments to international organisations, and conventions, treaties and agreements of which Brazil is a signatory (Brazil, 2016b).

South-South relations are well-defined in the defence documents, particularly the PND, when establishing as priority areas of Defence interest, 'the Brazilian strategic environment, which includes South America, the South Atlantic, the countries of the coast' (Brazil, 2016b:6), emphasising 'integration with South American countries' and 'seeking to maintain the South Atlantic as a zone of peace and cooperation' (Brazil, 2016b:11).

The regional level also remains a main focus of the defence sector in the END, as can be seen in the strategies for achieving the ODN of contributing to regional stability and to international peace and security. The END states that, in order to promote regional integration, it must 'encourage the development of a South American identity' and 'intensify strategic partnerships, cooperation and military exchange with the Armed Forces from Union of South American Nations countries (UNASUL in Portuguese)' (Brazil, 2016b:39).

Brazil's defence diplomacy

The Brazilian military has played a prominent role in South America, especially in foreign policy and international relations. According to Garcia (1997), the connection between the military and international politics was more profound during the Military Regime (1964-1984), but there were historical antecedents of the military, and particularly the Army, playing a role in politics. In contrast, greater participation in domestic affairs increased interest in foreign policy, since domestic decisions reflected the country's international participation options and vice versa (Garcia, 1997:21).

Felix Martin (2001) extends this hypothesis to all countries in South America. According to the author, the interconnection between military participation in domestic affairs and perceptions of the regional security environment explains the external-peace/internal-violence paradox in South America. From this perspective, the decrease in South American military campaigns since the end of the Chaco War between Bolivia and Paraguay (1932-1935) is rooted in an evolutionary social process, where the militaries developed common socioeconomic values, beliefs, principles, and objectives. This fostered the Brazilian armed force's increasing identification with the interests, progress and success of the transnational and national dimensions of other military institutions in the region. The increasingly transnational identity of the militaries transformed their traditional missions, as protectors of the state from external threats, to national political players and guardians of the state from internal political foes in their respective polities (Martin, 2001).

The lack of military campaigns between South American nations since the 20th century has contributed to increased cooperation between the armed forces of the region, especially since the 1990s when the process of regional integration in the Southern Cone of South America intensified due to the economic and political agreements that arose from the institutionalisation of the Southern Common Market (MERCUSUL in Portuguese).

The sense of transnational identity and solidarity constructed between militaries during state-building processes also played an important role in this matter. An illustrative example of this is the cooperation between Brazil and Argentina in the nuclear field, a case where the attempt at reconciliation between two authoritarian rivals came before political democratisation or social and economic interdependence. These countries started inching towards a stable peace under the scrutiny of the military dictators in charge, and while the international press was reporting that Argentina and Brazil were moving towards nuclear weaponisation due to mutual suspicion, officials were actually engaging in quiet diplomatic attempts to establish the terms of a bilateral nuclear engagement (Mallea, Spektor & Wheeler, 2015).

Under democratic regimes, Brazil and Argentina have adopted mechanisms of transparency and mutual trust, benefiting from what was already practised by the military in terms of exchanges and cooperation. In the Brazilian case, this helped the MOD to achieve the ODN of contributing to regional stability and to international peace and security.

This sense of transnational identity and shared perception of security and defence issues in South America also helps to explain why the Brazilian proposal to create a Defence Council within UNASUL was so well-received by the other countries in the organisation. In a set of interviews carried out in 2009 with military members of the Amazon Cooperation Treaty Organization (ACTO) countries, one year after Colombia bombed a camp of the Revolutionary Armed Forces of Colombia (FARC) in Ecuador, one could see that this diplomatic incident had not changed the decision of the Amazonian countries to cooperate in matters involving protection of the region's natural resources. In this sense, it is interesting to note that the perception that the natural treasures of the Amazon are coveted by the rich countries of the North is shared by the militaries of all the ACTO countries, regardless of the degree of exchange that these countries have with the armed forces of the United States (the case of Colombia is remarkable), the United Kingdom (which maintains close cooperation with Guyana and Suriname) or Russia (which seeks to replace the United States as the main military reference in Venezuela) (Marques, 2010).

This shared perception is expressed in the first version of the END (Brazil, 2008). The document emphasises that the country will reject any attempt at external imposition on its decisions regarding the preservation, development and defence of the Amazon region.

It will not allow organisations or individuals to serve as instruments for foreign interests, political or economic, that are aiming to weaken Brazilian sovereignty (Brazil, 2008). This served as a primary motivation for the increase in Brazilian defence diplomacy in the Amazon region in the last decade.

The Guidelines for the Activities of the Brazilian Army in the International Area (DAEBAI in Portuguese), published in 2013, convey what Brazil and its Army consider defence diplomacy activities: (1) permanent missions abroad with diplomatic representatives, military organisations of education or instruction, international organisations, commissions and others; (2) permanent missions of foreign military personnel in Brazil in the military sector; (3) conferences and meetings, bilateral or multilateral, with the participation of Army representatives in Brazil or abroad; (4) courses, internships and visits, both by Brazilian military officers abroad and by foreign authorities and military personnel in Brazil, in order to deal with matters of interest to the Army; (5) cooperation and military exchanges of various natures; (6) exercises with foreign troops in Brazil and abroad; (7) participation in peace missions; (8) participation in humanitarian missions in Brazil and abroad; (9) sales and purchase of Defence Materials (PRODE in Portuguese), its components and raw materials; (10) signature of agreements, covenants, additive terms, technical arrangements, letters of intent and related documents; and (11) other occasional missions (Brazil, 2013c:13-14).

According to DAEBAI, these activities would aim to: (a) maintain a regular dialogue on bilateral and multilateral issues of mutual interest in the fields of defence, fostering cooperation, integration and mutual trust with the armies of other countries; (b) contribute to maintaining a stable global order through participation in humanitarian aid and peace operations under the aegis of international and regional organisations; (c) support and contribute to the structural consolidation efforts of the armies of friendly countries; (d) facilitate the achievement of a legal framework that regulates the development, within the Defence environment, of bilateral and multilateral relations; and (e) strengthen the national defence industry in order to reduce technological dependency and overcome unilateral restrictions on access to sensitive technologies (Brazil, 2013c:20-21).

Based on this framework, the tables below show the international agreements involving military diplomacy signed between Brazil and other South American countries during the Cardoso and Lula presidencies.

TABLE 1.2 Summary of Brazil's international agreements on defence issues with South American countries from 2003 to 2010

Country	Bilateral agreement
Argentina	- Memorandum of Understanding on Consultation and Coordination between the MOD and MRE of the two countries, as well as follow-up on defence issues of mutual interest (1997) - Catalogue Agreement (1997) - Creation Statement of Bilateral Defence Working Group (2000) - Joint Declaration agreeing to develop Cooperative and Mutual Support Activities in areas of Human Resources, Logistics, Operational Training, Technical Assistance and other (2001)
Bolivia	- Creation Statement of Bilateral Defence Working Group (2000)
Colombia	- No defence agreement was signed in the period
Chile	- Creation Statement of Bilateral Defence Working Group (2000)
Ecuador	- Declaration of Peace Agreement between Ecuador and Peru by the Armed Forces of the Guaranteeing Countries (1996) - Agreement on Provision and Support to Military Observers Mission Ecuador-Peru (MOMEP in Portuguese) (1998) - Joint Declaration Establishing Bilateral Defence Working Group (2002)
Guyana	- No defence agreement was signed in the period
Paraguay	- Military Cooperation Agreement (1995)
Peru	- Joint Declaration Establishing Bilateral Defence Working Group (2002) - Plan for Provision and Support to MOMEP (1998) - Action Plan Brazil-Peru (1999)
Suriname	- Declaration of Interest on Military Cooperation (1995)
Uruguay	- Agreement on Cooperation in the Field of Defence (2010)
Venezuela	- Joint Declaration on Military Cooperation (1998) - Joint Declaration Agreeing to Develop Cooperation and Mutual Support Activities in Areas of Common Interest (2000)

SOURCE: Landim (2015)

TABLE 1.3 Summary of Brazil's international agreements with South American countries from 2003 to 2010 in defence issues

Country	Bilateral agreement
Argentina	- Framework Agreement on Cooperation in Defence Fields (2005) - Adjustment to Agreement for Scientific and Technological Cooperation in the Military Technology Area GAÚCHO Vehicle (2005) - Brazil-Argentina Joint Declaration (2008) - Supplementary Protocol to the Cooperation Agreement (2008)
Bolivia	- Agreement on Cooperation in the Field of Defence (2007)
Colombia	- Agreement on Cooperation in the Field of Defence (2008) - Memorandum of Understanding for Cooperation in Combating the Illicit Manufacturing of and Trafficking in Firearms, Ammunition, Accessories, Explosives, and Other Related Materials (2008)
Chile	- Agreement on Cooperation in the Field of Defence (2007)
Ecuador	- Agreement on Cooperation in the Field of Defence (2007)
Guyana	- Agreement on Cooperation in the Field of Defence (2009)

Country	Bilateral agreement
Paraguay	- Memorandum of Understanding for the sending of a Marine Squad to the Brazilian Armed Forces (2006) - Agreement on Cooperation in the Field of Defence (2007) - Technical arrangement relating to Cooperation in the Maintenance of Military Armoured Vehicles (2007) - Joint Statement creating the 2 + 2 Mechanism for Strategic Consultation and Evaluation involving the MD and MRE of the two countries (2007)
Peru	- Memorandum of Understanding on Cooperation in Protection and Surveillance of the Amazon (2003) - Agreement on Cooperation in the Field of Defence (2006) - Statement creating MRE + MD Consultation Mechanism (2006) - Declaration of Cooperation on Protection and Surveillance of the Amazon (2006)
Suriname	- Agreement on Cooperation in the Field of Defence (2008)
Uruguay	- Agreement on Cooperation in the Field of Defence (2010)
Venezuela	- No defence agreement was signed in the period

SOURCE: Landim (2015)

Under Cardoso's administration, Brazil signed security and defence agreements with all South American countries, except Colombia and Guyana. However, according to Landim (2015), even without these agreements, the Brazilian Army maintained its international activities, carrying out various acts of military diplomacy. It is noteworthy that during Cardoso's administration, the MOD was still embryonic and service branches still managed their own priorities, even in matters affecting the international area (Marques, 2004).

Similarly, under Lula's administration, the Brazilian government also concluded security and defence agreements with all the countries of South America, except Hugo Chávez's Venezuela. However, regardless of agreements signed at the governmental level, the Army maintained its diplomatic links with all South American armies, including Venezuela's, whose absolute numbers in terms of exchanges and vacancies for courses and internships in the military were behind only Paraguay, Peru and Ecuador (Landim, 2015). Under Lula's government, the MOD became stronger and began to jointly lead projects of the three service branches. This is well-illustrated by the MOD's initiative, through Minister Nelson Jobim, of creating the South American Defence Council of UNASUL.

Another important aspect is that Brazil's defence diplomacy in the region is predominantly through activities that do not require many resources or investments, such as exchanges, meetings and education, even though South America has been a priority for foreign policy in both Cardoso and Lula's governments. Despite this, Brazil's defence diplomacy has supported continued cooperation between the armed forces of the region, and thus its "good neighbour policy", contributing to the increase of mutual trust amongst South American countries.

Dilma Rousseff's administration has continued the defence diplomacy initiatives of its predecessors, and some indicators relating to the Army have drawn particular attention.

TABLE 1.4 Summary of Brazilian Army's international activities with South American countries from 2011 to 2016

Country	Courses, internship exchanges	Conferences, meetings	Visits	Operations, exercises, manoeuvres, events	Permanent missions
Argentina	289	25	98	42	23
Bolivia	72	14	14	0	10
Colombia	110	28	72	13	19
Chile	106	27	81	12	6
Ecuador	96	10	28	1	9
Guyana	83	10	17	1	5
Paraguay	117	25	87	3	20
Peru	131	15	48	7	13
Suriname	39	8	27	2	2
Uruguay	123	19	38	3	6
Venezuela	98	11	4	0	14

SOURCE: Adapted by Marques and Maia Neto from data provided by Brazilian Army Staff

Throughout Rousseff's administration, there has been a significant increase in participation by the Army in international activities in South America, in spite of the economic and political crisis that Brazil has been undergoing since 2015. Compared with data from previous periods, the Army increased its presence in several countries in the region, particularly Colombia and Peru. Since the peace agreements in Colombia between the government and FARC, the Colombian Army has been studying the structures of the Brazilian Army, which is considered to be a model for the reorganisation of the armed forces in a country.

If Brazil's defence relationship with South American countries has been improving in recent years, Venezuela is the exception to this trend. The Brazilian Army has significantly reduced the number of its military personnel in that country, and sent a single colonel to attend a course there during 2017. In contrast, Venezuela has increased the number of Venezuelan military personnel attending courses in Brazil. The impeachment of Rousseff and the worsening political crisis in Venezuela have contributed to a growing gap between the two countries, culminating in the cancellation of scheduled bilateral meetings.

The strategic projects of Brazilian armed forces

Since the enactment of the END in 2008, three strategic areas for the defence sector have been outlined: nuclear (coordinated by the Navy); cybernetic (managed by the Army); and space (under the responsibility of the Air Force). The priority in these areas is to seek a growing nationalisation of the scientific-technological field, and the development of civilian and military human resources (Brazil, 2016a).

Together with the above-mentioned strategic sectors, and seeking to support the medium- and long-term strategic goals in the END (Brazil, 2008, 2012c, 2016b), the military has laid out plans to enable the Armed Forces to meet the defence challenges that may arise from the development of the country. The services' strategic projects have sought to re-establish their operational capabilities, as well as reduce the technological gap with developed countries. Through the Defence Deployment and Equipment Plan (PAED in Portuguese), the MOD seeks to consolidate these projects, support the Forces' demands for equipment, and enable them to act within the national territory.

With a focus on the Defence – Development nexus, the projects were developed not only to support the services' needs, but also to increase the defence industrial base, either through new legislation to regulate defence products and fiscal incentives to the sector, or by the nationalisation of the technology used in these products.

All three services have projects that aim at Obtaining Full Operational Capacity (OCOP in Portuguese), that is, they seek to revitalise the existing structure by 'recovering the strategic and operational levels of subsistence supplies, stewardship, fuels and lubricants, ammunition and supplies, critical parts and spares' (Brazil, 2016a:146).

Several projects already existed before the implementation of the END. However, it was from these guidelines that the strategic repositioning of these and subsequent projects occurred, allowing the country to develop capacities for defence of its sovereignty and its interests in a manner more integrated and aligned with the ONDs. The 2016 END defines the term 'national defence capabilities', which in turn supports the elaboration of a new PAED, with possible revisions of the current strategic plans of the Armed Forces. The main projects of the Forces are explained in the National Defence White Paper:

Navy

- Construction of Naval Power Nucleus, which aims to expand the operational capacity of the Navy. This includes the Submarine Development Programme (PROSUB in Portuguese), whose objective is the construction of four new conventional submarines and one nuclear-propelled submarine, in addition to a shipyard and submarine base to support these units, and the acquisition of surface means (PROSUPER-1) to develop the ability in Brazil to design and build five escort vessels, five ocean patrol vessels, and one logistical support vessel.

- Naval Nuclear Programme (PNM in Portuguese), which initially aimed to dominate the nuclear fuel production cycle achieved in 2012. The PNM is now seeking the construction of a prototype pressurised water reactor, as the basis for the reactor in the first Brazilian Submarine with Nuclear Propulsion (SNBR). The PNM and the PROSUB are closely linked, with the success of the PROSUB depending on the development of the nuclear propulsion system through the Naval Nuclear Programme.

- The Blue Amazon Management System (SisGAAz in Portuguese),[4] a system that will allow monitoring and control of the Brazilian jurisdictional waters, increased efficiency in inspection and search and rescue operations in the Blue Amazon, and more efficient interagency operations (Federal Police, Brazilian Institute of the Environment and Renewable Natural Resources, etc.).

Army

- The Integrated Border Monitoring System (SISFRON) is based on border monitoring, control, mobility and presence. It will allow the Army to monitor national borders and promptly respond to any aggression or threat. The system will contribute to unified socioeconomic initiatives which promote the sustainable development of the country's border regions. The system will be interlinked with similar systems of the other Armed Forces, of the MOD, and of other federal agencies.

- The Guarani Project covers the implementation of the New Family of Armoured Wheeled Vehicles (NFBR in Portuguese) of the Brazilian Army. The Project intends to provide mechanised units with new armoured vehicles which incorporate the most recent trends and technological developments. The Project calls for the acquisition of 2,044 Brazilian-designed Guarani armoured personnel carriers over a period of 20 years.

- ASTROS 2020, a defence system that aims to provide the Army with elevated fire support capacity through the national development of a missile with a range of up to 300 km. The Army will have two groups of missile and rocket launchers.

Air Force

- Recovery of Operational Capacity, a process of performance evaluation and selection of alternatives to replace, modernise, develop or revitalise aircraft and their systems, in order to strengthen and maintain the operational capacity of the Air Force. This project involves training and instruction of pilots, replenishment of weapons stocks, and technological upgrading of aircraft including: the fighters AMX and F-5 (projects A-1M and F5-M), maritime patrol P-95 (Project P-3-BR), transportation and refueling (projects KC-130 and C-95M), reconnaissance (Project R-99), and airborne early warning and control (Project E-99).

- Reinforcing the integration of the aerospace and defence industry with the MOD. It also aims to contribute to the competitiveness of products offered by that sector in internal and foreign markets. This project is nationally oriented, and the development and production of a National Aircraft for Transportation and Refueling (KC-390) is therefore noteworthy.

- The Space Systems Strategic Programme, which aims to develop and acquire the means to launch space platforms, and the construction of the relevant infrastructure. An important phase was the launch of the 2016 Geostationary Defence and Strategic Communications Satellite (SGDC in Portuguese), which will allow access to broadband internet throughout the country, as well as encrypted communications throughout South America.

Since the 2008 version of END, the Brazilian defence sector has strived to create an integrated monitoring and control system, including airspace, boundaries, jurisdictional waters and, with the launch of the SGDC the Portuguese acronym for its Geostationary Defence and Strategic Communications Satellite System), the space environment. To this end, structures are being created to enable this integration in the medium- and long-term.

With this focus on system integration, the Strategic Space Systems Programme will provide infrastructure for the operation of several strategic projects, amongst them the systems that focus on monitoring and control, such as SISGAAz, SISFRON (the Portuguese acronym for the Border Monitoring System), the Brazilian Aerospace Defence System (SISDABRA in Portuguese), and the Amazon Protection System (SIPAM in Portuguese). This will enable national system integration, serving to support both the defence of the territory and aspects such as public security, and fight against transnational crimes (Brazil, 2016a:60).

Strategic projects are the most visible face of national defence objectives and their respective strategies, enabling the integration of the Defence–Development nexus, which is the main scope of defence documents.

Final remarks

Brazil's National Defence Strategy is aligned with the country's development and the place it intends to occupy in the international arena. Since the 1970s, Brazil has pursued strategic autonomy and, in order to achieve this objective, has sought to intensify cooperation with the countries within its strategic environment, encompassing the countries of South America and coast of the South Atlantic.

Since Cardoso's presidency, Brazil's diplomatic actions concerning defence cooperation have been conducted by the MOD in accordance with the principles advocated by the

Ministry of Foreign Affairs. The military has an essential role in this process and, as has been outlined in this chapter, has aimed to establish a cooperative relationship with their counterparts since the beginning of the 20th century.

Establishing cooperative relations with South American Armed Forces at the regional level allows Brazil to peacefully project power and secure support for the achievement of its main national defence objectives: sovereignty, national treasures, and territorial integrity. These cooperative relationships also contribute to national development, as Brazil assumes that South American countries represent an important market for their defence materials. Therefore, the country has attempted to regionalise some of its strategic projects, such as SIPAM, SISFRON and the SGDC.

Finally, it is important to note the stability and continuity of Brazil's defence diplomacy efforts in South America, from the presidencies of Cardoso to Rousseff. Throughout this period, Brazil played a fundamental role as mediator of conflicts and inducer of integration processes in the region. The recent diplomatic impasse between Brazil and Venezuela is a new stage in the decades-old dynamics established between the militaries of the two countries, and will require the attention of analysts in the coming years. Nevertheless, based on the normative documents that guide the activities of the Armed Forces, defence diplomacy will continue to play a central role in Brazil's defence strategy.

Notes

1. According to President Cardoso, the creation of the Ministry of Defence in Brazil had as main objective to rationalise the preparation and the use of the Brazilian Armed Forces, through a greater strategic and operational integration of the three branches of the Armed Forces (Marques, 2004).

2. Law 12,598 of 21 March 2012, established that:
   - Defence Material (PRODE) is any goods, service, work or information, including weapons, ammunition, means of transport and communications, uniforms and materials for individual and collective use in the defence activities, with the exception of those that are assigned for administrative use;
   - Strategic Materials (PED) are all defence products that are of strategic importance for national defence, due to their technological content, scarcity or indispensability;
   - Defence System (SD) is the interrelated or interactive set of PRODE that serves a specific purpose;and
   - Strategic Defence Company (EED) is any legal entity accredited by the Ministry of Defence. These companies will have access to special tax schemes and funding for programmes, projects and activities related to national defence goods and defence strategic products, in accordance with law (Brazil, 2012a).

3. The defence ministers were (in this order): Elcio Álvares (from the Liberal Front Party), Geraldo Magela da Cruz Quintão (no party affiliation), José Viegas Filho (diplomat), José Alencar Gomes da Silva (from the Liberal Party), Francisco Waldir Pires de Sousa (from the Workers' Party), Nelson Azevedo Jobim (from the Brazilian Democratic Movement Party), Celso Luiz Nunes Amorim (diplomat affiliated to the Workers' Party), Jaques Wagner (from the Workers' Party), José Aldo Rebelo Figueiredo (from the Communist Party of Brazil), Raul Belens Jungmann Pinto (from the Popular Socialist Party) and Joaquim de Silva e Luna (retired military).

4. Brazil's jurisdictional waters are the South Atlantic region over which Brazil has territorial rights and other exploration and control prerogatives is the country's jurisdictional waters. These waters have recently been named the Blue Amazon, and are roughly equal, in geographic area, to the Brazilian Amazon (Brazil, 2012b:21).

References

Amorim, C. 2015. Grand Strategy: Foreign and Defense Policy in a Changing World. *Austral: Brazilian Journal of Strategy & International Relations*, 4(7):9-21.

Aron, R. 2002. *Paz e Guerra entre as nações*. Brasília: Editora Universidade de Brasília; São Paulo: Imprensa Oficial do Estado de São Paulo.

Brazil. 1988. *Constituição da República Federativa do Brasil*, de 05 de outubro de 1988. Diário Oficial (da) República Federativa do Brasil, Poder Legislativo, Brasília, DF, 5 October.

Brazil. 1998. Presidency of the Republic. *Brazilian National Defense Policy*. Brasília: Presidência da República. https://bit.ly/2W7bNBj

Brazil. 1999. Lei Complementar Nº 97, 9 de Junho de 1999. *Diário Oficial (da) República Federativa do Brasil*. Poder Executivo, Brasília, DF, 10 June.

Brazil. 2005. Ministry of Defense. *Brazilian National Defense Policy*. https://bit.ly/2QbcjKl

Brazil. 2008. Ministry of Defense. *National Strategy of Defense*. https://bit.ly/2TZlpLP

Brazil. 2010. Lei Complementar Nº 136, de 25 de Agosto de 2010. *Diário Oficial (da) República Federativa do Brasil*. Poder Executivo, Brasília, DF, 26 August.

Brazil. 2012a. Lei 12.598, de 21 de março de 2012. Diário Oficial (da) República Federativa do Brasil, Poder Executivo, Brasília, DF, 22 March.

Brazil. 2012b. Ministry of Defence. *Defense White Paper*. https://bit.ly/2vdpgMO

Brazil. 2012c. Ministry of Defence. *Política Nacional de Defesa e Estratégia Nacional de Defesa*. Brasília, DF.

Brazil. 2013a. Decreto 7.970, de 28 de Março de 2013. *Diário Oficial (da) República Federativa do Brasil*. Poder Executivo, Brasília, DF, 1 April.

Brazil. 2013b. Decreto 8.122, de 16 de outubro de 2013. *Diário Oficial (da) República Federativa do Brasil*. Poder Executivo, Brasília, DF, 17 October.

Brazil. 2013c. Exército Brasileiro. Diretriz para as Atividades do Exército Brasileiro na Área Internacional (DAEBAI). https://bit.ly/33b7ere

Brazil. 2016a. Ministry of Defence. *Livro Branco da Defesa Nacional*. Brasília, DF. https://bit.ly/3cRGHnb

Brazil. 2016b. Ministry of Defence. *Política Nacional de Defesa e Estratégia Nacional de Defesa*. Brasília, DF. https://bit.ly/2U5ovxI

Cepik, M. & Bertol, F.L. 2016. Defense policy in Brazil: bridging the gap between ends and means. *Defence Studies*, 16(3):229-247. https://doi.org/10.1080/14702436.2016.1180959

Cottey, A. & Forster, A. 2004. Reshaping Defence Diplomacy: New Roles for Military Cooperation and Assistance. *Adelphi Paper 365*. Oxford: Oxford University Press.

De Oliveira, E.R. 2005. *Democracia e Defesa Nacional: a criação do Ministério da Defesa na presidência de FHC*. Barueri, SP: Manole.

De Oliveira, E.R. 2009. A Estratégia Nacional de Defesa e a Reorganização e Transformação das Forças Armadas. *Interesse Nacional*, 71-83.

Farrell, T., Rynning, S. & Terriff, T. 2013. *Transforming Military Power since the Cold War: Britain, France, and the United States, 1991-2012*. Cambridge, UK: Cambridge University Press. https://doi.org/10.1017/CBO9781107360143

Freire, G. 1987. *The Masters and the Slaves*. Berkeley: University of California Press.

Garcia, E.V. 1997. O pensamento dos militares em política internacional (1961-1989). *Revista Brasileira de Política Internacional*, 40(1):18-40. https://doi.org/10.1590/S0034-73291997000100002

Khanna, P. 2011. *Como governar o mundo*, Rio de Janeiro: Editora Intrínseca.

Landim, H.G.C. 2015. *O papel da diplomacia militar brasileira exercida pelo Exército para a consolidação de um arranjo de defesa na América do Sul*. PhD thesis. Escola de Comando e Estado-Maior do Exército, Rio de Janeiro: ECEME.

Maia Neto, J. 2015. *As novas demandas de segurança e defesa nacional e seus impactos na transformação organizacional dos ambientes militares, em especial, do exército brasileiro*. PhD thesis. Escola Brasileira de Administração Púlica e de Empresas, Rio de Janeiro: FGV.

Mallea, R., Spektor, M. & Wheeler, N.J. 2015. *The Origins of Nuclear Cooperation: a Critical Oral History of Argentina and Brazil*. Rio de Janeiro: Woodrow Wilson Center for Scholars/FGV.

Marques, A.A. 2003. Concepções estratégicas brasileiras no contexto internacional do pós-Guerra Fria. *Revista de Sociologia e Política*, 20:69-85. https://doi.org/10.1590/S0104-44782003000100007

Marques, A.A. 2004. El Ministerio de Defensa en Brasil: Limitaciones y perspectivas. *Revista Fuerzas Armadas y Sociedad*, 18(18):27-51.

Martin, F.E. 2001. Os militares e a paz regional na América do Sul, 1935-1995, in H.L. Saint-Pierre & S.K. Mathias (eds.), *Entre votos e botas: as forças armadas no labirinto latino-americano do novo milênio*. Franca, SP: Ed. Unesp.

Muthanna, K. 2011. Military Diplomacy. *Journal of Defence Studies*, 5(1).

Singh, P.K. 2011. China's Military Diplomacy. *Strategic Analysis*, 35(5):793-818. https://doi.org/10.1080/09700161.2011.591252

Silva, Golbery do Couto. 1967. *Geopolítica do Brasil*. Rio de Janeiro: José Olympio.

02

Chilean Defence Policy
Moving forward

Andrés Villar and Francisco Rojas

Abstract

In this chapter, we review Chile's perspective on some of the matters most relevant to its defence policy, particularly those related to Latin America and international security. We present the challenges that emerge in these environments, and the contribution Chile can make to them.

Chilean foreign policy aims to be global and balanced. Based on the interdependent nature of the globalisation process, Chile performs at the global level according to their strategic capabilities and expectations. However, above all, Chile has built its reputation on its immediate priority, which is its role in Latin America, and South America in particular. That is Chilean identity, and where the root of Chilean security lies.

It is from this standpoint that Chile seeks to realise and contribute to a community that assists in building a more peaceful, more democratic, more prosperous, fairer and more sustainable global community in the 21st century. That is why, in order to understand the Chilean defence policy construct, it is fundamental to first explain the dynamics of international security in the Latin American region and, from there, to analyse past and current events.

Introduction

Given the current era of interdependence, political and strategic realities affect all countries and regions. We are going through a period of uncertainty, where the order and architecture that previously existed in international security have begun to show signs of important changes. Current scenarios, including risks and threats, are complex in nature and variable in time. No country or region is exempt from this level of uncertainty, which has three dimensions: the erratic signals of great powers, the structure of international security, and the international security agenda.

The signals from the great powers are confusing, making it difficult to develop a coherent agenda of priorities and strategic response. Extreme nationalism, terrorist attacks, and inability to cope with global challenges such as immigration, cyber-attacks and global warming have hit the legitimacy of international political actors. In this context of international confusion, some national leaders have begun looking for populist and short-term solutions to complex global challenges. Uncoordinated international actions and analytic errors undoubtedly prevent accurate strategic defence planning, thereby affecting international security.

This is partly because the traditional international security institutions, created more than 50 years ago to prevent, contain and confront crises and conflicts, have been delegitimised or surpassed, or are incapable of solving new international security phenomena. As a direct consequence, some countries have opted for unilateral strategies of conflict resolution. The paradox of this trend is that threats to peace and security are mostly regional or global in nature.

Regional security complex in South America

The regional goal of South America is to achieve a Zone of Peace, and this is the starting point of our contributions to the international security order. However, despite Latin America being an interstate zone of peace, it is also the most violent region in the world in terms of intentional homicides. Thus, non-state threats, such as organised crime, have a major impact.

Latin America, and South America in particular, exhibits the fewest conflicts in the world in terms of regional security. In part, this is because it has a culture of peaceful settlement of disputes, which has proven to be very effective. It is not that there have been no conflicts, but since the late 19th century, with only two or three exceptions during the 20th century, the region has built a normative political paradigm that has allowed it to maintain interstate peace.

How do we explain these evolving patterns of interstate security?

The goal of regional security has been the major frame of reference for management and resolution of territorial disputes amongst the Latin American states. Although the region is part of the International American System, security concerns have first and foremost been referred to the immediate neighbourhood, rather than to the extra-regional or global contexts (Hurrell, 1999; Mares, 2001; Kacowicz, 2003:125).

While the sources of interstate violence have changed since the independence period, it is possible to find some trends. Violence in the region has predominantly arisen from four causes: (a) boundaries and territorial disputes; (b) competition for resources; (c) imperial and other power disputes; and (d) ideological competition (Atkins, 1999; Kacowicz, 2003).

In this context, South America has a unique profile. Like other regions of the world, it has suffered a relatively high incidence of internal wars, but there have been no wars of secession. More remarkably, there has been only one war between South American states since 1941, between Peru and Ecuador in 1995 (Holsti, 1996). In this sense, scholars agree that South America constitutes a distinct international system that contains its own unique properties and dynamic (Burr, 1965; Atkins, 1999; Hurrell, 1999). This is what Buzan has called 'regional security complexes' (1991:210).

19th century: A balance of power model

In less than 100 years, six wars were formally declared in the region in the 19th century. According to most scholars, the most devastating and significant were between Paraguay and Argentina, Uruguay and Brazil (1865-1870), and the War of the Pacific between Peru, Bolivia and Chile (1879-1884), with consequences lasting into the 20th century. There were also five major armed invasions and interventions, resulting in a total of 44 militarised disputes between 1816 and 1900. Central America and the Caribbean was also the region where the United States (US) developed military intervention policies, although these were limited in South America, and virtually non-existent in the Southern Cone (Hensel, 1994, Holsti, 1996; Hurrell, 1999; Mares, 2001; Kacowicz, 2003:125).

The rivalry between Argentina and Brazil for control of the Rio de la Plata region, which centred on Uruguay in the early 19th century, influenced the behaviour of South American countries and the characteristics of the period. Both countries sought control of the zone, but after several bilateral disputes and the intervention of Britain, they signed the Treaty of Montevideo (1828), in which both countries agreed to recognise Uruguayan independence so as to create a buffer state between them. However, in 1851 Brazil forced a treaty in which Uruguay gave up almost half its territory along the northern frontier, and the Paraguayan War (1865-1870), known as the War of the Triple Alliance, resulted from the alliance between the Uruguayan Colorados (political faction), Argentina and Brazil against the Paraguayan dictator, Francisco Solano López. After five years of war, Paraguay was completely destroyed, most of its male population was killed, and Argentina and Brazil took portions of its territory (Atkins, 1999:320-321).

Prior to 1914, and with few exceptions, the leading states in the international context were successful at managing challenges to the established order and attempts at expansion by emerging states were generally put down. Europe was predominantly committed to the status quo, and this included the maintenance of state boundaries in Europe. Acquisition of territory by using military force generally took place at the periphery of the system, such as the War of the Pacific between Bolivia, Peru and Chile (Goertz & Diehl, 1992:98). Indeed, this was the last important war of the 19th century in South America.

The War of the Pacific was an economic war, and the commercialisation and exportation of nitrate through Bolivian coastline by Chilean companies was the source of the conflict. The rise of taxes was the reason given to start to a war over control of the economic strategic zone, but when the Chilean government attacked in the Bolivian desert, Peru entered the war on the side of Bolivia. Major actions were fought at sea, where Chile had supremacy over Peru, and the Chilean army invaded Peru and occupied Lima. The US and European countries unsuccessfully attempted to mediate a truce, and Chile finally defeated the Peru-Bolivian alliance (Atkins, 1999).

Through this brief description of the main war in the South Cone, we highlight the characteristics of the region during this period. Looking at 19th-century South America, we find patterns of peace and war, intervention, territorial predation, alliances, arms races and power balancing quite similar to those found in 18th-century Europe. On one hand, this reaffirms the political-diplomatic influence of European ideas, and that South American countries were still under the aegis of the *Pax Britannica*, so it is not a coincidence that Great Britain was nominated the permanent arbitrator between them (Ferrari, 1969 quoted by Kacowicz, 2005:138). On the other hand, South America was also embedded in the international society, meaning that their practices and behaviours were not so different to the policies of the great powers during the *Pax Britannica*. According to Holsti, this lends support to neorealist, structural characterisations of international politics as a game of conflict, war, struggle and survival (1996:152).

20th-century South America: A no-war zone

Latin America has seen war relatively infrequently since the late 19th century. Anchored in successful deterrence, the balance-of-power system was developed in South America during the second half of the 19th century and first part of the 20th. The ententes between Brazil and Chile on the one hand, and Argentina, Bolivia, and Peru on the other, were the basis of this balance-of-power system. States assessed their relative capabilities effectively, interacting with and deterring one another. This system provides one important explanation for the low incidence of warfare amongst South American states (Burr, 1967; Dominguez, 2003:18).

As Dominguez highlights (2003), South America saw only five wars during the last 70 years of the 20th century. Three of these broke out in the 1930s, as Bolivia and Paraguay fought over the Chaco area, Peru and Colombia over the Leticia region, and Peru and Ecuador over the Zarumilla region. Argentina and the United Kingdom went to war in 1982, and Ecuador and Peru again in 1995. The number of casualties was characteristically between 500 and 1,500 battlefield deaths, except for the war over the Chaco, with about 100,000 deaths. The duration of these wars was typically measured in weeks, except for the much longer Chaco War and the 1939-41 Ecuador-Peru war (Dominguez, 2003:18).

How do we explain these evolving patterns of interstate security? Scholars have taken different views. The realist approach has pointed to geopolitical location, to varying degrees of insulation from extra-regional influences, and to the hegemonic or policing role of

Britain and the US on the continent. Within the region, scholars highlight the emergence of relatively autonomous regional balances of power in countries like Argentina, Brazil and Chile, as well as the absence of transport links, borders that were geographically moved from centres of political and economic activity, and the gap of military technology between countries (Burr, 1967; Holsti, 1996, Hurrell, 1996:535). Meanwhile, international society theorists stress the extent to which a shared cultural and historical experience, particular patterns of state formation, and ongoing international interaction all combine to produce a strong regional diplomatic culture (Hurrell, 1996; Kacowicz, 2005). In sum, South America is 'a regional society of states which, although still often in conflict, conceived themselves to be bound by a common set of rules and shared in the working of common institutions' (Hurrell, 1996:535).

In the 20th century, South America was essentially a no-war zone, although there were high levels of violence and mistrust between neighbouring countries. In this context, conflict resolutions were settled by governments, and from bilateral bargains to arbitration or mediation channels, diplomatic strategies were characterised by a reduced number of actors.

Great powers, mediators and regional organisations

The US and regional organisations have not played a significant role in the settlement of international disputes in the South American region. Historically, the US has reacted in a range of ways to deal with security and promoted the use of force and interventions in South America during the 20th century. For instance, during the war between Ecuador and Peru (1939-1940), and in the Beagle Channel dispute in the 1970s, the US did not intervene at all. In contrast, the country was willing to support the use of force in the Central American crisis during the 1980s. In this sense, it is important to note that the use of force in the region has predominantly been informed by whether the US approves or opposes its use (Hurrell, 1996:531; Mares, 2001:83). However, the evidence shows that the most important external actor in the region did not play a key role in settling conflicts and avoided the use force in South America. As we can see in Table 2.1, during the global economic crisis in the 1920s and 1930s, there were ten active international disputes in Central and South America. According to Dominguez (2003), 35 countries served as intermediaries in containing or settling those conflicts. Yet even at that early stage, while an inter-American system of conflict resolution was emerging, the US played a limited role as an intermediary (Dominguez, 2003:23).

TABLE 2.1 Intermediary activity in South and Middle American regions* location of dispute, 1925-1942

Intermediary governments	South America	Middle America	Total
South American	15	3	18
Middle American	3	2	5
USA	5	2	7
European	5	0	5
Total	28	7	35

* Middle America refers to Mexico, Central America and the Caribbean.

The same patterns can be seen in the role played by regional and international organisations. As Holsti (1996) notes, since 1945 not a single territorial/resource conflict in the region has been resolved through the intervention of an international organisation. Governments have favoured ad hoc arbitration and mediation procedures outside of the context of international organisations (Holsti, 1996:171).

However, we do not want to create the misleading idea that security problems have been overcome in Chile and in the region. Along with the traditional security agenda, the globalisation process has introduced security problems of a different nature. In some cases, we face new actors, non-state and transnational in scope, who pose new threats, and with different intensities in each region. In the case of Latin America, the most important problem is transnational organised crime, whose main activity is drug trafficking, although it is not limited to drugs. Trafficking in persons and small arms are also serious problems, amongst other illicit activities that overwhelm the capacities of states and demand an urgent strengthening of statehood and international cooperation.

Along with these are problems of international security stemming from global dynamics, which in turn demand growing and perhaps new forms of international cooperation of an increasingly cosmopolitan character. Climate change and global warming are perhaps the most important and challenging of the new issues on the international security agenda, although they are by no means the only ones. However, they are non-volitional phenomena which pose a risk to the human species and all life on the planet, making them risks rather than threats.

Defence diplomacy

In the 90s, Chile, together with others in the region, ratified or adhered to the most relevant international agreements regarding non-proliferation and limitation of weapons of mass destruction. Amongst these are the Nuclear Non-Proliferation Treaty, the Treaty on the Prohibition of Nuclear Tests, the Chemical Weapons Convention, and the Biological Weapons Convention. Along with this, Chile substantially increased its contribution to the operations of United Nations (UN) peacekeeping, ratified the Antipersonnel Mines Convention, and showed its willingness to join the Missile Technology Control Regime. Likewise, after the 9/11 attacks, Chile supported the policies and treaties adopted by the Security Council of the UN, including the Proliferation Security Initiative.

In the strategic arena, the democratisation process gave way to a new type of regional relationship amongst Latin American countries. Along with the pacification of Central America, these included the Argentine-Brazilian approach, and Argentine-Chilean distension. From 1990, Chile joined this process of strategic regional transformation, giving it a renewed impetus in the neighbourhood. They distinguished two strategic areas: bilateral and multilateral.

In terms of bilateral strategy, the transformation of the relationship with Argentina was key (Van Klaveren, 1998:129; Robledo, 2010). During the 90s, Argentina and Chile agreed to resolve pending territorial litigation, identifying 24 problems linked to the demarcation of the international boundary. 22 of these were resolved directly in 1991, while the other two (Laguna del Desierto and Campo de Hielos Sur) were resolved by international arbitration in 1994 and a treaty in 1998 respectively (Van Klaveren, 1998:129). Ongoing measures were implemented to promote mutual trust (MCM), such as the Treaty of Peace and Friendship of 1984, and the Permanent Chilean Security Committee (COMPERSEG) in 1995 which was aimed at increasing the transparency of bilateral strategic relationships, thereby reducing mistrust and allowing progress towards more advanced relationships. This resulted in the elaboration of the Common Standardized Methodology for the Measurement of Defense Expenses, with the support of the Economic Commission for Latin America (ECLAC 2001).

In 2004, based on the experience of joint work during the UN Observation Mission in Haiti (MINUSTAH), and despite the difficulties that would begin to emerge in the bilateral relationship in the gas sector, the countries agreed to constitute a combined and joint military force for operations of peace (Southern Cross Brigade). The progression from cooperation under a security dilemma towards cooperative security was the result of a long process, timidly initiated in 1984 and re-launched with new impetus from 1990, finally crystallising at the end of the 20th century. In 1999, Argentina published its first Book on National Defense, affirming for the first time in its bilateral relationships with Chile that it no longer had basis for conflict with the country. Meanwhile, in 2000 during his first trip abroad after assuming the presidency, President Ricardo Lagos made a state visit to Argentina, declaring before its Plenary Congress that Chile no longer had a conflict hypothesis with Argentina (Lagos, 2000).

Thus, the Chilean-Argentine relationship evolved from one characterised by conflict over numerous territorial differences, to cooperative security, to eventual association, reflected in the constitution of the Cruz del Sur Brigade. In this stage, both states acted in a joint and coordinated manner, together with Brazil and a growing number of other countries, but they ultimately failed to consolidate progress and come to an agreement on common agenda and policy.

At the multilateral level, since 1990 Chilean foreign policy has placed a strong emphasis on the creation and strengthening of cooperation institutions at the subregional, regional, and inter-American level. At the inter-American level, security threats emerged in two dimensions: the interstate or traditional security agenda, and the agenda of new threats, usually of societal origin and with a transnational scope.

In the traditional agenda, one of the first efforts was oriented to the development of mutual confidence measures on a regional scale. After several academic meetings held in Argentina and Chile, in 1995 the countries carried out the first Regional Conference on Measures of Mutual Confidence, thus beginning a process that would continue in 1999 and 2001, would be extended and consolidated in the region, and would finally be institutionalised in the System Inter-American Commission at the 2003 Special Conference on Hemispheric Security. This regime would add Chile's support to the Inter-American Convention on Transparency in Conventional Weapons Acquisitions, adopted in 1999. Along with this, the Summits of the Americas process was begun in 1994, and began a new dynamic of cooperation between the US and the region, which would be extended to the field of security with the development of the Ministerial Conferences of Defence from 1995.

At the Latin American level, cooperation was also developed, although the most relevant achievements have been in the traditional agenda. After the end of the Argentine-Brazilian nuclear competition, there was a regional move towards nuclear non-proliferation. The Treaty of Tlatelolco in 1994 created the conditions for the incorporation of Chile and, a few years later, of other countries as well (Chile signed the non-proliferation treaty in 1993, Argentina in 1995, Brazil in 1997, and Cuba in 2002). Over time, all countries in the region joined the regional and international regimes for the prohibition of weapons of mass destruction (nuclear, biological and chemical): the Nuclear Non-Proliferation Treaty, and the Chemical Weapons Convention, which was complemented by a regional agreement, the Commitment of Mendoza. In this way, Latin America was consolidated as a Zone of Peace and completed a long process of transformation of regional policy.

In terms of the new threats such as trafficking, Chile is part of a number of conventions and mechanisms, such as the Inter-American Convention Against the Illicit Manufacturing and Trafficking in Firearms, Ammunition, Explosives and Other Related Material (CIFTA) (1997), as well as the Inter-American Drug Abuse Control Commission (CICAD). Similarly, efforts related to the protection of democracy and human rights were applied after the

Declaration of Santiago, in the cases of Peru, Haiti, Guatemala and Venezuela. These also contributed to regional stability, producing indirect strategic effects.

In the early 2000s, Chilean foreign policy and regional policy was marked by the beginning of Latin American cooperation in peace operations, specifically around Haiti and MINUSTAH in 2004. Although peace operations are part of the collective security system, in some cases they enable cooperative agreements between countries. Because they are not conceived as military alliances against a common enemy, but rather generators of a common security, under certain conditions, such as those indicated in the case of Chile and Argentina with the Southern Cross Force, they can give way to processes of political association.

From the 1990s, Chilean defence and foreign policy converged, contributing to bilateral, subregional, regional and inter-American cooperation processes, joining existing treaties, such as the Treaty of Reciprocal Assistance; and the UN Charter. This dynamic enabled a shift from a militarised and highly conflictual regional policy to a new dynamic of greater cooperation, fewer traditional interstate conflicts, and the development of new regimes to cope with transnational problems. Ultimately, this led to a dynamic of flexible security architecture, which described the emergence of a network of cooperative regimes and groups that operated simultaneously at different levels (Bachelet, 2002; Robledo, 2011).

The Zone of Peace: An important legacy and asset

The Zone of Peace is an important political and diplomatic outcome, a regional contribution that the developed world usually ignores. Latin America today is not a source of global insecurity. Rather, it is a contributor to global security, both through its own stability as a continent, and through its participation in international cooperation for peace and global stability. It is from this extraordinary and positive Latin American regional reality that Chileans define the priorities of their international activity in the field of security. These priorities are, first, consolidating our Zone of Peace and the construction of a community of security; second, constructing global security; and third, strengthening cooperation between the regions and their member states.

Regionalism and security in Latin America

Chile's first priority is to consolidate the achievements described in the previous paragraphs. To this end, the country promotes regional security cooperation through the construction and development of a network of multilevel regimes, both neighbourhood and subregional, Latin American and inter-American. This is what the Chilean Defence Policy has called a complex, collective and cooperative security architecture.

In turn, the regional security agenda has two important political purposes: to move from the Zone of Peace towards more advanced and ambitious stages of regional cooperation, such as the idea of a pluralistic security community; and to renew the inter-American institutions, which we consider a fundamental space for dialogue between the US and Latin America.

In terms of the first objective, Latin American regionalism has taken important steps in recent years with the creation of the Community of Latin American and Caribbean States, the birth and rapid development of the Pacific Alliance, and the creation of the Union of South American Nations (UNASUR), whose South American Defence Council (CDS) is a central tool for further progress in regional security and contributing to international peace.

For Chile, the strengthening of this regional architecture and the contribution that it has and continues to make represents one of its main objectives in the field of international security, which is why Chile makes significant efforts to strengthen both UNASUR and CDS. Since their origins, Chile has shown a great commitment to these institutions, by both promoting their foundation, and actively contributing to their development and improvement, which President Michelle Bachelet ratified. In its Government Programme, it was stated that, 'during the period 2014-2018, the main objective of the National Defense Policy will be to create a Security Community in South America … with the Defense Council of UNASUR the institution to advance in this matter'.

The strengthening of the CDS made it possible to consolidate the region as a Zone of Peace and establish the political basis for what in the long term could become a security community in South America. To do this, it was necessary to continue to build trust and transparency, and to lay the foundations for common policy. Chile collaborates on all initiatives of the CDS, paying special attention to areas of growing relevance. An example of this is the promotion of UNASUR member countries' commitment to international peace and security within the framework of the UN, such as the formation of the Combined Joint Binational Peace Force, 'Cruz del Sur', an agreement with Argentina.

Other areas of relevance are cyber defence; citizen participation in defence issues; incorporation of a gender perspective; and explicit attention for equal rights and obligations of minorities. Chile also aims to promote the relevance of cooperation for the preservation of the environment and biodiversity in our region, as well as to address natural disasters.

One of the areas that the Chilean Defence Policy has strongly focused on is the extension of measures of mutual trust and crisis prevention, as well as collective and verifiable commitments to a policy of full transparency in terms of military budgets and acquisitions. Chile has played a leading role in both initiatives.

All these actions are part of one of the priority areas for Chilean defence, with the aim, as former President Bachelet said, to transform the Chilean strategic environment through cooperation, peacebuilding in the region, and overcoming the security problems facing the international community. Recent history has shown that this is possible, as Chile was able to transform its conflictual relationship with Argentina into a cooperative one. Chile now aims to consolidate that by moving towards a strategic partnership and pursuing a similar process with Peru.

From this perspective, the strategic transformation has been more complete, profound and successful in Argentina, because it included both Chile and Brazil (pending the question of the Malvinas [Falkland] Islands). In the case of Chile, despite developments with Bolivia and Peru, the results have been different. The most relevant transformation in the region occurred in the Brazilian-Argentine relationship, although this has not been the only one. Ecuador and Peru resolved their protracted border dispute, experiencing a transformation similar to the Argentine-Brazilian and Argentine-Chilean relationships, overcoming border conflicts and solving security dilemmas. Therefore, the question in the cases of Chile-Peru and Chile-Bolivia is what is possible, and under what conditions.

Regarding the war between Ecuador and Peru (1995), it is important to note how this conflict delayed the expansion of cooperation in defence in the region in the post-Cold War period. In fact, the conflict froze such measures for a few years, maintaining mutual distrust in South America during the early 1990s.

National security strategy

Based on studies carried out by the Chilean Ministry of Defence between 2012 and 2017, the implementation of a new defence planning model was outlined in the new White Paper in 2018. The process begins at the political level, guiding both the use of force and the development of capabilities through the preparation of respective management documents. The strategic level planning process is constituted by Employment of Force plans and the Strategic Capacity Development Plan, which will be carried out under the responsibility of the Joint Chiefs of Staff.

The promulgation of Law 20.424 (the National Defence Policy) in 2010 introduced several norms related to the planning of national defence, which gave rise to a system with a greater number of participating actors, civilian and military, and with more precise links between the different levels of responsibility of the system (political, strategic and institutional). In general, the law identifies the actors that must participate in the system and establishes their functions. In particular, it broadened the participation of the actors at the political level, since the so-called primary planning or policy development resides at this level. However, Law 20.424 does not indicate how each actor's responsibilities must be performed. Some norms, in particular those related to the use of force, were only developed subsequently, by means of Supreme Decree 113, published in 2014.

This new Decree (March 2018) provided some important details, such as that the National Defence planning process is composed of both a primary and a secondary segment, and described the documentation that makes up the primary and secondary planning of defence, with an emphasis on the use of force. It explained that primary documentation refers to sectoral documentation, not national documentation, which has a political nature, while secondary documentation is of a military nature and produces joint strategy in terms of general processes and unique planning. Regarding the normative and conceptual frameworks of the defence planning system, the Ministry of Defence has made progress in developing a methodology that is no longer based on threats, but rather focuses on satisfying requirements in the face of a specific threat.

Management of strategic resources

Development of natural resources will be a major objective for many countries in the future, since natural resources are the basis for sustainable economic growth. Chile is no exception, with natural resources including oil, natural gas, coal, and precious metals, such as copper and lithium. Given increasing demand due to rapid industrialisation in China, Japan and Korea, the competition over these natural resources will remain acute. Anticipation of oil exhaustion, decreasing oil supply from the Middle East owing to political instability and military conflicts, and the quick rise in oil prices, all inevitably exacerbate leaders' anxiety and spur their willingness to show their muscle if they think it necessary. 'Rising energy prices, fears of supply scarcity, and rapid increases in oil-import dependency in China and other regional powers such as Indonesia have helped drive resource nationalism amongst regional governments' (Collins & Erickson, 2011). Energy nationalism in many regions is 'often inextricably tied to disputes over territorial and maritime claims and is exacerbated by the geographical proximity of states with a history of conflict' (Collins & Erickson, 2011).

The contemporary exercise of sovereignty over strategic resources is key, resulting in a relatively great reliance on defence policy, with two interrelated effects. It raises complex questions of intertemporal law and, because early international law required less for a state to gain sovereignty (particularly over terra nullius), it leads claimants to base arguments on weakly or inconsistently documented indications of sovereignty that would be much too thin to be valid today. These include asserted discovery or sporadic use by a state's nationals or patrols by its navy, inclusion in the state's territory on maps or in documents setting forth a government's administrative structure, and so on. Not surprisingly, such evidence is relatively weak and mixed in terms of which party it supports, at least in contrast to cases of territorial sovereignty over substantial, populated landmasses.

As a result of economic transformations, technological, demographic and environmental processes were developed globally in recent decades, guaranteeing access, control and sustained availability, in quantity, variety and price, of natural resources. This is currently a priority issue on national agendas, as well as a conditioning element of the international agenda.

Climate change: A new dimension

Many of the challenges in security and defence require cooperative responses. Based on the initiatives being carried out by the defence sector in Chile, climate change, science and technology, and cyberspace have been considered here.

The care of the environment and the risks associated with climate change have been at the centre of the debate in recent years. Although these matters were not part of the traditional security and defence agenda, they have increasingly been included as challenges that should be addressed. Climate change is growing in importance as a strategic issue. Although there is no evidence that climate change increases the likelihood of interstate conflict, it is certain that the various consequences of global warming pose risks to the security of countries. From the reports prepared by the Intergovernmental Panel on Climate Change (IPCC), it can be deduced that climate change would more strongly affect the countries with greater vulnerabilities, decrease the amount of available resources, alter territorial and maritime borders, as well as affect the military installations and modus operandi of the armed forces.

This is why several countries have begun to implement sectoral policies on the subject. The armed forces are major users of fossil fuels, so there is a challenge to establish measures that reduce their greenhouse gas emissions, with a focus on the use of new technologies and clean energies as the main alternative to help contain global warming. Much of this can be approached in a cooperative way, on the one hand creating common risks and challenges and, on the other representing an opportunity to change the patterns of use of energy resources.

Final remarks

To sum up, we argue that security and defence require a broad and global view that considers the different elements that affect them. Although traditional and non-traditional threats remain, and adapt in new ways that challenge our policies, the general principles and norms that guide our country's international cooperation are the best tool to deal with new threats and actors.

In this sense, Chile works from its own successful experience as part of a Zone of Peace, to contribute to the construction of a stable and peaceful international environment, within our region, with Asia Pacific and Europe, and now also with Africa. It is fundamental to deepen Chilean international commitments and actions worldwide, as well as to strengthen interregional relations and Chile's own internal fields of action, in a coordinated and convergent manner.

Chilean Defence Policy has taken up this challenge, working on greater participation in the global context, such as by expanding its peace missions; strengthening its relations with other regions, as in the case of agreements with the European Union; and promoting cooperation in its closest environment, particularly through the CDS.

We believe that this relationship, through the institutionalisation of cooperation, is the main way to address the current challenges associated with security and defence. Countries have common challenges, but also common principles and norms with which Chile has agreed, and that guide the country to continue deepening its relationships and building a safer region, together with Latin American countries.

References

Agüero, F. 1988. Legacies of transition: Institutionalization of the Military and Democracy in South America. *Mershon International Studies Review*, 48:384-404.

Atkins, P.G. 1999. *Latin American and the Caribbean in the International System*. Boulder: Westview Press.

Bull, H. 2002. *The Anarchical Society. A Study of Order in World Politics, 3rd edition*. New York: Palgrave. https://doi.org/10.1007/978-1-349-24028-9_1

Buzan, B. 1990. *People, States, and Fear: An Agenda for International Security Studies in the Post-Cold War Era*. Boulder: Lynne Rienner Publishers.

Collins, G. & Erickson, A.S. 2011. Energy Nationalism Goes to Sea in Asia. *NBR Special Report #31*. Seattle: The National Bureau of Asian Research.

Dominguez, J.I., Mares, D., Orozco, M., Palmer, D.S., Aravena, F.R. & Serbin, A. 2003. *Boundary disputes in Latin America*. Washington, DC: United States Institute for Peace.

Donadio, M. & Tibiletti, L. 1998. Strategic Balance and Regional Security in the Southern Cone, in J.S. Tulchin & F.A. Rojas (eds.), *Strategic Balance and Confidence Building Measures in the Americas*. Washington: The Woodrow Wilson Center Press.

Ferris, E.G. & Lincoln, J.K. 1981. Foreign Policy: the pragmatic pursuit of political goals, in E.G. Ferris & J.K. Lincoln (eds.), *Latin American Foreign Policies: Global and Regional Dimensions*. Boulder, CO: Westview Press.

Garrison, J.A. 2005. Foreign Policymaking and Group Dynamics: Where We've Been and Where We're Going. *International Studies Review*, 5(2):155-202. https://doi.org/10.1111/1521-9488.5020015

George, A.L. & Bennett, A. 2005. *Case Studies and Theory Development in the Social Sciences*. Cambridge, MA: BCSIA.

Gerson, A. 1977. The Beagle Channel Affairs. *The American Journal of International Law*, 71(4):733-740. https://doi.org/10.1017/S0002930000123966

Giacalone, R. 2012. Latin American Foreign Policy Analysis: External Influences and Internal Circumstances. *Foreign Policy Analysis*, 8(4):1-19. https://doi.org/10.1111/j.1743-8594.2011.00176.x

Goertz, G. & Diehl, P. 1993. Enduring Rivalries: Theoritical Constructs and Empirical Patterns. *International Studies Quarterly*, 37(1):147-171. https://doi.org/10.2307/2600766

Goldstein, J. & Keohane, R.O. 1991. Ideas and foreign policy: an analytical framework, in J. Goldstein & R.O. Keohane (eds.), *Ideas & Foreign Policy. Beliefs, Institutions, and Political Change*. Cornell: Cornell University Press.

Gourevitch, P.A. 1978. The Second Image Reversed: International Sources of Domestic Politics. *International Organization*, 324:881-911. https://doi.org/10.1017/S002081830003201X

Hill, C. 1993. The capability–expectations gap or conceptualising Europe's international role. *Journal of Common Market Studies*, 31(3):305-328. https://doi.org/10.1111/j.1468-5965.1993.tb00466.x

Hill, C. 2003. *The Changing Politics of Foreign Affairs*. New York: Palgrave Macmillan.

Holsti, K.J. 1996. *The State, War and the State of War*. Cambridge: Cambridge University Press. https://doi.org/10.1017/CBO9780511628306

Hudson, V.M. 2007. *Foreign Policy Analysis. Classic and Contemporary Theory*. Lanham, MD: Rowman & Littlefield.

Hurrell, A. 2007. *On Global Order. Power, Values and the Constitution of International Society*. Oxford: Oxford University Press.

Jervis, R. 1976. *Perception and Misperception in International Politics*. Princeton, NJ: Princeton University Press.

Jervis, R. 1978. Cooperation under the Security Dilemma. *World Politics*, 30(2):167-214. https://doi.org/10.2307/2009958

Kacowicz, A. 2005. *The impact of norms in international society: the Latin American experience 1881-2001*. Notre Dame, IN: University of Notre Dame.

Lobell, S.E. 2009. Threat assessment, the state, and foreign policy: a neoclassical realist model, in S. Lobell, N. Ripsman & J. Taliferro (eds.), *Neoclassical Realism, the State, and Foreign Policy*. Cambridge: Cambridge University Press. https://doi.org/10.1017/CBO9780511811869

Mani, K. 2011. *Democratization and Military Transformation in Argentina and Chile. Rethinking Rivalry*. Boulder, MA: Lynne Rienner Publishers.

Mares, D. 2001. *Violent peace. Militarized interstate bargaining in Latin America*. New York: Columbia University Press. https://doi.org/10.7312/mare11186

Mintz, A. & DeRouen Jr., K. 2010. *Understanding foreign policy decision making*. Cambridge: Cambridge University Press. https://doi.org/10.1017/CBO9780511757761

Parish Jr., R. 2006. Democrats, Dictators, and Cooperation: The transformations of Argentine-Chilean Relations. *Latin American Politics and Society*, 48(1):143-174. https://doi.org/10.1111/j.1548-2456.2006.tb00341.x

Putnam, R. 1988. Diplomacy and Domestic Politics: The logic of two-level games. *International Organization*, 42(3):427-460. https://doi.org/10.1017/S0020818300027697

Ripsman, N.M. 2009. Neoclassical realism and domestic interest groups, in S. Lobell, N. Ripsman & J. Taliferro (eds.), *Neoclassical Realism, the State, and Foreign Policy*. Cambridge: Cambridge University Press.

Rojas Aravena, F. 1992a. *Gasto militar en América Latina, procesos de decisiones y actores claves*. CINDE/FLACSO.

Rojas Aravena, F. 1992b. De la reinserción a los acuerdos: la política exterior chilena en 1991, in *Chile y el Mundo*, Cono Sur.

Rojas Aravena, F. 1996a. *Balance estratégico y medidas de confianza mutua*. Santiago, Paz y Seguridad en las Américas/FLACSO-Chile/The Woodrow Wilson Center.

Rojas Aravena, F. 1996b. *Medidas de confianza mutua: verificación*. Santiago, Paz y Seguridad en las Américas/FLACSO-Chile/The Woodrow Wilson Center.

Rojas Aravena, F. 2006. Una comunidad de seguridad en las Américas: una mirada a la conferencia especial de seguridad, in J.S. Tulchin, R.B. Manaut & R. Diamint (eds.), *El Rompecabezas. Conformando la seguridad hemisférica en el siglo XXI*. Prometeo Libros/Bononiae Libirs.

Rojas Aravena, F. & Álvarez-Marín, A. 2011. *América Latina y el Caribe: confianza, ¿un bien escazo?* FLACSO/AECID/Gobernabilidad y convivencia democráctica en América Latina/TESEO.

Rose, G. 1998. Neoclassical Realism and Theories of Foreign Policy. *World Politics*, 51(1):144-172. https://doi.org/10.1017/S0043887100007814

Russell, R. 1990. El proceso de toma de decisiones en la política exterior Argentina (1976-1984), in R. Russell (ed.), *Política exterior y toma de decisiones en América Latina*. Buenos Aires: Grupo Editor Latinoamericano.

Russell, R. & Tokatlian, J.G. 2003. From Antagonistic Autonomy to Relational Autonomy: A Theoretical Reflection from the Southern Cone. *Latin American Politics and Society*, 45(1):1-24. https://doi.org/10.1111/j.1548-2456.2003.tb00230.x

Tickner, A.B. 2003. Hearing Latin American Voices in International Relations Studies. *International Studies Perspectives*, 4(1):325-350. https://doi.org/10.1111/1528-3577.404001

Van Klaveren, A. 1984. The Analysis of Latin American Foreign Policies: Theoretical Perspectives, in H. Muñoz & J.S. Tulchin (eds.), *Latin American Nations in World Politics*. Boulder, MA: Westview Press.

Van Klaveren, A. 1997. Continuidad y cambio en la política exterior chilena, in T. Di Tella (ed.), *Argentina-Chile: ¿desarrollos paralelos?* Buenos Aires: Nuevo Hacer Grupo Editor Latinoamericano.

Varas, A. 1980. Foreign Policy and National Security Doctrines. *Documento de Trabajo*, n°100, FLACSO-Chile.

Waltz, K. 1979. *Theory of International Politics*. Reading, MA: Addison Wesley.

03

Colombia – Not So Unusual After All
A case study on the transnational making of the boundary between 'defence' and 'public security'

Manuela Trindade Viana

Abstract

Colombia is often mentioned as an anomaly within the expected framing of defence and public security, an anomaly that arises from a faulty division of labour between the police and the military. In this chapter, I offer a different interpretation: I use Colombia as an entry point to analyse the processes through which the boundary distinguishing 'defence' and 'public security' has historically been built. The argument unfolds in two parts. Firstly, I analyse how counterinsurgency was raised to a privileged position in the Colombian military doctrine in the second half of the 20th century. The second analytical move looks at the dynamic between the United States and Colombia in the making of a counterinsurgency *a la colombiana* and inscribes this dynamic in the hemispheric circulation of military *savoirs*. By dissecting the main direction of transmission in this circuit, I show how defining Colombia as a 'malfunction' in the division of labour between police and military is misleading, as it does not account for the transnational impact on what has come to constitute 'defence' in Colombia. Moreover, the framing of Colombia as an anomaly avoids questioning the assumptions upon which disputes of anomaly/normality rest. I argue that, by focusing on the circulation of military *savoirs*, it becomes apparent that the domains of public security and defence are not only constitutively merged, but also transnationally so. This claim is important, given that the boundary separating these domains came to characterise a central part of our institutional imaginaries of democracy since the 20th century, and perhaps more strongly since the late 1980s in Latin America.

Introduction

In March 2015, in an interview[1] I conducted in the Colombian Superior War College (ESDEGUE, in Spanish), I was told that Colombian defence and public security came to be organised as inextricably associated spheres due to the armed conflict: 'Without basic internal security conditions, it is not possible to turn our attention to traditional defence issues, for the integrity of the Colombian territory has been under threat for decades'. The connection made here between defence and public security points to the latter as a condition of the former: the violence of the armed conflict prevents the Colombian military forces from performing their 'traditional' defence role. It also suggests that the military would only be able to perform their traditional role in a post-conflict scenario, when threats to the Colombian territory and population cease to exist, as there would be no longer be a need for the military to engage in public security. This could be seen as an attempt to justify an anomaly within the expected framing of defence and public security, one arising from a faulty division of labour between the police and the military in Colombia.

However, I offer a different interpretation. Instead of viewing the boundary between defence and public security in Colombia as flawed, I use it to problematise the recurrent framing of this country as an anomaly in terms of the division of labour between the police and the military (as in Rouquié, 1984; Pizarro, 1987a, 1987b; Atehortúa & Vélez, 1994; Vargas, 2003; Ciro & Correa, 2014; Velásquez, 2015). Importantly, my objective here is not to justify and defend the involvement of the military in Colombian public security matters. Rather, my point is that the framing of the problem as such misses the fundamental question regarding the assumptions upon which disputes about Colombia's status as an anomaly rest.

The objective of this chapter is to use Colombia as an entry point to analyse how the boundary between defence and public security has historically been built. I argue that by focusing on the military *savoirs* – technical knowledge whose authority derives from the experience in a specific professional domain – it becomes apparent that public security and defence are not only constitutively merged, but also transnationally so. In other words, public security and defence are intertwined, not as a Colombian idiosyncrasy, but globally through the circulation of military expertise, or military *savoir*. This claim is of fundamental importance, given that the boundary separating those domains came to characterise a central part of our institutional understanding of democracy since the 20th century – perhaps more strongly since the late 1980s in Latin America, when the region was going through a so-called "re-democratisation" processes.

One might say that using Colombia as a case study to argue that the boundary between the terms is blurred is an easy task, for nothing else can be expected from a country where the Military Forces have for decades been engaged in public order affairs. However, my point is precisely that we cannot understand how the spatial and functional limits of defence have been historically constituted without looking at Colombia in the broader context of military *savoirs* in the hemisphere – what I call a 'circuit of military *savoirs*' (Viana, 2017). In the next pages, I show that it is key for us to grasp how the role of Colombian military professionals in public security as defence has been defined.

The argument unfolds in two parts. First, I analyse how counterinsurgency attained a privileged position in Colombian military doctrine in the second half of the 20th century. I focus on the Colombian Army[2] as the branch of the military forces which, throughout the second half of the 20th century, has more systematically been the focus of the military *savoirs* here analysed. In this process, it becomes clear that we need to bring the United States (US) to the fore if we want to identify how the national security doctrine took shape in the making of defence policy in Colombia, and thus also of public security. The emergence of counterinsurgency as a privileged military *savoir* helps to understand the systematic entanglement of the Colombian military with public security affairs.

The second aspect of the analysis looks at the broader context of military *savoirs* in the hemisphere. Through this, I show how defining the division of labour between the police and military in Colombia as malfunctioning is misleading, as it does not account for the transnational influences on what constitutes defence in Colombia. The section also looks at Colombia's recent re-positioning in the hemispheric circuit of military *savoirs*. If Colombia has been seen as an anomaly when it comes to distinguishing defence from public security, what is its status in relation to other countries?

Colombia and the US in the making of a counterinsurgency a *la colombiana*

The literature on the professionalisation of the military in Colombia associates the prominent role of the army in public security with the close relationship between Colombian and US military officers in the second half of the 20th century (Rouquié, 1984; Pizarro, 1987b; Atehortúa & Vélez, 1994; Leal, 2002; Rodríguez, 2006; Vargas, 2014). What are the main features allowing for such a claim, and why is the US used as a reference in the Colombian military's engagement with public security?

In order to address these questions, we need to turn our attention to the 1950s, as it was in this period that interaction with the US army started to crystallise into assistance programmes, instruction materials, and training programmes. A starting point for our discussion is the Korean War (1950-1953), presented by military officers in Colombia such as General Álvaro Valencia Tovar, as 'a source of extraordinary experiences […] which divides the modern history [of the army] in two eras: before Korea and after this experience, when the army was modernized and learned how to fight accordingly to modern concepts' (Pizarro, 1987b). Although the Korean War was the Colombian Army's first experience in battle with the US military forces, the way it is portrayed in Colombian military historiography does not match the occasional character of interactions with the US military prior to the war, or the improvised character of recruitment.[3] Nevertheless, this experience was used by military officers as an opportunity for the intensification of the professionalisation of the army along 'US lines' (Atehortúa, 2008:67-70). More specifically, high-ranking military officers who returned from the Korean War translated their experience into 'technical' improvements in the Army (Pizarro, 1987b:32; Leal, 2002:20; Rodríguez, 2006).

For example, General Alberto Ruiz Novoa, who commanded the Colombia Battalion No. 1 from July 1952 to June 1953, registered what he considered the main contributions from this experience in three different books (1956a, 1956b, 1965). At the tactical level, the aspects he highlighted derive from guerrilla warfare, shown in the importance he attributes to the role of infantry, small-units patrol, and training infantry soldiers not only for body-combat, but also for long-distance marching, rather than counting on motor vehicles for that purpose (Rodríguez, 2006:64). He also pointed to the need to replace heavier and costlier non-portable artillery used in conventional warfare, like cannons, howitzers, and war tanks (Rodríguez, 2006:65). According to the general, one of the main benefits Colombia could gain from closer interaction with the US army was specifically related to psychological operations. He argued that the use of propaganda, rumours and information campaigns could be useful in demoralising communist guerrillas (Rodríguez, 2006:65-66). It is thus noteworthy that he offered a justification of the position of the US army as a reference point for professionalisation that was more attuned to the 'problem of communism' facing Colombia.

Furthermore, General Ruiz Novoa is known for having conceived the main aspects that came to constitute 'Plan Lazo', a set of military operations launched in 1962, when Novoa was Minister of War. Aiming at 'pacifying' Colombia, the rationale of the Plan was that violence had social and economic root-causes (Leal, 2002:43). Specifically, 'the philosophy of the Plan was "to remove the water from the fish", that is, to remove the peasant's support to the guerrilla' (Ruiz, 1992, in Leal, 2002:44) through a set of social and economic policies that were added to the military intervention. This tactical component was referred to as 'civil-military action' (*acción cívico-militar*) by Novoa, in a speech published in 1964 (Ruiz, 1964:247). In practice, civil-military action in Plan Lazo often involved the distribution of pamphlets with information on the mission of the Colombian army, in addition to very occasional services offered by the military in small villages, such as shoe repair and tooth extraction. Importantly, the provision of those services always coexisted with armed confrontations and psychological techniques, such as infiltration and torture, aimed at gathering information on the insurgents.

The forces participating in Plan Lazo had been trained in irregular warfare in the Lancers' School (Escuela de Lanceros), established in 1955 as a specialised unit of the infantry. Months before the foundation of the school, a commission of five Colombian high-ranking military officers visited Fort Benning in Georgia, US, in order to attend the 'Ranger Course' (Leal, 2002:44; Rodríguez, 2006:77). Formalised in 1951 as a specific department within the US Army Infantry School, the rangers are agile and flexible small-unit soldiers engaged in irregular warfare, whose training constituted short-term courses based on counter-guerrilla warfare for jungle and urban terrains, instruction on how to perform ambush and infiltration, and a set of exercises focused on physical preparation and resilience (Rodríguez, 2006:77). With the assistance of the US army's Captain Ralph Puckett, the Escuela de Lanceros was built as a mirror of the Rangers School in terms of training and military procedures.

In an article published in 1959 in the official review of the US Army Infantry School (*Infantry Review*) and then in the Colombian *Revista Militar*, it was claimed that the Colombian Army's interest in the Ranger Course derived from the massive presence of guerrillas and *bandoleros* in specific regions (Puckett & Galván, 1959:94, in Rodríguez, 2006:78):

> These irregular groups have been, for a long time, a continuous threat to the peace and security of the Colombian people; being experts on the mountains and jungle paths, they are very difficult to find and defeat, and the Army has not been successful in dominating them. To overcome this difficulty, it was necessary to put forth a specific training program for a special kind of operation; since small units have been used to combat the anti-socials, the solution became evident: selected officers and non-commissioned officers had to be trained in order to fight the enemy in its own terrain and with its own methods. This was the mission of the Lancers' School, and it excelled at it.

As the excerpt above shows, the creation of the Escuela de Lanceros was considered a concrete response to a security necessity, given the 'continuous threat to the peace and security of the Colombian people'. This version of the national security doctrine became the main axis around which defence practices were developed in Colombia. In this context, the Escuela de Lanceros excelled in fighting 'the enemy in its own terrain and with its own methods', not only through the mobility that such irregular warfare required, but also a specialised *savoir* in the terrains that guerrillas and *bandoleros* were experts on: the mountain and the forest. According to a campaign manual dated 1944, translated and adapted by the US military mission to the Colombian Military Forces, 'In the war in the jungle, the soldier fights two different enemies: man and nature. Between them, nature is often the most impressive one' (Estado Mayor General de las Fuerzas Miltares. República de Colombia, 1944:5).

Such a statement has two main implications. Firstly, it highlights the reliance on the 'native population'. In order to make the soldiers more familiar with the hostile conditions of the jungle, the manual instructs troops to count on 'carefully selected local guides, whose loyalty and integrity are undisputable' (Estado Mayor General de las Fuerzas Miltares. República de Colombia, 1944:50). However, while necessary for the military to feel safer in a terrain they are not familiar with, the 'native population' constitutes a potential danger, for there may be enemy infiltration, a risk which a careful selection process aims to minimise. Furthermore, according to the manual, 'The use of organized native troops … will not only help dissipate any opposition to the presence of our troops, it will also bolster solidarity against a common enemy' (Estado Mayor General de las

Fuerzas Miltares. República de Colombia, 1944:51). The population is thus portrayed as either an enemy to be defeated or an asset to be explored so that the operation succeeds, constituting a source of knowledge on the terrain, as well as a source of intelligence and legitimacy.

The second implication of fighting where and how the 'anti-socials' fight is the format of the training programme. With the assistance of the US military, the Escuela de Lanceros dedicated a significant part of its training programme to familiarising soldiers with the hostile environmental conditions of the jungle.[4] The first groups who graduated from the Escuela de Lanceros were attached to brigades operating in regions considered to be 'infested with guerrillas' (Vásquez & Negret, 1960:60, in Rodríguez, 2006:81). The 1960 memoirs of the Minister of War, Rafael Hernández Pardo (1959-1960), celebrated the efficiency of the *lanceros* in controlling "subversion" foci in those regions. Within a few years, this infantry specialisation constituted the backbone of Plan Lazo.

The features of Plan Lazo correspond to the main pillars characterising what we have come to know as counterinsurgency (Porch, 2013): (i) an emphasis on tactics, mobility, and the small units deriving from it; (ii) a population-centric approach and a 'winning hearts and minds' motto, due to the idea that the population acts as both the key to the success of the operations and the risk of infiltration of the enemy; and (iii) an emphasis on intelligence, given the difficulty of discerning an enemy from an ally in a given population. These features remained the main axes guiding military operations in Colombia throughout the following decades.

The analysis so far has shown how Plan Lazo was central to the elevation of counter-insurgency to a privileged position in Colombian military doctrine, as well as to a more systematic interaction with the US in terms of the professionalisation programme of the Colombian Army in the second half of the 20th century. I now turn my attention to another fundamental piece in our puzzle: Plan Colombia. On the one hand, the analyses about Plan Colombia often underestimate the importance of the war in Korea and Plan Lazo to the consolidation of the features mentioned above. However, if understood as an important point within a broader trajectory, Plan Colombia is an unavoidable subject if we want to discuss the implications of the so-called "post-conflict" context in Colombia for defence doctrine in this country. This is because Plan Colombia takes the features mentioned above to another level, in terms of: (i) the intensity of the relations with the US; (ii) the resources mobilised in the Plan; (iii) the areas covered by the specialisation of the military in Colombia; and (iv) the scale of the professionalisation of the Colombian Army.

The first two aspects are intrinsically linked. Between 2000 and 2006, US foreign assistance to Colombia amounted to US$ 4.7 billion, 80% of which was concentrated in military and police training, equipment, weapons, and vehicles (Isacson, 2006), making Colombia the main recipient of military aid from the US in Latin America, and the third in the world, after Israel and Egypt. Amongst the many ways one can interpret the scale of Plan Colombia, one is that the regime of justification mobilised by the Colombian Army evoked a "military crisis" in a context marked by an intensification of violence in the country. Ongoing military defeats to the FARC in fronts considered as strategic by the Armed Forces resulted in the claim that military reform was both necessary and urgent (*El País*, 1998; Rangel, 1998; Revista Semana, 1998; Villamizar, 2003). Based on this, the Minister of Defence, Rodrigo Lloreda Caicedo (1998-1999), created the Commission for the Restructuration and Modernization of the Armed Forces in 1998, with the objective of developing a comprehensive reform plan.

One of the main components of Plan Colombia was the procurement of aeroplanes and helicopters aimed at strengthening the air power of the Colombian Army, and based on this, 74 helicopters were supplied by the US, and additional ones were procured by the Colombian government (Vargas, 2014:140). Four years after Plan Colombia had been implemented, Colombia had the third largest fleet of helicopters in the Americas, after the US and Brazil (Villamizar, 2003:50). As of 2003, the police and military forces in Colombia had 230 helicopters, of which 30 are of the assault kind, mostly produced in the US (Black Hawk, Bell, Huey, and Hughes) (Villamizar, 2003:51).

If Plan Lazo was characterised by the specialisation of the combat forces within the Colombian Army, this specialisation was further deepened with Plan Colombia, and organised according to different criteria: (i) the geographical characteristics of the Colombian territory, as in the case of the four Mountain Battalions (*Batallón de Alta Montaña*); (ii) specific skills mobilised by military operations, as in the four Mobile Brigades and the Rapid Deployment Force (*Fuerza de Despliegue Rápido* – FUDRA, in Spanish); and (iii) the category of threat, as in the case of the Counternarcotic Brigades (*Brigadas Contra el Narcotráfico* – BACN, in Spanish).[5]

Amongst those specialised forces, the BACN is emblematic of how the US engaged with training in the context of Plan Colombia. Created in 1999, the Counternarcotic Battalions were trained by the 7th Group of US Special Forces in Fuerte Tolemaida.[6] The training programme combined a focus on physical preparation with the familiarisation of the soldiers with terrains such as the jungle and mountain, highlighting the persistent relevance of the rangers in the irregular form of warfare characteristic in Colombia.[7] What is important in Plan Colombia in this regard is the explicit incorporation of counternarcotic policies into military expertise – a domain which until then had been part of the scope of the Colombian National Police (Vargas, 2012).

Finally, an additional key feature of Plan Colombia was how quickly it expanded the manpower of the Colombian Army, predominantly through "professional soldiers" (*soldado profesional*), those who, after having concluded the mandatory military service (18-24 months), decided to remain in the Military Forces, receiving specific training and a salary for their work (Villamizar, 2003:61). In 1998, there were 22,000 professional soldiers in Colombia, while by 2002 there were 55,000 (Vargas, 2014:141). The increase stemmed from the so-called *Plan 10,000*, issued in 1999 with the objective of substituting 10,000 "regular soldiers"[8] for the same number of "professional soldiers" each year until 2001 (Villamizar, 2003:61).[9] The short-term process in the conversion of a regular soldier into a professional soldier allowed for the rapid increase of combat soldiers in Colombia: most professional soldiers were incorporated into the Counter-guerrilla Battalions (BCG, in Spanish) and Mobile Brigades (BRIM, in Spanish) (Villamizar, 2003:61-62) after a 14-week training programme.[10]

Preparing thousands of soldiers for combat required dedicated infrastructure, and the School of Professional Soldiers (ESPRO, in Spanish)[11] was created in December 1999, based in Nilo (Cundinamarca), offering training facilities and short-term courses focusing on the physical preparation of soldiers. Interestingly, the polishing of those who were to become instructors in the ESPRO was undertaken in Fuerte Tolemaida,[12] which was founded in the department of Cundinamarca in the 1950s, during general Gustavo Rojas Pinilla's administration (1953-1957). Under Plan Colombia, Fuerte Tolemaida received massive investments aiming at developing its infrastructure and transforming it into a centre of excellence in military training.[13]

This analysis of Plan Colombia highlights the re-definition of counterinsurgency in Colombia so as to encompass counterterrorism and counternarcotic tactics in a more systematic way. More recently, as Colombia claims to have overcome the violence of the late 1990s, these domains correspond to the military *savoirs* the Colombian Army has been increasingly taken as a reference for to its counterparts in Latin America. In the next section, we describe the transnational influences leading to defence being viewed as public security in Colombia and discuss how the country has come to enjoy a privileged position in more recent years.

The circulation of military *savoirs* in the Americas and the recent re-positioning of Colombia

In mapping the main defence practices of the Colombian Army in the second half of the 20th century, the previous section revealed a fundamental aspect: the role of the US Army as an example for the Colombian Army in the structure, organisation, and execution of their professionalisation programmes. In this section, I argue that this is a specific example of a broader circulation of military *savoirs* in Latin America,[14] which also characterises the US as a diffusion hub, and counterinsurgency as the most valorised concept. For us to grasp the texture of this circuit, we need to identify the main mechanisms through which these military *savoirs* circulate: the military schools operating as diffusion sites; courses taught and manuals useds in those schools; military missions travelling from one country to the other in the hemisphere; and specific military doctrines.

The hemispheric circulation of military *savoirs* started to gain shape in the 1940s, in the context of the Cold War, and contributed to synergies between military forces across the Americas. For example, the organisation of regular meetings and competitions and the creation of permanent commissions on specific topics allowed for the exchange of doctrine and instruction materials, along with the comparison of forces (such as equipment and personnel), the design of cooperation mechanisms, the articulation of a "common" agenda, and networking. These practices are shared, compared, and discussed in inter-American institutions: the Inter-American Defense Board, the Organization of the American States (OAS), and the School of the Americas (SOA). Such an institutional system – and the interactions it allowed for – has two main effects. Firstly, it contributed to the harmonisation of military *savoirs* throughout Latin America during the second half of the 20th century. Secondly, its weight created a reluctance to change the direction of this harmonisation.

A closer look at the SOA will illustrate this point. Colombia only figured prominently in the student population of the SOA from the 1970s onwards (Gill, 2004:74).[15] Between 1970 and 1979, Bolivia, Chile, Colombia, Honduras, Panama, and Peru sent between 1,100 and 1,800 students each, accounting for 63% of total enrolment in the School (Gill, 2004:78). Returning from those courses in the SOA, Latin American military officers often had the content of the material translated into Spanish/Portuguese, so that it could be used as reference for the courses taught in their home countries (Gill, 2004:99). This form of knowledge sharing has continued: in the second half of the 20th century, training manuals on counterinsurgency were created in Fort Levenworth, and then translated to Spanish at the SOA (Gill, 2004:54).

As the definition of what constitutes a threat was developed through the decades, the configuration of the SOA changed, both in terms of the courses offered and in student demographics. For example, while the Central Intelligence Agency (CIA) and the US Army Special Warfare School sent their civil and military professionals to the SOA to teach Latin American students, the Drug Enforcement Agency (DEA) and the Federal Bureau Agency (FBI) undertook similar practices as drug trafficking increasingly became seen as the main threat facing the Americas by the 1980s. In terms of the student population, Mexico, El Salvador and Colombia accounted for 9,000 students in the 1980s – 72% of the total student population (Gill, 2004:83). However, it was only in the 1990s that the Colombian Armed Forces – both police and military personnel – attended specific courses on drugs at the SOA. The SOA Watch database[16] illustrates the changing curriculum offered by the SOA, as well as revealing For instance, the "Patrol Operations" course, attended by 129 low-rank military officers[17] and non-commissioned officers (*suboficiales*) from Colombia during the 1980s, disappeared as such in the following years.[18] Only 30 high-ranked Colombian officers[19] attended courses at the School from 1960 to 1989. Similarly, some of the courses were "tailor-made" for a specific state or group of states – as in the case of "Jungle Courses".

On one hand, the best-attended courses in a given historical context might suggest a transformation of military *savoirs* throughout the second half of the 20th century. On the other hand, the changes mentioned above are all organised under a broader category of military *savoir*: counterinsurgency. The transformations identified must thus be read as a re-articulation within a specific military *savoir* or, more specifically, as refinements in counterinsurgency tactics based on contextual interpretations of what "insurgency" is being combatted, and information on how this "enemy" operates. In other words, the changing curriculum during the second half of the 20th century is not a transformation of military *savoirs* in the same way as the displacement of conventional warfare by counterinsurgency in mid-20th century Latin America.

There is another fundamental aspect related to the courses offered in military schools such as the SOA since the second half of the 20th century. As shown above, while the US enjoys a position of authority in the diffusion of counterinsurgency to other countries in the hemisphere, the tactical refinements and adjustments point to the agency of Latin American military professionals in this process. Since the mid-20th century, the US Army has indeed been the reference point for others in the region when building their professionalisation programmes. However, this does not imply a unidirectional flow. As mentioned above, there is a demand-driven component to courses taught in these institutions, an institutional response to what was considered a priority by key military partners in the region. Indeed, the circulation of Latin American military officers amongst these schools allowed for a solid hemispheric network of military professionals, as well as the legitimisation of the discourse on the "threats" facing societies in the hemisphere, contributing to the fabric of military institutions in those countries.

Enabling this circulation of Latin American military professionals was one of the remarkable features of the history of this institutional fabric. For instance, the economic constraints facing many Latin American states since the end of the 1970s led to a significant decrease in the number of students at the SOA. As an effort to facilitate the flow of students by that time, in 1976 the Gerald Ford administration initiated the International Military Education and Training (IMET) programme, funding the training of foreign troops (Gill, 2004:78). By the 1980s, when many Latin American states were immersed in economic crises, these resources funded Mobile Training Teams (MTTs), small teams formed by US military officers who trained troops *in situ* (Gill, 2004:75, 85). With time, this came to constitute the main platform through which military training was provided in Latin America.

As shown in the previous section, military missions were also important channels through which military expertise on intelligence and irregular combat (the *lanceros*, for instance) were transmitted. The format of such missions varied in duration (the 1962 intelligence mission to Fort Holabird lasted for 8 months, for instance) and scope (to attend a course, to instruct troops, to create a military school and build its curriculum, etc.). As in the case of the *Escuela de Lanceros*, the purpose of the US military mission to Colombia was not only to crystallise a *savoir* on irregular warfare in the form of a specialised school, but also to create the conditions for the transmission of that *savoir*. It was for this reason that a group of high-ranking military officers visited the facilities at Fort Benning to attend the "Ranger Course", making sure that they were in a position to teach others when they returned. Importantly, the SOA was only one of the destinations for Colombian military personnel to familiarise themselves with a specific technique, domain or doctrine.

This circuit of military *savoirs* seems to have changed in recent years, with Colombia coming to operate as a hub for the diffusion of military knowledge in the region. In Fuerte Tolemaida from 2009 to 2013, the Colombian Army and Colombian National Police trained 10,310 professionals from Mexico; 3,026 from Panama; 2,609 from Honduras; 1,732 from Guatemala; 1,132 from Ecuador; 510 from Peru; 465 from El Salvador; and 377 from Costa Rica (Tickner, 2014:3). In April 2013, the *Escuela de Lanceros*, one of the nine training schools in Fuerte Tolemaida, concluded its 367th course, resulting in the training not only of Colombian military professionals, but also of 582 international students from 19 different countries (including Brazil, Canada, Ecuador, El Salvador, France, Peru and the United States) (CENAE, 2013). These numbers reveal that other countries in the world, and particularly in Latin America, have come to take Colombia as a reference in the training of their military and police units in counterinsurgency. Colombia's position in the circuit of military *savoirs* is predominantly based around Fuerte Tolemaida, a facility whose modernisation and transformation into a centre of excellence in military training relied on significant shares of the resources from Plan Colombia.

However, the re-positioning of Colombia in the Latin American circuit speaks not only to the range of courses that came to attract attention from other armies in the region, but also to a specific category of military professional. For example, ESPRO, the school specialising in preparing *soldados profesionales* through short-term courses focused on irregular warfare, appears as a key destination for military personnel in the region. The most-attended courses on 'tactical military operations against illegal organisations' include elite units; mobile units; explosive units; demolitions; and demining (ESPRO, n.d.).

In this sense, ESPRO trains soldiers in both the highly-ramified specialisation that came to characterise the Colombian Army, and a form of "professionalisation" in other armies in Latin America. Being the only school of its kind in South America, ESPRO has received students from Brazil, Chile, China, Israel, Paraguay, Peru, the United Kingdom (UK) and the US (ESPRO, n.d.).

The training of Latin American military professionals in Colombia in recent years is a result of the country overcoming the problem of insurgency in its territory, and now being in the position to teach others based on its expertise. In the words of the Minister of Defence (2011-2015) at the time in Colombia, Juan Carlos Pinzón (2015:8):

> Because of the sustained progress since the turn of the century, and their exceptional expertise and experience, the Colombian Armed Forces are well positioned to evolve into a regional leader in training, education, and actively participate in international peacekeeping, humanitarian assistance, and disaster relief missions around the globe. Colombia's experience successfully combating insurgent groups, illicit facilitators, transnational criminal organizations, and drug trafficking organizations, makes it uniquely capable and qualified to assist other nations that today, or one day, may face similar threats.

Of course, it is important to explore how this re-positioning of Colombia affects the privileged position that the US has enjoyed in the hemisphere for so many decades. Although this is outside the scope of this chapter, it is noteworthy that this recent dynamic is more like a trilateral organisation – preserving the US as a key piece in this arrangement – than a full displacement of the US as the main authority on counterinsurgency. Two elements arising from my fieldwork in Colombia[20] account for this hypothesis. Firstly, the Colombian Ministry of Defence reserves a whole section of its main building in Bogotá for military staff from the US. Second is the significant numbers of military instructors and high-ranked military officers from the US going to Fuerte Tolemaida and the Superior War College (ESDEGUE, in Spanish) respectively.

For the purposes of this chapter, however, the main argument emphasises another aspect in this dynamic, which is the boundary allegedly differentiating defence from public security. In the introduction to this chapter, I highlighted that Colombia is repeatedly framed as an anomaly for the practices undertaken by its Military Forces which are not considered part of a traditional defence agenda. According to this understanding, the historical and systematic engagement of the Colombian Army with public security constitutes a problem in terms of the principles underlying the differentiation of defence and public security.

Within these terms, Colombia's position as an authority in the region in recent years leads to a puzzle, as even countries whose military forces are not seen as anomalies, such as Chile, France, and the UK, have been learning from Colombia's experience in public security matters. In post-conflict Colombia, the debate on the role the Military Forces can perform in peacetime reinforces the need for the Colombian National Police to take the lead in internal affairs. Along with this, the Colombian Army should emphasise civil-military action which, as we have seen, is not that different from counterinsurgency, and export its expertise to 'nations that today, or one day, may face similar threats' (Pinzón, 2015:8). Thus, if Colombia is considered to be a post-conflict context, but the "disturbing" participation of the military in public security continues, the position of the country as a provider of solutions to counterinsurgency operations must be taken as an analytical puzzle. As the analysis here shows, Colombia's position in a broader circuit of military *savoirs* suggests that the term "anomaly" should apply to the whole hemispheric circuit, not just to Colombia. However, this is tantamount to saying that we should question the standard of normality against which this so-called anomaly is assessed.

This chapter has problematised the supposed boundary between defence and public security. By offering an account of how military *savoirs* circulate in the hemisphere, it highlighted that defence and public security are transnational social constructs. Accordingly, the labelling of Colombia as an anomaly when it comes to traditional defence practices is challenged, because it makes it difficult for us to identify the historical processes that resulted in a specific contextual understanding of defence. It is not a matter of shifting the responsibility for "problematic" institutional design from Colombia to the US, for we must also recognise the agency of Colombian military professionals in the history of military *savoirs*. Similarly, we cannot limit our understanding of public security to a given space or function, precisely because it requires broader definitions of internal and external.

Final remarks

What are the assumptions behind the boundary we draw between defence and public security? This chapter has taken up this question through a focus on Colombia as an analytical point of entry. What makes Colombia relevant as a case study is the recurrent framing of the country as an anomaly in light of persistent and pervasive engagement of the Military Forces with public security. This chapter has a twofold argument.

First, I explored how it is necessary to account for the active role of the US Army in the emergence of counterinsurgency as the main military *savoir* guiding the engagement of the Colombian Army with public security. I argued that it is impossible to understand the Colombian Army's notion of defence without including the US Army in the analysis. My second move involved looking at this interaction within a hemispheric circuit of military *savoirs*. The influence of the transnational idea of defence as public security on Colombia points to the limits of confining the anomaly to a specific territorial context. After all, the blurred boundary between those two domains stems from the relation between US and Colombian military professionals, a dynamic which itself is inscribed in a circuit of military *savoirs*.

Furthermore, exploring the circulation of military *savoirs* in Latin America in the second half of the 20th century allows us to more closely examine the common valorisation of counterinsurgency as more relevant to the "threats" that the military in the hemisphere were believed to be facing. Importantly, however, the re-positioning of Colombia in the circuit of military *savoirs* does not refer exclusively to the military. In the post-conflict context, both police and military professionals from other countries have sought Colombian expertise to solve the problems they claimed to be facing.

In this sense, the chapter displaces the spatial (from Colombia to the circuit) and temporal (from internal war to post-conflict) lenses through which we frame "problems" in the supposed boundary between defence and public security. This transnational perspective of how the military came to perform public security functions in Colombia is thus of fundamental importance if we are to question the notion of the two as distinctive spheres of policy, involving contrasting tasks and different professionals of the public force. Considering the position of authority that such a boundary enjoys in our beliefs about democracy, the discussion here acquires particular significance, and particularly in Latin America, where militarisation has increasingly been debated.

One might say that a key aspect is the transformation of warfare. Indeed, the multiple forms that counterinsurgency has taken all share at least one constitutive element: the population-centric approach. This is an essential component, for it is this element that leads to an inherent confusion between police and military functions. If we accept counterinsurgency as a central tenet of defence on the one hand, and public security on the other, then we must also be prepared to accept the modalities of war that constitute social ordering practices in our daily lives.

Notes

1. The interview took place in ESDEGUE on 9 March 2015. Personal information about the interviewee are not public, under the request of the interviewee. For more details on the content of the interview, however, please contact the author: m.trindadeviana@gmail.com

2. The Colombian Armed Forces are constituted by the Military Forces (Army, Air Force, and Navy) and the National Police.

3. Indeed, at least 15 volunteers joined the Battalion right before it departed to Korea: although they were formally enlisted, many of them did not have any previous military instruction (Atehortúa Cruz, A.L., 2008:66).

4. Its main course comprised a twelve-week instruction, structured into four phases. The first one was a six-week course focused on the physical preparation of the soldier through military gymnastics, fencing with bayonet, personal defence, swimming, and survival. During this period, the soldier was also taught on intelligence and tactics, as well as on how to read aerial-photographic maps, to work with explosives, and to lead. The second phase (two weeks and a half) corresponded to patrolling in a flat, jungle terrain, where the soldiers were given eight different counter-guerrilla missions. In the two weeks constituting the third phase, the soldiers patrolled in mountainous terrains and participated in technical and tactical exercises on how to prepare and protect from an ambush. Moreover, in this part of the course, the soldiers engaged in combat simulations, with a mission, a target, and a weapon, and were trained on how to jump on the river with their equipment and uniform. In the final week of the Lancers' Course, the soldier went through several tests on command, patrol and physical resistance (Rodríguez, H., 2006:80).

5. It is important to mention that this process had been accelerated since the 1980s, in the context of the intensification of the "war on drugs". Indeed, in 1985, the Colombian Army created the Urban Anti-terrorism Special Forces Group (*Agrupación de Fuerzas Especiales Antiterroristas Urbanas* – AFEUR, in Spanish), with the objective of countering and neutralising terrorist actions in the main urban areas of Colombia. In 1996, the Army created the Unified Action Groups for the Personal Liberty (*Grupos de Acción Unificada por la Libertad Personal* – GAULA, in Spanish), exclusively dedicated to avoiding and finding solutions to practices of kidnapping and extortion. Currently, the FUDRA, the AFEUR, the GAULA, and the BACN are 4 of the 6 Special Forces of the Colombian Army. For more information, see https://bit.ly/3aPpysq [Accessed 7 September 2018]

6. Currently, the Brigade is constituted by three maneuver units (BACN No. 1, 2 and 3), and one support unit – the Counternarcotic Services and Support Battalion (*Batallón de Apoyo y Servicios Contra el Narcotráfico* – BASCN, in Spanish), responsible for the provision of materials, budget and logistics to the maneuver units (Ejército Nacional de Colombia, 2017).

7. The training programme is constituted by four pillars. The first one involves a technical preparation in which the soldier learns how to master weapons and equipment such as compass, GPS and night vision devices, as well as techniques such as how to build an improvised vessel. In this phase, soldiers are also trained on "ranger operations". The second pillar corresponds to training on physical tactics, including physical resistance exercises such as marching, trotting and training in specific formations (polygonal) and self-defence, in addition to the emphasis on swimming for river crossing and rescue. The third component of the training programme is focused on the psychological preparation of the soldiers, mainly through simulations on how to deal with situations under pressure. Finally, the programme aims at familiarising the soldiers with the legal frameworks on human rights and humanitarian law. In this last phase, the courses instruct soldiers on how to deal with local authorities, and how to proceed with invasion, capture and confiscation.

8. The category "regular soldier" refers to a military professional whose career is prepared from the basis in the Escuela de Cadetes (School of Cadets). In the latter, the military students remain for 4 to 5 years, as the starting point of the military career programme for the low-ranked military in Colombia.

9   The category "regular soldier" refers to a military professional whose career is prepared from the basis, in the Escuela de Cadetes (School of Cadets). In the latter, the military students remain for 4 to 5 years, as the starting point of the military career programme for the low-ranked military in Colombia.

10   See https://bit.ly/2w6kYr5 [Accessed 15 September 2018].

11   See https://bit.ly/3aSMFlW [Accessed 15 September 2018].

12   Ibid.

13   In this context the fortress had its name changed to National Training Center (CENAE, in Spanish). Currently, Fuerte Tolemaida has nine schools specialized in lancers (ESLAN), military parachuting (ESPAM), army tactics (ESERT), support and services for training (BASEN), special forces (ESFER), professional soldiers (ESPRO), shooting (ESTIR), high mountains (ESAMO) and jungle (ESSEL). For more information, see http://www.cenae.mil.co/ [Accessed 15 September 2018].

14   Actually, we could also picture it as a global phenomenon. Porch (2013), for instance, shows how military professionals from France and the United Kingdom travelled to the United States in the 1960s so as to engage in conversations on how their experience could be mobilized in counterinsurgency tactics that were being advanced by the United States in Southeast Asia. In a book edited by Arielli and Collins (2012), a compilation of chapters reminds us how the circulation of military professionals is not a phenomenon confined in a specific geography, nor in a specific time frame.

15   According to Gill (2004:74), after the Cuban Revolution, the SOA had a 42% increase in the number of students in comparison to the 1950s. During the 1960s, when the SOA was transferred from Fort Benning (United States) to Fort Gulick (Panama), 13,500 students attended courses at the School. Venezuela, Nicaragua, Bolivia, Panama, and Peru represented the greatest shares: from 1960 to 1969, between 1,000 and 2,000 trainees were sent by each of these states.

16   https://bit.ly/2WeJG36 [Accessed 17 February 2017].

17   From Second Lieutenant (*Subteniente*) to Major (*Mayor*).

18   From 1978 to 1988, the course was attended by 823 Latin American students.

19   From Lieutenant Colonel (*Teniente Coronel*) to General (*General*). However, only Lieutenant Colonels and Colonels attended courses at the SOA in the period mentioned above.

20   My fieldwork involved interviewing military professionals from diverse ranks in the Ministry of Defense and military schools in Colombia. Focused on the training and schooling of military personnel, I also had access to specific manuals which were used in those schools. The work comprised four 15-day visits to Bogotá from 2014 to 2016.

References

Atehortúa Cruz, A.L. 2008. Colombia en la Guerra de Corea. *Folios*, Segunda época, 27:63-76. https://doi.org/10.17227/01234870.27folios63.76

Atehortúa Cruz, A.L. & Vélez Ramírez, H. 1994. *Estado y Fuerzas Armadas en Colombia.* Cali: TM.

Centro Nacional de Entrenamiento. 2013. *Ser Lancero, honor que cuesta.* https://bit.ly/38yz95n [Accessed 16 September 2018].

Ciro Gómez, A.R. & Correa Henao, M. 2014. Transformación estructural del Ejército colombiano. Construcción de escenarios futuros. *Revista Científica General José María Córdova*, 12(13):19-88. https://doi.org/10.21830/19006586.155

Ejército Nacional de Colombia. 2017. *Historia de la creación Brigada Especial contra el Narcotráfico.* 1 January. https://bit.ly/2PXb4Pe [Accessed 24 September 2018].

El País. 1998. 'El Ejército colombiano recupera una ciudad ocupada'. 5 November. https://bit.ly/39DgDKA [Accessed 24 September 2018].

ESPRO (Escuela de Soldados Profesionales). n.d. *Reseña Histórica.* https://bit.ly/3aKExDR [Accessed 16 September 2018].

Estado Mayor General de las Fuerzas Miltares. República de Colombia. 1944. *La Guerra en La Selva. Manual de Campaña.* Bogota, D.C.: Sección Imprenta y Publicaciones.

Gill, L. 2004. *The School of the Americas: Military Training and Political Violence in the Americas.* London: Duke University. https://doi.org/10.1215/9780822386001

Isacson, A. 2006. Plan Colombia – six years later: Report of a CIP staff visit to Putumayo and Medellín, Colombia. *International Policy Report.* Center for International Policy.

Leal Buitrago, F. 1984. Los militares en el desarrollo del Estado. *Estado y política en Colombia.* Bogota: Siglo XXI.

Leal Buitrago, F. 2002. *La Seguridad Nacional a La Deriva.* Del Frente Nacional a la Posguerra Fría. Mexico, DC: Alfaomega.

Pinzón, JC. 2015. Colombia Back from the Brink: From failed state to exporter of security. *PRISM*, 5(4):2-9.

Pizarro Leongómez, E. 1987a. La Profesionalización Militar en Colombia (1907-1944). *Análisis Político*, 1 (May-August).

Pizarro Leongómez, E. 1987b. La Profesionalización Militar en Colombia (II): El Periodo de La Violencia. *Análisis Político*, 2 (September-December).

Porch, D. 2013. *Counterinsurgency: Exposing the Myths of the New Way of War.* Cambridge: Cambridge University Press. https://doi.org/10.1017/CBO9781139226301

Rangel, A. 1998. El Desastre del Caquetá. *El Tiempo*, 8 March. https://bit.ly/2xgENvZ [Accessed 24 September 2018].

Revista Semana. 1998. *El sindrome de Jacobo.* Nación. 7 December. https://bit.ly/2TPreLD [Accessed 24 September 2018].

Rodríguez Hernández, S.M. 2006. *La influencia de los Estaos Unidos en el Ejército colombiano, 1951-1959.* Medellín: La Carreta.

Rouquié, A. 1984. *El Estado Militar en América Latina.* Buenos Aires: Emecé,

Ruiz Novoa, A. 1956a. *El Batallón Colombia en Korea, 1951-1954.* Bogotá: Empresa Nacional de Publicaciones.

Ruiz Novoa, A. 1956b. *Enseñanzas de la Campaña de Corea aplicables al Ejército de Colombia.* Bogotá: Antares.

Ruiz Novoa, A. 1964. Discurso del Señor Ministro de Guerra, Mayor General Alberto Ruiz Novoa. *Revista de las Fuerzas Armadas*, IX(26):237-247. https://bit.ly/39BZl0t [Accessed 9 February 2017].

Ruiz Novoa, A. 1965. *El gran desafio.* Bogotá: Ediciones Tercer Mundo.

Tickner, A.B. 2014. *Colombia, the United States, and Security Cooperation by Proxy.* Washington, DC: WOLA. http://www.wola.org/files/140318ti.pdf [Accessed 24 September 2018].

Vargas Velásquez, A. 2003. 'Los militares en el Postconflicto'. *El Tiempo*, 9 January. https://bit.ly/2TQUfGL [Accessed 24 September 2018].

Vargas Velásquez, A. 2012. *Las fuerzas armadas en el conflicto colombiano: antecedentes y perspectivas.* Medellín: La Carreta.

Vargas Velásquez, A. 2014. The profile of the Colombian Armed Forces: A Result of the Struggle against Guerrillas, Drug Trafficking and Terrorism, in D.E. Mares & R. Martínez (eds.), *Debating Civil-Military Relations in Latin America.* Brighton: Sussex Academic Press. pp. 130-154.

Velásquez, R., C.A. (Coronel r.). 2015. La fuerza pública que requiere el postconflicto. *Working Papers*, No. 13. Fundación Ideas para la Paz. Bogotá: FIP.

Viana, M.T. 2017. Preparing for War, Preparing for Peace: the Colombian "success story" and the transformation of the military professional. PhD dissertation, Institute of International Relations, Pontifical Catholic University of Rio de Janeiro, Rio de Janeiro, Brazil.

Villamizar, A. 2003. *Fuerzas Militares para la guerra*: La agenda pendiente de la reforma militar. Bogotá: Fundación Seguridad & Democracia.

04

Cuba's Defence Diplomacy
Hard and soft power, 1959-2018

Dirk Kruijt

Abstract

Cuba, a country with eleven million people, played a significant military and development role from the 1960s to the late 1980s, and is still an influential donor country. Its reputation was built on support to revolutionary and national liberation movements in Latin America and in Africa. Additionally, Cuba also was a provider of medical and humanitarian assistance to the global South.

Cuba's military were involved in training and advising Latin American revolutionaries and provided assistance in several African colonial and postcolonial wars. During the 'special relation' with the Soviet Union and the COMECON countries, Cuba had a redoubtable military and intelligence apparatus, at the same time procuring explicit defence against a potential invasion by the United States (US) and supporting multiple revolutionary and resistance movements in Africa, Latin America and the Caribbean.

After the disintegration of the Soviet Union and the COMECON, Cuba restructured its economy, strongly supported by its Armed Forces as a management instrument and as a food and security provider. In the 1990s, when its strong military position was weakened, Cuba still preserved and even expanded its medical and literacy assistance to many countries. During the period of the Latin American Pink Tide governments (2000-2015), Cuba was again a high-profile player in Latin American and Caribbean politics.

Introduction: Cuba's diplomacy and 'revolutionary internationalism'

Cuba, a country of eleven million inhabitants, was a significant power in the international political arena from the 1960s to the late 1980s, and it is still an influential donor country. Its reputation was built on support to revolutionary and national liberation movements in Latin America (providing training and assistance to guerrilla movements) and in Africa (through a strong military presence). However, it is less well-known that Cuba is also an innovative and significant provider of medical assistance to the Global South, beginning in the early 60s and intensifying until the present. To this day, the country is a significant development actor in terms of medical and literacy expertise, especially in Africa and Latin America.

In this chapter, I will trace the emergence and evolution of Cuba's formal and informal diplomatic networks which supported and influenced the political and social agendas of Latin American, Caribbean and African countries.[1] This will be done through an interpretation of Cuba's 'Revolutionary Internationalism' and its motives, the modus operandi of its diverse hard and soft power institutions, and its large-scale personnel involvement. The chapter traces the results of Cuba's internationalism in the context of their foreign relations with the two superpowers during the Cold War, and with Latin America and the Caribbean, Africa and the Middle East. My guiding research question is: how did Cuba cope with its singular position of enmity with the US and relatively stressful friendship with the Soviet Union during the Cold War without losing its own long-term objective, which was not only to survive but also produce radical changes in the so-called Third World? How did Cuba maintain its influence and prestige when the military muscle and generous economic assistance of the Soviet Union ended?

With its strategic position in the Gulf of Mexico, and its proximity to the US (Florida, 90 miles), Mexico (Yucatan, 120 miles), Haiti (50 miles) and Jamaica (90 miles), Cuba is a key country in the Caribbean. However, it is precisely this geopolitical location that made Cuba, the largest island of the Caribbean, an object of the expansionist policies of its larger neighbours, especially the US. Several 19th century American presidents tried to annex or buy the island and its population when it was still a Spanish colony, and during the last of its three consecutive liberation wars, the US intervened and occupied the island in 1898.

Formally declared independent in 1902, it remained an American protectorate until 1 January 1959, when the Cuban Revolution triumphed. However, it remained economically vulnerable until the end of the 20th century, reinforced by the centuries-long tradition of sugar production, lack of energy sources, and need for a strong defence structure against external threats. Cuba's economic vulnerability was intensified by an economic embargo imposed in 1962 by the US, which also meant economic sanctions against third party commercial relations.

Senior Cuban diplomat, Carlos Alzugaray, former ambassador to the European Union, clarified 'Cuban national interests' as follows (2017):

> Preserving and defending the independence, sovereignty, self-determination, and security of the Cuban nation as the primary mission; establishing external economic relations that will promote its development without being used as a means of external pressure; assuming and protecting a popular, democratic, and participatory form of government based on its own traditions; establishing and promoting of a prosperous and fair socio-economic system in which "the full dignity of the human being should be the first law of the Republic (...)"; safeguarding and protecting Cuba's cultural identity and socio-political values; and projecting Cuba's cultural

and ideological values internationally at a level of involvement proportional to its real possibilities as an effective member of international society.

In the course of this contribution, it will become clear that, as a guiding principle, Cuba always sought and acquired political support from the non-aligned (NO-AL) countries and became an eminent member state of this organisation, accompanying its military endeavours with humanitarian aid as long as it had one of the largest standing armies in the region. After the Cold War, it continued its humanitarian assistance and maintained a position of influence far beyond its 'country class' of a relatively small country.

I will analyse two distinct phases in Cuba's relations with the outside world. The timespan covers the period from 1959 to 1989 during which Cuba, with Soviet support, had created the second-largest military force in the Western hemisphere and participated in large-scale expeditionary operations in Africa, as well as providing continuous support to left-wing movements and governments in Latin America and the Caribbean. During the 60s, its revolutionary objectives and defensive and stability priorities sometimes clashed with those of the Soviet Union, but in the period thereafter, keen diplomacy and military expeditionary support to Africa were balanced. From the early 70s to the late 80s, Cuba experienced relative welfare under Soviet support. However, a new phase was initiated with the implosion of the Soviet Union, when Cuba's 'Special Period' began, a period of internal austerity and drastic changes in its foreign policy that continued in the 21st century, based on soft power and peace facilitation.

Cuba's overtures towards the Soviet Union were initiated in February 1960, when Soviet Vice-Premier Mikoyan visited Cuba and negotiated a trade agreement on the importance of Cuban sugar, Soviet oil and commercial loans. In May 1960, diplomatic relations with Moscow were re-established; they had been ruptured in 1952. Che Guevara headed the first significant Cuban mission to the Soviet government and, in May 1962, the Soviet Union became Cuba's self-appointed military protector by soliciting Fidel Castro's permission to deploy nuclear missiles on the island. Kruschev intended to kill two birds with one stone (Pavlov, 1994:40-42):

> ...positioning nuclear weapons on the doorstep of the United States with the noble justification of the "defence of Cuba against possible American aggression". An agreement was reached about the deployment of intermediate and tactical nuclear missiles and specialized Soviet forces, a total of 45,000 enlisted men and officers with munitions and other supplies for thirty days of combat, while authorizing Field Commander Pliyev in Cuba to exercise his own flexible response ... without asking for Moscow's permission.

This caused the so-called Cuban Missile Crisis. After this, Khrushchev and Kennedy cut a secret deal without consulting the Cubans, who heard of the deal through the radio and were deeply offended (Ramonet, 2008:312). The Soviet government tried to soften Cuban feelings with multi-billion-dollar grants, abundant military assistance, and the continued presence of the Soviet military on the island with a combat brigade of 2,800 men.[2] However, the mutual relations only improved during the Brezhnev years (Bain, 2007:27; Latrèche, 2011).

Part I: Cuba's hard power (1960s to 1980s)

After 1959, Cuba had to handle three main concerns: redesigning its relationship with the US, whose growing enmity had become obvious; reshaping an economic and political support structure with new allies in Europe, Asia and Africa; and remodelling its formal and informal diplomacy to support and promote similar revolutionary efforts elsewhere while maintaining its sovereignty, and economic and commercial interests, and building a broad international support structure. That meant simultaneously building an army; developing formal and informal diplomacy; establishing an economic support structure with new allies; and creating an internal security system and foreign intelligence service.

Army and militia (the FAR and MINFAR)

Fidel Castro, the political and military leader of the insurgency, resisted a counterinsurgency campaign by the regular army of dictator Batista, before taking the initiative in a successful offensive strategy that finally caused the collapse of Batista's forces (Castro, 2010a, 2010b). Cuba's new armed forces were created from the structures of the guerrilla forces, the Rebel Army in the Eastern mountains of the Sierra Maestra, and the armed resistance groups of students and youth in the flat lands and the cities. Along with this, rebellious army, navy and air force officers who had been incarcerated by the former dictator were reintegrated in the new army (Graña, 2008). In February 1959, Fidel Castro became prime minister (and president in 1976), while his brother Raúl Castro took over command of the Armed Forces.

Cuba's first armaments were donated by the Venezuelan government of that time, or captured by the rebel leaders, while the first military training of the newly appointed officers was sometimes given by former sergeants of Batista's army (Báez, 1996). The new military ranks still referred to the former rebel army ranks, and anyone above the rank of captain was *comandante* (major), even the commanders of brigades (Bell, Caram, Kruijt & López, 2004; Kruijt, 2017). In 1961, the government structure was reorganised, and the Ministry of Defence became the Ministry of the Fuerzas Armadas Revolucionarias (FAR and MINFAR). Raúl Castro was the minister from 1959 to 2006 when he succeeded his brother as (interim) presiden, before being formally elected Cuba's president in 2008, retiring in 2018 while remaining first secretary of the Communist Party.

The FAR had a double mission in the 1960s (Dominguez, 1978:342-246). The first was to suppress internal insurgencies of 'counterrevolutionary forces', mainly in the mountainous Escambray region in Central Cuba where around 180 smaller and larger rebellion groups were contesting the new government. The second was to protect the country against invasions, as in the Bay of Pigs (Playa Girón) in 1961, when a group of 1,300+ CIA-trained mercenaries undertook a failed invasion. After two days of severe fighting, the invaders had suffered casualties of 114 dead and 1,200 captured. Immediately before the invasion, the government had also created a system of militias (currently called the Milicias de Tropas Territoriales, MTT), youth members with light weapons who protected Cuba's infrastructure and assisted the FAR. However, before the Missile Crisis of 1962, the Soviet Union had already provided support to the Cuban Armed Forces in the form of equipment.

In 1970, after a failed sugar harvest, the Cuban leadership had to publicly recognise that its economy needed Soviet support. Sugar was Cuba's only real export commodity, and at the time both capitalist and Soviet economists were unanimous about the wisdom of continuing this mono-product culture, despite all previous efforts of industrial diversification and import substitution. Numerous Soviet experts visited the island for economic planning, business management, engineering projects, infrastructural design, military and technological advancement, and even higher education. In 1972, Cuba became a full member of the COMECON (an association for economic integration), and the contingent of Soviet specialists increased from 1,000 in the early 1960s to 6,000 by 1975; of them, 50% were military specialists (Duncan, 1985:87ff., 101).

Soviet investments and development assistance contributed to a remarkable growth of new industrial plants, and the reconstruction of out-of-date enterprises, mostly sugar plants (Pavlov, 1994:76). The Soviet Union had essentially become Cuba's mono-supplier of essential products, oil and raw materials, its principal provider of fertilisers, trucks, cars, and road-construction equipment, and also paid the running costs of transportation in both directions, dispatching about 300 cargo vessels on a permanent basis (Pavlov, 1994:83).

One of the institutions that strongly benefitted from Soviet support was FAR (Báez, 1996; Vellinga, 1976). The Cuban military maintained warm relations with their Soviet counterparts and commanding officers received training in Moscow or Leningrad (Baez, 1996). The FAR were modernised along Soviet lines, and until the late 90s, nearly all Cuban generals had been trained in the Soviet Union.

In the early 70s, a re-equipment programme was launched with the most sophisticated weaponry (MIG fighter-bombers, T-62 tanks and BM-21 missile launchers) and military technology at the time (Duncan, 1985:101). During the three decades of 'fraternal cooperation' between the Soviet Union and Cuba, the FAR was annually provided with supplies, training and equipment worth about US$1 billion (Latell, 2003:10). By the late 1970s, the Armed Forces had expanded hugely and at its peak by the end of the 1970s, and during its Africa campaigns, the FAR had between 470,000 and 510,000 members (Latell, 2003:11; 2009):

> It was the largest military force in Latin America and vastly bigger than those of countries Cuba's size anywhere in the world. Furthermore, man for man during the 1970s and 1980s, it may have been the best and most experienced fighting force of any small nation, with the single exception of Israel.

In the early 1970s, military officers also started to perform managerial functions beyond the soldierly realm. There had always been cabinet ministers with a military rank, and from that point on, a process started in which eight to ten senior members of the FAR were permanently in charge of strategic ministerial portfolios (Duncan, 1985:108-109).

The FAR also implemented large-scale expeditionary operations in Africa LeoGrande, 1980; Gleijeses, 2002, 2013; George, 2005; Liebenberg, Risquet & Shubin, 2016). By the 60s, the Cuban leadership had sent military deployments to Algeria and Syria, to Congo Brazzaville and Congo (Zaire), and it operated in the Horn of Africa in the 70s. However, its most prominent role was in Southern Africa. Cuba sent 380,000 soldiers and 70,000 additional civilian technicians and volunteers to Angola, equipped with 1,000 tanks, 600 armoured vehicles and 1,600 pieces of artillery (Risquet, 2007:xlvii; 2008:102). Along with this, Cuba had a military presence in Ethiopia, Eritrea, Guinea Bissau and Mozambique, and sent civilian 'internationalists' to at least ten African countries. However, the FAR operated only sporadically in Latin America, especially in the 1960s (Ramonet, 2008:733), although it was often not the FAR members who participated, but rather special envoys or instructors of the Special Forces within the Ministry of the Interior (MININT), under the leadership of Piñeiro (see the section below on Foreign Intelligence).

Diplomacy (MINREX and ICAP): The managing of Cuba's foreign relations

Whatever the Soviet influences and pressures on matters of foreign policies in Latin America, especially with respect to the political actors of the left, Fidel Castro was never an obedient subscriber to Soviet politics (Pavlov, 1994:97ff.). While the Soviets assisted with credit lines, commercial activities, technical and military assistance, and arms delivery, the Cubans acted as political advisers and provided military training to national liberation movements in Latin America and in Africa. In fact, over several decades, Cuba was the 'general hospital' for many wounded or crippled revolutionaries and welcomed insurgents and political exiles onto the island.

Militarily, Cuba became engaged in African wars, while politically it heavily supported Latin America's guerrilla movements in the 60s and continued to help new politicians and actors of the left in Latin America and the Caribbean. Fidel Castro personally monitored Cuba's foreign policy closely, and this is perhaps illustrated in an observation by the then-Minister of MINREX, Carlos Rafael Rodríguez. In 1972, at the request of Cuba's spy master Manuel Piñeiro, three senior members of Cuba's foreign intelligence requested an interview about the Central Committee's policy with respect to the US. Rodriguez told them bluntly (Suárez & Kruijt, 2005:47ff., 233ff.):

> Look ... if Fidel instructs me that I explain to you Cuba's policy with respect to the United States, I think that I'm able to do it. But don't worry too much. Here, [even] the members of the Politburo do not know what our policy is about. We're going to give you instructions and you follow what Fidel and I tell you to do. Because here, [the two] who handle it, are Fidel and me.

Cuba was one of the 20 founding members of the Organization of American States (OAS) in 1948, but in 1962 its membership was suspended by a majority vote, under strong American pressure. The island was excluded because 'Marxism–Leninism was incompatible' with the principles and objectives of the inter-American system (Birsen, 2015), although the two US neighbours, Canada and Mexico, never ruptured diplomatic relations with Cuba. During the Reagan administration, Cuba was put on the US 'State Sponsors of Terrorism' list in 1982, and there is no other country in the world that was the subject of American sanctions for so many decades (Bernell, 2011).

Cuba's formal and informal diplomacy was in support of the group of NO-AL countries, of which the island became an influential member, and in 1979 and 2006, the country hosted the sixth and the 14th NO-AL summits. Cuban diplomacy was also explicitly aimed at establishing and maintaining good relations with all member states of the United Nations (UN), and it participated and participates in nearly all organisations of the UN system. It took special care to nurture its relations with Latin America and with the many small Caribbean states, all of them voting members of the UN General Assembly (Ceceña, Barrios, Yedra & Inclán, 2011; Suárez & Amézquita, 2013). Its prestige and reputation as an important international and regional ally made the persistent economic embargo a yearly dispute in the UN meetings.

Many of Cuba's political alliances with leftist movements and their leaders were based on personal friendships with Fidel Castro, who developed a strong affinity for Caribbean leaders, becoming close with Chile's Allende, Panama's General Torrijos, Peru's General Velasco, and Venezuela's Hugo Chávez after 1994. He also occasionally hand-picked Cuban diplomats who he thought would be appreciated by these leaders and become 'friends of the president', even before the establishment of formal bilateral relations.

An additional instrument of informal policy was and is the Instituto Cubano de Amistad con los Pueblos (ICAP, Cuban Institute of Friendship with the Peoples), initially an organisation created to accommodate foreign visitors and sympathisers, but which gradually became an institution where semi-diplomatic relations were nurtured with countries still not officially tied to Cuba. These included the overseas territories of American and European countries, especially in the Caribbean before independence, with relevant political and popular organisations in other countries, and the Caribbean islands with American, British, Dutch and French statehood.

The ICAP identified other actors and movements beyond the traditional 'revolutionary movements', searching for other nationalist-leftist regimes and movements:

> We realized that by being more open-minded and using a more delicate tone, we penetrated sectors to which we otherwise would never have gotten access. That is what we called "popular diplomacy", going beyond the sectors we traditionally reached, the so-called "revolutionary sectors".[3]

The ICAP also created 'visiting brigades' when American, European, African and Asian delegations came to the island. Notwithstanding the official Cuban 'scientific atheism', the ICAP and the Departamento América tried to invite the representatives of Liberation Theology of to the island:

> During a long period, we maintained good relations with many of the progressive religious believers … A large number came to Cuba and it facilitated the ideological and political insight of Cubans into that even so important issue. On matters of religion many Latin Americans and some Europeans, like François Houtart, assisted us. I conversed and dined twice with Gustavo Gutiérrez, the founder of Liberation Theology, and transmitted him Fidel's invitation to come to Cuba. But he didn't dare to make that trip.[4]

The famous Dominican Frei Betto (1985) came to Havana and interviewed Fidel Castro about religion and revolution. In the early 1990s, ICAP co-organised solidarity flights from Brazil (with theologists Frei Betto and Leonardo Boff), accompanied by entrepreneurs, politicians, students and artists. ICAP also assisted in masses celebrated by progressive priests with solidarity groups from Argentina and Colombia.[5]

Foreign intelligence (MININT and Central Committee)

The most publicly acknowledged Cuban organisation for relations with Latin American rebel movements was the Departamento América, which was formally created in 1975 but had operated under other names since early 1959. Its chief was the veteran *comandante* Manuel Piñeiro, a close friend and confidant of Fidel and Che Guevara. This small but efficient organisation was hidden in the corridors of the MININT, until 1961 called the Ministry of Government, and initially was called section 'M'.[6]

'M' had several sections, and section M-OE was reserved for Special Operations (M-Operaciones Especiales), the paramilitary unit that trained many Latin American guerrillas. Section M (and its successors) always operated autonomously as they were created with the consent of Fidel Castro, who wanted a swift and agile organisation without bureaucracy. Originally, Piñeiro was also in charge of State Security and Foreign Intelligence, as Technical first Vice-Minister of MININT. In the early 70s, State Security, Intelligence and 'National Liberation' were split in three, and 'National Liberation' became a 'civilian' committee of the Central Committee of the Communist Party. The Departamento America was an elite organisation, with members hand-picked by Piñeiro.

Algeria and Mexico were of crucial importance for Cuba. Algeria was the pre-eminent country for diplomatic and other contacts with liberation movements in Africa and Asia, and in 1962, Piñeiro formed a "working group" for strategic cooperation. Cuba assisted with a mission during the Algerian-Moroccan conflict in 1963, followed in 1965 by an agreement on intelligence cooperation between the two countries. Also in 1965, a special unit was created to accommodate relations with other African liberation movements. Che Guevara travelled to Africa for three months in 1964-1965, establishing more direct contacts, and Algeria was instrumental in establishing these relations.

Mexico was the only Latin American country that did not rupture its diplomatic contacts with Cuba in the 60s under strong American pressure. Thus, Mexico, and by the late 1960s Panama under General Torrijos as well, were the bridgeheads for travel and contact with clandestine movements in the region. In Mexico City and Panama City, many revolutionary refugees found a home, and institutional contacts were established during the decades of military dictatorship. From the Cuban embassy in Mexico to the legation in Panama, intensive contacts with the Central American guerrillas were maintained.[7]

Latell, the former CIA officer at the Cuba desk in 1964 and the National Intelligence Officer for Latin America in the 90s, considered the Cuban intelligence as 'one of the five or six best such organizations in the world, and has been for decades' (Latell, 2007:192).

Part II: Cuba's soft power (1989 to present)

Civilian assistance has always been another hallmark of Cuba's policy, even during interventions in war contexts. During the Central American civil wars, the future FPL representative of the largest military organisation within the Salvadorian guerrilla army FMLN, Jorge Juárez, was severely wounded. He remembers the treatment he received during his periods of convalescence:

> It is surprising, but nobody wrote a study about the enormous efforts of the Cubans to attend to the many injured of the wars in Central America. Nearly all patients received literacy courses, primary or secondary education as well; the blind were trained in braille. It was probably the most important contribution of Cuba to the combatants of Central America.[8]

In fact, most military missions in Africa were accompanied by medical and literacy campaigns, albeit on a smaller scale. The most striking example was the spontaneous post-war development assistance in Angola. When the Cuban military contingents were to return after their tour of duty in Angola, the authorities asked Raúl Castro for urgent reparation and reconstruction assistance. Many common soldiers and officers, mechanics, drivers, engineers and paramedics took off their uniforms and continued working for weeks, or sometimes months, as civilian volunteers, applying their own professional experience. However, soft power diplomacy became the first priority after the implosion of the Soviet Union and the Socialist bloc in the late 80s and early 90s.

The FAR and national defence after 1991

When the Cold War came to an end and the US emerged as the only military superpower, the consequences for Cuba were disastrous. Cuba had become highly dependent on economic and military support from the Soviet Union and Eastern Europe, in the form of credits, soft loans and export subsidies. Its economic structure had been transformed into a mono-exporter of sugar and agricultural products to the COMECON countries, and while not a member of the Warsaw Pact, its military standing had benefitted enormously from special training and favourable delivery of equipment and spare parts. However, the collapse of the Socialist bloc was not the only catastrophe that struck Cuba, as the US intensified their already-damaging embargo. The Cuban government announced a 'Special Period in Peacetime', as the standard of living was drastically reduced.

Cuba's economy and society were transfigured into a system of extreme austerity and belt-tightening. Food was incredibly scarce, and nutritional deficiencies began to develop, while the desperate shortage of fuel nearly caused a standstill of the public transport system. The government prevented hunger and starvation by distributing packages of essential food and clothing, and the situation slowly improved after the turn of the century. Cuba's economy was in part refinanced by the 'special relationship' between Cuba and Venezuela after the election of Chávez as president (Clem & Maingot, 2012; Trikunas, 2012; Piccone & Tricunas, 2014). The dependency on incoming hard currency (euros from tourism and medical tourism) grew, and dollar remittances from the Cuban diaspora increased from US$1,2 billion in 2006 to US$3,5 billion in 2014 (Erisman, 2018:51-55. Nickel exports, medical missions abroad, medical services for paying foreign visitors, and Canadian, European and Latin American tourism became the primary source of foreign currency. President Putin pardoned 90% of the unsettled foreign debt, and Cuba restructured its foreign debt with the member states of the European Union. Finally, in 2015, after decades of silent diplomacy, diplomatic relations with the US were re-established (LeoGrande & Kornbluh, 2014; Ramírez & Morales, 2014), but the effects of 25 years of the 'special period' are ongoing.

Cuba's military was also hit hard by the downfall of the Socialist bloc, and in December 1982, Soviet Party leader Andropov explicitly told Raúl Castro that the Soviet Union would not defend Cuba by sending troops. Subsequently, the MINFAR created a defensive tunnel structure and a voluminous militia system with the 'nationwide capabilities to revert to guerrilla warfare in the event of major military hostilities' (Latell, 2003:11). Economic and military support by the Soviets continued on a diminishing scale after 1985, but fell dramatically by the end of 1991, when the Soviet Union morphed into Russia. Delivery of new weapons and spare parts was very difficult, and the FAR's only option to remain operational was cannibalising older equipment. Fuel was another crucial shortage.

When Chávez negotiated with Cuban diplomats about an invitation to travel to Cuba in 1994, the Departamento America let him know, 'that Cuba not even could buy him a matchbox', and Chavez decided to buy the ticket himself.[9] When a Guatemalan army delegation visited the island in 1996 during the reconciliation sessions with the guerrillas, the pilots were shown MIGs, but they were not ignited, as this was only permitted in emergency situations.[10]

Trainings in Russia were cancelled, intelligence hardware was restricted, and military service was reduced from three to two years. The FAR's personnel was officially halved, although the reductions probably went further, to one third or less of its previous strength, while the budget was cut in half (Klepak, 2000:3ff., 2005:47ff., 2014; 2018:26ff.; Diamint & Tedesco, 2018). A similar process occurred within the MININT's military structures, and in 1994, the Special Forces of the MININT, the training specialists of the Latin American guerrillas in former decades, were dissolved.

Thus, Cuba's hard power diplomacy came to an end. During the 80s, Cuba had supported Central American guerrillas in El Salvador and Guatemala, and the victorious post-guerrilla Sandinista government in Nicaragua. However, in 1990 it had to retire all of its military presence, and in 1991 the last troops departed from Africa. The reduced FAR received new tasks. There had always been military veteran generals in key posts of the government, and now, with an economy in crisis, these veterans were selected to fulfil management functions in most of the strategic Cuban industries (Klepak, 2018:30-31). During the 1990s and early 2000s, approximately 60% of state enterprises had a military manager, and in the early 90s, promotion to lieutenant-colonel required a management course in agricultural or industrial economy. During the twelve years of government by Raúl Castro (2006-2018), the budget of the FAR slowly increased.

Public health care and medical brigades

Cuba's internationalism, which until the mid-1980s had been predominantly expressed through support for guerrilla movements in Latin America and the Caribbean and large-scale military operations in Africa, had now turned to provision for humanitarian assistance by medical and literacy teams (Feinsilver, 1993; Kirk & Erisman, 2009; Kirk, 2015, 2018; Erisman & Kirk, 2018). Cuba's civilian development aid aims to provide poor citizens in underdeveloped or poor countries with assistance in fields in which Cuba has expertise: public health provisions and literacy campaigns, post-disaster reconstruction, and sport (training and facilities). According to the statistics of the MINREX, from 1959 to 2011, around 156,000 Cuban civilians worked as 'internationalists' worldwide: 81,000 in Africa, 47,000 in the Americas, and 10,000 in the Middle East. In the same period, around 40,000 academic professionals, of whom 30,000 came from Africa, graduated in Cuba.[11] Cuba assisted in the establishment of medical schools in Yemen (1976), Guyana (1984), Ethiopia (1984), Guinea Bissau (1986), Uganda (1988), Ghana (1991), Luanda (1992), Gambia (2000), Equatorial Guinea (2000), Haiti (2001) and Eritrea (2003).[12]

The first Cuban medical mission abroad was in Algeria (1963), and by 1978, around 2,000 Cuban health personnel worked abroad, which increased to 3,000 in 1999, 3,800 in 2001, 15,000 in 2003, 25,000 in 2005 and 30,000 in 2007 (Kirk & Erisman, 2009:8, 12). During the administration of Raúl Castro, this number grew and other medical initiatives, such as medical schooling for foreigners, were continued or expanded. In July 2016, 55,000 medical professionals (of which 25,000 were doctors) were working in 67 countries (Kirk, 2018:59). This brought and brings Cuba an enormous amount of prestige in the Global South (Huish, 2014:188ff.).

In October 1998, Fidel Castro launched the idea of a special Medical School for Latin American students, the Escuela Latinoamericana de Ciencias Médicas (ELAM). The university opened its doors in September 1999 with students from 18 Latin American and Caribbean countries. By the mid-2000s, it started to attract students from other continents and from 2012, students from 98 countries graduated from ELAM. The ELAM system and study allowances also expanded to other countries when Venezuelan President Chávez co-financed and co-developed the Cuban initiative. ELAM-like medical schools were established in Bolivia, Nicaragua and Venezuela, and undergraduate schools were set up in Guyana and Nicaragua.[13]

In 2004, Cuba launched the programme Operación Milagro (Operation Miracle) to cure cataract and other eye diseases, co-financed by Venezuela. It started in Venezuela and was extended to many other countries in Latin America, the Caribbean, Africa and Asia. According to official data, 2,577,000 persons benefitted from this Cuban-Venezuelan initiative between 2004 and 2015 (Misión Milagro, 2016) Medical brigades operated and still operate in many Latin American and Caribbean countries, especially after natural disasters (Kirk, 2018:63-66ff.). In 2016, the countries which most benefitted from Cuban medical support in Latin America were Venezuela (28,351 medical personnel), Brazil (10,994), Bolivia (721), Ecuador (567), Guatemala (415) and Guyana (181); while those in Africa were South Africa (9,344), Angola (1,712), Mozambique (303), Guinea (221), Namibia (125) and Gambia (113). During the Ebola outbreak in West Africa, 258 medical specialists were sent to Sierra Leone, Liberia and Guinea (Anderson, 2014).

Literacy campaigns

A second instrument of international assistance is literacy campaigns. In Cuba, a massive literacy campaign was organised in 1960, and in 1961 the island had been officially declared 'free of illiteracy'. Based on these experiences, Cuban teachers advised on, assisted in and implemented literacy programmes in Angola and Nicaragua, and in other assistance missions in Latin America, the Caribbean and Africa.

In 2000, the instrument was standardised in an audio-visual programme called 'Yo, sí puedo' (Yes, I can) (Artaraz, 2012). In the early 2000s, it was implemented in Venezuela on a massive scale, with half a million unemployed students incorporated as teachers, and around 500 Cuban experts assisting in the specific design. In 2006, Venezuela was also declared 'free of illiteracy', and the programme was then adapted for the multinational and multilingual country of Bolivia. Of the indigenous population, around 40,000 Quechua and Aymara monolingual Bolivians benefitted from the programme, while Cuban and Venezuelan teachers adapted the design for a second campaign during assistance to Haiti in the aftermath of the 2010 earthquake.[14] Meanwhile, Cuba had implemented adapted versions of 'Yes, I can' in 30 countries (Abendroth, 2009).

Peace negotiations

By the late 80s, Cuba became engaged in peace negotiations in the Latin American region. Fidel Castro and Piñeiro convinced the leaders of the M-19 and members of the Colombian Coordinadora Guerrillera Simón Bolívar (CGSB) to engage in a political rather than a military solution, and Piñeiro organised meetings between the CGSB and the Salvadorian FMLN to facilitate formal and informal peace dialogues. Cuba continued to play a leading role in the peace process in Colombia and in Guatemala, the last two countries in which guerrilla movements were still fighting in the last decade of the 20th century.

After the brutal years of counterinsurgency (1978-1983) under the military governments of Lucas García and Ríos Montt, the guerrillas lost the war, and retired to remote indigenous regions, retaining some smaller urban pockets in the western highlands and the northern jungle (Balconi & Kruijt, 2004; Kruijt, 2008:144-153). The leadership of the URNG lived in exile in Mexico City, from where the chief commanders directed the war by fax and telephone.

After the return to democracy, informal conversations were initiated in Costa Rica and Spain, and formal discussions in Oslo. From 1991 to 1996, the peace negotiations continued, but the real breakthrough came when two key negotiators, Rodrigo Asturias (of the

Guatemalan URNG) and General Julio Balconi (an army general), reached an agreement about informal consultation, extended to extra-official sessions between the army and the guerrillas, with the silent approval of the civilian presidents. Norway and Cuba acted as facilitators, and in March 1996, Cuba organised a three-day session of reconciliation between the army and the guerrillas in Havana, after which the guerrillas announced a unilateral cease-fire, and a timetable for disarmament was drawn up.[15] The peace negotiations were successfully ended after the Havana session, and Cuba's relationship with Norway on matters of peace in Latin America would continue throughout the larger period of the Colombian peace talks in the 1990s and 2000s.

Colombia's peace process had a history of pacts, ceasefires, amnesties, demobilisation and reintegration into society (Pizarro, 2017; Villamizar, 2017). During one of the most important peace processes, which lasted from 1989 to 1991, Cuba acted as a peace facilitator, at the request of both the Colombian government and the guerrilla movements. Thereafter, only the two oldest guerrilla movements, the FARC and the ELN, continued their insurgency operations. From then until the present, nearly all consecutive Colombian presidents asked for Cuba's assistance to re-initiate informal dialogues, re-open informal peace talks, provide facilities in Cuba, and ask for peace diplomacy and missions of Cuban diplomats (Castro, 2017).

After the peace agreement with FARC in 2016, peace negotiations were initiated in and then suspended by the new government of President Duque.

Conclusions

Ninety miles away from the US, the most powerful military world power, Cuba's diplomacy was based on defence alliances and support from Asian, African and Latin American countries. With its relatively weak economic structure and its history of sugar exportation, it relied largely on monocultural sugar production and generous credits and grants during its alliance with the Soviet Union and the European Socialist bloc. This was also true of its military capability. It supported guerrilla and national liberation movements in Latin America, largely through training, medical support and facilities on the island, and in Africa, with expeditionary military forces as well as medical and civilian support.

After the collapse of the Soviet Union, Cuba's soft power became the defining characteristic of its defence policy. During more than 15 years of intimate relations with Venezuela (1999-2015), Cuban-Venezuelan soft policy favoured manifold countries. It was during the time of ALBA (the Alianza Bolivariana para los Pueblos de Nuestra América, Bolivarian Alliance for the People of Our America) that a special bond between Cuba and Venezuela was created in 2004, and afterwards expanded to Bolivia (2006), Nicaragua (2007) and Ecuador (2009), and a further six Caribbean island-states between 2008 and 2014.

The first 15 years of the 21st century were also Latin America's Pink Tide, with friendly socialist or reformist governments in Argentina, Bolivia, Brazil, Chile, Ecuador, El Salvador, Guyana, Nicaragua, Paraguay, Peru, Surinam, Uruguay, and Venezuela, and good relations with most Caribbean island-states. Cuba and Venezuela opted for new Latin American bodies, where the US was absent or not dominant: UNASUR (the Union of South American Nations, the Unión de Naciones Suramericanas, although Cuba did not become a member); CELAC (the Community of Latin American and Caribbean States, Comunidad de Estados Latinoamericanos y Caribeños, a kind of OAS but excluding Canada and the US); and the Sao Paulo Forum, a side group of leftist Latin American political and social movements.

Cuban defence policy has always been interwoven with its internationalism, which became part of the daily life of many Cuban families, where husband or wife, daughter or son participated in missions abroad. 'Roughly a tenth of Cuba's population of eleven million has taken part in some form of internationalism: as soldiers in foreign wars, disaster relief personnel, teachers, doctors, cultural workers, and specialists in a vast variety of fields' (Randall, 2017:209).

During the long consecutive government periods of Fidel Castro (1959-2006) and Raúl Castro (2006-2018), 'internationalism' and international solidarity were the backbone of Cuba's foreign relations and defence diplomacy. Bilateral relations with Asian, African, Latin American and European countries, and membership of nearly all organisations of the UN system, were and are nurtured. While Cuba's military capabilities have shrunk dramatically and its economy, even after the prudent reforms of former president Raúl Castro, is still seeking its stability and self-sustained growth, it enjoys significant international goodwill. For example, year after year, the UNGA has voted against the continuance of the US embargo, with a growing majority of countries condemning it. By November 2017, only two countries opposed the resolution – Israel and the US. Cuba's defence policy is therefore not based on military presence or sophisticated equipment, but on humanitarian assistance and medical expertise. It even downgraded its pretences of being an offensive force promoting revolutions worldwide. In June 2019, the Cuban government closed the offices of the OSPAAAL, the former Organization of Solidarity with the People of Asia, Africa and Latin America, founded in Havana in January 1966 after the Tricontinental Conference, when it had acclaimed to be the forerunner of revolutionary support to the socialist cause.

Notes

1. This article draws on research published as Kruijt (2017) and Suárez and Kruijt (2015).
2. The combat brigade remained in Cuba until September 1991, a month after the coup attempt against Gorbachev.
3. Interview with Giraldo Mazola (Havana, 3 February 2012) and Luis Morejón (Havana, 1 March 2012). Mazola was the founding Director and Morejón was the Vice-Director of the ICAP (see Suárez & Kruijt, 2005:15ff., 422ff.).
4. Interview with Fernando Martínez Heredia, Cuba's leading philosopher until his death in 2017 (Havana, 2 March 2012); see Suárez and Kruijt (2005:703ff.).
5. Interview with Luis Morejón (Havana, 1 March 2012); see Suárez and Kruijt (2005:422ff.).
6. I use the term 'Departamento América' to cover all institutions that evolved from G2 in M in Vice Ministerio Técnico (VMT) of the MININT: Dirección General de Inteligencia (DGI), Dirección General de Liberación Nacional (DGLN), all operating within the MININT, and then Departamento América after 1975. Eventually, the Departamento América was incorporated into the Departamento de Relaciones Internacionales of the Central Committee.
7. Interviews with Ramiro Abreu (19 and 25 October 2011), Jorge Luis Joa (27 October 2011), and Fernando Ravelo Renedo (interview 17 October 2011); see Suárez and Kruijt (2005:520ff., 95ff., 120ff.).
8. Interview with Jorge Juárez Ávila (16 July 2015).
9. Interview with Carlos Antelo, then the minister councillor at the embassy in Caracas (Havana, 24 and 27 October 2011); see Suárez and Kruijt (2015:600ff.).
10. Conversations with General Julio Balconi in Cuba (October 2003).
11. Presentation by and discussion with Noemí Benítez y de Mendoza (Sociedad Cultural José Martí), "Internacionalismo y política exterior de la Revolución Cubana", at the International Symposium La Revolución Cubana. Génesis y Desarrollo Histórico, organised by the Instituto de Historia de Cuba (13-15 October 2015.)
12. https://bit.ly/2w5KgFQ [Accessed 12 January 2016].
13. Interview with Maritza González Bravo, academic vice-rector of the ELAM system (9 November 2012); see Suárez and Kruijt (2015:656ff.).
14. Interview with Javier Labrada (Havana, 8 November 2012). Labrada was a senior adviser in Venezuela, Bolivia and Haiti; see Suárez and Kruijt (2015:634ff.).
15. Interview with Ramiro Abreu, the long-time Cuban overseer during the Central American civil wars (Havana, 25 October 2011); see Suárez and Kruijt (2005:520ff.).

References

Abendroth, M. 2009. *Rebel Literacy: Cuba's National Literacy Campaign and Critical Global Citizenship*. Sacramento: Litwin Books, LCC.

Alzugaray, C. 2017. *Cuban Revolutionary Diplomacy, 1959-2017*. Cubadebate 28 September. https://bit.ly/2QbmoY3 [Accessed 25 May 2018].

Anderson, J.L. 2014. 'Cuba's Ebola Diplomacy', *The New Yorker*, 14 November. https://bit.ly/33bBSAG [Accessed 6 June 2018].

Artaraz, K. 2012. 'Cuba's Internationalism Revisited: Exporting Literacy, ALBA, and a New Paradigm for South–South Collaboration', in P. Kumaraswami (ed.), *Rethinking the Cuban Revolution Nationally and Regionally: Politics, Culture and Identity*. London: Wiley–Blackwell (The Bulletin of Latin American Research Series), pp. 22-37. https://doi.org/10.1111/j.1470-9856.2011.00645.x

Báez, L. 1996. *Secretos de generales*. Havana: Editorial SI-MAR S.A.

Bain, M.J. 2007. *Soviet–Cuban Relations 1985 to 1991. Changing Perceptions in Moscow and Havana*. Plymouth: Lexington Books.

Balconi, J. & Kruijt, D. 2004. *Hacia la reconciliación. Guatemala, 1960-1996*. Guatemala: Piedra Santa.

Bernell, D. 2011. *Constructing US Foreign Policy. The Curious Case of Cuba*. New York: Routledge. https://doi.org/10.4324/9780203829264

Birsen, F. 2015. The Cuban Revolution, the U.S. Imposed Economic Blockade and US-Cuba Relations, *Global Research*, 27 February. https://bit.ly/2W5TZq6 [Accessed 13 July 2018].

Castro Ruz, F. 2010a. *La victoria estratégica*. Havana: Oficina de Publicaciones del Consejo de Estado.

Castro Ruz, F. 2010b. *La contraofensiva estratégica. De la Sierra Madre a Santiago de Cuba*. Havana: Oficina de Publicaciones del Consejo de Estado.

Ceceña, A.E., Barrios, D., Yedra, R. & Inclán, D. 2011. *El Gran Caribe. Umbral de geopolítica mundial*. Havana: Editorial de Ciencias Sociales.

Clem, R.S. & Maingot, A.P. 2012. *Venezuela's Petro-Diplomacy. Hugo Chávez's Foreign Policy*. Gainesville: University Press of Florida.

Diamint, R. & Tedesco, L. 2018. 'Incertidumbres cubanas: Las Fuerzas Revolucionarias en el proceso de transformaciones', paper presented at the XXXVI International Congress of the Latin American Studies Association LASA), Barcelona, 23-26 May.

Dominguez, J. 1978. Cuba: Order and Revolution. Cambridge: Belknap Press of Harvard University Press.

Duncan, W.R. 1985. *The Soviet Union and Cuba. Interests and Influences*. New York: Praeger.

Erisman, H.M. 2018. Cuba's International Economic Relations: A Macroperspective on Performance and Challenges, in H.M. Erisman & J.M. Kirk, (eds.), *Cuban Foreign Policy: Transformation under Raúl Castro*. Lanham: Rowman and Littlefield, pp. 43-57.

Erisman, H.M. & Kirk, J.M. (eds.). 2018. *Cuban Foreign Policy: Transformation under Raúl Castro*. Lanham, MD: Rowman and Littlefield.

Feinsilver, J.M. 1993. *Healing the Masses: Cuban Health Politics at Home and Abroad*. Berkeley: University of California Press.

George, E. 2005. *The Cuban Intervention in Angola, 1965-1991. From Che Guevara to Cuito Cuanavale*. London: Frank Cass.

Gleijeses, P. 2002. *Conflicting Missions. Havana, Washington, and Africa (1959-1976)*. Chapel Hill: The University of North Carolina Press.

Gleijeses, P. 2013. *Visions of Freedom. Havana, Washington, Pretoria, and the Struggle for Southern Africa, 1976-1991*. Chapel Hill: The University of North Carolina Press. https://doi.org/10.5149/9781469609690_Gleijeses

Graña Eiriz, M. 2008. *Clandestinos en prisión*. Havana: Editorial de Ciencias Sociales.

Huish, R. 2014. The Heart of the Matter. The Impact of Cuba's Medical Internationalism in the Global South, in C. Krull (ed.), *Cuba in a Global Context. International Relations, Internationalism, and Transnationalism*. Gainesville: University Press of Florida, pp. 176-207. https://doi.org/10.5744/florida/9780813049106.003.0011

Kirk, J.M. 2015. *Healthcare without Borders: Understanding Cuban Medical Internationalism*. Gainesville: University Press of Florida. https://doi.org/10.5744/florida/9780813061054.001.0001

Kirk, J.M. 2018. The Evolution of Cuban Medical Internationalism, in H.M. Erisman & J.M. Kirk (eds.), *Cuban Foreign Policy: Transformation under Raúl Castro.* Lanham: Rowman and Littlefield, pp. 59-75.

Kirk, J.D. & Eirsman, H.M. 2009. *Cuban Medical Internationalism. Origins, Evolution and Goals*. New York: Palgrave Macmillan.

Klepak, H. 2000. *Cuba's Foreign and Defence Policies in the 'Special Period'*. Ottawa: FOCAL Paper 00-4. February.

Klepak, H. 2005. *Cuba's Military 1990-2005. Revolutionary Soldiers during Counter – Revolutionary Times*. New York: Palgrave Macmillan.

Klepak, H. 2014. A Model Servant. The Revolutionary Armed Forces and Cuban Foreign Policy, in C. Krull (ed.), *Cuba in a Global Context. International Relations, Internationalism, and Transnationalism*. Gainesville: University Press of Florida, pp. 44-57. https://doi.org/10.5744/florida/9780813049106.003.0003

Klepak, H. 2018. The Defense Contribution to Foreign Policy: Crucial in the Past, Crucial Today, in H.M. Erisman & J.M. Kirk (eds.), *Cuban Foreign Policy: Transformation under Raúl Castro*. Lanham: Rowman and Littlefield, pp. 25-41.

Kruijt, D. 2008. *Guerrillas: War and Peace in Central America*. London: Zed Books.

Kruijt, D. 2017. *Cuba and Revolutionary Latin America. An Oral History*. London: Zed Books.

Latell, B. 2003. *The Cuban Military and Transition Dynamics*. Miami: Institute for Cuban and Cuban-American Studies.

Latell, B. 2007. *After Fidel. Raul Castro and the Future of Cuba's Revolution*. New York: Palgrave Macmillan.

Latell, B. 2009. *The Revolutionary Armed Forces: Cuba's Institutional Linchpin*. Miami: Institute for Cuban and Cuban American Studies.

Latrèche, L. 2011. *Cuba et L'USSR. 30 ans d'une relation improbable*. Paris: L'Harmattan.

LeoGrande, W.M. 1980. *Cuba's Policy in Africa, 1959-1980*. Berkeley: University of California, Institute of International Studies.

LeoGrande, W.M. & Kornbluh, P. 2014. *Back Channel to Cuba. The Hidden History of Negotiations between Washington and Havana*. North Carolina: University of North Carolina Press. https://doi.org/10.5149/northcarolina/9781469617633.001.0001

Liebenberg, I., Risquet, J. & Shubin, V. 2016. *A Far-Away War: Angola 1975-1989*. Stellenbosch: African Sun Media. https://doi.org/10.18820/9781920689735

Misión Milagro: 12 años al servicio de los más necesitados'. 2016. *TeleSUR*, 7 July. https://bit.ly/38OJvhy [Accessed 29 November 2017].

Pavlov, Y. 1994. *Soviet-Cuban Alliance: 1959-1991*. New Brunswick: University of Miami, North-South Center, Transaction Publishers.

Piccone, T. & Tricunas, H. 2014. *The Cuba-Venezuela Alliance. The Beginning of the End?* Policy Brief, June 2014, of the Latin America Initiative – Foreign Policy at BROOKINGS. https://brook.gs/2wPclkT [Accessed 22 June 2018].

Pizarro, E. 2017. *Cambiar el futuro. Historia de los procesos de paz en Colombia (1981-2016)*. Bogota: Penguin Random House Grupo Editorial.

Ramírez Cañedo, E. & Morales Domínguez, E. 2014. *De la confrontación a los intentos de "normalización". La política de los Estados Unidos hacia Cuba*. Havana: Editorial de Ciencias Sociales (2nd edition).

Ramonet, I. 2008. *In Conversation with Fidel*. Havana: Cuban Council of State Publications.

Randall, M. 2017. *Exporting Revolution: Cuba's Global Solidarity*. Durham: Duke University Press. https://doi.org/10.1215/9780822372967

Risquet Valdés, J. 2007. 'Prólogo a la edición cubana', in Piero Gleijeses. *Misiones en conflicto. La Habana, Washington y África, 1959-1976*. Havana: Editorial de Ciencias Sociales (3rd Cuban edition), pp. vii-xlviii.

Risquet Valdés, J. 2008. 'La epopeya de Cuba en África negra', in P. Gleijeses, J. Risquet & F. Remírez (eds.), *Cuba y África. Historia común de lucha y sangre*. Havana: Editorial de Ciencias Sociales.

Suárez Salazar, L. & Amézquita, G. 2013. *El Gran Caribe en el siglo XXI. Crisis y respuesta*. Buenos Aires: Consejo Latinoamericano de Ciencias Sociales (CLACSO).

Suárez Salazar, L. & Kruijt, D. 2015. *La Revolución Cubana en Nuestra América: El internacionalismo anónimo*. Havana: RUTH Casa Editorial (e-book).

Trinkunas, H.A. 2012. The Logic of Venezuelan Policy during the Chávez Period, in R.S. Clem. & A.P. Maingot (eds.), *Venezuela's Petro-Diplomacy. Hugo Chávez's Foreign Policy*. Gainesville: University Press of Florida, pp. 17-31. https://doi.org/10.5744/florida/9780813035307.003.0002

Vellinga, M. 1976. The Military and the Dynamics of the Cuban Revolutionary Process. *Comparative Politics*, 8(2):245-270. https://doi.org/10.2307/421328

Villamizar, D. 2017. *Las guerrillas en Colombia. Una historia desde los orígenes hasta los confines*. Bogota: Penguin Random House Grupo Editorial, serie Debate.

05

Venezuela's Defence Diplomacy under Chávez and Maduro (1999-2018)

Dirk Kruijt

Abstract

Between the 1950s and the late 1980s, Venezuela's economy and welfare attracted many migrants. An economic crisis, subsequent mass uprising and riots, and brutal repression by the armed forces was a watershed. Mid-career officers conspired; one of them, Hugo Chávez, a Lieutenant-Colonel staged a coup that failed (1992). Imprisoned and amnestied, he founded a political movement, won the presidential elections and took office in 1999.

Chávez and Castro became revolutionary brothers-in-arms. Venezuela supported Cuba by subsidised oil, Cuba provided military and intelligence experts, and medical and literacy personnel on a massive scale, around 50,000 in 2013. Chávez launched an extraordinary pro-poor reform programme, the 'socialism of the twentieth century'. Meanwhile, he strengthened the armed forces both numerically and budgetarily, buying Russian and Chinese equipment. He also created militias of armed civilians up to 365,000 members.

Gradually the military occupied more strategic positions as cabinet ministers or supervisors of state institutions. Chávez death in 2013 coincided with the fall of the oil prices, dramatic budget cuts, mass demonstrations, and mass outmigration, in the context of a galloping inflation and a polarised society. His successor Maduro governs by decree (there are two contending parliaments) and turned nearly all significant cabinet and top administrative positions in the public sector and the nationalised economy to the military, his staunch allies.

Introduction: Venezuela's natural resources under previous governments

Venezuela has the second largest oil deposits in the world, owns huge gas reserves, and has the second largest hydropower facilities in Latin America. For almost the entire twentieth century, Venezuela was blessed with abundant natural resources that enriched the national elite and a growing middle-class population. Oil was discovered in the 1920s, and in the first three decades after World War II, the booming oil prices made Venezuela a wealthy country. From the 1950s to the early 1980s, Venezuela's economy experienced consistent growth, and the country enjoyed one of highest standards of living in Latin America, attracting many migrants. Particularly in the 1960s and 1970s, oil revenues guaranteed generous public spending on welfare programmes, health care and education, and food and transport subsidies. Venezuela was also one of the founding members of the Organization of the Petroleum Exporting Countries (OPEC). In 1976, the oil industry was nationalised and by 1980 the new conglomerate, *Petróleos de Venezuela S.A.* (PDVSA), was the third largest oil company in the world after the purchase of refineries in the United States (US) and Europe.

From the late 1950s onwards, Venezuela had a bipartisan political system, the result, after a period of dictatorship, of a pact between two parties: *Acción Democrática* (AD), a social democratic party with a strong labour base; and the *Comité de Organización Electoral Independiente* (COPEI), a centre-right Christian Democratic party. For 40 years, they largely alternated office, but in the late 1980s this political structure deteriorated, as a result of internal leadership disputes and widespread corruption amongst public officials (Levine, 2002). The political decline was accompanied by a collapse of world oil prices, a process of devaluation and double-digit inflation (84% in 1989 and 99% in 1996).

An IMF-assisted adjustment programme, launched by government technocrats as shock therapy for the economy, prompted mass uprising and riots in the country's capital Caracas, which were repressed by the armed forces (Bertelsmann Stiftung, 2018:5). This so-called 'Caracazo', with a death toll of at least 500 citizens, was a watershed event.

The advent of Chávez

Venezuelan mid-career officers, members of a group called COMACATE (in English: Comandantes [Lieutenant-Colonels], Mayors, Captains and Lieutenants) began to conspire against the government and planned a reformist coup. There were also other parallel military opposition groups, one of which was headed by Hugo Chávez, then a Lieutenant-Colonel who, along with his brothers-in-arms, formed a clandestine movement (MBR-200) and staged a failed coup in 1992. He received only a light prison sentence and he retained a considerable popularity as someone who had stood up to government corruption. After his release, he founded another political movement with a programme of social reforms and presented himself as a presidential candidate.

After his release from jail, he was discreetly monitored by Cuban diplomats. When he launched his new movement and campaigned in the slums and rural villages, they were impressed by the adoration he attracted, and when they heard religious villagers saying, "The Messiah has come, I want to touch the Messiah", they were convinced that Chávez would be the next Venezuelan president. His campaign for social and economic reforms won him the favour of both the rural poor and urban slum dwellers, the working class and the impoverished middle classes. When he wanted to visit Cuba, he was told that

"Cuba not even could buy him a matchbox" and he bought his own ticket. When the plane landed, Fidel Castro greeted him as if he already were a Chief of State. It was the beginning of a special bond: Fidel the wise old mentor, Chávez his young revolutionary successor and colleague.

Chávez was not the first revolutionary Venezuelan military president. In 1958, after the overthrow of Venezuelan dictator Pérez Jimenez and before the bipartisan pact between AD and COPEI, leftist Rear Admiral Wolfgang Larrazábal became interim president. He sent a large stock of weapons to Castro's Rebel Army in December 1958, when they were at the brink of victory. Similarly, Chávez was a life-long devotee of Simon Bolívar and admirer of leftist military reformists Velasco (in Peru, 1968-195) and Torrijos (in Panama, 1968-1981), and he built on their legacy. Bolivar, Velasco, and Torrijos believed in the ideal of an indivisible unity between people and the army, and identified themselves as military reformers with a special calling to break the power of the economic and political oligarchy, restore national control over the economy, and carry out social reforms, implemented by the Armed Forces. Their public discourses and they are basically identical: soldiers of poor descent, familiar with poverty, educated within the army which let them grow beyond their expectations, extremely loyal to the armed institution, and acting as structural reformers for the benefit of the poor and underprivileged. However, Chávez was the most outspoken and emphasised the role of the military as the vanguard of his future revolutionary process. In his own words: 'We can say that it is like the formula of water: H_2O. If we say that the people are the oxygen, the armed force is the hydrogen. Water doesn't exist without hydrogen' (Bilbao, 2002:28-29). The new president decided to trust his loyal brothers-in-arms and other military senior officers.

He campaigned as a presidential candidate against the two existing but disintegrating political parties (Carnevali, 2014), and won the elections in 1998. In 1999, he organised a Constituent Assembly where he obtained a large majority. He later won three consecutive presidential elections: in 2000 (with 60%), 2006 (with 63%) and 2012 (with 55%).

Like Simon Bolivar, the national and Latin American hero of the War of Independence, Chávez envisioned a 'civil-military alliance'. Before Chávez's presidency, the Venezuelan military was constitutionally restricted to safeguarding public security and protecting the national territory. They could not vote in elections and were not expected to participate in public debates. The new Chávez Constitution drastically changed the role of the armed forces, turning it into an instrument of national development and a service provider to the poor and underprivileged. His initial political movement, and later the United Socialist Party of Venezuela (*Partido Socialista Unido de Venezuela*, PSUV), was built on the sympathy and the loyal votes of the poor classes of society; by the time he took in office in 1999, approximately half the population lived below the poverty line (ECLAC, 2001:44).

He also received support from grassroots organisations that emerged during his presidency, and more than 30,000 'communal councils' (*consejos comunales* in Spanish), elected by the community to initiate and oversee local activities and policies.

However, there was also growing opposition from military elites, and segments of the middle- and upper-classes. In 2002, Chávez survived an attempted military coup, and a failed general strike, organised by a heterogeneous alliance of military and opposition party leaders, which left the already-divided political opposition discredited. As a result, Chávez purged the higher military echelons, and loyalty to the president and the 'Bolivarian Revolution' became a career requirement.

The Venezuelan armed forces under Chávez

The Venezuelan Armed Forces have four branches: the Army, the Navy, the Air Force, and the National Guard (a kind of militarised police). These were renamed the "National Bolivarian Armed Force" (FANB, *Fuerza Armada Nacional Bolivariana* in Spanish). Gradually, the FANB became the executive instrument of the charismatic President-Comandante, who had organised his sympathisers into a political party, militias, trade unions, and neighbourhood associations. The higher echelons of the military and the mid-ranking officers became part of the transformed army, used as a state-building institution and the right arm of the president. The nationalist-leftist ideology of the 'military as guardians of the nation', acting for the benefit of the entire nation, especially the poor, contributed to their institutional status. Since the beginning of the Chavez's presidency, the armed forces had been used for civil tasks, and this role was later expanded, such as in the management of gigantic housing projects and other infrastructural provisions.

The appointment of the military to management positions in these projects, the administration, and the nationalised economy helped to increase their loyalty to the president, who styled himself as following in the footsteps of Bolivar. It also helped that military salaries were increased, and that lower-class popular access to the military and militias was encouraged. After the removal of adversaries within the armed forces after the failed coup of 2002, Chávez rapidly promoted loyal non-commissioned officers to officers and mid-career officers to top jobs, and members of the armed forces were permitted to vote in elections.

Between 2008 and 2015, the armed force's budget grew from 1.06% to 4.61% of the GDP, while military personnel increased from 117,400 in 2010 to 197,744 in 2014 (from 40 to 63 per 10,000 citizens). In 2015, the number of militias was 365,046, organised in 100 'integral defence areas' (RESDAL, 2016:210-215; Jácome, 2018). Chávez named these popular auxiliary forces the 'People-in-Arms' (*Pueblo en Armas*) to emphasise the bond between the armed forces and the civilian population.

Venezuela's sources of weaponry changed over time. At first, Chávez tried to match the much-larger armed forces of Colombia (around 400,000 effectives due to its 'internal armed conflict') by buying sophisticated Russian equipment especially for the Venezuelan air force and navy. In later years, that was complemented by Chinese multipurpose airplanes. He also tried to acquire Brazilian and Spanish aircraft and French submarines, but US pressure prevented the delivery (IISS, 2009:57-58). In 2005, Chávez also signed a contract with Russia for the assembly of Kalashnikov assault rifles, ammunition and drones for popular defence purposes, in the case of a US invasion. As long as world oil prices were high, the Venezuelan government heavily invested in weaponry.

Socialism of the 21st century, Cuba and petro-diplomacy

In the first ten years of Chávez's presidency, he expanded on his notion of 'socialism of the 21st century'. World oil prices were booming, and the oil revenues were the basis for an extensive redistribution programme. Chávez's socialism consisted of extensive nationalisation and expropriation, more than 20 major social and economic reforms, new political structures, the incorporation of the army as an executive body, and a charismatic *President-Comandante*. He launched a large series of domestic social and economic 'missions', headed by trusted military personnel and civilians, in the process creating a system of presidential ministers and cabinet members who depended directly on the president's orders.

Research NGO *Transparencia Venezuela* worked out that, of all 526 Venezuelan state-owned enterprises, 74% were nationalised or expropriated under presidents Chávez and Maduro. Oil giant PDVSA, nationalised in 1975 and extended to a conglomerate of interlinked corporations, became the financial draft horse of the reforms, while the nationalisation of banks facilitated financial control by the government. In 2003, a policy was issued on foreign exchange and on consumer prices in the hands of the state (Transparencia Venezuela, 2017:3-4, 12, 32).

After 2002, Castro provided Chávez with Cuban bodyguards, as in the case of Allende in the early 1970s. Chávez also began to arm civilian militias as had been done in Cuba, where militias had been created immediately before the Bay of Pigs invasion in order to prevent domestic difficulties or counter an invasion by foreign mercenaries or soldiers. In later years, the Cuban and Venezuelan security apparatus reached an agreement of mutual cooperation, enabling operations in one another's territory.

Chávez and Castro built a relationship as two equal partners with Venezuela as financier, which became a mutually beneficial agreement: Cuban doctors, literacy trainers and educational experts went to Venezuela, while Cuba received generous oil deliveries at preferential rates. In 2013, the year of Chávez's death, around 50,000 Cuban teachers, literacy experts, university professors, doctors, dentists, paramedical personnel and other experts were employed in Venezuela. Chávez also became the financier of a network of like-minded Latin American countries, the ALBA countries (Bolivarian Alliance for the Peoples of Our America): with Bolivia (2006), Nicaragua (2007), Ecuador (2009) and six Caribbean island-states, with Surinam and Haiti receiving observer status. Honduras's affiliation in 2009 was prevented by a military coup.

The Cuban and Venezuelan leaders considered a kind of further political unification, with Cuba's Vice-President of the Council of State in 2005 claiming that, "there was only one country with two presidents". In 2007, Chávez launched the idea of a Cuban-Venezuelan confederation: 'In the near future we, Cuba and Venezuela, could perfectly establish a confederation of republics: one confederation, two republics in one, two countries in one.'[1] However, Venezuela and Cuba had two decidedly different economies and political structures, and Venezuela's was already strongly polarised. As a result, the project was never realised.

The Cuban-Venezuelan health programme and the many other missions initiated in those first years were a great success, giving Chávez huge popularity. Undeniably, the quality of life for the poorer people of Venezuela greatly improved during the first ten years of his presidency (ECLAC, 2017:47, 50). According to the Venezuelan Institute of statistics (INE), the poverty percentage decreased from 44% in 1999 to 27% in 2010.

Chávez's foreign policy was aimed at a Latin American integration policy that was not dominated by the US. He was one of the main architects of a new hemispheric integration model, with the Bolivarian Alliance for the Americas (ALBA) in 2004, the Union of South American Nations (UNASUR) in 2008, and the Community of Latin American and Caribbean States (*Comunidad de Estados Latinoamericanos y Caribeños*, CELAC) in 2012. These organisations were created to bypass US and OAS political and military influence, and to exclude those Caribbean islands with US or European statehood. Most of the ideological underpinning was a fervent pro-poor, pro-socialist and 'Our America' discourse, accompanied by vitriolic anti-US rhetoric.

There is good reason to use the term 'petro-diplomacy' (coined by Clem & Maingot, 2011) when discussing Venezuelan foreign policy. Financial support was given from Venezuelan oil revenues or on the basis of highly favourable oil-supply programmes, like PetroCaribe, PetroSur, PetroNica and PetroAndina. Chávez was an important contributor to institutions like the Forum of São Paolo, founded in 1990 by Lula and Castro, that comprises more than 100 organisations and movements, and he also co-financed the World Social Forum, a Brazilian initiative created in 2001. In 2003, Castro and Chávez initiated the Network of Intellectuals and Artists in Defence of Humanity, presided over by Mexican sociologist Pablo González Casanova.

However, with respect to Chávez's domestic policy, while poverty and income inequality declined, urban crime grew. Between 1999 and 2010, the number of murders per 100.000 inhabitants increased from 25 to 57, and this is at least partly due to radical changes in the institutional order. The new government encouraged land invasions, the establishment of a new social order destabilised the existing institutions of law and order: a new criminal legislation curtailed the role of the police, there were public conflicts between the president and the armed forces during the failed coup in 2002, conflicts with the old political structures, and half-hearted government action against armed gangs in communities (Briceño-León & Camardiel, 2015).

Along with this, political opposition proliferated. A divided segment of the two former political powers (AD and COPEI), as well as 18 smaller opposition parties of all political orientations, formed the Democratic Unity Roundtable (*Mesa de la Unidad Democrática*, MUD) in 2009. In June 2009, former social democratic politician Antonio Ledezma was elected as Mayor of Caracas and re-elected in 2013. The onset of an economic recession, double-digit inflation, increasing levels of poverty and insecurity, and reports of corruption affected Chávez's popularity in his last years, but did not stop him from winning an electoral victory just before his death. However, under the presidency of his successor Maduro, the problems multiplied exponentially.

Maduro's Venezuela (2013-2018)

Nicolás Maduro, son of a prominent union leader and later a union leader himself, followed cadre courses in Cuba and was a loyal 'Chavista'. He made a career under Chávez as President of the National Assembly, Minister of Foreign Affairs, Vice President and, after Chávez's death, as Interim President. He won the presidency in 2013 with a narrow majority, and was soon confronted by a deep economic malaise, conflicting power blocs within the governing PSUV, and growing popularity of his political opponents.

In the last quarter of 2013, Venezuela's economy entered a recession, and in 2014, world oil prices fell dramatically. The government's course of action was monetary financing. Venezuela became heavily indebted to Russia and China, and the 'parallel dollar' (the price setting of nearly all consumer goods) went up explosively. Analysts can only use estimates because the Central Bank has not published inflation statistics since 2015, but most foreign analysts describe the Venezuelan economy at present (May 2019) as in free-fall or meltdown with an inflation rate of 815,194 percent. The circulation of cash is restricted, and there is an acute shortage of essential goods and services, particularly medicine and food.

The social and political divide in Venezuela, already visible during Chávez's last years, became catastrophic under Maduro's presidency, resulting in opposition marches and wide-spread discontent. However, the opposition MUD is also internally divided. The most government-friendly sector wants clean elections and the release of political prisoners, others would welcome a coup by the armed forces, while the most radical wing would opt for an invasion by the US.

When the crisis started to impact the daily budget and national diet, Maduro's government organised a new clientelist instrument, *Comités Locales De Abastecimiento y Producción* (CLAP), local production and distribution committees who provide a three-weekly food package per household. It is a national programme that sustains the core of the Maduro vote. In 2014, only 8% of Venezuelans received a package, but this had jumped to 28% by 2016, while structural poverty escalated to 38% in 2016 (ENCOVI, 2017). It is generally agreed that by August 2018, poverty had reached the same percentage (around 50%) as when Chávez took office. The 'Carnet de la Patria' (Certificate of the Fatherland) and CLAP are the new political loyalty programmes of the government, and the food packages are distributed by the military or the local party representatives (López Maya, 2018:69).

Since 2014, the number of Venezuelan migrants seeking refuge in Latin America, the US and Spain has grown (Freier, 2018), although the exact amounts are hard to ascertain. According to UNHCR and OIM data, 328,888 official asylum-seekers and other legal migrants had left Venezuela by 31 August 2014, the asylum-seekers predominantly to Peru, the US, Brazil and Spain, the other legal migrants principally to Colombia, Chile, Ecuador and Argentina. However, that is only the tip of the iceberg, and Venezuelan scholars estimate that the exodus already numbers between three and three and a half million Venezuelans, predominantly economic migrants (May 2019). The first wave was the academic brain-drain: engineers, doctors, architects, and other professionals. After this, mass migration increased.

Corruption and crime also increased, particularly in Caracas, the larger cities and the long border region with Colombia, where violent non-state actors operate, such as former guerrilla units, drug gangs and armed criminals. It is widely-known that of the 50 most lethal cities of 300,000 inhabitants or more in the world in 2016, 42 are located in Latin America, and Caracas is the most violent city of all, with 130 assassinations per 100,000 inhabitants (Seguridad, Justicia y Paz, 2017).

Researchers have noted the nebulous or non-existent government publications about crime and crime statistics and, in 2015 and 2016, two renowned scholars published on the structural character of corruption in the country, drawing attention to the large Colombian and Venezuelan criminal and drug networks (Tablante & Tarre 2015; 2016). Journalists and academic researchers can only speculate about the extent of illegal import and export of drugs and valuables, gold and capital, but there are strong indications that

Rampa 4, the government airfield, is a site from which gold, monetary instruments and stockpiles of cash are transferred to accounts at foreign banks in Europe and Panama, or as deposits for residences and other properties in foreign countries (Briceño Torrealba, 2016). The researchers also highlighted substantial corruption within the oil giant, PDVSA, and other state-owned enterprises, such as production and distribution consortium, Pdval (Tablante & Tarre, 2016:104ff., 168ff.).

In information about the 526 state-owned or nationalised companies, only 21% of the shareholder structure, 6% of the names of the board members, and 24% of the names of the CEOs have been published, and of the identified CEOs, 30% are active duty or retired military (Transparencia Venezuela, 2017:8). The military oversee and administer CLAP, and also manage the entire electrical and hydro-power sector, the Metro of Caracas, and the Corporación Venezolana de Guyana, the source of nearly all national natural and mineral resources. Additionally, they operate the entrepreneurial industrial complex associated with the Ministry of Defence (Ramos Pismarato, 2018:271ff.).

Along with this, Maduro governs by decree, supported unconditionally by the upper echelons of the armed forces. In early 2015, the Mayor of Caracas, Ledezma, was detained on charges of supporting an attempted coup, then put under house arrest, confined again, and again put under house arrest. In November 2017, he fled to Spain where he received political asylum. In December 2015, the united opposition MUD won the parliamentary elections with 56% of the vote, and in response, Maduro by decree organised the election of a Constituent Assembly in June 2017. The MUD parties boycotted the elections and the governing PSUV won a massive victory in the absence of rivals. At present, the Constituent Assembly 'cohabits' with the elected parliament but has assumed all legislative functions.

In two subsequent elections, for the governors of the federal states in October 2017 and the mayors of the municipalities in December 2017, the PSUV again achieved victories. The MUD was divided on participation, and Maduro won 19 of the 23 seats, and surprisingly obtained a (disputed) majority in states where even Chávez was defeated at the height of his popularity, although the opposition considers these elections as flawed. In the municipal elections of December 2017, only some of the MUD parties presented candidates. With a turnout of only 47% of the electorate, Maduro won 300 of the 335 municipalities, even in the principal districts of Caracas, recently seen as an opposition city. In May 2018, with a turnout of 46%, and with the MUD parties again boycotting, Maduro won the presidential elections with 68% of the votes, his closest challenger oppositional 'Chavista' candidate Falcón, who won 21%. In January 2019, Juan Gaidó, president of the parliament, declared himself interim president disputing the legitimacy of both Maduro's presidency and the Constituent Assembly. The country has again two presidents in one country, but not exactly what Fidel Castro and Hugo Chávez had intended.

The Venezuelan armed forces under Maduro

After Maduro's inauguration, civilian ministries and management functions were increasingly transferred to the military. Active or retired military officers occupied key cabinet positions; and important sectors and strategic public instruments, like tax collection, budgeting, public contracts and tendering, purchases and acquisitions in the public sector, public imports, and control of the public banks are also managed by military officers (Tablante & Tarre, 2015; Ramos Pismarato, 2018).

Under Chávez, the FANB were already a powerful instrument, acting as both the right (defence and internal security) and left hand (in charge of ministries, missions and economic management) of the president. However, Chávez's charisma was undisputed and he maintained control by annual appointments of new senior commanders, resulting in career mobility of more junior officers.[2] He also rewarded loyalty with promotion, thus creating a system of rank inflation within the armed forces. Some recently retired high-ranking senior commanding officers estimate the number of generals (and their equivalents in the navy, air force and national guard) at 700.[3]

At present, the armed forces still act as both the defence and management, and control and repression forces of the ruling government. Maduro also developed a new mass promotion programme to reward loyalty. On 5 July 2018, the Independence Day of Venezuela, Maduro promoted 183 officers to general or admiral (*El País*, 2018), and topped up the salaries of the officers' corps, so that in terms of national salary scales in the public sector, an army colonel earns 15 times more than a university professor. During the 20th century, Venezuelan ministers of defence could be either a civilian or a high-ranking military officer, but under Chávez, 12 loyal senior military officers were appointed first as commander-in-chief of the armed forces, and subsequently as minister of defence.

Maduro extended this system of selecting only fierce 'Chavista' military loyalists, such as General Vladimir Padrino, who was commander-in-chief in 2013, and was made minister of defence in 2014. Confronted with political mayhem and economic calamity, Maduro issued an 'emergency economic decree' in July 2016, creating a 'sovereign and safe supply' of food and goods, to be headed by his minister of defence. Padrino appointed 24 flag officers as section heads: for rice, fruits, chickens, beans, etc., and because food provision is politically vital in present-day Venezuela, the military effectively controls the government and the ministers. Large-scale corruption within the armed forces is a common research topic in the academic and journalistic fields, and according to information published in *El País* (2018), in the first half of 2018 the Ministry of Defence received 35% more budget than the Ministry of Education, and 17 times more than the Ministry of Agriculture.

General Padrino is now in charge of national defence and management of the national economy, at the same time overseeing all other social missions, acting as a kind of super-premier, and the armed forces oversee 51% of the entire national budget (Transparencia Venezuela, 2017:7; Jácome, 2018). In November 2017, Maduro appointed the commander of the National Guard, General Manuel Quevedo (another loyal 'Chavista'), as both the Oil Minister and as president of the PDVSA, the state-owned industrial complex of oil enterprises on which the Venezuelan economy is so dependent. Consequently, senior military members are strongly intertwined with government. In the present (September 2018) 32-member cabinet, 12 members are military, controlling the most vital positions: Defence, Interior, Justice, Alimentation, Housing, Public Works, Transport, and Electricity.

The close collaboration between Cuba and Venezuela in terms of intelligence and state security has been consolidated (Trinkunas, 2005; Ramos Pismarato, 2008; Ramos Pismataro, Francesca & Andrés Otálvaro, 2008; Jácome, 2011; Sánchez Medero, 2014; Strønen, 2016; Giacalone, 2017). Cuban assistance and training have strongly influenced the military defence strategy, as well as the ideology of high-ranking officers of the armed forces, and the intelligence and counterintelligence services in their efforts to 'control external and internal threats' (Jácome, 2017). Civilian, military and political intelligence tend to overlap, and the distinction between the functions and operations of the Servicio Bolivariano de Inteligencia Nacional (National Intelligence Service, SEBIN), the Dirección General de Inteligencia Militar (Military Intelligence, DGIM) and the Dirección General de Contrainteligencia Militar (Military Counterintelligence, DGCIM) is unclear in practice (Ramos Pismataro, 2018:268).

Conclusions

On 3 May 2018, President Maduro published a page-long article in *El País*, arguing that Venezuela's democracy is quite different from all others, 'Because all others – in practically all other countries of the world – are democracies created by and for the elites ... class based democracies ... For us, the essence of our democracy is that the economy serves the people and not [that] the people are at the service of the economy ... For us ... the economy is justice and democracy, protection.'

The declaration is hopeful, but less encouraging is the phenomenon of growing autocracy, and militarisation of the economy, society and political structures. Less hopeful, too, is the hyperinflation and mass emigration, not only by the elites and upper-middle classes, but by poor people arriving at refugee camps and bivouacs in other Latin American countries at the mercy of perhaps distant family members or former Venezuelan refugees, other people with compassion, or foreign governments overwhelmed by the sheer volume of the continuing migration stream.

Venezuela's democracy is based on an alliance between the elites of a political party and the military establishment, supported by a core of roughly 30% of the electorate.

However, in general, military institutions have a better life-expectancy than political parties, political careers and political leaders. At present (September 2018), the political fate of the president is largely dependent on the loyalty of his military supporters, while Venezuela is a house divided, economically and politically. The military sustains the president and oversees a large part of governing the country and managing the economy. But what if the Venezuelan economic and political crisis grows deeper, the protest movements become more desperate, and the armed forces, instead of loyal supporters, feel the need to become the national arbiter?

With two conflicting parliaments, a serious national division, an economy in hyperinflation, a failed refinancing of foreign debt, and rapid impoverishment of a considerable part of the population, the future of the country is depressing. In the near future, Venezuela's stormy years may turn into a hurricane.

Notes

1   Carlos Lage quoted in Pérez Marcano and Sánchez García (2007:176) and Hugo Chávez quoted in Martínez Heredia (2010:79).
2   Traditionally, the general commanders of the four branches have the highest seniority. If a more junior commander is appointed, all higher-ranking officers are invited to retirement.
3   Author's interviews in November 2017 in Caracas.

References

Bilbao, L. 2002. *Chávez y la Revolución Bolivariana. Conversaciones con Luis Bilbao.* Santiago de Chile: Capital Intelectual S.A. and LOM Editores.

Briceño Torrealba, J.G. 2016. Rampa 4 de Maiquetia, trampolín oficial del narcotrafico. *La Patilla, Noticias, Información e Investigación*, 20 November. https://bit.ly/3aD9k5J [Accessed 11 September 2018].

Carnevali, D. 2014. *El hundimiento de los partidos políticos tradicionales venezolanos: el caso COPEI.* Bogotá: Villegas Editores.

Clem, R.S. & Maingot, A.P. 2011. *Venezuela's Petro-Diplomacy: Hugo Chávez's Foreign Policy.* Gainesville: University Press of Florida. https://doi.org/10.5744/florida/9780813035307.001.0001

ECLAC. 2001. *Panorama social de América Latina 2000-2001.* Santiago de Chile: United Nations – Economic Commission for Latin America and the Caribbean, October.

ECLAC. 2017. *Social Panorama of Latin America 2016.* Santiago de Chile: United Nations – Economic Commission for Latin America and the Caribbean, October.

El País. 2018. 'Maduro asciende a militares venezolanos "leales" a su Gobierno'. 6 July. https://bit.ly/3ayuRwm [Accessed 28 August 2018].

ENCOVI. 2017. *Encuesta sobre Condiciones de Vida Venezuela 2016.* https://bit.ly/338B8MD [Accessed 7 December 2017].

Freier, L.F. 2018. Understanding the Venezuelan Displacement Crisis. *E-International Relations*, 28 June. https://bit.ly/3aAmPmy [Accessed 29 August 2018].

IISS. 2009. *The Military Balance 2009.* Abingdon: Routledge for the International Institute for Strategic Studies.

INE. 2015. *Pobreza por línea de ingreso, 1er semestre 1997–1er semestre 2015.* Caracas: Instituto Nacional de Estadisticas. https://bit.ly/2U4vKX1 [Accessed 29 August 2018].

Giacalone, R. 2017. Posición y participación militar venezolana en la controversia del esequibo: Estudio comparativo1982 y 2015. *Aldea Mundo*, 22 (January-June). https://bit.ly/3cIO6XD [Accessed 27 August 2018].

Jácome, F. 2011. *Fuerza Armada, estado y sociedad civil en Venezuela.* Caracas: Instituto Latinoamericano de Investigaciones Sociales (ILDIS).

Jácome, Francine. 2017. Venezuela: ¿un nuevo tipo de régimen militar? *Foreign Affairs Latinoamérica*, 17(4):44-52.

Jácome, F. 2018. Los militares en la política y la economía de Venezuela. *Nueva Sociedad*, 274 (March-April):119-128. https://bit.ly/2TXeEdA [Accessed 16 August 2018.]

Kruijt, D. 2016. L'armée vénézuélienne, le peuple et la mystique révolutionnaire. *Le Monde diplomatique*, Décembre. https://bit.ly/2TTBjqO

Kruijt, D. 2018. Venezuela na vijf jaar "Chavista" Maduro [Venezuela after five years of Chavista President Maduro]. *Clingendael Spectator* (February). https://bit.ly/3cMQWJl

Levine, D.H. 2002. The Decline and Fall of Democracy in Venezuela: Ten Theses. *Bulletin of Latin American Research*, 21(2):248-269. https://doi.org/10.1111/1470-9856.00042

López Maya, M. 2018. Socialismo y comunas en Venezuela. *Nueva Sociedad*, 274 (March-April): 59-70. http://nuso.org/articulo [Accessed 3 September 2018].

Maduro, N. 2018.'Nuestra democracia es proteger'. *El País*. 3 May:11.

Martínez Heredia, F. 2010. *Si breve…* Havana: Editorial Letras Cubanas.

Pérez Marcano, H. & Sánchez García, A. 2007. *La invasión de Cuba a Venezuela. De Machurucuto a La Revolución Bolivariana.* Caracas: Los Libros de El Nacional.

Ramos Pismataro, F. 2018. Los militares y el deterioro democrático en Venezuela. *Estudios Políticos*, 53:260-282. http://doi.org/10.17533/udea.espo.n53a12 [Accessed 5 September 2018].

Ramos Pismataro, F. & Otálvaro, A. 2008. La Fuerza Armada Nacional en la Revolución Bolivariana. *Revista Desafíos*, 18(1):11-49.

Ramos Pismataro, F. & Rodríguez, R.F. 2017. Venezuela y la revolución perpetua. *Razón Pública*, 25 July. https://bit.ly/2Q11g73 [Accessed 31 August 2018].

RESDAL. 2016. *Atlas comparativo de la defensa en América Latina y Caribe, edición 2016.* Buenos Aires: Red de Defensa y Seguridad de América Latina.

Sánchez Medero, G. 2014. Fuerza Armada en la Revolución Bolivariana de Venezuela (1999-2012). *Revista Venezolana de Gerencia*, 19(68):598-617. https://doi.org/10.31876/revista.v19i68.19123

Seguridad, Justicia y Paz. 2017. *Metodología del ranking (2016) de las 50 ciudades más violentas del mundo.* México, DF. https://bit.ly/2VUantX [Accessed 27 August 2018].

Strønen, Å. 2016. *"A Civil-Military Alliance": The Venezuelan Armed Forces before and during the Chávez Era.* Bergen: Chr. Michelsen Institute (CMI Working Paper WP 2016:4).

Tablante, C. & Tarre, M. 2015. *El gran saqueo. Quiénes y cómo se robaron el dinero de los venezolanos.* Caracas: La Hoja del Norte.

Tablante, C. & Tarre, M. 2016. *El estado delincuente. Cómo actúa la delincuencia organizada en Venezuela*, 4th edition. Caracas: La Hoja del Norte.

Transparencia Venezuela. 2017. *Empresas propiedad del estado en Venezuela. Un modelo de control del Estado.* https://bit.ly/2wHzKoh [Accessed 5 April 2018].

Trinkunas, H. 2005. *Crafting Civilian Control of the Military in Venezuela: A Comparative Perspective.* Chapel Hill: University of North Carolina Press. https://doi.org/10.5149/9780807877036_trinkunas

UNHCR, IOM. 2018. *Venezuela Situation: Asylum-seekers from Venezuela 2014-18 per 31 August 2018.* United Nations Refugee Agency (UNHCR) and International Organization for Migration (IOM). https://bit.ly/38CkUN9 [Accessed 10 September 2018].

06

South Africa's Defence Diplomacy in Africa

Ian Liebenberg and Raymond Steenkamp-Fonseca

Abstract

South Africa's defence posture in Africa changed radically between 1950 and 2018. From a garrison-minded state mired in diplomatic isolation, the country 'returned to Africa' following its negotiated transition to democracy. As South Africa's relations on the continent evolve, so too does the country's use of various instruments of foreign policy. This chapter primarily considers the military instrument in foreign policy, and in particular the country's policy and practice of defence diplomacy. Shaped in part by the presidential styles of Nelson Mandela, Thabo Mbeki, and Jacob Zuma, the interplay between foreign policy and defence has required South Africa to ensure it is not perceived as a hegemon by its neighbours in Africa, but as a declared partner – albeit often as the dominant partner. Even so, expectations continue that South Africa should extend its role in the African Union (AU), and through the African Peace and Security Architecture (APSA) it helped to establish. As the chapter notes, significant gains have been made in advancing South African interests through defence diplomacy, but real limitations exist and these should be considered rationally before unrealistic demands or inflated expectations are uncritically accepted.

Introduction

Under apartheid policy (1948-1994), the quest to impose internal control required a complementary external policy. South Africa's defence posture therefore created an intolerant and aggressive power on the continent, and while confident of its policies, the Pretoria regime fundamentally misjudged the evolving international setting. In the years to come, its actions were based on a fundamental strategic flaw, misreading both developments in and reasons for conflict in southern Africa – both within South Africa, and in the region.

For decades, South Africa acted both as an exporter of armed conflict and as an economic destabiliser in the region, particularly in the neighbouring frontline states (Ispahani, 1984). This was ultimately an untenable defence posture. The People's Armed Forces of Liberation of Angola (FAPLA) and its Cuban allies forced the South African Defence Force (SADF) to a standstill in Angola, and eventual withdrawal from Angola and Namibia. Namibia became independent in March 1990 under United Nations (UN) Resolution 435, and in February 1990, the African National Congress (ANC), the Pan-Africanist Congress (PAC), and the South African Communist Party (SACP) were unbanned and restrictions were lifted on internal political organisations, such as the United Democratic Front (UDF) and the National Forum (NF). The negotiated transition that resulted in constitutional democracy in South Africa allowed the country to re-enter world politics and the socio-politics and economy of the African continent, as a potentially constructive actor and peace multiplier. With this transformation and demilitarisation of security policies, a new posture saw South Africa framing its role as peacemaker and agent for change towards reconstruction, development, growth and, to an extent, democratisation. Thus, between 1990 and 2000, South Africa arguably transformed from an imposing hegemon to a relatively benevolent partner on the continent.

However, one should be cautious of over-simplifying this transformation. The dichotomous approach, understanding South Africa's defence and foreign policy as neatly divided between the apartheid-era and a post-apartheid era, risks being too simplistic. The primary shortcoming is that by focusing on South Africa's own political trajectory, this perspective does not adequately take into account the changing context of African security and African development. Neither does it account fully for the rapidly changing macro-political international context. In order to appreciate South Africa's defence diplomacy in Africa more completely, it is essential to consider public policy as having an internal trajectory as well as being a response to changes in the regional and international political and security environment. We begin in the next section by setting out the historical context, using the example of South Africa's involvement in Namibia and Angola, and the use of the military instrument in foreign policy. The subsequent section looks at the transition to a democratic dispensation and explains the broader policy context under the 1996 Constitution. The discussion is structured around the country's Foreign and Defence policy under the Mandela, Mbeki, and Zuma presidencies, in terms of their principles, policy formulation, and implementation.

It is within the wider spectrum of policy choices in the deployment of soft power that the concept of peace diplomacy becomes relevant. Peace diplomacy is not a frequently-used concept, despite the use of 'peace' and 'diplomacy' as central to the study of international relations (Van Nieuwkerk, 2012), and one may also choose to refer to conflict management (Van Nieuwkerk, 2012). Our use of the term follows closely that of Van Nieuwkerk, where peace diplomacy refers to 'the activities associated with peacemaking, peacekeeping and peacebuilding' and thus in the South African case, as the government's 'involvement in continental peacemaking (diplomatic interventions in the form of mediation or negotiation processes), United Nations mandated peacekeeping operations (also known as multidimensional peace support) and peacebuilding (in line with the AU framework for post-conflict reconstruction and development)' (2012:84). It is important to note that multiactor coalitions and policy implementation entities are involved (Van Nieuwkerk, 2012).

The remainder of the chapter looks at SA defence policy, and structural and organisational changes since 1994; the principles on defence engagement through multilateral institutions like the UN, the AU, and the Southern African Development Community (SADC); bilateral relations with countries with whom defence agreements have been signed on training, VIP protection, joint operations, or peace missions; South Africa's role in the region, including its involvement in (southern) African peacekeeping; South Africa's role in the African Standby Force and the African Command, and the relationship with the current APSA; and South Africa's defence policy and the challenges of defence diplomacy in the medium term.

From apartheid to transition and transformation

From being a well-regarded actor on the international stage under the rule of Field-Marshall Jan Christiaan Smuts, South Africa's image deteriorated after the electoral victory of the National Party in 1948. Apartheid policies were implemented at all levels of society, based on a system of racial discrimination which was underpinned by racial classification, largely benefiting the white population. Black South Africans had no voting rights, and hence no right to citizenship, and the voting rights of so-called coloured people were scrapped. The policy of apartheid, including rigid racial separation, the withholding of full citizenship rights, discrimination, and the displacement of the internal population along racial lines, was coupled with increasing repression, particularly from 1963. This repression was first carried out by the police and later by military structures, enforcing the whites-only minority regime and resulting in the militarisation of state and society. Thus, the apartheid system and its grave social injustices was clearly a form of structural (state) violence imposed in an authoritarian way.

Initially, Pretoria sided with the (perceived Christian) West and the capitalist states. Aligned with the Allied Forces during World War II, South Africa participated in the 'Berlin Lift', the air-relief operation in Germany (1948-1949), and in the UN-mandated multinational operation in the Korean peninsula from 1950. Though nominally supported as a bulwark against Communist expansion in southern Africa, South Africa's political stance was increasingly questioned at the UN. South Africa had argued from the start that its government policies fell within the country's domestic jurisdiction, and as a sovereign state, it need not subject itself and its domestic affairs to international scrutiny. However, this defence proved baseless and apartheid was labelled as a crime against humanity by General Assembly Resolution 2202 A (XXI) of 16 December 1966. Strong opposition to apartheid came from most of the developing countries in Africa, Asia, the Caribbean, and Latin America. Even in Europe, voices of protest rose, starting in the East European countries and social-democratic states such as the Scandinavian countries, and eventually from some members of the Security Council (Pampallis, 1991:278). Sanctions were to become a large part of the anti-apartheid struggle. On the African continent, the Organization of African Unity (OAU) helped bolster a broader 'Third World' voice through the Non-Aligned Movement (NAM) bloc within the UN General Assembly. In the face of an international anti-apartheid movement, and especially from the 1970s onwards, South Africa's defence posture was driven by a siege mentality. The dominant ideology of the political leadership was that of a garrison state, perceiving itself to be under a 'total onslaught' from Soviet/Chinese Communism, a hostile Africa (through which the disconcerting winds of change of independence were blowing), and an increasingly unappreciative West.

One can draw parallels between South Africa's internal and external policies. Internally, the government used strong-arm tactics and ignored the feelings of the majority of South Africans. Externally, this was mirrored in the government's disregard of international criticism, including criticisms voiced at the General Assembly. 'South Africa [provided] a dramatic illustration of the internationalisation of a domestic situation' (Pampallis, 1991:205). Heavy-handed domestic policies and repressive actions inside the country reflected a diplomatic but hard-fisted foreign and defence policy. Pretoria's policies led South Africa to international pariah status, aptly described as 'diplomacy of isolation' (Geldenhuys, 1984).

Namibia

South Africa's treatment of the Namibian people should be considered alongside its domestic record of repression. Mandated after World War I by the League of Nations to protect German West Africa (later South West Africa – SWA), neither the Smuts government nor the apartheid government saw fit to withdraw from Namibia. The South African political elite and their followers started referring to Namibia (still called SWA) as South Africa's 'fifth province', but in spite of this, the Namibian people persevered in their attempts at independence, combating superior armed forces from South Africa who believed SWA was rightfully theirs (UN, 1974). In this, the Namibians, and specifically the South West African People's Organization (SWAPO), were supported in their international efforts by persistent objections at the UN from India, Liberia, Mexico, and numerous others that joined the call for Namibians to choose their own destiny, an opportunity denied them ever since the brutal German colonial occupation during the 1880s (Liebenberg, 2015:17-34, 2018:16).

As in South Africa, territorial segregation between 'ethnic' groups was envisaged and South African legislation, including security laws, was applied in the territory (Seegers, 1996:135). The Odendaal Commission (1962-1964) made it clear that 'a policy of differentiation must be followed' and 'ethnic groups are basic units of development' (Seegers, 1996:22-24). In the eyes of many, this was a clear attempt to structure Namibia along apartheid lines. This all took place despite the visit to Namibia by a UN Special Committee for South West Africa, to which Pretoria reluctantly agreed. Members of the Committee pointed out that the Pretoria government was intent on the subordination of the people of Namibia to their own likes. Pretoria obstinately forged ahead (Seegers, 1996:21) and requests to solve the tensions around segregationist policies and the issue of Namibia fell on deaf ears (Frankel, 1984:278, 279; Pampallis, 1991:278; Geldenhuys, 1984:205). Despite resistance and protest, Namibia's status remained that of a mandate (UN, 1974). In 1961, the UN General Assembly asked for collective action against South Africa, and by November 1962 the Assembly called for specific diplomatic and economic sanctions against the apartheid government (Geldenhuys, 1984:206).

For a brief period in 1966, South Africa's mandate over Namibia seemed confirmed when the International Court of Justice (ICJ) ruled that Liberia and Ethiopia did not have any legal rights or interest in the matter of SWA. In a way, many Namibians felt that their long struggle for self-determination since the 1880s had been betrayed by this ruling, and it affirmed their need to pursue an armed struggle. In response, South African authorities introduced emergency regulations, security operations, and detentions, while maintaining its position in the face of international criticism. The UN Security Council revoked South Africa's mandate in Namibia, and by 1971, the ICJ re-affirmed that South Africa's occupation of Namibia was in contravention of international law. In his special report for 1973, the Secretary-General of the UN, Kurt Waldheim, emphasised the 'special responsibilities of the international community towards the Territory and the people of Namibia', and urged the UN organs, and the Security Council in particular, 'to seek effective approaches to bring about a solution based on the inalienable rights of the Namibian people to self-determination, national independence, and the preservation of the unity and territorial integrity of Namibia' (Geldenhuys, 1984:42).

Following a Resolution by the UN General Assembly, governments from Scandinavia, Eastern Europe, the NAM, and other countries recognised SWAPO as Namibia's sole representative (Geldenhuys, 1984:14ff.; Du Pisani, 1986:6ff.). When the UN adopted Resolution 435 in 1978, the so-called Western Five – the US, UK, West Germany, Canada, and France – temporarily agreed that Namibia should be granted independence and that a UN Transition Assistance Group (UNTAG) was to assist in ensuring free and fair elections. However, covert support to South Africa continued, notably from the US, UK and France

(Stockwell, 1978:272-273; Jaster, 1985:92, 114; Namibia Support Committee, 1988:698-701; Liebenberg, 2011:72-73).

Angola

South Africa invaded Angola in 1975 to bolster the 'anti-communist' forces amongst the rebel movements. After the coup in Portugal against the Caetano government in 1974, three liberation movements in Angola vied for power, but only one was a legitimate liberation movement: the Popular Movement for the Liberation of Angola (MPLA). The Union for the Total Liberation of Angola (UNITA) was implicated in earlier dealings with Portuguese security forces, while the leader of the third, the National Front for the Liberation of Angola (FNLA), was hardly on Angolan soil, having chosen Kinshasa in Zaire as his headquarters, and was in the pay of the USA's Central Intelligence Agency (CIA). In contrast, the MPLA had significant support in urban areas, including trade unions, and since 1954 had demonstrated its ability to mobilise in towns and the countryside, and to fight and survive in the field, despite setbacks (Liebenberg, 2008:66-68). South Africa's support for Jonas Savimbi's UNITA, and supply of hardware and advisors to Holden Roberto's FNLA guerrillas, escalated the regional cycle of violence, and both Namibia and Angola were to suffer for decades from the destabilising conflicts that they experienced. Even if they had combined their resources, the frontline states could not match the military power of South Africa, as the consistent build-up of South African forces led to an arms race in southern Africa. South Africa's aggressive posture forced the frontline states to spend money on arms, rather than much-needed development, all while South Africa deliberately destabilised the frontline states through punitive economic steps.

In summary, as the examples of Namibia and Angola show, South Africa's isolation forged a unilateral foreign policy to ensure regional hegemony. This 'total strategy' led to the country's militarisation, and the destabilisation of its neighbours. The primacy of the military as an instrument of foreign policy saw the SADF engaging in cross-border conflict and a geopolitics of war, in the face of pressure from the international community.

A new era dawns

South Africa's negotiated transition (1990-1996) marked a significant advance in the country's political development, and a clear break in how it sees and is seen by its neighbours. The anti-apartheid struggle was an international one, and South Africa was subsequently welcomed into a new world that, at least temporarily, had left behind the bipolar Cold War schisms (Dyer, 2009:186, 198).

As South Africa returned to the international community, there was a wide range of international actors with whom to interact, and the country engaged broadly with other nations and continents through both bilateral and multilateral agreements. However, it is clear that, rather than being swayed to join a specific power bloc, South Africa could act from its position as an emerging middle power. For example, South Africa returned to the British Commonwealth, yet was also a leader of the NAM; it deepened relations with European countries, the EU, and with the US (particularly under Clinton), but simultaneously further enhanced long-standing connections with Libya and Cuba, and acted independently in its relations with countries like China, India, and Iran. Van Wyk argues that 'South African scholars predominantly evaluated the Mandela presidency as a period of (new) foreign policy-making, the establishment of new relations and the continuation of old relations' (2012:277). South Africa thus was able to forge a balanced stance, arguably based on moral principles, yet asserting that the new democracy also identified its own interests.

South Africa developed a new diplomatic orientation and stepped out of its self-declared alliance with the West and close association with military regimes in Latin America and aggressive pariah states such as Israel, preferring a 'foreign policy of peace' and multilateral international participation and engagement. South Africa demonstrated its solidarity with the developing world and became a member of the NAM, as well as being involved with what was to become the AU, initiating the New Partnership for Africa's Development (NEPAD) and the African Peer Review Mechanism (APRM), despite initial differences on how to unify Africa and on what economic pathway to follow to ensure sustainability and stability. Within the southern Africa subregion, South Africa entered the Southern African Development Coordination Conference (SADCC), the precursor to SADC. Thus, South Africa moved from a destabiliser to a cordial beneficiary and partner in solidarity on the continent, at least in the new political elite's view. Recognised as a regional economic core and possessing a relatively strong military, this leadership role seemed a natural position, but the challenge was how to be a benevolent partner, rather than a selfish hegemon. Any hegemonic enterprise reminiscent of apartheid power policy would rightly invite scepticism from other African states.

South Africa's policy context

Partly as a result of the Cold War, there was extensive armed conflict on the African continent during the 1960s, 70s and 80s. The year 1991 also saw widespread conflict, both globally and on the African continent, but Cilliers (2014) observed that this was followed by a steep decline in conflict occurrence, which reached low levels from 2002 to 2005. However, since 2009 there has been a rise in armed conflicts, especially in Africa, partly because of the so-called War on Terror and intervention by Western core states (Cilliers, 2014).

For South Africa, the end of the Cold War required an adjustment of foreign policy within a changed international environment, from one based on Cold War rivalry to a post-

Cold War global order. This international context provides a necessary but incomplete understanding of the setting of South Africa's foreign policy, which requires consideration of the context of South Africa's transition, which we will address below.

Foreign policy

The new South Africa's foreign policy and diplomacy closely echoed its expressed domestic values. Achievements in the domestic domain, such as being able to successfully find a negotiated resolution to long-standing conflict and formalise a commitment to peace, reconciliation, and democratisation of state and society, understandably shaped how the country saw itself internationally. The new Constitution (Act 108 of 1996), based on a Bill of Rights and principled constitutionalism, envisaged a democratic non-racial society that focused on peace and conflict resolution internally and externally. Van Nieuwkerk argues that 'the link between foreign policy and peace diplomacy (as an instrument of foreign policy)' created the image of South African presidents, especially Mandela and Mbeki, 'as foreign policy actors and peacemakers' (Van Wyk, 2012:277). This approach saw a shift from hard power to soft power, entailing an opportunity for defence diplomacy.

This domestic context can be seen in the light of the personalities of the leaders who made the democratic transition possible. Under presidents Mandela and Mbeki (1994 to 2008), South Africa's experience of resolving national conflict through negotiation strongly influenced the formulation of foreign and defence policies shaped by a commitment to values, and not just interests. With their global presence, these leaders were influential in carrying out foreign policy themselves, perhaps under-utilising their foreign ministers, and ultimately failing to ensure the development of diplomatic expertise at the departmental level.

Under presidents Mandela and Mbeki, South Africa embarked on a range of bilateral and multilateral agreements, diplomatic, political, economic and cultural, with SADC, the rest of Africa, and countries on other continents. Foreign policy under these presidents was consistent with attempts to: (1) advocate South Africa's negotiated transition as a model of conflict resolution; (2) stress South Africa's commitment to the region and the African continent; (3) affirm South Africa's relationships with past supporting nations outside of and including the NAM (i.e. Russia, Cuba, Libya), and with friendly nations on the European continent such as the Scandinavian countries and The Netherlands; and (4) re-orientate South African engagement with states outside South Africa's normal ambit, such as Brazil, China, Iran, and others. The foreign policy approach also demonstrated that South Africa was ready and willing to work with Western core economies such as Germany, the UK, and the US, and subsequent bilateral agreements testified to this. However, despite the diplomatic projection reflecting re-alignment with Africa, affirmation of old friendships and a willingness to act as peacemaker on and off the African continent, foreign policy under Nelson Mandela to an extent remained ad hoc. Some would even argue that it was greatly reliant on Mandela as president, his international profile, personal actions, and preferences.

When Thabo Mbeki assumed the presidency, foreign policy was still thoroughly influenced by the executive branch of government, and it has been argued that under Mbeki, the role of Parliament diminished (Van Wyk, 2012:279). Along with this, the Mbeki administration organised government functions into 'clusters', as coordinating mechanisms of integrated governance (Alden & Le Pere, 2004). This applied at cabinet ministerial level (policy), but also at the Director-General level (implementation), and foreign policy and defence policy are considered together within the International Relations, Peace and Security (IRPS) Cluster. The cluster included the South African National Defence Force (SANDF), the externally-directed intelligence agency (the SASS), and Foreign Affairs who led the work of policy formulation and implementation (Africa, 2011). The cluster approach underlines the primacy of political action through diplomatic channels, and the necessity to engage peaceful instruments of foreign policy before considering military engagement.

Mbeki's vision of an African Renaissance saw South Africa push for the AU, for its economic programme NEPAD, and for internal accountability through the APRM. Although not everyone accepted Mbeki's views on the future continental strategy, especially in the economic realm, South Africa pushed for greater regional integration between West, East and Southern Africa (Ngwenya, 2012) with the AU as the foundation stone for continental cooperation and, perhaps, closer integration.

Under Jacob Zuma, the Department of Foreign Affairs (DFA) was renamed the Department of International Relations and Cooperation (DIRCO) to help enhance 'public diplomacy' and 'facilitate domestic constituency engagement'. There was a shift from conflict resolution to economic diplomacy (Vickers, 2012), which was emphasised in 2011 in the Draft White Paper on Foreign Policy (Masters, 2012:27-28).

Soft power

South Africa sought to internationalise itself with a new more inclusive approach, presenting principled aptitude to furthering peace, reconstruction, and development. The promotion of human rights, derived from the experience of apartheid and the attainment of a liberal constitution, played an important role in the early years of South Africa's foreign policy orientation (Masters, 2012:145; Neethling, 2012:479-482), and some observers argue that soft power from 1994 until 2012 was the very essence of South Africa's foreign policy (Smith, 2012:69). The use of soft power stems partially from South Africa's value-laden approach (involving conflict prevention, conflict resolution, preference for negotiation, and democratisation) and partially from the realisation of the limits of their economic and military power. In reality, there are limits to what a middle power such as South Africa can do, despite its relative strength in a region (Hughes, 2001).

South Africa embraced multilateralism as a way to solve diplomatic challenges, and its foreign policy emphasises the importance of working through multilateral institutions. Ten years after independence, Nathan (2005) summarised that, 'South Africa promotes multilateralism in the international system as the best means of maintaining global order, addressing global problems, mitigating the domination and unilateralism of powerful states, and empowering weaker countries.' However, more than just participating in international institutions, the idea was to actively promote a reformist programme in these institutions (Alden, 2014). 'South Africa embraced multilateralism as an approach to solving the challenges confronting the international community … it took up a leading role in various multilateral forums' (Monyae, 2012:139). South Africa promoted peace and security with a definite emphasis on Africa and developing nations in general, and attempts were also made to improve interaction with, and cooperation between, the UN Security Council and others (Monyae, 2012). Some even talked about these activities as an 'evolving doctrine of multilateralism' by South Africa, as a 'realist middle power' and a 'pluralist middle power' (Monyae, 2012:139, 141, 142).

South Africa entered African politics as a regional power on the continent and an aspiring middle power internationally (Hughes, 2001), and it changed from regional hegemon to benevolent partner – at least in terms of its discourse. However, there were on one side those who advocated a stronger role, and on the other side those who dreaded such a possibility.

Defence policy

The South African Constitution (Act 108 of 1996), the White Paper on Defence (May 1996) subtitled 'Defence in a Democracy', and the Defence Review (April 1998), and the Defence Act (Act No. 42 of 2002) collectively set the direction of the Department of Defence (today the Department of Defence and Military Veterans, DOD) and the SANDF. Though the main issues were the transition to democracy and the transformation of the DOD, the White Paper also set out a foreign policy and defence posture based on a principled preparedness to engage constructively with states in the region. The policy foresaw armed forces with a primarily defensive orientation, and thus envisaged a change from animosity to friendship with South Africa's neighbours. The process of publishing 'Defence in a Democracy' can itself be seen as a necessary change from the past, as it was a relatively transparent and inclusive process, with extensive domestic consultation across Ministries and other government departments, but also with academic experts and broader civil society (Africa, 2011). The second Defence Review was less inclusive, but did not deviate much from its predecessor in terms of defence posture, force projection, and South Africa's role in Africa with regards to peacekeeping operations. The latest defence review also raised some concerns, such as the need to rejuvenate the SANDF and to update and replace obsolete equipment, including the need for modernised aerial troop transport, and a highly-educated officer's corps. Ignoring these issues may impact on South Africa's obligations and defence diplomacy, but so far very little has been done by the DOD to implement their obligations in terms of the 2015 Defence Review.

A clear philosophy was reflected of constructive involvement in preventive diplomacy, peacebuilding, peacemaking, development based on pro-active resolution of conflict, and moral leadership. Peace Missions were defined as including 'participation in Preventative Diplomacy, Peacemaking, Peacekeeping Operations, Peace Enforcement, Peace Building, Humanitarian Assistance and Humanitarian Intervention' (Department of Government Communications and Information Systems (GCIS), 2003). South African policy also reflects the change in how international peacekeeping is carried out under UN mandates, in particular the increased attention of Peace Support Operations (PSO) on post-conflict reconstruction, security sector reform, and humanitarian assistance (GCIS, 2003). On paper, this orientation is consistent with a foreign policy based on liberal humanitarian principles.

However, if South Africa expected to play a larger role in regional stability and international peace missions, then the SANDF force structure and modernisation plans needed to accommodate this new role. Granted, the primary role of the armed forces remains defence of the homeland, but even as a secondary mission, external deployment to enhance regional stability requires proper training, preparation, and equipment. It is in this light that one must understand the arms acquisition process, or Strategic Defence Procurement (SDP), commonly referred to in South Africa as the Arms Deal, announced in September 1999. The acquisition of submarines, frigates, helicopters, fighter jets, and training aircraft for the air force and the navy indicate an orientation towards traditional conventional threats, contradicting the stated defensive posture of the SANDF, and contributing little to South Africa's peacekeeping role on the continent. The exclusion of any significant procurement for the army at the time highlighted these contradictions, and still raises questions about operational readiness. Moreover, investigations into the irregularities of the Arms Deal, which led to charges of corruption against members of parliament and the executive, including Jacob Zuma, significantly eroded the public perception that the military could be trusted by broader civil society. Put another way, the fallout from the Arms Deal controversy and corruption has prevented a clear picture of anything good being done by the civilian and military leadership, resulting in an increasing civil-military relations gap.

South Africa's defence policy should be understood in its multilateral policy context, and specifically the regional dimension, through the common security arrangements for the SADC region. 'South Africa has not flinched from active engagement, both within its own region and on the global stage' and this against a background of high expectations from the international community about [South Africa's] role' (Sidiropoulos, 2007:1; DOD, 2009).

Within SADC, South Africa aimed at a new security orientation, and seemingly committed itself to future conflict resolution, mediation, and conflict management through the creation of the SADC Organ on Peace, Defence and Security Cooperation. The SADC Organ has a strong security mandate, as it is endowed in Article 2 of the Protocol with the power to 'consider enforcement action' as a last resort to prevent, contain, resolve inter- and intra-state conflict (Hammerstad, 2005). In theory, SADC has power to intervene in the domestic affairs of member states, but this has not been the case in practice. The discourse on regional security in SADC arguably hinged on differing interpretations: Zimbabwe, Angola and Namibia preferred a mutual defence pact with a military response to conflict, while the camp led by South Africa preferred a common security regime based on conflict resolution and political solutions (Nathan, 2005:42). The SADC Standby Brigade, as part of the AU's African Standby Force, can be seen as an effort driven by South Africa to create coherence between the subregional and continental security architecture.

The Future SA Army Strategy (Strategy 2020) was released in 2009 and includes reference to the army's role in peacekeeping and peace enforcement on the continent. The primary role, constitutionally defined, remains protection of national sovereignty and territorial integrity, but there was recognition from army planners that peacekeeping operations will dominate in the future (Baker, 2009:12). The Defence Review 2015 indicates the broader role of the SANDF within a developmental state, and re-affirms South Africa's African focus and its role in post-conflict reconstruction and development (PCRD), while the country's role in 'regional and continental processes to respond and resolve crises' is stressed (Neethling, 2012:474-479). Some theorists saw the Draft Defence Review 2012 as a positive development, 'given the demands placed on the SANDF in the field of post-conflict reconstruction and development' (Neethling 2012:472), arguing that this may impact positively on the evolution of developmental peacekeeping. Most recently, the Minister of Defence formulated a Directive on 'Execution of Defence Diplomacy Policy in the DOD'. The challenge, as revealed in the Annual Report 2016/17, is that there needs to be synchronisation between the Ministers' Directive and the DIRCO policy, as set out in 'Anchor State Document on Defence International Engagements' (DOD, 2017).

This policy background therefore demonstrates the gap between acquisitions and the conceivable external deployment missions of the SANDF. Some illustrative examples will be useful, and the chosen cases are Lesotho, Burundi, Democratic Republic of Congo (DRC), Sudan, and Central African Republic (CAR), each demonstrating a particular aspect of South Africa's use of the military as defence diplomacy in Africa. First, it is necessary to briefly consider the range of bilateral agreements on defence issues.

Defence diplomacy engagement

Defence dialogue and cooperation are inherent in defence diplomacy arrangements, and aim to avert misunderstandings and ease mistrust by promoting transparency. In practical terms, this can be done through exchange of defence attachés, and exchange of information on a number of topics, such as defence budgets, force structure, modernisation plans, and deployments. A second feature of defence diplomacy is establishing bilateral and multilateral agreements, as well as participating in multinational organisations, such as the UN, the AU and SADC (especially in the Interstate Defence and Security Committee) (GCIS, 2017). Bilateral defence diplomacy and cooperation take place at a number of political levels and institutions, although as Blake reveals, there is a dearth of information on South Africa's defence cooperation generally, and his position as a military practitioner means his study provides useful insights (2016). At a deeper level of connection, states may participate in military education and joint military exercises. Following the framework of Cottey and Forster (2004), defence diplomacy engagement can be divided into a number of areas of activity:

High-level political ties: The Bi-National Commission (BNC) is a forum for dialogue at the presidential level. The BNC is usually chaired by the South African President, and includes the Minister of Defence and Department officials. In contrast, a Joint Commission on Cooperation (JCC) is chaired by the Minister of DIRCO, but usually includes other government ministers, including the Defence Minister, and other senior officials. The Minister of Defence chairs meetings at the Joint Permanent Commission on Defence and Security (JPCDS), which are annual bilateral meetings with representatives of states contiguous to South Africa. At the level of Secretary for Defence (equivalent to a Director-General), meetings are held as a Defence Committee (DC) with senior departmental officials in attendance (Blake, 2016).

Military-to-military contacts: As set out in the Defence Review 2014, the relationship with other armed forces is carried out through a DOD Foreign Relations Strategy. Defence International Affairs (DIA) formulates and provides policy advice on Defence Foreign Relations, which administers support to the SANDF defence attaché offices abroad and to foreign military dignitaries (DOD, 2015).

TABLE 6.1   SA defence diplomacy involving SADC states (2011-15)

SA defence diplomacy involving SADC states (2011-15)	Total
Defence dialogue:	125
- Bilateral meetings	61
- Multilateral meetings	64
Defence agreements	8
Defence ties at diplomatic level	11
Defence cooperation programmes:	33
- Exercises	10
- PSO	7
- Training	2
- Anti-Piracy Operations	4
- HADR	2
- Border Liaison Forums	4
- Conference and Symposia	1
- Other	3

SOURCE: Developed from Blake (2016)

Defence diplomacy in South Africa's continental peacekeeping operations

Lesotho

South Africa moved beyond its stated preference for diplomatic conflict resolution with its first foreign deployment of the military to Lesotho in 1998. The post-election constitutional crisis in that country resulted in Prime Minister Mosisili requesting assistance to prevent a possible coup. Peaceful diplomatic solutions had been tried, including through the SADC Troika, but Mandela's preventive diplomacy efforts and calls for constitutional reform were not sufficient to avoid the crisis following the disputed general election of April 1998. The crisis was compounded by members of the Lesotho Defence Force (LDF) staging a mutiny in September 1998, and an increase in civil disorder and public violence which led to internal instability. The SANDF deployed under Operation Boleas to prevent an unconstitutional take-over of power and secure law and order, a military action that Du Plessis called the 'intrusive use of the military instrument in the form of military intervention' (2003:130). South Africa maintained that it was a peace operation under a SADC mandate and not an invasion, as the Botswana Defence Force (BDF) had been involved.

The issue remains whether South Africa gave up on negotiating a political settlement too quickly, deploying the military without a full understanding of how the enforcement action would be viewed. There were also questions about the requirements for regarding a military response as a SADC response since, as Neethling points out, there were no clear guidelines from SADC regarding military responses in internal conflicts (2012). At the time of Mosisili's request, the SADC Chair and the president of South Africa were the same person (Likoti, 2007). Moreover, South Africa had not participated in the August 1998 intervention operation in the DRC after requests from President Laurent Kabila for military assistance, while Angola, Zimbabwe, and Namibia did intervene. In both Lesotho and the DRC, regional security cooperation under the SADC banner in intrastate conflict proved controversial. From an international perspective, De Coning argues that, 'South Africa, Botswana and SADC, appeared to have failed to obtain prior authorization from the UN Security Council as required by Chapter VIII of the Charter' (1998:22), while others hold that, although there is debate about the strict legality of the operation, South Africa's actions were legitimate (Southall, 2006:7). Nevertheless, South Africa was aware that acting unilaterally could be interpreted as hegemonic dominance, and leading up to the 2002 election, they continued to engage Lesotho via SADC.

Burundi

The Burundi intervention can be seen as one of South Africa's most successful uses of the military in foreign policy in support of diplomatic negotiation and peacemaking (Du Plessis, 2003:126; Southall, 2006:12). Nelson Mandela became involved as the key peace mediator in the OAU peace process after the death of Julius Nyerere in 1999 although, as Van Eck notes, Nyerere's facilitation was flawed as two Burundian political-military movements had been excluded (Van Eck, 2009:168-170). Mandela's diplomatic efforts resulted in the Arusha Agreement of Peace and Reconciliation of August 2000, the basis of which was a three-year transitional government based on power-sharing between Tutsi- and Hutu-dominated political parties.

Given the resistance from the excluded armed movements, the peace process required ongoing ceasefire negotiations, and South Africa was prepared to back up its diplomatic efforts with a military presence. With Jacob Zuma, then the country's deputy president, taking the lead, South African negotiations resulted in armed groups, political parties, and regional neighbours maintaining a fragile peace. South Africa deployed a military force to Burundi in support of the Arusha Peace Agreement, facilitating the return of exiled political leaders and providing protection to those participating in the Burundi Transitional Government. The military deployment of the South African Protection and Support Detachment (SAPSD) was referred to as Operation Fibre, a protective military deployment in the context of a negotiated settlement.

There was also a multilateral track to South Africa's involvement, as the Department of Foreign Affairs had approached the UN for assistance in gaining international support for the deployment (Makwetla, 2012). This support was confirmed in Security Council Resolution 1375 (20 October 2001) which 'Endorses the efforts of the Government of South Africa and other member States to support the implementation of the Arusha Agreement, and strongly supports in this regard the establishment of an interim multinational security presence in Burundi, at the request of its Government, to protect returning political leaders and train an all-Burundian protection force.'

Along with this, South Africa also worked through the newly created AU. The AU Mission in Burundi (AMIB), established in May 2003 as the first AU peacekeeping mission, had a South African as its first Force Commander, and South Africa participated alongside Ethiopia and Mozambique as the major military contributors. It must be pointed out that South Africa had an authoritative role in the creation of the AU, and that a number of initiatives regarding the deployment of the mission were carried out by President Thabo Mbeki in his capacity as AU chairperson (Landsberg, 2012). South Africa also continued to play a major role in Burundi when the UN Operation in Burundi (ONUB) was established in June 2004. South African Major General Derrick Mgwebi was the first ONUB Force Commander, a first for a South African in an international peacekeeping force (Makwetla, 2012).

Democratic Republic of the Congo

The DRC case presents a range of examples of South Africa's use of the military instrument. As noted above, in contrast with South Africa's more pacific approach within SADC, the trio of Zimbabwe, Angola, and Namibia pursued a militarist line. This resulted in their participation in the hostilities in the DRC, and consequently to a cleavage on this issue in SADC and antagonism between SADC states. Nevertheless, the diplomatic initiatives of Thabo Mbeki between 1999 and 2002 promised political stability to the DRC and resulted in the signing of the Lusaka Peace Agreement in July 1999. This paved the way for the establishment of the UN Organization Mission in the Democratic Republic of the Congo (MONUC), and diplomatic efforts were bolstered by the deployment of the SANDF as part of the internationally-mandated mission. South Africa's participation in MONUC from September 1999 was code-named Operation Mistral.

South Africa's multilateral participation in MONUC increased, particularly after the assassination of President Laurent Kabila in January 2001 placed renewed pressure on the UN to expedite the implementation of MONUC. The UN allocated a number of staff officer posts to South Africa, and SANDF personnel were deployed for 12 months. South

Africa was also requested to deploy its specialist elements, the South African National Defence Force Specialist Contingent (SANDFSPECC), as well as the SANDF Aero Medical Evacuation team. South African Military Police members were also deployed to establish the MONUC Military Police Unit, and in July 2002, the UN DPKO requested that South Africa deploy a Task Force to MONUC.

South Africa entered into the DRC with bilateral or trilateral defence diplomacy agreements. South Africa had signed an agreement with the DRC and Belgium to support security sector reform in respect of the DRCs Armed Forces (FARDC). This deployment of the South African Detachment Assisting with Integration and Training (SADAIT) in the DRC from January 2005 was named Operation Teutonic, and its primary role was to provide assistance with the identification and registration process. This was expanded later in 2005 (Teutonic II) with the deployment of additional personnel to the Eastern DRC to facilitate with training centres.

The situation in the DRC continues to evolve. In July 2010, the UN mission received a new mandate and was renamed the United Nations Organization Stabilization Mission in the Democratic Republic of the Congo (MONUSCO). The SANDF presence in the DRC in support of MONUSCO consisted of three military observers, 12 staff officers, and a contingent of 1200 members. In 2014, a new mandate was decided by UN Security Council Resolution 2098, which saw South Africa deploying a battalion as part of the MONUSCO Force Intervention Brigade.

Sudan

The Sudan example sheds light on the deployment of an AU mission, although it was also partly a hybrid AU-UN mission (Khadiagala, 2014). The SANDF launched Operation Cordite in July 2004 with the deployment of staff officers and military observers to Darfur, Sudan. This was in support of the AU Mission in Sudan (AMIS), and to supplement the existing Sudan deployment. An infantry protection company and an explosive ordnance disposal unit were also deployed. AMIS was terminated at the end of 2007 by the UN African Mission in Darfur (UNAMID), becoming the first AU-UN hybrid mission. The South African contingent remained in Darfur in support of this hybrid mission, and the UN requested that South Africa increase the contingent to a standard UN Infantry Battalion-size force in 2008. However, challenges regarding the infrastructure within the mission area made it impossible to comply. By 2012, the contingent totalled 760, including eight military observers and seven staff officers. In assessing South Africa's participation in the AU-led mission, we can nevertheless conclude that 'The mobilisation of the AU Mission in Darfur failed to stem the genocide committed by the Sudanese government of Al-Bashir against defenceless civilians seeking autonomy for the region' (Khadiagala, 2012:278). A full account of South Africa's participation, beyond the scope of the present chapter, should include Thabo Mbeki's diplomatic role on behalf of the AU/UN and the wider implications of South Africa's changing relationship with the International Criminal Court (ICC).

Central African Republic

South Africa's involvement in CAR signalled a significant change in foreign policy. As has been noted above, foreign policy is shaped by the Presidency, and in the case of President Zuma, there was a significant shift from the policies of his predecessors. However, some argued that there was continuity in both personnel and the vision for an African Agenda in foreign policy (Habib (2009:143). While it is true that the African unity rhetoric continued to underpin foreign policy narratives, Khadiagala (2014:279) characterised the Zuma period as 'muddling through' rather than leadership, and criticised the economic diplomacy in Africa as leading to the 'conflation of national and party interests as ANC elites and Zuma's family members joined in the scramble for economic opportunities'.

It is in this context that one must try to understand the military deployment to CAR. According to some allegations, the CAR involvement may have partially been caused by business interests that included the Zuma family. While all of the facts are not yet in the open, this may change with the initiation of the Commission on State Capture on 20 August 2018. What is known from a briefing by deputy Defence Minister Makwetla is that the original mission to CAR of March 2007, Operation Vimbezela, was primarily comprised of training and engineer personnel. This was in response to a request from the CAR for assistance with training and refurbishment of training facilities. The 2007 bilateral military agreement was signed by then President Mbeki and CAR's president Francois Bozize, and was apparently renewed in December 2012 under Zuma's rule, by which stage Bozize's authoritarian rule was coming under significant pressure from the armed rebel coalition known as Seleka. For reasons that are not entirely clear, South Africa deployed an estimated 200 paratroopers during January 2013. What is clear is that the SANDF troops that were dispatched to CAR were not for training or infrastructure refurbishment, and that they were deployed with neither parliamentary approval, nor coordination with DIRCO (Römer Heitman, 2013). Along with this, neither the AU nor the SADC security organ were consulted.

The rationale of the deployment of forces to CAR remains opaque and thus speculative. We can dismiss the argument that there was a need to defend a national security interest or substantial economic interests, since CAR does not feature as a significant security or commercial partner (Khadiagala, 2014:279). Neither is the argument one based on historical ties, as the CAR leadership was not involved in the anti-apartheid struggle. One reason offered by Khadiagala is that South Africa's pan-Africanist credentials are strengthened by its involvement in French-speaking Africa, but this view is in reference to Mbeki's 2007 bilateral agreement, not to Zuma's unilateral adventurism. From the perspective of the Seleka rebels, who entered into power-sharing negotiations with the Bozize government in January 2013, the South African troops were propping up the Bozize regime (Khadiagala, 2014:279). Seleka's military offensive to capture Bangui in March 2013 resulted in 13 South African soldiers being killed, with 27 wounded and one missing in action.

This ill-fated involvement in CAR remains controversial. There was domestic criticism because the deployment happened with less parliamentary oversight than was necessary, and because there were inconsistencies in the explanations offered after the deployment ended in tragedy. Similarly, there was insufficient consultation within SADC, of which CAR is not a member, and with the Economic Community of Central African States (ECCAS), of which CAR is a member. This failure of domestic oversight of defence diplomacy has led to media speculation that South African soldiers were deployed to CAR to protect mining companies with links to the ANC, and to protect the financial interests of the Zuma family.

While President Zuma maintained that those killed in Bangui 'died in defence of the country's foreign policy', there were considerable efforts to avoid full accountability (Khadiagala, 2014:285). Instead, Zuma was quoted as saying (Khadiagala, 2014:285):

> There must be an appreciation that matters of military tactics and strategy are not to be discussed in public ... No country reveals and discusses its military strategies in the manner that South Africa is expected to do. Those who are engaging in this game should be careful not to endanger both the national interest and the security of the republic.

However, an analysis by two professors of Military Strategy at the South African Military Academy concluded that the CAR deployment is indicative of the deep-seated strategic failures of South African military action on the continent (Vreÿ & Esterhuyse, 2016). Despite the CAR incident as a low point in South Africa's defence diplomacy, expectations continue that South Africa should extend its role in the AU and through the APSA it helped to establish. Significant gains have been made in advancing South African interests through multilateral diplomacy, including in the continental security institutions, but caution is advised.

Defence diplomacy on the continent

Under Mbeki's diplomatic initiative between 1999 and 2002, South Africa played a key role in transforming the OAU into the AU. The AU's Constitutive Act condemned genocide, war crimes, and crimes against humanity, and the AU thus has the right to intervene against military coups and in defence of human rights. With its creation in July 2002 came a framework for APSA, based on a collective security approach from a human security perspective (Hutchful, 2009). The AU's 15-member Peace and Security Council (PSC) is the most important African institution for the management of peace and security issues, authorising peace operations and coordinating conflict management strategies (African Union, 2002). Since 2004, the AU has intended to build its capacity to respond to conflicts rapidly and effectively through the creation of the African Standby Force (ASF), but while initially scheduled for operation by 2010, the delay in creating the ASF reveals the weaknesses of Africa's institutional capacity at the subregional level.

In contrast, SADC declared its new regional military formation, the SADCBRIG, operational in August 2007 (Mandrup, 2009). South Africa was crucial, and described as 'very active in the formation of the ASF, and SADCBRIG', which was modelled on the Nordic Stand-by High Readiness Brigade (Mandrup, 2009:18). South Africa's ambitions were also evident at the AU itself: in 2012, South Africa aggressively campaigned for the candidacy of Nkosazana Dlamini-Zuma for the position of AU Commission Chair. This was controversial as it went against the unwritten rule that no major African power should occupy this position. By May 2013, the AU Assembly established the African Capacity for Immediate Response to Crises (ACIRC), based on individual African states deploying troops. South Africa strongly championed ACIRC, but key continental players such as Nigeria, Ethiopia, Egypt, and Kenya expressed reservations (Brosig & Sempijja, 2015:2-3). Some argue that South Africa's push for ACIRC diverted resources and political energy away from finalisation of the ASF (Warner, 2015), while critical observers hold that the AU had been used as a tool of South Africa's foreign policy. Dlamini-Zuma served only one four-year term as Chair.

Conclusions and recommendations

South Africa's involvement in Africa via its defence diplomacy aimed to show the country as a potential peace multiplier. However, as this role has expanded, both in terms of geography and complexity, new demands and expectations must be met with realism. On the one hand, South Africa's diplomacy demonstrates a commitment to Africa, its people, and the continent. On the other hand, a lack of reflection or poorly-calculated pragmatism has introduced discrepancies. Despite South Africa's appearance of relative strength, there are real limitations that should be considered rationally before unrealistic demands or inflated expectations are uncritically accepted (Brooks, 2001; Nibishaka, 2011; Dube, 2013; Fabricius, 2013; Schuenemann & Cilliers, 2013). These are the fundamental issues that impact South Africa's defence diplomacy.

As we noted, the 'new' South Africa's approach to conflict resolution on the continent and elsewhere was to advocate its own internal solution to other conflict-ridden societies: that of transition through negotiation and the attainment of constitutional democracy. Promoting peace through advocating negotiated settlement was taken seriously, especially under Presidents Mandela and Mbeki, as South Africa's diplomacy after 1994 moved from a militarist to a moralist approach in its external relations. The country's foreign policy centred on the themes of Africanism, promoting human rights and democracy, a holistic approach to security, pacific forms of conflict resolution, and multilateralism. As Nathan (2005) points out, these five themes have value when they are mutually-consistent, conceptually-linked, and consolidated.

Although Nathan (2005) was referring specifically to the early years of the Mbeki presidency, he also identified significant contradictions. One such inconsistency was an absence of common values in the region, which inhibited collective action and policy consensus. An example of this disconnect between declared democratic commitments and foreign policy in action was the policy towards Zimbabwe. Far from being 'quiet diplomacy', Nathan (2005) shows South Africa's foreign policy as expressing support for Mugabe, even in response to state repression and the undermining of the rule of law. This position on Zimbabwe was also inconsistent with South Africa's stated holistic approach to human security. Nathan (2005) argued that South Africa's foreign policy is constrained by deep political divisions in the region and in SADC, and this chapter demonstrates that this has had an impact on how the country carries out its defence diplomacy, and on the effectiveness of such policy.

Relative to the region, South Africa has both a strong and vibrant economy and a capable military force. Expectations therefore run high for South Africa to be actively engaged in peace missions. Simultaneously, the country also has to guard against the perception of behaving as an imposing hegemon. It has also had to steer clear of involvement with other international actors, such as the US, UK and France, that may be perceived as colonial or neo-imperial powers. Yet the expectation that South Africa, as the regional power in SADC and one of the significant powers in Africa, has to be more involved in a spectrum of peace missions, including peace enforcement, persists (Tlhaole, 2013:13; Williams, 2011:1). South Africa's mission-based approach, including peace-support operations and defence diplomacy, must be seen as selective engagement, depending on force levels, capabilities and resources in support of properly articulated foreign relations (Liebenberg & Mokoena, 2014:8). The challenge is to align expectations with real capabilities, or to align ends and means.

South Africa is currently constrained by having a weak economy, limited capacity for external action, and a number of domestic problems, including poor service delivery. Real limitations exist in the military too, such as the age profile of SANDF staff, the levels of available skills, budgetary constraints, and the state of readiness of equipment, some of which was bought in the 1990s and is now not immediately deployable. These limitations should be kept in mind by political and military leadership, even if South Africa has a coherent foreign policy. The challenge to be able to deliver effectively without promising too much requires a coherent long-term national security strategy. A solid document on a National Security Strategy is required.

Once this national security strategy is properly articulated, South Africa's defence diplomacy as an extension of its foreign policy needs to focus on coordination with its partners. Aside from the greatest obstacle of financing, coordination and leadership are huge challenges. States on the continent have different abilities and capabilities, and how to streamline coordination between the militaries of states, regional organisations and the AU requires continuous attention. As Hughes argues, 'some states must in practice come to take a greater initiative than others' (2001:296), and South Africa would do well to work through the organisations it has been instrumental in creating: SADC and the regional organisations (West, East and in the Maghreb) within the continental realm (AU, ASF, APSA). Responsibilities should be shared and cooperation enhanced through task division that keeps in mind the asymmetric nature of the economic power and relative influence of African countries in the broader partnership. Future success will depend on how well-coordinated, planned and executed operations will be, how cost-effective within a set time-frame, and to what extent states with differing economies in each region and on the continent can contribute to missions.

A fundamental aspect, however, has to underpin all of South Africa's international action and that is its democratic status and respect for the constitutionally-mandated rule of law. Effective civilian oversight is necessary, and political and military leaders must be held accountable for the availability of funding, material capacity, human capacity, and skilled resources. There must be informed debate on the conditions for intervention: When to go and when not to go? Here, capacity, expectations, skills, and finances are of great importance, as timely, rather than reactive, intervention is necessary. Of importance is that the decision for intervention be thoroughly agreed upon by all the actors. Force generation should match cooperation, consultation, entrance, and exit strategies. These are all factors that require military expertise but need to have civilian oversight. In this regard, the recent criticisms can be summarised as: (1) the undue influence of the ruling party on political decision-making, especially under Jacob Zuma; (2) the relatively low levels of participation by parliament; (3) the relative lack of influence of the Defence Secretariat (Fourie, 2012); and (4) the lack of coordinated policymaking and development of a long-term vision for South Africa's security position and engagements in the region and on the continent. Critical observers also point out that 'parliament's reactive rather than pro-active foreign policy role has often been criticised' (Van Wyk, 2012:279).

Assuming that this is true, a lot of work remains to ensure closer interaction between DIRCO, the Presidency, parliament, the Defence Secretariat (as a significant independent institution), and the DOD. As foreign policy impacts so closely on defence diplomacy, a more integrated approach is necessary, while civilian oversight is simultaneously strengthened. This is a necessary approach as the country combines its soft power and hard power capabilities. The challenges from earlier remain. If South Africa oversteps the line between benevolent strong partner and imposing hegemon, some diplomatic gains will be lost and replaced with underlying tensions. On the other hand, if the benevolent partner overstretches or over-estimates its capacity, it may lead to loss of face and diminished trust between continental actors. There are no easy choices here.

References

Africa, S. 2011. The Transformation of the South African security sector: lessons and challenges. Policy Paper 33. Geneva Centre for the Democratic Control of Armed Forces (DCAF). Geneva: DCAF.

African Union. 2002. *2002 Protocol Establishing the Peace and Security Council.* https://bit.ly/2PX5Raa [Accessed 8 November 2018].

Alden, C. 2014. BRICS and Africa: A Partnership for Sustainable Development? SAIIA Conference at Crown Plaza Rosebank, 12-13 November.

Alden, C. & Le Pere, G. 2004. South Africa's Post-Apartheid Foreign Policy: From Reconciliation to Ambiguity? *Review of African Political Economy*, 31(100):283-297. https://doi.org/10.1080/0305624042000262293

Baker, D.P. 2009. New Partnerships for a New Era: Enhancing the South African Army's Stabilization Role in Africa. Strategic Studies Institute. June.

Blake, R. 2016. Defence diplomacy for conflict prevention: A strategic analysis with reference to the South African Defence Review 2015. Unpublished Master's thesis, University of Pretoria.

Brooks, D. 2001. From Destabilising to Restabilising: South Africa's Military Transition and Capacity for Peacekeeping. *South African Yearbook of International Affairs, 2000/2001.* Johannesburg: SAIIA.

Brosig, M. & Sempijja, N. 2015. The African Capacity for Immediate Response to Crisis: Advice for African Policymakers. *Policy Insights no. 22*, South African Institute of International Affairs. Johannesburg: SAIIA.

Cilliers, J. 2014. *Africa's conflict burden in a global context*. ISS Paper 273, October. Pretoria: Institute for Security Studies (ISS). https://doi.org/10.2139/ssrn.2690123

Cottey, A. & Forster, A. 2004. *Reshaping defence diplomacy: New roles for military co-operation and assistance*. Oxford: Oxford University Press.

De Coning, C. 1998. Conditions for intervention: DRC and Lesotho. *Conflict Trends*, 1(4):20-23.

Department of Defence. 2009. *Annual Report FY 2008-2009 (Safeguarding South Africa for A better Life for All)*. Pretoria: DOD.

Department of Defence. 2015. *Department of Defence Strategic Plan (2015-2020)*. Pretoria: DOD.

Department of Defence. 2017. *Department of Defence Annual Report 2016/17*. Pretoria: DOD.

Department of Government Communication and Information System (DGCIS). 2003. *South African Yearbook 2002/2003*. Pretoria: DGGIS.

Department of Government Communication and Information System (DGCIS). 2017. *South African yearbook 2016/17*. Pretoria: DGGIS.

Dube, M. 2013. BRICS Summit 2013: Strategies for South Africa's Engagement (South African Institute of International Affairs, SAIIA). *SAIIA Policy Briefing*, 62.

Du Pisani, A. 1986. South Africa in Namibia: Variations on a Theme (South African Institute of International Affairs, SAIIA). *International Affairs Bulletin*, 10(3):6ff.

Du Plessis, A. 2003. The Military Instrument in South African Foreign Policy: A Preliminary Exploration. *Strategic Review for Southern Africa*, XXV(2):106-143.

Dyer, G. 2009. *Future Tense: The Coming World Order*. London: Serpent's Tail.

Fabricius, P. 2013. OAU Milestone: The Focal Shift from Decolonisation to Democracy. *Weekend Argus*, 25 May:25.

Fourie, D. 2012 Decline and Fall: Why the South African Civilian Defence Secretariat was dissolved in 1966. *Scientia Militaria*, 40(3):40-70. https://doi.org/10.5787/40-3-1032

Frankel, P.H. 1984. *Pretoria's Praetorians: Civil-Military Relations in South Africa*. Cambridge: Cambridge University Press.

Geldenhuys, D. 1984. *The Diplomacy of Isolation: South Africa's Foreign Policy Making*. Johannesburg: Macmillan. https://doi.org/10.1007/978-1-349-17501-7

Habib, A. 2009. South Africa's foreign policy: hegemonic aspirations, neoliberal orientations and global transformation, *South African Journal of International Affairs*, 16(2):143-159. https://doi.org/10.1080/10220460903265857

Hammerstad, A. 2005. People, States and Regions, in A. Hammerstad (ed.), *People, States and Regions: Building a Co-operative Security regime in Southern Africa*. Johannesburg: South African Institute of International Affairs.

Hughes, T. 2001. South Africa: The Contrarian Big African State, in C. Clapham, J. Herbst & G. Mills (eds.), *Big African States: Angola, Sudan, DRC, Ethiopia, Nigeria, South Africa*. Johannesburg: Wits University Press.

Hutchful, E. 2008. From Military to Human Security, in J. Akokpari, A. Ndinga-Muvumba & T. Murithi (eds.), *The African Union and its Institutions*. Auckland Park, South Africa: Fanele.

Ispahani, M.Z. 1984. Alone Together: Regional Security Arrangements in Southern Africa and the Arabian Gulf. *International Security*, 8(4):152-175. https://doi.org/10.2307/2538567

Jaster, R.S. 1985. *South Africa in Namibia: The Botha Strategy*. Lanham: University Press of America.

Khadiagala, G.M. 2014. South Africa in Africa: Groping for leadership and muddling through, in G.M. Khadiagala, P. Naidoo, D. Pillay & R. Southall (eds.), *New South African Review 4: A fragile democracy – Twenty years on*. Johannesburg: Wits University Press. https://doi.org/10.18772/22014047632

Landsberg, C. 2012. Towards a post-apartheid South African foreign policy review, in C. Landsberg & J-A. van Wyk (eds.), *South African Foreign Policy Review* (Vol. 1). Pretoria: Africa Institute of South Africa.

Liebenberg, I. 2008. Talking Small Wars in Far Away Lands: Three Incidences in Angola's "Second War of Liberation", in T. Potgieter, A. Esterhuyse & I. Liebenberg (eds.), *Regions, Regional Organisations and Military Power*. Stellenbosch: African Sun Media.

Liebenberg, I. 2011. From Racialism to Authoritarianism: South Africa, Militarised Politics and the Implosion of State Legitimacy under Apartheid. *ISPAIM Occasional Paper*, 10(16).

Liebenberg, I. 2015. On our Borders: Namibia seeks its own Destiny, in I. Liebenberg, G. Risquet & V. Shubin (eds.), *A Far-Away War: Angola 1975-1989*. Stellenbosch: African Sun Media. https://doi.org/10.18820/9781920689735

Liebenberg, I. 2018. 'Tussen vryheid en massamoord in Hornkranz-skadu'. *Beeld*, 5 May:16.

Liebenberg, I. & Mokoena, B. 2014. 'South Africa's role in African Peace'. *Daily News*, 26 September.

Likoti, F.J. 2007. The 1998 Military Intervention in Lesotho: SADC Peace Mission or Resource War? *International Peacekeeping*, 14(2):251-263. https://doi.org/10.1080/13533310601150875

Makwetla, T. 2012. South Africa's Contribution to Peace in Africa. *SA Army Journal*, 5:24-32.

Mandrup, T. 2009. South Africa and the SADC standby force. *Scientia Militaria, South African Journal of Military Studies*, 37(2):1-24. https://doi.org/10.5787/37-2-66

Masters, L. 2012. Opening the 'black box' – South Africa's foreign policy making, in C. Landsberg & J-A. van Wyk (eds.), *South African Foreign Policy Review* (Vol. 1). Pretoria: Africa Institute of South Africa.

Monyae, D. 2012. The Evolving "Doctrine" of Multilateralism in South Africa's Africa Policy, in C. Landsberg & J-A. van Wyk (eds.), *South African Foreign Policy Review* (Vol. 1). Pretoria: Africa Institute of South Africa.

Namibia Support Committee. 1988. *Namibia 1884-1984: Readings on Namibia's History and Society*. Lusaka: United Nations Institute for Namibia.

Nathan, L. 2005. Consistency and inconsistencies in South African foreign policy. *International Affairs*, 81(2):361-372. https://doi.org/10.1111/j.1468-2346.2005.00455.x

Neethling, T. 2012. Considerations on Defence Thinking in Post-1994 South Africa with Special Reference to Post-Conflict Reconstruction and Development (PCRD). *Scientia Militaria*, 40(3): 472-500. https://doi.org/10.5787/40-3-1037

Ngwenya, N.X. 2012. South Africa's relationships with African anchor states, in C. Landsberg & J-A. van Wyk (eds.), *South African Foreign Policy Review* (Vol. 1). Pretoria: Africa Institute of South Africa.

Nibishaka, E. 2011. South Africa's Peacekeeping Role in Africa: Motives and Challenges of Peacekeeping. *International Politics*, 02.

Pampallis, J. 1991. *Foundations of the New South Africa*. Cape Town: Maskew Miller Longman.

Republic of South Africa. 1996. *Defence in a Democracy: White Paper on National Defence for the Republic of South Africa*, May. Pretoria: Government Printing Works.

Republic of South Africa. 1998. *South African Defence Review*. Pretoria: Government Printing Works.

Römer Heitman, H. 2013. *The Battle in Bangui: The untold inside story*. Johannesburg: Parktown Publishers.

Schuenemann, J. & Cilliers, J. 2013. 'OAU Milestone: The Continent Looks Better than Before'. *Weekend Argus*, 25 May:25.

Seegers, A. 1996. *The Military in the Making of Modern South Africa.* London: IB Taurus.

Sidiropoulos, E. 2007. South Africa's regional engagement for peace and security. *Fride Comment*, October. Madrid: Fundación para las Relaciones Internacionales y el Diálogo Exterior.

Smith, K. 2012. Soft Power: The Essence of South Africa's Foreign Policy, in C. Landsberg & J-A. van Wyk (eds.), *South African Foreign Policy Review* (Vol. 1). Pretoria: Africa Institute of South Africa.

Southall, R. 2006. A long prelude to peace: South African involvement in ending Burundi's war, in Southall, R. (ed.), *South Africa's role in conflict resolution and peacemaking in Africa*. Cape Town: HSRC Press. pp. 105-133.

Stockwell, J. 1978. *In Search of Enemies: A CIA Story.* London: Andre Deutsch.

Tlhaole, L. 2013. SANDF briefs media on DRC deployment. *South African Soldier*, 20(9), September.

United Nations (UN). 1974. *A Trust Betrayed: Namibia*. New York: UN Office of Public Information.

Van Eck, J. 2009. Lessons from the Burundi Peace Process, in K. Shillinger (ed.). *Africa's Peacemaker? Lessons from South African Conflict Mediation*. Johannesburg: South African Institute of International Relations.

Van Nieuwkerk, A. 2012. A Review of South Africa's Peace Diplomacy Since 1994, in C. Landsberg & J-A. van Wyk (eds.), *South African Foreign Policy Review* (Vol. 1). Pretoria: Africa Institute of South Africa. https://doi.org/10.1080/10220469409545105

Van Wyk, J-A. 2012. Reflections on South Africa's post-apartheid foreign policy and preliminary comments on future, in C. Landsberg & J-A. van Wyk (eds.), *South African Foreign Policy Review* (Vol. 1). Pretoria: Africa Institute of South Africa.

Vickers, B. 2012. South Africa's Economic Policy in a Changing Global Order, in C. Landsberg & J-A. van Wyk (Eds.). *South African Foreign Policy Review* (Vol. 1). Pretoria: Africa Institute of South Africa.

Vreÿ, F. & Esterhuyse, A.J. 2016. South Africa and the search for strategic effect in the Central African Republic. *Scientia Militaria*, 44(2):1-27. https://doi.org/10.5787/44-2-1174

Warner, J. 2015. Complements or Competitors? The African Standby Force, the African Capacity for Immediate Response to Crises, and the Future of Rapid Reaction Forces in Africa. *African Security*, 8:56-73. https://doi.org/10.1080/19392206.2015.998543

Williams, P.D. 2011. Peace Operations in Africa: Lessons Learned Since 2000. *Africa Security Brief*, 25.

07

National Security in Complex Times
The South African military dimension

Shadrack Ramokgadi, Tobie Beukes and Ian Liebenberg

Abstract

Having returned to the international gallery of nations in 1996 after its apartheid pariah status was lifted, South Africa had to adjust its defence posture, defence diplomacy, and general national security framework to new conditions. The Cold War was over, interstate wars in the region were unlikely, and if undertaken at all, military deployment was to participate in peacekeeping operations. With the apartheid garrison state mentality a thing of the past, a new national security strategy became a necessity. This chapter discusses the need and guidelines for a national security strategy suited to a democracy and a developmental state aware of current and future socio-economic challenges, and its role in the region and on the African continent.

Introduction

In South Africa, an official National Security Strategy (NSS) is prepared and reviewed periodically by the executive authorities, who are required to outline national security priorities, and suggest policy responses. Post-1994, the NSS process began with the White Paper on National Defence for the Republic of South Africa (1996), followed by the Defence Review 1998, and Defence Review 2015. The latest NSS is currently being developed, but it faces challenges. This chapter exclusively uses publicly available sources as it attempts a fresh look at a future NSS, highlighting lessons from the national security strategies of other countries, and providing some comparative insights.

Methodology

The methodology used here is qualitative and involved an extensive literature study of open source documents. While the goal was to gain insights on a possible security strategy for post-apartheid South Africa, we limited our country comparisons, choosing not to focus on core aggressive states, self-perceived 'world policemen', or societies that see themselves as beleaguered by a hostile world, such as the US. The authors assume that regional and international cooperation remain important tools, and that multipolarity in the future is a given.

National security in a new democracy

This contribution will do the following:

- Define the concept of national security;
- Describe current and future challenges to national security;
- Discuss the mandate of the South African National Defence Force (SANDF);
- Provide an outline of the role and functions of the military in national security;
- Discuss the SANDF Military Strategy;
- Discuss security as a concept and its links with perceived national values;
- Discuss regional challenges; and
- Indicate the threats that face the population of South Africa.

Defining the concept of 'National Security'

The challenges experienced by states have changed since the end of the Cold War and the temporary lessening of the East-West divide. Increased globalisation and hyper-capitalism brought with them intensive international integration, yet simultaneously increased social alienation, fragmentation, and the rich-poor divide (Giddens, 1993). These have also led to new tensions and (armed) conflicts between multiple stakeholders (including non-state actors), often expanding into hybrid conflicts.

'National security' has no single definition (D'Anieri, 2014:69), but a broad description of a national security strategy, focusing on a diverse array of global threats including political, social, economic, health and environment, is relevant for the purposes of this chapter. The South African White Paper on Defence (1996: chapter 2) described national security as follows:

> In the new South Africa national security is no longer viewed as a predominantly military and police problem. It ... broadened to incorporate political, economic, social and environmental matters ... Security [became] an all-encompassing condition in which individual citizens live in freedom, peace and safety; participate fully in the process of governance; enjoy the protection of fundamental rights; have access to resources and the basic necessities of life; and inhabit an environment which is not detrimental to their health and well-being ... At national level the objectives of security policy therefore encompass the consolidation of democracy; the achievement of social justice, economic development and a safe environment; and a substantial reduction in the level of crime, violence and political instability. Stability and development are regarded as inextricably linked and mutually reinforcing. At international level the objectives of security policy include the defence of the sovereignty, territorial integrity and political independence of the South African state, and the promotion of regional security in Southern Africa.

The above implies a move away from restrictive threat analysis to what may be described as a *new and broader security realism*, where the future safety of people is linked not only to armed threats, but also to threats to human life and life quality within communities and regions.

Current and likely future challenges to national security

In the current context, the threats and risks to the state and society encompass the military, economic, political-cultural and resource-environmental sectors (Mulaudzi & Liebenberg, 2017:29ff.; De Wet & Liebenberg, 2018; Mandrup, 2018:136ff.). However, economic, social and political dynamics also offer opportunities and challenges to enhance the interests of South Africa. The South African approach to national security, we argue, should be based on an agreement between state and organised civil society (or civil community) on the protection of social liberties and human security, and the readiness for managing threats and risks in the regional environment. Thus, economic, political-cultural and resource-environmental security must be clearly identified in terms of both traditional and non-traditional threats and risks, as well as the positive challenges and opportunities that can enhance the interests of South Africa, the region, and the continent.

Current and likely future challenges to national security for South Africa include, but are not limited to:

- Regional instability (i.e. deterioration of quality of life and increasing poverty);
- Climate change and disasters;
- Energy supply and water/food sustainability;
- Internal (violent) reactions related to service delivery, xenophobia, crime;
- Possible intervention by states outside the continent; and
- Possible cyber-attacks and terrorism.

The military and the Constitution

The Constitution of the Republic of South Africa, Act 108 of 1996 (hereafter, Constitution, 1996) holds that:

a. The defence force is the only lawful military force in the Republic;

b. The defence force must be structured and managed as a disciplined military force;

c. The primary object of the defence force is to defend and protect the Republic, its territorial integrity and its people in accordance with the Constitution and the principles of international law regulating the use of force;

d. The President as head of the national executive is Commander-in-Chief of the defence force, and must appoint the Military Command of the force; and

e. Command of the Defence Force must be exercised in accordance with the directions of the Minister of Defence under the authority of the President.

South African National Defence Force functions

According to the Defence Act, Act 42 of 2002 (Section 18 (1) (d)), the SANDF may, subject to the Constitution, be employed:

a. For service in the defence of the Republic, for the protection of its sovereignty and territorial integrity;

b. For service in compliance with the international obligations of the Republic with regard to international bodies and other states;

c. For service in the preservation of life, health or property;

d. For service in the provision or maintenance of essential services;

e. For service in the upholding of law and order in the Republic in cooperation with the South African Police Service under circumstances set out in a law where the said Police Service is unable to maintain law and order on its own;

f. For service in support of any department of state for the purpose of socio-economic upliftment; and

g. To effect national border control.

Along with this, according to the Constitution (1996, Schedule 6, section 24):

> (2) The National Defence Force shall exercise its powers and perform its functions solely in the national interest in terms of Chapter 11 of the Constitution of the Republic of South Africa, 1996.
>
> (3) The employment for service, training, organisation and deployment of the South African National Defence Force shall be effected in accordance with the requirements of subsection (2).

The role of the military

Development requires stability, and stability requires sound state and social structures which are seen and experienced as legitimate by the citizenry (Mulaudzi & Liebenberg, 2017). Thus, a well-trained and equipped military which holds legitimacy in the eyes of civil society is imperative. The military provides security for both internal crises (in cooperation with the South African Police Service [SAPS]) and external aggression or threats to peace, making it a potential tool to ensure regional and international security. After 1994, the new government replaced the militarist security project of the apartheid government with a more holistic approach, using the lessons learnt through negative experiences and the flaws in civil-military relations under apartheid. Currently, the primary threat to security is not military and cannot be dealt with by purely military means. Along with this, in a constitutional state civil-military relations and safe communities hold more value than the ability to suppress with force, and the military is bound to accept civil control. This has an influence on the role of the military, whether internal or external, and also impacts the national security strategy.

This new approach arose from the success of the country's negotiated settlement and the leadership preference for persuasion and negotiation. Force has been viewed as a limited mechanism, applicable only in exceptional situations, and rather than projecting military force, South Africa's aim is to project diplomacy and enhance cooperation and peace, meaning that all other options should be exhausted before the use of force.

Strategic national security functions of the South African government and SANDF

Security in all forms is seen as a core function, and the armed forces and other state organs are required by government to contribute to this. The SANDF, as an arm of the state, is required to respond to both internal and external security issues, as guided by national and international regulatory frameworks, and this provides the foundation for a comprehensive approach to national security. Arguably, the main role of the SANDF is the use of military capabilities to achieve identified policy objectives. One approach suggests that the security-creating role of the government can fall into six strategic functions: China after a period of relative disruptive Western Colonial intervention returned to what perhaps can be called the geographical space of a perceived "greater" China as many ages before. While China became a republic, it was to experience a wide-ranging and destructive Japanese invasion before World War II and a civil war between communists and nationalists that was to end with the defeated nationalists establishing a nationalist government in exile in 1949 on the island of Taiwan (the latter seen by the Chinese government as an errant province). In a sense then the European imposed model of nationalism (or in cases a paradigm widely accepted in current discourse) had long-term consequences, some of which we still see today: (1) Anticipation; (2) prevention; (3) deterrence; (4) protection; (5) intervention; and (6) stabilisation (Constitution, 1996; White Paper on Defence, 1996; Defence Review, 1998).

Anticipation

As a representative of a community of citizens, the government is to prepare for foreseen and unforeseen contingencies, including incidents that may threaten the interests of South Africa or international rule of law. The role of the SANDF is to prepare forces which can respond to any foreseeable circumstances for the protection of its sovereignty and territorial integrity, and if needed, secondary roles of various forms (Constitution, 1996: Chapter 11, Section 201(2)).

Prevention

The SANDF is required to proactively prevent possible future threats to the country or region. The Constitution (1996: Chapter 11, Section 2019(c)) provides for the deployment of the SANDF for services in compliance with the international obligations of the country, in line with international bodies and other member states. The most common obligation is the duty to protect people from any harm through prevention. Given the South African context and historical experience, the principle of 'self-defence' demands the prevention, management and resolution of conflict through non-violent means (White Paper on Defence, 1996: Chapter 4).

Deterrence

The South African government is expected to discourage any actions that are in conflict with the interests of the state or the international rule of law (White Paper on Defence, 1996:Chapter 4), including protection outside the geographical confines of the country and its inhabitants.. In effecting this, the government of SA states that the prevention of conflict and war is a primary course of action (Defence Review, 1998: Chapter 2). This includes self-defence, requiring a defence capability which is sufficiently credible to deter potential aggressors (Defence Review, 1998: Chapter 2). The credibility of the core force capability must therefore be maintained at all times, as per the core-force approach (Ministry of Defence, 2010). The Constitution prescribes the mobilisation of the SANDF for service in upholding law and order within the country in cooperation with the SAPS, under circumstances where the police services are unable to do so alone (1996: Section 201(2)(a)). Such cooperative arrangements require an awareness of the limitations of the armed forces for deployment within a civilian environment and should be treated with care in terms of 'deterrence'.

Civilian control over the military remains paramount. The deployment of the SANDF in cooperation with the SAPS should only be carried out with the awareness that military solutions to political problems are inherently limited. The Constitution (1996) prescribes that the president is the Commander-in-Chief of the defence force and appoints the Chief of the Defence Force. The White Paper on Defence, the Public Service Act, and the Public Finance Management Act provide for the Secretary for Defence (a civilian), who shall exercise their functions and powers as Head of Department and Accounting Officer (Defence Review, 1998:Chapter 9). Along with this, the Constitution established a Defence Secretariat to assist the Minister of Defence with functions related to issuing of orders, directives, and commands, and the execution of budgetary programmes, as well as oversight, in close cooperation with parliament and defence-related committees.

Protection

South Africa views itself as a member of the international community, and the SANDF is therefore expected to participate in international peace operations. For the purposes of the protection of the people, peace support operations are characterised by *military operations other than war* (MOOTW). Participation in MOOTW is founded on the understanding that regional peace and security is important to SA, as any spill-over from neighbouring countries will impact on its territorial integrity and national security (RSA Constitution, 1996; White Paper on Defence, 1996; Defence Review 1997/1998).

One has to note that international peace support operations are not limited to the deployment of troops, and can include providing equipment, medical personnel and facilities, logistical support, engineering services, communication systems, and staff (RSA Constitution, 1996; White Paper on Defence, 1996; Defence Review 1997/1998).

Intervention

A function of the state is to carry out offensive operations to enforce change in the behaviour of actors or alliances that threaten the interests of the state, the region or, where applicable, international rule of law (Ministry of Defence, 2010). This can include peace support operations, which for the purposes of intervention are characterised by peace enforcement entailing the application or threat of coercion (Ministry of Defence, 2010). The application of such force should aim to promote international peace and abide by international resolution (RSA Constitution, 1996; White Paper on Defence, 1996; Defence Review 1997/1998; Ministry of Defence, 2010).

Stabilisation

In terms of the above the South African security forces may be requested to assist in re-establishing security in any of the affected countries in the region. Thus, stabilisation refers to common security, regional defence cooperation, and confidence- and security-building measures in Southern Africa (RSA Constitution, 1996; White Paper on Defence, 1996; Defence Review 1997/1998; Ministry of Defence, 2010). In this context, the SA government is to be committed to political, economic and military cooperation with neighbouring states.

The Constitution (1996) also states that the SANDF may be employed in other roles in addition to self-defence, deployment in cooperation with the SAPS, and international peace support operations. These activities include disaster relief, the provision and maintenance of essential services, search and rescue, evacuation of South African citizens from high-threat areas, protection of maritime resources, and regional defence cooperation (Constitution, 1996).

Figure 7.1, compiled by the authors (see below), represents a summary of the proposed strategic functions of the South African government and the SANDF. Government is responsible for national security; the SANDF for activities to attain such goals, keeping in mind civilian control over the military.

Anticipation
Prevention
Deterrence
Protection
Intervention
Stabilisation

NATIONAL SECURITY AGENDA

1. Defence of the state, territorial integrity and citizens.
2. Support to national and regional interests.
3. Promoting international peace and security.

FIGURE 7.1 Strategic functions of the SANDF in pursuit of the National Security Agenda

SANDF and national security frameworks

At present, the South African Defence Review (2015) is the only national policy framework that guides the development of the NSS into an implementation and funding model in South Africa. Thus, the operational activities of the SANDF should be aligned with the prescripts of the Defence Review. For example, the alignment of the military's operational activities with the agenda for sustainable development within the Southern African Development Community (SADC) is important, along with military intervention in promoting international peace and security. While the Defence Review 2015 remains the only official statement that defines security concerns and prescribes the nature of acceptable policy responses, the White Paper on National Defence is the cornerstone in providing comprehensive and long-range planning on matters related to defence doctrine, force design, force levels, logistic support, armaments, equipment, human resources and funding (Defence Review, 1998:Chapter 1).

The aim in designing the White Paper on Defence and the Defence Review 1998 was to achieve national consensus on defence matters, subjected to consultation with multiple stakeholders and other interest groups (Defence Review, 1998). Defence reviews present proposals on themes such as defence posture and doctrine, force design options, and civil military relations, and act as an attempt to determine the appropriate size, structure, force design and posture of an armed force.

Defence posture and doctrine

In terms of defence posture, the SANDF should abide by the government's primary chosen course, which is the prevention and deterrence of conflict and war, and the government should go to war only when non-violent strategies and deterrence on all available levels have failed (Defence Review, 1998:Chapter 2). Thus, this needs to find expression in the NSS, keeping in mind political, economic, social and cultural rights, and primary needs of South Africa's citizens; the commitment to goals of arms control and disarmament at national, regional and international levels; and the country's vision to pursue peaceful relations with other states, including through military cooperation (Defence Review, 1998:Chapter 2).

In protecting the state and its people against external threats, the SANDF is to employ the following NSS guidelines (Defence Review, 1998): (1) Military cooperation with other states in pursuit of common security; (2) prevention, management, and resolution of conflict through non-violent means, such as diplomacy, mediation and arbitration; and (3) force employment, as the very last option. Similarly, the Constitution requires that the deterrent capability be established in line with international law on armed conflict, and related international humanitarian law (1996: Chapter 11, Section 200 (2)). For example, the show of force through joint multinational military exercises should also respect international environmental rules and regulations.

South Africa's defence doctrine is derived from its defence posture and the related policy frameworks, and encompasses the main principles and concepts that guide the conduct of military operations in support of national objectives. The SANDF doctrine is also founded on the Constitution's commitment to international rule of law governing aggression, and provides for military capability that is able to halt, contain and reverse the effects of offensive actions at operational level of conflict, although this approach does not rule out offensive operations as the last instance (Constitution, 1996).

Force design options

The SANDF is required to plan and prepare force structure elements (e.g. land, sea, air, and cyber defence; and health support) that are ready at all times to act in defence of South Africa and to respond to other defence contingencies (Defence Review, 1998). Force design is based on readiness to execute the primary functions of the SANDF, namely defence of the state, its people and its territorial integrity against military aggression (Defence Review, 1998). Force design options are also influenced by the required level of defence, the approved defence posture, and the defence budget. For the latter, a funding model remains a challenge to be addressed.

Given economic and political-constitutional constraints, political judgment and military expertise are at play throughout the process, implying the development of various scenarios, policy responses or conceived courses of action. Needless to say, the approval of a specific option is primarily determined by the maintenance of the specified capabilities at the approximate level (Defence Review, 1998). Force design is a multidimensional system and should be open for review and innovation, enabling flexible responses to various security challenges or threats. Affordability is dependent on the long-term sustainability of the design, while upgrading and replacement of equipment is dictated by the lifespan of the capability itself, both man and material (Defence Review, 1998). Thus, force design process should translate into manageable options, and strategic gaps and related risks need to be consistently considered (Defence Review, 1998).

Civil military relations

The democratic transition in South Africa is relevant here, despite conceivable shortcomings since 1996 (Defence Review, 1998:Chapter 9). Civilian control over the military is the assumed cornerstone of democratic practices in South Africa. Civilian control relates to constitutional and legal transformation, oversight mechanisms, normative and cultural transformation, and future organisational restructuring (Defence Review, 1998:Chapter 9). The SANDF is required to remain subordinate to the elected government and should retain ultimate respect for the principle of civil supremacy. This view should be reinforced through training and development programmes in the SANDF, with emphasis placed on the respect for civil control, as entrenched in the SANDF code of conduct for uniformed members (Defence Review, 1998:Chapter 9). In this regard, continuous rejuvenation, persistent education of personnel, and the creation of a tertiary-educated officer corps is of utmost importance, and currently in need of urgent attention.

The Constitution (1996) prescribes that the president is the Commander-in-Chief of the defence force and appoints the Chief of the Defence Force. The White Paper on Defence, the Public Service Act, and the Public Finance Management Act provide for the

Secretary for Defence (a civilian), who shall exercise their functions and powers as Head of Department and Accounting Officer (Defence Review, 1998:Chapter 9). Along with this, the Constitution established a Defence Secretariat to assist the Minister of Defence with functions related to issuing of orders, directives, and commands and the execution of budgetary programmes, as well as oversight, in close cooperation with parliament and defence-related committees.

The SANDF Military Strategy (SANDFMS) and envisioned national values

The SANDFMS (2002) plans for eventualities in the military environment and attempts to provide answers to military challenges in the foreseeable future. The strategy hierarchy stems from the Constitution, the Defence Act, White Paper, Defence Review, and other statutory prescripts, and is fed by national values. In turn, the Department of Defence (DOD) Military Strategy provides and employs force strategies inclusive of support strategies (SANDFMS, 2002). Military strategy documents provide the strategic profile through the DOD's Vision of Effective defence for a democratic South Africa, as a constitutional democratic state (SANDFMS, 2002).

The SANDFMS closely relates to the constitutional values of the country, and reflects on the use of the military outside its borders, seeking peace, and preventing or resolving conflict rather than acting belatedly and in a heavy-handed manner see in this regards the chapter by Liebenberg and Fonseca on South Africa's defence diplomacy). In the case of South Africa, these values are to be underpinned by the notions of democratisation of state and society, the constitutional state-principle, and unity in social diversity.

South Africa is a diverse community (Zegeye, Liebenberg & Houston, 2000; Van der Heyden, 2018), and one of the constitutional norms is unity in diversity. The SANDF should therefore reflect the values of diversity, tolerance, service to the community, representivity on all levels, and accountability for its actions (Polley, 1988; Corder, 1989; Van Zyl-Slabbert, 1992; Duncan & Seleoane, 1998; Seleoane, 2001; Houston, Liebenberg & Humphries, 2001). These national values need to be reflected within the SANDF and its deployment in the region, and should be seen to be part of practice and attitude wherever defence force members may find themselves. Other terms that crop up in the national discourse and that have a bearing on the SANDF are a non-racialist approach, respect for personal freedom and community safety, social cohesion, and a strong sense of service delivery. On a critical note, the interaction between civil society and the military should remain favourable, although a growing civil-military gap can be observed in South Africa, which needs urgent attention.

SANDF Military Strategy

At the core of SANDFMS are the military strategic objectives and military strategic capabilities, contained in the Strategic Plan 2011-2015 (DOD, 2011). The SANDF Military Strategic Objectives are to be aligned to a corresponding NSS, and are intended to highlight (1) the enhancement and maintenance of comprehensive defence capability; (2) promotion of peace, security and stability in the region and continent; and (3) providing support to the people of the Republic of South Africa (DOD, 2011).

The Military Strategic Missions are to be founded on a mission-based approach, using peace and war-time time missions to direct the strategy for force preparation and force structure (DOD, 2011), and accommodating both primary and secondary functions of the SANDF. The missions are to be aligned to a mandate-driven approach set out by parliament, and are to be implemented in non-conventional tasks, health support duties, peace support operations, special operations, defence diplomacy, support to other government departments, disaster relief and humanitarian assistance, presidential tasks, and conventional operations. The Military Strategic Concepts (Mission Based Approach) are guidelines on how to accomplish the Military Strategic Objectives. Specific concepts are mission-essential training, mission trained force, selective engagement and strategic positioning.

National values and interests; security arrangements regional and continental

South Africa changed from a society based on racial segregation to a constitutional state through an extended process of transition (1990-1996). New values and legal frameworks had to be negotiated in tenuous circumstances, a process which has yet to be completed. Some core values which entered the discourse during the transition are principled non-racialism and an ethos of service to the community. Along with this, various religious, linguistic and cultural entities exist in South Africa, and the Constitution requires that the public sector, which includes the military and broader security community, enact tolerance of differences, as well as equality between peoples of different communities. The South African socio-political vocabulary was extended with terms such as equity, service delivery (*batho pele*), *ubuntu*,[1] accountability, development, sustainable growth, and knowledge transfer.

These terms outline national values to be achieved, and future national values to be nurtured, and these should also be reflected within the SANDF in terms of internal and external interaction with other communities and the evolving security community in Southern Africa. South African's national values share a link with the broader security community.

In terms of regional involvement, South Africa abides by regional structures as well as the protocols of the African Union (AU), and also adheres to international agreements and the protocols of the United Nations (UN). In cases of intervention, diplomatic or military (i.e. peacekeeping or peace enforcement), South Africa is bound by its Constitution and by international agreements, and adherence to the role of a constitutional state and a facilitator of peacemaking on the continent should be the focus. However, values and interpretation of reality remain complex, and the country may also find itself in a situation where the push of powerful states will clash with South Africa's role as peacemaker. South Africa's NSS will therefore have to decide on how to deal with similar future challenges.

Regional challenges

Observers pointed out that South Africa has to move from a diplomacy of a dominant power in the region to one of engagement in diplomatic, political and military activities such as peacekeeping (Malan & Cilliers, 1997).

The expectations for the NSS are high, but the authors have important limitations to consider. There are massive economic differences between states in Southern Africa even while South Africa holds a lion's part of the collective GDP in the region.[2] Because of this other member states may expect much from South Africa in terms of a financial contribution to the region and the continent. In reality, the South African defence budget has not increased significantly over the past five years and is unlikely to experience large increases soon (see Appendix below). In terms of maintenance, the replacement and modernisation of equipment and manpower/human resource expenses limit the SANDF's capacity, and this must be kept in mind, both in defence diplomacy and in conceptualising an NSS.

Since the Declaration and Treaty of the SADC (1992) and the launch of the Organ for Peace, Defence and Security (OPDS) (1996), South Africa has been woven into the regional security architecture. In recognition of Chapter VIII of the UN Charter, southern African states agreed on the Protocol on Politics, Defence and Security Cooperation, which confirms respect for sovereignty, equality, interdependence, non-aggression and non-interference in the affairs of other states. The achievement of solidarity, peace and security, and the recognition of cooperation in political, defence and security measures both form part of this understanding. Add to this the promotion of peaceful settlement of disputes by negotiation, conciliation, mediation and arbitration, and the full picture becomes challenging in a region where there are large-scale economic disparities and occasional differences of opinion. The objectives of the protocol relate to curbing cross-border crime and promoting communities based on domestic security, as well as enhancing and nurturing regional capacity in terms of disaster management and international humanitarian assistance.

Against this background, South Africa is expected to play a role in both the region and the AU. Future security thinking will revolve around economic interdependence, closer cooperation, integration (without worsening social marginalisation) and awareness of outside influences and pressures. While positive growth rates are being experienced in the majority of countries in the region, these often do not translate into an abundance of funding for military and peacekeeping purposes. Interdependence is likely to remain in southern Africa for many years to come, and people will look towards South Africa for its contribution. Under current conditions, the expectations on what South Africa can do are unrealistically high. A consistent balance needs to be struck here when an NSS is framed.

Threats that face the population of South Africa

Traditionally, the concept of security has been interpreted in militarist terms, namely the simple military defence of the state or the offensive use of military power. However, since the 1994 Human Development Report of the UN Development Programme (UNDP), the concept of security has included human security, which implies a condition of freedom from pervasive threats to people's rights, their safety or their lives. It is seen as an all-encompassing condition in which individual citizens live in freedom, peace and safety; participate fully in the process of governance; enjoy protection of fundamental rights; have access to resources and the basic necessities of life; and inhabit an environment that is not detrimental to their health and well-being.

Within the human security paradigm, the South African population face some potential and real threats, and an NSS should reflect an awareness of these potential threats and contingencies. Examples are health (including HIV/AIDS), lack of social services at all levels of government, social insecurity (high levels of poverty and crime), and corruption (syphoning money from social upliftment and economic growth). Within this broad architecture, the roles and duties of the military should be outlined to ensure that military action in a secondary role remains within the set parameters, yet will be functional, effective and professionally available when the need arises.

By 2004, it was reported that South Africa had the highest HIV prevalence rates in the world, with 20% of the adult population (roughly five million people) being HIV positive (Nattrass, 2004). Although the health budget has increased and antiretroviral treatment has been rolled out, the situation is still not satisfactory. In 2001, there were 4.1 million people living with HIV in South Africa (9.4% of the total population), and this increased to 5.24 million by 2010, representing 10.5% of South Africans (SAIRR, 2010:52). The highest rates were recorded in KwaZulu-Natal, Gauteng and the Free State, with the Western Cape having the lowest prevalence rate of 6% (SAIRR, 2010:55). According to the SAIRR's future demographic projections, the situation is likely to worsen substantially from 2020 to 2040 (SAIRR, 2010:56).

AIDS impacts heavily on existing human capital, infecting mainly young adults, and affecting people's health and productivity, resulting in them becoming a burden on the state. It destroys a section of people capable of contributing to the economic and social life of the community, while care for the frail and sick demands financial resources from the state, the taxpayer, and the private sector. More worrying is the social dislocation caused by the loss of fathers, mothers, caregivers, guardians or children, which damages the social fabric of society. The disease has the potential to disrupt economic growth, the maintenance of a labour force and human/intellectual capital and contribute to greater inequality. The latter can in turn act as a trigger for internal conflict.

When considering an NSS, the military needs to make its contribution through educating its own personnel and their families, and the communities within which they are active, around diseases such as HIV/AIDS. The military health services should also be available to assist in problem areas, and with initiatives of government health services in a clearly defined and publicly acceptable secondary role, especially in rural areas.

Other threats, such as climate change and its conceivable negative spin-offs, also need to be factored in. The extent of such challenges (e.g. drought and floods followed by scarcity of resources) are not fully predictable, and the consideration of multidisciplinary task teams to act as early warning forums are necessary.

Communities and social divisions

Social conflict is multifaceted, and one of the main challenges to democratic consolidation in South Africa is the cultural divisions within the country. The country is divided across a variety of linguistic, ethnic, racial and religious lines, and there is a sharp rich-poor gap which creates tension and conflict through real or relative depravation. One of the worrying trends in South Africa is a growing class of people without access to any job or occupation – the *jobless class*. The existence of a jobless class can further tensions between those with jobs – even if only part-time or poorly paid – and those without access to jobs. The result of these tensions, confounded by suboptimal service delivery, may lead to active alienation from government or the state, and even active distrust of the state and the electoral process.

Another challenge is the inflow of migrants, both legal and illegal, which can trigger tensions and xenophobia, as the newcomers are seen as people who take jobs, and hence economic opportunities, from South Africans. In the past, this led to violent confrontations and tensions remain. The issue of national security is linked here with social tolerance and human security. While creating tolerance through education and with optimum immigration control, the military are also called upon to ensure the efficient patrolling of South Africa's borders, which have become porous since 1998. Those aware of national security challenges need to factor this in too.

In case of violent conflict within communities, the military (including the medical support services) may be called upon to assist in a strictly secondary role, and the ability and capability of officers and non-commissioned officers (NCOs) to negotiate, manage and facilitate conflict is important here. In this regard, training should be offered to officers and NCOs where possible, and the same applies where the military may be called upon to assist in crime reduction.

The framework for an NSS should take cognisance of all of the above. One of the adverse consequences of divisions or perceived schisms in society is political intolerance, with the potential for social conflict. In deeply divided societies, people typically develop strong in-group identities, often leading to strong out-group animosity that can culminate in alienation and violent civil conflict. The protracted conflicts in the region, such as in Sudan, are attributed to attempts by one group to subjugate or impose its will on other groups. With its numerous ethnic and linguistic groups and deep social stratification, South Africa may face similar challenges. As a constitutional extension of the state, the military should be aware of this and contribute to tolerance, inter-group communication, and maintenance and nurturing of principled non-racialism and caregiving to smaller or marginalised groups and communities.

Like schools, religious groups, the media and sport organisations, the military is an agent of socialisation for their personnel, their families and peer groups. It is important that the values of life-long education, knowledge sharing, tolerance and accommodation are reflected actively into the organisation and into the community.

The Grim Reaper(s): Unemployment, inequality and poverty

The policy of separate development implemented by the apartheid regime created one of the most unequal societies in the world, and South Africa's macro-economic policies since 1996 further contributed to inequalities. In 1996, 1,8 million South Africans were earning less than US$1 a day, but by 2005, the figure had risen to 4,2 million people (Johnson, 2010). The unique feature of this inequality is that, unlike in other countries, the disenfranchised group in South Africa is the numerical majority. This has left a large part of the society in a situation characterised by poverty and limited chances of emancipation. A further characteristic of inequality in South Africa is that inequalities within groups also deepened while, according to a Human Sciences Research Council (HSRC) report, households originally living in poverty had sunk deeper into poverty (Schwabe, 2004). 'In the past inequality in South Africa was largely defined along race lines. It has increasingly become defined by inequality within population groups as the gap between rich and poor within each group has increased' (Schwabe, 2004).[3]

Inequality has serious consequences, such as lack of social capital, lack of upward mobility, and social disorganisation, which frequently spill over into secondary problems such as crime, health threats, or intercommunity tensions. Despite the efforts of the new democratic government, couched in the National Development Plan, these challenges largely remained by 2018, and current inequality remains a serious challenge (Mulaudzi & Liebenberg. 2017:29ff.).

Along with this, unemployment in South Africa is very high, and rising. The country arguably has one of the highest rates of unemployment in the world, which in 2002 was 41% on a broad definition, and 30% on a narrow definition. Unemployment is especially high in rural areas and informal settlements. (Landman, Bhorat, Van der Berg & Van Aardt, 2003).

The economy is unable to productively absorb the current labour force, which is different from the patterns that exist in most developing countries, where scarcity of jobs in the formal sector translates into large informal sectors, rather than high levels of unemployment. Unemployment in South Africa remains a matter of serious concern due to its effects on economic welfare, production, human capital, social exclusion, crime and social instability. The level of unemployment and its rise is the most serious problem facing the country. Following the first democratic elections in 1994, the government's efforts to eliminate poverty have been frustrated by the ongoing shedding of jobs from the formal economy, resulting in continued poverty for sections of the population. Landman et al.(2003) came to the conclusion that 40% of people in South Africa are living in poverty, with the poorest 15% in a desperate struggle to survive, and the authors suggested that the most challenges facing South Africa following transition to democracy is to break the grip of poverty. Despite short spurts of growth, unemployment remains a major social challenge (Mulaudzi & Liebenberg, 2017:29ff.).

People who perceive their poverty as permanent or increasing may ultimately be driven by hostile impulses, rather than rational pursuit of their interests. Thus, a high level of poverty can result in the breakdown of values, and other undesirable behaviours such as high levels of crime.

Land

One of the damaging legacies of colonial and apartheid history in South Africa is the inequitable distribution of land between race groups. In addition to being a source of social tension, the result is that impoverished communities have little opportunity for providing for themselves through subsistence and commodity production. Many rural people are essentially landless, and those who have land find it too small or poor for production. In addition, these families and communities lack financial support for training and productivity.

Land reform is an accepted necessity, but when land reform takes place in an unplanned and haphazard way, tensions are created. Simultaneously, weak planning of land reform can have dire consequences for the agricultural output of the country and its ability to produce enough food for use and export. There should be awareness of the sensitivity of the issue in South Africa, which must be factored into the national and community security architecture.

It has been pointed out that, in view of the expected increase of the South African population (natural growth, as well as incoming people) between now and 2025, South African agricultural outputs need to increase drastically, but the need for growth in agricultural output acts as a double challenge. Agricultural output has to be enhanced, yet it may be tempered by land reform if the latter is not managed well and implemented with care. One challenge relates to a concrete negative outcome, namely food insecurity, while another relates to possible dissatisfaction with the speed of land reform. These challenges cannot be neglected and future needs and wants will have to be balanced carefully (De Wet & Liebenberg, 2017).

Crime

Crime is one of the most difficult challenges facing SA, with a crime rate amongst the highest in the world, and all South Africans are vulnerable to its effects. In 2007, South Africans had to live with the reality of around 19,000 murders per year, roughly 200,000 robberies and aggravated robberies, 300,000 burglaries (some violent), 85,000 stolen cars and 55,000 rapes (Altbecker, 2007:37-38). Crime diverts resources to protection efforts, increases health costs, and generally creates an environment unconducive to productive activity, and the exodus of professionals and specialists is largely attributed to this factor. All of this has the potential to discourage investment and hinder long-term growth in the country.

Rising crime rates are often typical in countries undergoing transition, as democracy tends to compound crime by weakening the overbearing controls put in place by a previously oppressive government, and even relatively affluent citizens have an incentive to participate in crime when controls are weakened. The South African crime situation is aggravated by relatively easy access to illegal firearms and the existence of numerous crime syndicates. Surveys suggest that South Africans are particularly exposed to violent crime and murder, and while crime statistics over the past years have shown a slight improvement, there is no room for complacency. Crime causes feelings of insecurity and undermines confidence in democratic governance and government policies.

The military can set an example to society by maintaining a crimeless military community. However, the military cannot and should not act as a police force, although it will have to be considered as an element to support the police in exceptional cases. Inwardly, the military as an institution should demonstrate that the military institution strives to be free of crime and corruption.

Corruption

The prevalence of corruption – or even the perception of corruption – can lead to deep discontent and loss of legitimacy for governments. To maintain legitimacy, governments should be able to prove that they are making positive changes to the negative experiences of citizens. The threat of criminalisation of state and society cannot be ignored. Not addressing it can invite social discontent and alienation. Post-apartheid South Africa saw many trials and tribulations, including high levels of corruption, especially under President Zuma's rule. The current investigation into 'state capture' hopes to unveil the truth, and the commission will ideally propose concrete steps to prevent future corruption. To create a secure society, these challenges cannot be ignored when reflecting on and framing security in South Africa.

While the military is not a tool to be used for corruption prevention, its role as a socialisation agent and example setter should not be underestimated. Leading by example by stamping out corruption is important.

Extremism and violence

Since the transition from authoritarian rule to democracy, the likelihood of extremist attacks has reduced substantially in South Africa. Some tensions remain, but the incorporation of most of the dominant white political parties has diminished the likelihood of right-wing extremism, although it must be mentioned that the majority of then white parties, with the exception of supporters of authoritarianism, in principle agreed with a parliamentary and representative system. There are also no left-wing groupings that advocate violent regime change, even if the rhetoric is fairly militant (i.e. the Economic Freedom Fighters or EFF); rather, the 'left' opposition generally work within the ambit of the democratic and labour structures available in South Africa. Some may argue that Muslim fundamentalists pose a danger to South African communities, but in terms of cultural and religious tolerance, the Muslim and Christian communities generally coexist peacefully in South Africa, and to a large extent are socially enmeshed/integrated.

Unfortunately, as a result of the US's 'war on terror', Muslim people are frequently associated in foreign media with 'terrorism' or as 'political Islamists', and such labelling causes intolerance and alienation. However, it seems unlikely that the South African state can be labelled as an extension of those countries that are waging a war on terror, given its non-alliance stance and interactions with other states (Latin-America, Middle East, China, Europe, India, Russia, African peers). Close association with countries that have declared a war on terror may be seen as guilt-by-association by their targets, but South Africa has so far steered clear of such associations in its multilateral relations and involvement on the continent.

Keeping a distance from states that habitually project military power outwards will benefit national security in South Africa and should be continuously on the agenda. Experience over the past two decades has shown that countries that uncritically associate themselves with the US's war on terror can become targets as a result of guilt by association, and the bomb attacks in Spain are but one example. The US chose to project military power far outside its own borders against those perceived to be part of a 'terrorist onslaught', and such power projection frequently caused social dislocation, insecurity, alienation, and destruction in the targeted communities, deeper animosity, alienation, and the urge to retaliate. Close association with those that fight a war on terror may well cause discontent in other communities, and apartheid is an example of a case where a wide definition of terrorism was uncritically applied. Attempts to suppress 'terrorism' eventually had the opposite effect, galvanising communities against the apartheid state and its policies.

The vulnerability of African states to extremism is attributed partly to porous borders, weak authority in governance and public finance, seemingly irrepressible internal conflict over scarce resources, criminal groups attempting to gain access to scarce resources (diamond, ivory, etc.), the reluctance of long-serving leaders/governments to step down after losing legitimacy or national elections, and the easy availability of weapons. Extremism is frequently founded on a lack of economic perspectives, social deprivation, a loss of cultural identity, political repression, and a dysfunctional state. Like any country, South Africa is a possible target for extremist action, but government foreign policy, African policies, and the constitutional commitment to religious and economic equality play important roles in reducing such a risk.

However, the likelihood of local protest over dissatisfaction with service delivery and infrastructure is greater and needs to be kept in mind. It is also important not to label such instances as extremism, or as that of people intent on anarchy or 'manipulated by dark forces'. The focus here should be on preventing and resolving such protest through awareness of the context, and by addressing the root of the problem, which is lack of services. It is of utmost importance that local discontent be solved through addressing the root causes, rather than forceful action and/or attaching negative labels to the discontented. The role of the military here can be educational or to lend a hand in community initiatives in order to improve perceptions and to demonstrate a willingness to assist, on the condition that such educational help is according to constitutional obligations and is non-partisan.

Nuclear weapons and national security

In the aftermath of the Cold War, the immediate risk of a nuclear war subsided. Despite the reality of mutually assured destruction (MAD), there was the possibility that a nuclear war could be triggered unintentionally or mistakenly. As a relatively small state ('middle power') under apartheid, South Africa, like Israel, was a nuclear-holding nation, projecting an aggressive foreign policy in the region. Since then, South Africa has signed the non-proliferation treaty and other relevant treaties, and is a non-nuclear power.

In reality, the mass holders of nuclear power are still in the West, while Russia also retains significant, if not competitive, numbers. Relative 'newcomers', such as India and China, do not seem inclined to use their nuclear power other than as a deterrent under serious provocation, and as a last resort. New 'newcomers', such as North Korea, do not have even vaguely competitive capacities, and if offensive nuclear capacity is reached, they will be unlikely to stockpile significant numbers. Thus, given the reality of limited arsenals and despite being labelled as 'rogue states', it remains highly unlikely that such a state will unleash a nuclear war, with the possible exception of Israel, which operates within a framework of 'being besieged' and threatened.

In short, the nuclear threat that new newcomers pose is overrated when measured against current stockpiles of nuclear arms. More likely, such attempts at building nuclear capacity are to boost confidence, as these countries are consistently criticised and threatened and may thus have developed the feeling of being besieged, which will have worsened the feelings of exclusion and isolation of their governments and significant chunks of their population. South Africa faces no nuclear threat in the short to medium term, as it is not geographically near to any of these powers, nor is it in competition with them. Realistically, the likelihood in the long-term is also limited. Any 'hard' military threat that may arise is likely to be from stronger powers in search of scarce resources, or who have strong ideological differences with South Africa or its leadership, and in this case the threat would be economic, rather than nuclear.

The vision, mission, structures and posture of South Africa's defence should include both conventional and non-conventional capabilities. The military have responsibilities to participate in peacekeeping operations and carry out border security. The capabilities for this need to be retained and honed in a cost-effective way, and the defence policy and NSS should take heed of this. Added to this is the challenge of planning a policy of rejuvenation within the current defence budget, as an increase is highly unlikely in the short to medium term, and savings will have to be incurred through piecemeal methods such as salary cuts for top management, and natural attrition in higher age categories.

In terms of disaster management, the military, in cooperation with civilian institutions, should be prepared to assist in case of a nuclear disaster, both on and off our soil. South Africa has one nuclear reactor, and may add more given the current power crisis, and the reality is that having nuclear power goes with the possibility of a nuclear disaster. A nuclear disaster around our shores also cannot be ruled out, as various maritime vessels that pass along the sea routes of South Africa are nuclear-powered of which some are ageing fast.

Armed intervention by core states

The risk of direct invasion does not face South Africa. However, as both Kosovo and Libya have proven, the responsibility to protect (R2P) can be used as a rationale to intervene in other smaller states that are rich in resources. In the case of Iraq, the action was taken by core industrial states (US, UK) with others in alliance ('the willing') using the excuse of weapons of mass destruction (WMD). In Libya's case, it was an abuse of the R2P.

Given the shortage of certain resources on the globe, African and regional states should be aware of this threat. Any attack on an African state can have negative consequences in surrounding states, as the Libyan example now demonstrates. Preparedness for such interference and contingencies in this regard should be considered and planned for.

Conclusion

South Africa's citizenry currently faces no direct threat from nuclear or conventional attack. Some countries on the continent may be vulnerable to armed intervention by core states, under pretences such as the war on terror or R2P, or simply because they hold scarce resources. However, South Africa faces numerous other socio-political and economic challenges. The country's population currently does not face a conventional threat or reactionary violence and, given South Africa's diplomatic stance and multiple relations on the globe, they are also not a priority for what is described as 'terrorism'.

Being viewed as a regional powerhouse, South Africa can expect to be called upon within SADC and on the continent (AU) to provide mutual security, and to contribute to peace operations and/or disaster relief. Such requests are likely to increase rather than decrease.

South Africans face numerous human security challenges. An NSS should be aware of this and, as far as the SANDF is concerned, it is in these areas that it may need to be prepared to render services within prescribed parameters when called upon. In terms of its constitutional position and social responsibilities, the SANDF has a role to play in leading by example in terms of health, service delivery, accountability, corruption and crime-eradication, and community interaction. Projected inside the country, this example should also be seen to be visible both in the region and more broadly.

APPENDIX
SANDF budgetary challenges

Introductory remarks

This appendix provides an overview of successive South African defence budgets and their effects on the SANDF during the period 2008-2017. Defence underfunding and its effects constitute arguably the most significant military security development in post-Mandela South Africa, and analysing the defence policy and its outcomes without taking defence spending into account is less than useful.

Sustained underfunding and a shrinking budget

TABLE 7.1 Overview of South African defence budgetary allocations during the past decade

Year	GDP R trillion	Defence Budget R billion	Defence as GDP percentage	Inflation rate	Rand per US $1	Active service personnel	Reservist personnel
2008	2.28tr	27.8	1.21%	11.8%	8.27	62,082	15,071
2009	2.08tr	32.0bn	1.58%	7.2%	7.36	62,082	15,071
2010	2.68tr	30.7bn	1.14%	5.8%	7.40	62,082	15,071
2011	2.95tr	30.4bn	1.03%	5.9%	7.09	62,082	15,071
2012	3.2tr	37.9bn	1.18%	5.64%	8.20	62,082	15,071
2013	3.46tr	44.6bn	1.28%	5.77%	9.20	62,100	15,050
2014	3.65tr	42.8bn	1.17%	6.3%	10.69	62,100	15,050
2015	4.03tr	44.6bn	1.11%	4.8%	12.72	62,100	15,050
2016	4.28tr	47.2bn	1.09%	6.4%	15.26	62,100	15,050
2017	4.61tr	48.6bn	1.05%	5.4%	13.40	66,350	15,050

SOURCE: *The Military Balance*, 2009-2018[4]

It is clear that the South African inflation rate over the past decade has neutralised the effects of any nominal growth in the defence budget. The table provides an indication of the extent to which the Rand (ZAR) declined in value against foreign currencies, and the increasingly unfavourable foreign exchange rate compounded the damaging effects of the inflation rate on South African defence spending. The currency exchange rate directly affects not only main equipment acquisition costs, but also the cost of refits, maintenance, training and other services provided by armament system suppliers.

Table 7.1 further demonstrates how the defence budget declined to about 1% of the South African GDP, although the current minister of defence (Nosiviwe Mapisa-Nqakula) and her predecessor (Lindiwe Sisulu) both called for a defence budget amounting to at least 2% of the GDP. That percentage, if provided and sustained, would have enabled the SANDF to rebuild itself over a period of about 20 years.

Sustained overstretch

Table 7.1 demonstrates that SANDF personnel numbers have changed little over the past decade. Amongst other things, growth in SANDF foreign deployments did not result in a significant growth of personnel numbers. Figure 7.2 below provides an indication of the annual number of SANDF members deployed on UN peacekeeping missions from 1999 to 2018.

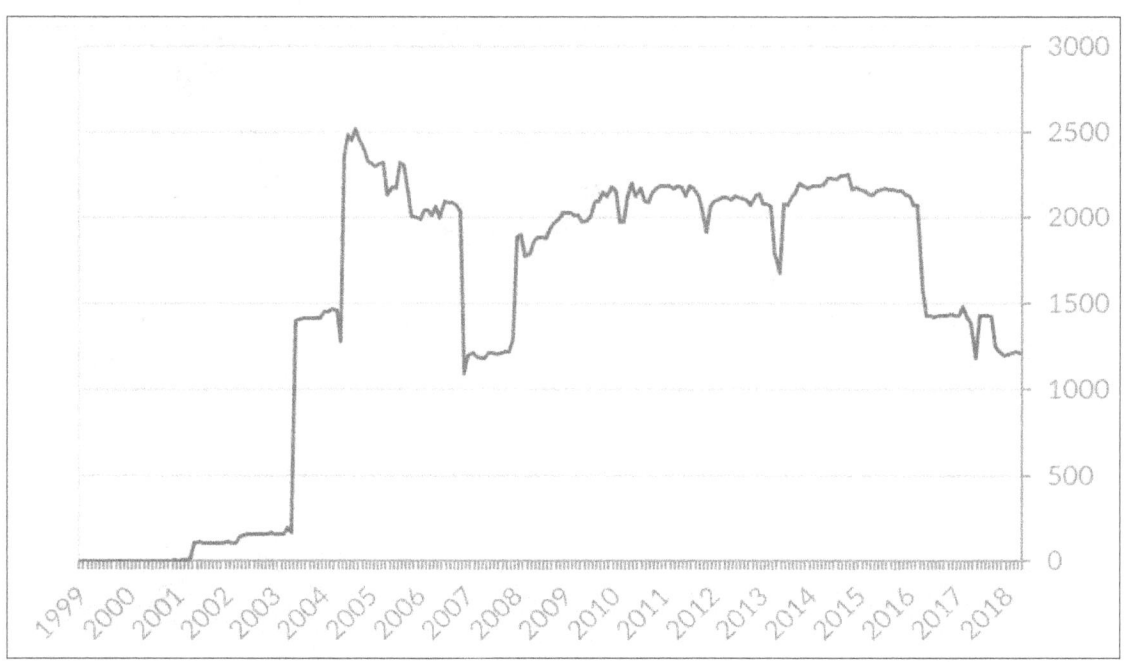

FIGURE 7.2 Number of SANDF members on UN peacekeeping missions, 1999-2018
SOURCE: De Carvalho, 2018

Unchanging personnel numbers had a direct impact on any personnel shortages experienced by the SANDF during the past decade. For example, in 2008 the SAAF had only 38% of its target strength in fighter pilots and 60% in fighter aircraft technicians. It also had only 72% of its helicopter pilots and 68% of its helicopter technicians. The air transport force had 68% of its target pilot quota and 59% of its technicians.[5] Persistent and significant personnel and budgeting shortages strain or overstretch a workforce, and the DOD Annual Report 2010/2011 mentioned overstretch specifically. The SA Army is referred to as 'severely overstretched, especially in the infantry, engineer and support capabilities.'[6] The Air Force fared no better,[7] while the SA Navy 'continued to experience critical shortages of personnel within the technical, combat, diver, submariner and logistics domains'.[8]

Any increase in personnel costs during the past decade cannot be attributed to a manpower increase, and this is especially interesting when one considers personnel costs as a percentage of the defence budget. Increasing percentages of the defence budget have been spent on personnel costs over the past 14 years. About 30% of the 2004 budget was allocated to personnel costs,[9] while the percentage of the 2016 budget was 57%[10] and 80% for the 2017 budget. During the course of 2017, the Defence Ministry announced plans to reduce the numbers of military personnel to 66,016 by 2019.[11] If the funding allocation for personnel cannot be increased, the Minister of Defence has no choice but to reduce their numbers, or at least cut remuneration and/or staff at high-ranking levels.

Defence policy implications

In May 2018, the Minister of Defence reminded parliament that they had endorsed the 2015 Defence Review as the national policy on defence but that the Defence Review remained unfunded. The declining budgetary allocation has reached the stage where the SANDF is losing essential capabilities. Given the expected current and future tasks of the SANDF, such expectations cannot be executed. The defence policy implications of sustained underfunding are clear. Sustained underfunding will increasingly amount to a contradiction of the South African defence policy, as articulated in the 2015 Defence Review, and continued underfunding reduced the status of the 2015 Defence Review to a relatively toothless policy.[12]

Notes

1. An African concept implying recognition of and abiding by reciprocal dignity and human-centredness.
2. In terms of the collective regional GDP in 2003/2003, South Africa held 74.9%, Angola 4,2%, Zimbabwe 4,2%, and Tanzania 3,9%, while Mozambique stood at 1,6%, the DRC at 2,6%, Zambia 1,6%, Swaziland at 0,5%, and Lesotho at 0,4%.
3. South Africa's Gini coefficient for the African population increased from 0,62 in 1991 to 0,72 in 2001 (HSRC, 2004). On the World Bank Gini Index, South Africa finds itself at 67%, ahead of Angola (59%), Bolivia (57%), the Central African Republic (56%), the Comoros (64%), Haiti (60%), Lesotho (53%), Zambia (51%) and Zimbabwe (50%). Within the region, only the Namibians were worse off at the time and rated 70% (Schwabe, 2004). In 2016, it was reported that the Gini coefficient increased from 0.61 (all population groups) in 1996 to 0.64 by 2014 (SAIRR, 2016:313ff.).
4. Table 7.1 is based on data collected from ten consecutive issues of *The Military Balance*, annually published online. These are: **109**(1):319-320, https://doi.org/10.1080/04597220802709910 [30 Jan 2009]; **110**(1):325-326, https://doi.org/10.1080/04597220903545858 [3 Feb 2010]; **111**(1):441-443, https://doi.org/10.1080/04597222.2011.559842 [7 Mar 2011]; **112**(1):452-454, https://doi.org/10.1080/04597222.2012.663218 [7 Mar 2012]; **113**(1):530-532, https://doi.org/10.1080/04597222.2013.757005 [14 Mar 2013]; **114**(1):457-459, https://doi.org/10.1080/04597222.2014.871886 [5 Feb 2014]; **115**(1):468-470, https://doi.org/10.1080/04597222.2015.996365 [10 Feb 2015]; **116**(1):467-469, https://doi.org/10.1080/04597222.2016.1127636 [9 Feb 2016]; **117**(1):534-537, https://doi.org/10.1080/04597222.2017.1271216 [13 Feb 2017]; **118**(1):433-434, 485-487, https://doi.org/10.1080/04597222.2018.1416986 [13 Feb 2018].
5. *The Military Balance*, 110(1):292, https://doi.org/10.1080/04597220903545858 [3 Feb 2010].

6   Annual Report 2010/2011, p. 61. Department of Defence, Republic of South Africa, 2011. Available on the DOD website: www.dod.mil.za
7   Ibid., p. 68.
8   Ibid., p. 74.
9   *The Military Balance*, 110(1):292, https://doi.org/10.1080/04597220903545858 [3 Feb 2010].
10 *The Military Balance*, 117(1):488, https://doi.org/10.1080/04597222.2017.1271216 [13 Feb 2017].
11 *The Military Balance*, 118(1):433-434, https://doi.org/10.1080/04597222.2018.1416986 [13 Feb 2018].
12 The following articles, published on defenceWeb (http://www.defenceweb.co.za), support the arguments made in the Appendix: 'Alarming issues' uncovered on border fact-finding mission (30 November 2018); 'Critical maintenance events' impact on SAAF maritime patrol capabilities (9 November 2018); Acknowledgement all is not well with the SANDF comes from the top (5 November 2018); Alternative funding, models needed for SA defence industry – Armscor (24 October 2018); Defence Legal Services will be impaired by lack of funds (11 April 2018); Defence Minister needs a hearts and mind campaign and a retrenchment plan (6 June 2018); Defence Review – no money, so no implementation (11 October 2018); Defence Review 2015 unlikely to ever be fully implemented (published on 29 November 2018); Navy Defence acknowledges it is in danger of sinking (5 June 2018); Navy deteriorating, Parliamentary Committee hears (26 November 2018); SA Navy funding and capacity need careful consideration – ISS (16 July 2018); SANDF suspensions cost millions (26 September 2018); Slow progress with DOD financial misconduct disciplinary proceedings (13 April 2018); Speech: Defence and Military Veterans Budget Vote 2018-19 (25 May 2018); Yam bemoans underfunded SANDF (18 October 2018).

References

Altbecker, A. 2007. *A country at war with itself: South Africa's crisis of crime*. Johannesburg: Jonathan Ball.

Corder, H. 1989. *Democracy and the Judiciary*. Mowbray: Institute for Democracy in South Africa (IDASA).

D'Anieri, 2014. *International Politics: Power and Purpose in International Affairs*. Wadsworth: Cengage Learning.

De Carvalho, G. 2018. *SA can use its position on the UN Security Council to be more than just a troop-contributing country?* 15 November. https://bit.ly/337hpNt [Accessed 3 April 2019].

De Wet, F. & Liebenberg, I. 2018. Food Security, wheat production and policy in South Africa: Reflections on food sustainability and challenges for the market economy. *The Journal for Transdisciplinary Research in Southern Africa (TD)*. https://doi.org/10.4102/td.v14i1.407

Duncan, J. & Seleoane, M. 1998. *Media & Democracy in South Africa.* Pretoria: HSRC and the Freedom of Expression Institute (FXI).

Dye, T.R. 2002. *Power and Society.* New York: Harcourt Publishers and Florida State University.

Giddens, A. 1993. *Sociology 2nd Edition*. Cambridge: Polity Press.

Houston, G., Liebenberg, I. & Humphries, R. 2001. *Public Participation in Democratic Governance in South Africa.* Pretoria: Human Sciences Research Council (HSRC).

Johnson, R.W. 2010. *South Africa's Brave New World*. London: Penguin.

Landman, J.P., Bhorat, H., Van der Berg, S. & Van Aardt, C. 2003. *Breaking the grip of poverty and inequality in South Africa, 2004-2014: Current trends, issues and future policy options.* https://bit.ly/2IBEbUk [Accessed 16 February 2012].

Liebenberg, I. 2011. Northern Africa, Arabian Springs, Oil and Arrogance: New uses for R2P in Africa. *Africa Renaissance*, 8(2 & 3):34-54.

Malan, M. & Cilliers, J. 1997. SADC organ on Politics, Defence and Security: Future development. *ISS Occasional Paper* No. 19, March. https://bit.ly/2TOGc4C [Accessed 2 April 2019].

Mandrup, T. 2018. An uncertain future: South Africa's national defence force caught between foreign-policy ambitions and domestic development. *Journal of Eastern African Studies*, 12(1):136-153. https://doi.org/10.1080/17531055.2018.1418166

Migdal, J.S. 1988. *Strong Societies and Weak States: State-Society Relations and State capabilities in the Third World*. Princeton: Princeton University Press.

Ministry of Defence (The Netherlands). 2010. *Future Policy Survey Final Report: A New Foundation for The Netherlands Armed Forces.* https://bit.ly/3cNlUkA [Accessed 1 April 2019].

Mulaudzi, M. & Liebenberg, I. 2017. Planning and Socio-Economic Interventions in a Development State: The Case of South Africa. *Journal of Public Administration*, 52(1):29-49.

Nattrass, N. 2004. *The Moral Economy of AIDS in South Africa*. Cambridge: Cambridge University Press. https://doi.org/10.1017/CBO9780511550454

Ngoma, N. 2003. SADC: Towards a security community. *African Security review*, 12(3). https://doi.org/10.1080/10246029.2003.9627230 [Accessed 2 April 2019].

Polley, J. 1988. *The Freedom Charter and the Future*. Mowbray: Institute for Democracy in South Africa (IDASA).

SAIRR. 2010. *South Africa Survey 2009/2010.* Johannesburg: South African Institute of Race Relations.

SAIRR. 2016. *South Africa Survey 2015/2016.* Johannesburg: South African Institute of Race Relations.

Schwabe, C. 2004. *Poverty in South Africa*. 26 July. https://bit.ly/3aIJaOV [Accessed 2 February 2019].

Seleoane, M. 2001. *Socio-Economic Rights in the South African Constitution: Theory and Practice*. Pretoria: Human Sciences Research Council (HSRC).

Van der Heyden, U. 2018. *De Dakar-Prozess: Der Anfang vom der Ende der Apartheid in Sudafrika*. Kiel: Solivagus Praeteritum.

Van Zyl-Slabbert, F. 1992. *The quest for democracy: South Africa in transition.* London: Penguin Forum Series.

Zegeye, A., Liebenberg, I. & Houston, G. 2000. *Resisting ethnicity from above: Social identities and democracy in South Africa.* Pretoria: Human Sciences Research Council (HSRC).

08

Namibia's Defence Diplomacy
A first exploration

André du Pisani

Abstract

Namibia's Defence Diplomacy and its Foreign, Defence and National Security Policies are products of a protracted liberation struggle of 23 years. The formative role that the United Nations (UN) played in the complex transition and protracted process that culminated in the independence of the country on 21 March 1990, too, left its imprint, while statutory provisions in the Constitution (especially the provisions contained in Chapter 11 on the Principles of State Policy) and the changing geopolitics and security environment within which the country finds itself, by-and-large shaped and continues to shape policy. As a small state, the domestic sources of defence diplomacy and policy, coupled to the country's key bilateral and multilateral relations and membership of regional bodies such as the Southern African Development Community (SADC) and the African Union (AU), and of the United Nations (UN), determine the topography of the country's international relations of which its defence diplomacy and defence policy are constitutive parts. Namibia has a number of defence attachés in its 33 missions and 3 consular missions.

In late October 2019, Namibia had 10 foreign military advisors/attachés attached to the Ministry of Defence (MOD). These came from the following countries: Angola, Botswana, Brazil, Canada, Poland, Ukraine, Italy, Zambia, Zimbabwe and the United States of America. Several other countries collaborate with Namibia in matters of training and policy design, most notably, the Federal Republic of Germany (FRG), India, South Africa and the People's Republic of China (PRC).

There is little evidence of defence intellectuals within the Ministry of Defence and the Namibia Defence Force (NDF), even if a few senior military officers have published on the defence and military posture of the country and its participation in peacekeeping operations under different mandates.[1] From a research point of view, the terrain of defence diplomacy and defence policy is under- explored with few available published sources on the topic.[2]

Introduction

In a memorable formulation a British diplomat once said, 'Foreign policy is what you do, diplomacy is how you do it'.[3] Although this basic distinction is useful, it is seriously incomplete, since all techniques for the implementation of foreign policy are, in the final analysis, political, and diplomacy engages with a range of actors, relationships and complexities. This goes for what some analysts call 'niche diplomacy' and also holds for public diplomacy.

The central feature of diplomacy in its different forms is communication. Historically, the basis for creating permanent diplomatic missions in the fifteenth century was the desire of kings and princes to have representatives in other courts to carry out continuous and systematic communication with other monarchs. The rules of protocol, diplomatic immunity, and non-interference in domestic politics, for example, were established to reduce conflicts over rank and status amongst diplomats, to prevent host governments from interfering with the diplomatic representatives of other states, and to prevent diplomats from engaging in the domestic affairs of their hosts. These legal rules codify diplomatic interactions.

In the contemporary international system, diplomacy has five substantive functions,[4] these are: First, conflict avoidance and management. Second, generating sustainable outcomes to different kinds of conflicts, thirdly, enhancing and facilitating cross-cultural communication as a means of confidence building, fourthly, facilitating negotiation and bargaining on specific issues, treaties, and agreements, and finally, providing a framework for managing programmes and activities of the foreign policy decisions of a range of state-based and non-state actors. Procedurally, these activities result foremost in communicating the views of a particular government and in exchanging information. After successful negotiation, diplomacy is often required to implement the agreement reached and to manage such agreements over time.

Modern diplomacy, however, unavoidably involves the presence and participation of third parties observing and supporting the diplomatic activities at hand, often to serve their own particular interests. Increasingly, also diplomacy is linked to economic- and trade relations, but also to cultural exchange, the environment, public health, peace and security and to science and technology.

In summary form, in foreign policy diplomacy refers to a policy instrument, often in association with other instruments such as economic or military force to enable an international actor to achieve its policy objectives. Diplomacy in world politics refers to a communication process between different international actors that seeks through negotiation to resolve conflict short of war. This process has been refined and institutionalised over many centuries and continues to evolve.

The corset of Namibia's defence diplomacy: On history and policy interfaces

The formation of the South West African People's Organization (SWAPO) on 19 April 1960 ushered in the beginning of almost three decades of struggle for an independent and democratic Namibia. Twenty-three of the 30 years were in the form of an armed liberation struggle. At the end of the all-important Consultative Conference held in Tanga, Tanzania, from 26 December 1969 to 2 January 1970, SWAPO established various departments, amongst these a Department of Foreign Affairs, tasked to execute the party's foreign policy and drive its diplomacy in exile.

Prior to independence, SWAPO had 27 foreign missions on all five continents and enjoyed observer status – the first African liberation movement to have been accorded such international recognition – at the United Nations (UN).[5]

This was the position from the beginning of 1970, when the party's Department of Foreign Affairs was established, up and till March 1990, when the country gained its independence under the auspices of the United Nations (UN). Table 8.1 shows SWAPO's international representation prior to formal independence in March 1990.

TABLE 8.1   SWAPO's international representation prior to independence

Africa	Europe	Asia	Americas	Australia	International organisations
Angola	Finland	India	Cuba	Australia	United Nations (observer status)
Algeria	France		United States of America		
Botswana	Federal Republic of Germany				
Congo					
Egypt	German Democratic Republic				
Ethiopia					
Libya	Iran				
Nigeria	Romania				
Senegal	Sweden				
Tanzania	United Kingdom (UK)				
Zambia	Union of Soviet Socialist Republics (USSR)				
Zimbabwe	Yugoslavia				

The SWAPO Mission in Finland was closed in 1972 and the responsibility resorted to the Mission in Sweden. The actual office stayed open and was run by SWAPO students in Finland, who dealt mostly with education, health and related concerns.

It is noteworthy that despite the fact that SWAPO had no diplomatic representation in countries such as the People's Republic of China (PRC), the Democratic People's Republic of Korea (DPRK) and Brazil, these countries and their commercial interests, as this chapter will show, became very important in the foreign relations and defence diplomacy of the independent State, for reasons that will become evident.

In the post-independence period, Namibia's bilateral relations with the PRC strengthened and deepened significantly. Such relations include the training of navy military personnel and the procurement of coastal defence vessels to protect the country's rich marine resources. The military training that the PRC provided during the protracted liberation struggle became the springboard for robust bilateral relations in the post-independence period. As this chapter will show, diplomatic and defence relations with the PRC, Brazil and India, became more salient since March 1990 when the country took its independence.

Apart from bilateral relations, SWAPO in exile, also had diplomatic relations with several other countries, amongst these, with the former Eastern bloc countries (under the ideological mantra of the Cold War), which, by 1984, provided roughly 60 percent of the total funds donated to the former liberation movement.[6] In addition to students who were members of SWAPO in exile studying in countries where the movement had diplomatic missions, there were students in Bulgaria, the former Czechoslovakia, the Gambia, Ghana, Kenya, Nigeria, Sierra Leone and Uganda. The People's Republic of China (PRC) provided military training to members of the People's Liberation Army (PLAN), the military wing of SWAPO, while humanitarian and material assistance came from 'progressive organizations and countries' such as Belgium, Denmark, The Netherlands, Norway, Portugal and Switzerland.[7] The Nordic countries were particularly generous with their political support and material assistance to SWAPO.[8]

It is also important to point out that prior to independence SWAPO participated in and maintained meaningful relations with several international organisations. As early as 1976, the United Nations General Assembly gave special diplomatic recognition to SWAPO in exile. The United Nations General Assembly's (UNGA) Resolution 31/152 of 1976, recognised SWAPO as the 'sole and authentic representative of the Namibian people'.[9] Subsequently, SWAPO was accorded observer status in the UNGA – at the time, a unique privilege accorded to an African liberation movement.

In terms of its other multilateral relations, SWAPO maintained diplomatic relations with the Organization of African Union (OAU), the antecedent of the African Union (AU). Since its inception in May 1963, the OAU's Liberation Committee provided SWAPO with material and financial support. Later, in 1978, SWAPO was admitted as a full (non-state) member of the Non-Aligned Movement (NAM), and as the liberation struggle deepened and expanded, the movement received support from the Commonwealth and the then frontline states (FLS). Moreover, SWAPO President Sam Nujoma and other senior leaders such as the late Theo-Ben Gurirab, regularly attended and addressed high-level meetings of many intentional organisations, amongst these: the UNGA and the UN Security Council, different UN agencies, Heads of State Summits, and meetings of the OAU, NAM and the FLS.[10]

While SWAPO in exile developed foreign policy capacity, the actual foreign policy decision-makers were limited to a few individuals, such as the President of the Party, the Secretary for Foreign Affairs, the Deputy Secretary of Foreign Affairs and the Permanent Observer to the United Nations (UN).[11]

The other important foreign policy actors, as distinct from key decision-makers, included members of the SWAPO Central Committee and Political Bureau (Politburo) who mostly formed part of several delegations to the UNGA, the UN Security Council and other international conferences that focused on advancing the independence of the country. Many such conferences took place in cities such as Geneva, London, Oslo, Stockholm, Brazzaville and Lusaka. In a related context, SWAPO also interacted over a long period with the former Western Contact Group (WCG), comprising of Canada, France, West Germany, the United Kingdom and the United States of America (USA).

When Namibia gained independence on 21 March 1990, the Ministry of Foreign Affairs was established and the newly independent Government entered into formal diplomatic relations with a number of countries. Significantly, the new Government continued diplomatic relations with all countries that it had relations with while in exile. New relations were also established, amongst these with Belgium that hosts the headquarters of the European Economic Community (EEC), the antecedent of the European Union (EU).

During the first year of independence, Namibia opened thirteen (13) diplomatic missions. Of these, four (4) were newly opened in Africa, six (6) in Europe and three (3) in the Americas. By then, a total of 156 agreements were entered into with foreign governments, as well as with international, inter-governmental and non-governmental organisations. These agreements covered health, economic and development cooperation, diplomatic relations, military cooperation, education and culture, scientific and technical cooperation, consular matters and aviation.[12] One such bilateral agreement was with Brazil, that facilitated military cooperation and training of the nascent Namibian Navy and became important for procuring naval vessels. Twenty-nine years after independence, Namibia has 31 embassies abroad and three consulates.

At the time of independence, the Ministry of Foreign Affairs (MFA) advanced five key objectives for the country's post-independence foreign policy. These were:

- To promote Namibia's security and territorial integrity and ensure the return of Walvis Bay and the offshore islands to Namibia;
- To promote Namibia's national identity and counter any vestiges of apartheid and colonialism;
- To promote Namibia's economic development and prosperity, by working to secure better terms of trade for Namibian commodities;
- Enhancing peace in the region like the end of civil war in Angola and the transformation of South Africa into a non-racial and democratic state, and
- To promote world peace through an active role in international organisations, such as the UN, OAU and NAM.[13]

What is interesting about these five key foreign policy objectives, is that they were formulated in a context where the SADC-region was not at peace, with civil war in

Angola, internal conflict in South Africa as that country was edging towards a transition to democracy and when Namibia's own independence and sovereignty were not complete, because of the non-integration of the port of Walvis Bay and the off-shore islands. Regional geopolitical and security concerns and fractures directly shaped the way foreign policy and later defence diplomacy, were configured. At the same time, a strong emphasis was retained on multilateralism in international bodies such as the UN, the former Organization of African Union (OAU) and the Non-Aligned Movement (NAM). Namibia also joined the Commonwealth, and that, too, impacted upon its foreign policy and defence diplomacy postures.[14]

These five objectives mentioned above, rest upon Article 96 of the Constitution (as amended), that states that the State shall endeavour that in its international relations it:

'(a) Adopts and maintains a policy of non-alignment;

(b) Promotes international cooperation, peace and security;

(c) Creates and maintains just and mutually beneficial relations amongst nations;

(d) Fosters respect for international law and treaty obligations;

(e) Encourages the settlement of international disputes by peaceful means'.[15]

The principle of non-alignment harks back to the Cold War and to SWAPO's diplomacy in exile as this chapter argues. Taken together, the principles reflect realist, idealist and liberal conceptions of foreign policy and relations. The belief in peace through law approach, coupled to the encouragement of conflict by peaceful means is a marker of the country's foreign policy and of its defence diplomacy, as will be shown in the following sections of this contribution.

Having introduced the diplomacy of SWAPO in exile and the objectives and principles that inform the foreign policy and relations of Namibia, of which the country's defence diplomacy is an integral part, the focus now shifts to structural and policy aspects of the Ministry of Defence (MOD) and the evolution and practice of the country's defence diplomacy.

Ministry of Defence (MOD) and the Namibia Defence Force (NDF)

The Ministry of Defence (MOD) was established in terms of Article 118 of the Constitution, a mere month after the country achieved its independence. The MOD was responsible for creating the organisational and administrative structure needed to manage the Namibia Defence Force (NDF).

Through its various directorates and divisions, the MOD has a number of key responsibilities. Chief of these are:

1. To formulate and implement defence policies for the Government;
2. To provide central operational and administrative headquarters for the Namibia Defence Force (NDF), and
3. To procure equipment for the NDF, mostly through a commercial company, August 26.

The principal roles of the NDF are:

- To ensure the maintenance of national sovereignty and the territorial integrity of the country;
- To provide various forms of humanitarian assistance to civil authorities and communities as and when required;
- To undertake ceremonial and diplomatic functions, and
- To assist the process of national reconciliation.[16]

Structure of the Ministry

The Ministry if headed by a minister who also chairs the Defence Staff Council, the highest management committee of the Ministry, and represents the Ministry in the National Assembly (NA) and Cabinet. The minister is supported by the Chief of the Defence Force and the Permanent Secretary, the financial officer of the Ministry.

The key directorates and divisions that formulate policy and operational concepts are:

First, the **Directorate Policy and Operations** with responsibility for policy and operational concepts formulation, such as organisation, deployment, planning of force design, policy for support arms, management of day-to-day military cooperation, and combat support services. This Directorate is headed by the Chief of Staff: Operations, who also serves on the Senior Management Committee (SMC) and the Military Steering Committee (MSC).

Secondly, the **Directorate Logistics** that is responsible for combat supplies and materials required for the efficient functioning of the NDF. This Directorate is headed by the Chief of Staff: Logistics who is also a member of the SMC and MSC.

Thirdly, the **Directorate Military Intelligence** regarding all issues regarding defence and security, inclusive of providing security advice to the Ministry; ensuring the security of all military installations, personnel and equipment; collection, analysis and dissemination of security information; managing the Ministry's communication policy, and managing relations with the print and electronic media. The Directorate is headed by the Chief of Staff: Military Intelligence who is a member of the SMC and MSC.

Finally, the **Division Procurement, Research and Development**, an independent division, established to coordinate capital procurement for the NDF, which includes the procurement of all military equipment, ammunitions and materials. The Division also enters into contract negotiations with suppliers and attends military exhibitions, liaising with manufacturers in the military industry to establish business contacts and securing supply channels. The Division is also responsible for researching, designing and developing (R&D) military materials to keep abreast of a fast-changing technological environment and operational needs.

The Namibia Defence Force (NDF)

The Namibia Defence Force (NDF) consists of the army, the Namibia Air Force and the Namibian Navy. Of these, the army is the largest and the Namibian Navy, the most recent. The legal basis for national defence is provided by Article 118 of the Constitution, as amended, which states that a Namibia Defence Force should be established by an Act of Parliament, in order to 'defend the territory and national interests of Namibia'. This was further developed in the Defence Amendment Act (Act No. 20 of 1990) that amended the earlier South African Defence Act (Act No. 44 of 1957) which set out various legal requirements for the composition and organisation of the Defence Force. The Defence Amendment Act of 1990 was also supported by a Military Discipline Code that emanated from the earlier 1957 Act.

The chief roles of the Army are to safeguard the sovereignty and territorial integrity of the country; to provide assistance to civil authorities and communities when required; to undertake ceremonial functions on behalf of the State, and to assist in the process of reconciliation. The Army comprises of former combatants of the People's Liberation Army of Namibia (PLAN) – the military wing of SWAPO in exile – and the minority South West Africa Territorial Force (SWATF), after these two formations were demobilised and many of them were integrated into a unified Namibia Defence Force (NDF).

The Air Force is envisaged in the policy and mission statement of the Ministry and was established after the Army and has since evolved into an important part of national defence. It is headquartered in Grootfontein in the central north of the country. The key roles of the Namibia Air Force are: to operate in support of the army and navy, to engage in surveillance; transportation of personnel and or supplies and equipment; rendering support to civil authorities or communities; and engaging in training.[17]

The Navy was established to defend the country's maritime domain and resources against illegal fishing, piracy and external attack. The core officers of the Navy underwent their naval training in Brazil, and subsequently also in China, once the country sourced vessels from there. Training was provided under various International bilateral agreements.[18] and over time, Namibia procured naval vessels from both Brazil and China. The most meaningful transformation started on 7 October 2004, when the navy was transformed from a wing to a fully-fledged navy. In October 2019, the Navy celebrated its fifteenth year of existence in Walvis Bay. The key role of the Navy lies in the domains of maritime security and the protection of the resources associated with the blue economy.

Late in October 2019, Namibian President Dr Hage G. Geingob officially opened the Chinese-funded Namibia Command and Staff College in Okahandja, north of the Capital City, Windhoek. The College was completed in 2016 with the purpose of enhancing the country's capacity to train army officers based on Namibian military doctrine. The doctrine covers aspects such as tactical and operational warfare both at command and staff level, as well as a sound understanding of the military's role within a democratic polity. At the official inauguration of the College, it was said by the Acting Chief of the Defence Force, Air Vice Marshall Martin Kapolo Pineas, that the facility would be providing training to other ministries and individuals. The College boasts a library, laboratory and syndicate room.[19]

Policy development: The early years

In February 1993, the then Minister of Defence, Peter Mwesihange a former combatant, presented to Parliament what is known as a Statement on Defence Policy.[20]

From its inception, defence and defence diplomacy, were posited as key parts of the new Government's foreign- and security policies, which were decided collectively by Cabinet. Since then, the main elements of Defence Policy have been set out annually in the Statement on the Defence Estimates (SDE). The SDE is built on the Government's assessment of developments that affect the country's security, its responses to such developments and the resources available that it proposes to allocate to defence. A similar Annual Security Estimate (ASE) is undertaken by the Namibia Central Intelligence Service (NCIS) for the President and Cabinet – particularly for members of the Cabinet Committee on International Relations, Defence and Security (CCIRDS).

The 1993 Statement on Defence Policy articulated the following key values and principles for directing the roles and functions of the NDF. These included:

- Apolitical – organised, trained and managed to serve the Government of the day and all the citizens of the State;
- Accountable – well-disciplined and accountable to the political leadership and the 'people through clearly defined political mechanisms of control';
- Capable to meet its primary role – that is, defence of the territorial integrity of the country – while playing a constructive role in promoting peace; and
- Affordable – bearing in mind national resource constraints, 'defence should not represent an unaffordable burden on the economy'.[21]

The February 1993 Statement on Defence Policy made it clear that future defence policy would be shaped by the above values and principles, even if policy implementation would have to 'reflect practical developments of all kinds affecting the country, both directly and indirectly', adding that 'in particular, it will need to take account of up-to-date assessments of potential threats to our security interests'.[22]

The initial 1993 Defence Policy articulation concluded by saying that, while the disengagement 'of the global powers from involvement in the conflicts of Southern Africa is a positive, though recent development; however, the continuing instability in the region means that the general risk remains high enough to justify the maintenance of an independent national defence capability'.[23]

As early as February 1993, and indeed in subsequent policy framings, Namibia's security was directly linked to, and dependent upon, regional stability. As a result, as will be shown in this contribution, regional security cooperation and coordination became and continues to be an important string in the bow of Defence and Security Policy more generally.

Procurement Policy, too, was premised on the principles of 'best quality equipment and materiel, provided that it suited the local terrain, climate, personnel, storage, accounting and other requirements; can be supported logistically, maintained and repaired in Namibia, as far as is practicable; can be delivered to or supplied in Namibia within the required time, and is available at the cheapest all-inclusive price, and with the most favorable terms of payment'.

The NDF made much of the nascent local armaments industry and made it clear, as early as February 1993, that the Ministry of Defence, 'intends to trade freely throughout the world' and that given the nature of defence business, the NDF would not become dependent on any one source of supply[24] The key holding company is August 26 and its affiliates.

In addition to procurement, the February 1993 policy statement also covered specific aspects relevant to defence diplomacy. These included the following five specific aspects: foreign military materiel aid and training assistance; the employment of advisers on technical and programme-related matters; the employment of consultants when such skills do not exist within the Namibian Public Service; the Employment of Contract Staff in areas where critical skills gaps exist, subject to the development of specific policies, and the deployment of military attachés to those countries 'with whom Namibia has significant defence relations, or where a future relationship will necessitate a permanent presence'.[25]

On the matter of defence resources, the 1993 policy statement stated:

> A central aim of the policy is to ensure that defence continues to account for no higher proportion of Government expenditure that is affordable. The MOD is,

therefore, beholden to ensure both its own management systems and those of the NDF represent the best value for money possible. It is also recognized that the implications of this policy for the defence programme are considerable and that its full implementation will therefore, depend upon the economy's ability to pay for them. The programme will be implemented as resources permit.[26]

This chapter will return in a subsequent section to the matter of defence budgeting and economics, as the share allocated in the various national budgets to the MOD, has grown exponentially since independence in 1990.

The 2011 Defence Policy represents the most recent and comprehensive statement on Policy, risks, the strategic environment, military strategy, military posture and force design, International Law and Agreements, human resources and research, development and procurement to date.[27]

While long awaited, this Policy and subsequent policy framings on Namibia' International Relations and Cooperation[28] provide the most comprehensive and recent policy frameworks for discussing the country's defence diplomacy. It is to these framings that the chapter next turns.

The 2011 Defence Policy: A précis

The introduction to the Defence Policy makes it clear that the Policy has been developed to complement other policies, particularly the National Security- and Foreign Policy. In this sense, the 2011 Defence Policy should be seen as a complementary policy to other security policies, with two key aims: assuring the security of the country, so as to allow it to pursue by just and peaceful means, its national interests at home and abroad, and maintaining a credible defence capability to any potential hostile intentions and actions.[29]

The legal basis for the 2011 Defence Policy derives from Article 118 of the Constitution (as amended), while the Defence Act 2002 (Act 1 of 2002), under Section 2, provides for the composition and organisation of the Namibia Defence Force's three Arms of Service: the Army, Air Force and Navy.

As one of the constitutive elements of the national strategy that aims at protecting the survival and National Interests of the State, the Policy advances guidelines for the development of the NDF, sets out is principal roles and functions, provides for programmes to enhance its development and locates Policy within a regional, SADC framework, and internationally in terms of several bilateral and multilateral agreements.

The Policy derives its orientation and thrust from the country's Policy on International Relations and Cooperation, as newly revised in 2017. The latter, International Relations and Cooperation, is anchored on Article 96 of the Constitution, with its provisions for non-alignment, the promotion of international cooperation, peace and security, respect for international law and treaty obligations and the settlement of international conflicts by peaceful means. These constitutional principles, in conjunction with the provisions of the Defence Act 2002 (Act 1 of 2002), frame the 2011 Defence Policy and provide it with legal import.

The national vision for the country derives from Vision 2030, the long-term development frame of the country with the core objective of transforming Namibia into an industrialised and knowledge-based economy. The national values come from the Constitution and is rights-based following the provisions of Chapter 3 of the Constitution that provides for a justiciable Bill of Fundamental Rights and Freedoms. In addition to these values, 'patriotism' has been added as a core value that underpins the Policy.

The national interests have been defined along two registers: 'vital interests' and 'peripheral interests'. The former, 'vital interests' typically involve the survival of the nation, protecting the territorial integrity of the State, guaranteeing the Nation's sovereignty, protecting democratic values and the economic resources of the country. The category of 'peripheral interests' includes, but is not limited to the following: cooperate with SADC to promote peace and stability in the region; cooperating with the African Union (AU) in ensuring economic prosperity and the entrenchment of democracy on the African continent; promoting global economic and greater social justice based on equality amongst nations, respect for international law and human rights and justice and fairness in global trade; promoting the collective security interests and system of SADC and working with the United Nations (UN) in terms of the provisions of the UN Charter.[30]

Collective security, which in essence is state-centric, remains the keystone of Namibia's defence policy and diplomacy. As summarised above, the 2011 Defence Policy does mention aspects of human-, economic- and environmental security, but in political and organisational terms, the country invests most of its time and resources in more traditional forms of collective security.

The strategic assessment contained in the 2011 Defence Policy, focuses sharply on the regional security environment and emphasises the responsibilities of SADC Member States under the SADC Protocol on Defence and Security Cooperation of 2001, as well as the various bilateral Joint Commissions on Defence and Security that Namibia has with all its neigbours, Angola, Botswana, South Africa, Zambia and Zimbabwe, as well as with Tanzania. Additionally, the Policy identifies various international security concerns that Namibia must take into account. These include, amongst others: environmental degradation that speaks to drought, water stress and the impact of global warming; global demographics and refugees; international terrorism and the proliferation of small arms and light weapons.[31]

The threat assessment that informs the Policy lies at two registers: internal and external. In respect of internal threats, the Policy specifically mentions secessionist sentiments in the former Caprivi Region (now the Zambezi Region); claims to ancestral land and for radical land redistribution; the plight of ex-combatants; youth unemployment; the unsustainable use of land in communal areas; the effects of global warming and the social impact of the HIV/AIDS pandemic. External threats include, amongst others: threats that emanate from extensive and porous international borders, illegal economic migration and the presence of foreign military on African soil.[32]

The Defence Diplomacy of Namibia comes out most clearly in the part of Policy that deals with potential scenarios for the deployment of the NDF. Apart from the obvious threat to the territorial integrity of the State, other scenarios include: Raids and blockades, especially in protection of the vital sea route, the country's most important trade route; engagement in counterinsurgency and 'low intensity conflicts' in support of the United Nations, the African Union and SADC; deployment in the context of natural disasters such as floods, earth quakes, fires and famine and participation in Peace Support missions as provided for in Section 32 (2) (a) and (b) of the Defence Act, Act 1 of 2002 and when called upon under the provisions of Chapters 6 and 7 of the United Nations Charter, as well as peace missions authorised and mandated by the African Union's Peace and Security Council in Chapter 8 of the UN Charter.[33]

Since the 2011 Policy, Namibia through the MOD and the NDF has become an active member of the SADC Standby Force. The country hosts a logistics support facility near Gobabis in the East of the country and has participated in various military exercises under the aegis of SADC and its security architecture. The NDF participated in the following military exercises with other SADC member states who contribute to the SADC Standby Force: Exercise Pabalelo (which loosely translated means 'safety' in Tswana) conducted from 14 to 29 November 2018 in Maun, Botswana a Level III exercise in medical support by health professionals from all participating SADC countries; a SADC Command Post Exercise code-named Umodzi, held in Malawi in October 2018; the SADC Special Forces Exercise, code-named Matumbawe, which was held in Tanzania in August 2017, and the SADC Military Aviation Exercise, code-named Blue Kunene held in Namibia in September 2017. These military exercises have been timely especially as SADC will go into the African Standby Force Roster duties from January 2019, whereby SADC will be expected to provide rapid deployment capability towards peace support efforts as part of the African Union's conflict resolution mechanisms. Namibia pledged a Battalion to the SADC Standby arrangement.

At policy level, regional security cooperation remains an important priority to the country. This is evidenced in Namibia's participation in the SADC Inter-State Defence and Security Committee (ISDSC), the SADC Mutual Defence Pact, the SADC Protocol on Defence and

Security Cooperation of 2001, the Southern African Regional Police Chiefs Commission (SARPCCO), the Harare-based Regional Peacekeeping Training Centre (RPTC) and as mentioned earlier in this chapter, in various Joint Commissions on Defence and Security.

As far as aspects of internal security are concerned, the NDF was engaged in operations between 1998 and 2002 in the Ohangwena, Kavango (now Kavango East) and Caprivi (now Zambezi) regions against elements of UNITA and the secessionist rebels of the Caprivi Liberation Army (CLA) in the then Caprivi Region. The work of the NDF, with technical and financial assistance from International Cooperating Partners (ICPs), in de-mining operations, in the Oshana-, Ohangwena- and Omusati Regions in the north of the country are especially noteworthy. These de-mining operations were undertaken by the Engineer Regiment of the NDF over a period of five years and successfully cleared all known landmines and unexploded ordinances. These operations also included the clearance of 402 electrical power pylons from Ruacana south wards. These pylons were heavily mined by the former South African Defence Force (SADF) at the time of the bush war in the country.

Peacekeeping operations

The engagement of the NDF, together with soldiers from Angola and Zimbabwe, between 1998 and 2001 in the internal conflict in the Democratic Republic of Congo (DRC) was the most controversial to date. The NDF intervened militarily following a request from former president Laurent Dessire Kabila to SADC Member States to help his newly formed government repulse a rebel attack that threatened the capital city of Kinshasa. A divided SADC gave the mandate to intervene militarily in the conflict in the DRC that soon took on regional and international dimensions. Compared with Namibia's earlier engagement in Angola, in 1996, the DRC operation was less successful, more complicated and significantly more secretive. The cost of the operation, as well as the circumstances under which two Namibian peacekeepers died, have yet to be made public. The Namibian Parliament was informed only after the NDF had dispatched a brigade to the DRC. During the intervention in the DRC, the NDF dispatched training instructors, to train the Congolese Armed Forces at the Kamina military base.[34]

Namibia's participation in various international peace missions constitutes one of the most visible forms of the country's defence diplomacy and of its international relations. With limited peacekeeping experience, the NDF deployed its first contingent of peacekeepers to Cambodia in early 1993 under the aegis of the United Nations. Since then, Namibia has become a significant troop and police contributor to the United Nations, African Union (AU) and SADC peace support operations (PSOs). The country's participation in peace support operations included the deployment of units up to battalion strength and individual peacekeepers such as Staff Officers and Military Observers. To date, the NDF participated in more than 15 peace support missions, under various mandates,[35] of which the SADC-led Preventive Force in Lesotho is the latest, while the NDF has seconded senior officers to the UN Department of Peace-Keeping Operations (UNDPKO) in New York at the request of the said department.

Participation in joint military exercises

Since 1997, the NDF has been a regular participant in various joint military exercises, chief amongst these: Exercise Blue Hungwe conducted in Nyanga, Zimbabwe, involving armed forces from various SADC member states from 1 to 20 April 1997; Joint Combined Exercise for Training, code-named Ex-Flintlock II B, conducted in Namibia from May to August 1997 and sponsored by the US Special Forces, European Command; Battle Group Exercise (B-GEX) at Oshivelo Training Area in northern Namibia; Exercise Blue Crane, which took place in South Africa from 7 to 30 April 1999; Operation Dolphino held in Namibia along the coast in 2014; Regional Air Force Exercise Blue Kunene (August to September 2017) held in Kunene Region of Namibia, and Battle Group Exercise held in Malawi in September 2018.

From 16 to 27 March 2019, Namibia together with several other African nations entered a new chapter in their military cooperation with India when they met in that country to participate in the inaugural version of the Africa-India Field Training Exercise (Afindex-19). The stated objective of the Exercise was to acquaint the contingents with each other's operational procedures to ensure improved operability in consonance with the requirements of the United Nations as outlined in Chapter 7 of the UN Charter.

Contingents from 17 African nations – Namibia, Benin, Botswana, Egypt, Ghana, Kenya, Mauritius, Mozambique, Niger, Nigeria, Senegal, South Africa, Sudan, Tanzania, Uganda, Zambia and Zimbabwe – along with a contingent of the Maratha Light Infantry (Jangi Paltan) representing India, came together for the first edition of the training exercise. Each African country sent 10 military personnel to the Aundh Military Station in Pune, India.

As part of the defence cooperation, India over the years, provided training to a large number of African military officers in various countries. India is one of the largest contributors to peacekeeping in Africa. The importance of engaging with Africa had been identified at the highest political level and been encapsulated in the India-Africa Forum Summit 2015.

In mid-September 2019, the Indian naval battleship, *INS Tarkash* (which means 'quiver') called at the Port of Walvis Bay as part of a routine exercise and as a gesture of peace to Namibia. The *Tarkash* is considered a modern stealth frigate commissioned in 2012 and is part of the Western Fleet of the India Navy based in Mumbai, India, under the Western Naval Command. The *INS Tarkash* visited many ports such as Djibouti, Alexandria (Egypt), Tangiers (Morocco), Lagos (Nigeria), Dakar (Senegal) and Maputo (Mozambique).[36]

Arms transfers

Since independence in March 1990, the Ministry of Defence (MOD) has been procuring armaments and other equipment from a number of countries, chief amongst these: India, Brazil, Russia, South Africa and China. The Federal Republic of Germany donated transport and other logistical equipment. Significant arms transfers occurred over the past decade or more, even in a context of a faltering economy in the 2016-2018 fiscal years.[37]

By far the most controversial bilateral relationship since independence has been the one with the Democratic People's Republic of Korea (DPRK). Apart from construction companies from that country that built most of the post- independent memorials such as Heroes Acre and the Museum of the Liberation Struggle, the NDF entered into a secret agreement with the DPRK to set up a munitions factory south of the capital city Windhoek. This agreement and the subsequent activities were a clear violation of several United Nations Security Council Resolutions and late in 2017, the Namibian Government had to eat humble pie when sanctioned individuals and the company were declared persona non grata in the country. This followed initial denials that Namibia was in violation of any United Nations Security Council Resolutions at the highest level of government. At the same time, a contract to build the new Defence Headquarters by the same company, Mansudae Overseas Projects, from the DPRK had to be cancelled, even if the same company built a building that houses August 26 Holdings in Academia, a suburb of Windhoek.[38]

Defence budget

For a small, stable and peaceful state, with a population of 2.5 million (2017) and faced by many developmental challenges, Namibia has a rather large defence budget that in 2010 reached 4.2 percent of GDP. Table 8.2 shows the defence budget of the country over the 2000-2018/19 period.[39]

TABLE 8.2 Defence Budget (2000-2018/19)

Defence Budget (2000-2018/19)	In Namibia $ 0000	As a percentage of GDP
2000	3.2	2.3
2001	3.15	2.2
2002	3.4	2.6
2003	3.7	2.8

Defence Budget (2000-2018/19)	In Namibia $ 0000	As a percentage of GDP
2004	3.5	3.5
2005	3.2	3.1
2006	3.0	2.8
2007	3.1	2.8
2008	3.6	3.2
2009	3.8	3.8
2010	4.2	4.1
2011	4.0	4.0
2012	3.8	3.9
2013	4.2	4.0
2014	4.6	4.0
2015/16	5.9	4.0
2016/17	6.1	4.3
2017/18	6.045	4.2
2018/19	5.9	4.0

Analysts of Namibia's defence budget, and of defence economics more generally, face special difficulties in obtaining reliable and comprehensive data on all aspects related to defence spending. The variances under the main divisions in the budget, such as Office of the Minister, Training, Army, 21st Guard Battalion, Air Force, Military Hospital, Navy and Procurement, are very difficult to calculate accurately. Procurement and modernisation programmes are even harder to determine. In the latest Defence Vote under the Defence Appropriation Bill 2018/2019, for example, the formal statement by the Minister simply reads on the targets provided for in the corresponding Medium-Term Expenditure Framework (MTEF): 'Carry out research on modern equipment and acquire 16,5% of Defence equipment by 2018/2019 and replace obsolete and outdated equipment with at least 16,5% latest technology by 2018/2019.'[40]

In the absence of a strong opposition and a robust system of parliamentary committees, there is precious little parliamentary oversight over the defence budget and expenditure. To make matters worse, August 26 Holding Company that has the mandate for research and development (R&D) and for procurement on behalf of the MOD, has never had its books publicly audited since its establishment more than a decade ago.

Conclusions

As an integral part of the country's Policy on International Relations and Cooperation, more so as reiterated in January 2017, it is to be expected that the Namibia's defence diplomacy will continue to mirror closely what happens in the country's foreign relations. Especially noteworthy are new elements in Policy that have taken on significantly more salience on account of the country's geopolitics as a logistics hub for SADC and the special emphasis put in Agenda 2063 of the African Union (AU). Such elements include, but are not limited to the following: the Blue Economy Initiative of the AU; more effective protection of the country's marine resources; trade and investment; infrastructure development; oil and gas and strategically positioning the country, especially for landlocked states, as a logistics hub for SADC within which the Port of Walvis Bay will play a vital role.

The fact that Namibia's defence diplomacy is mutually constitutive of its wider international relations, means that the latter defence diplomacy privileges a few strong bilateral relations such as with South Africa, Botswana and for training, technical support and procurement, the Federal Republic of Germany (FRG), India, Brazil and China. At the time of writing, November 2019, Namibia hosted military attachés from a number of foreign states, amongst these: the United States of America (USA), the United Kingdom, the Federal Republic of Germany, Argentina, South Africa, Turkey and Tanzania. The country's defence diplomacy is new realist and draws on the doctrines and diplomatic practice of a range of nations, inclusive of Western countries and those of the Global South.

The provision of higher-level academic education in security and strategic studies at the Military School housed within the University of Namibia (UNAM) and the Military Academy in Okahandja, holds much promise for developing defence intellectuals and diplomats for the 21st century.

Notes

1   One recent example is that of Lt. Gen. (rtd). Epaphras Denga Ndaitwah in his informative book, *A Life and Views of a Soldier Author's Perspective*. Beau Bassin (Mauritius): Lambert Academic Publishing, 2017.

2   Since independence in March 1990, a single edited volume appeared on the country's foreign relations, namely: Anton Bösl, André du Pisani and Dennis U Zaire (eds.), *Namibia's Foreign Relations Historic contexts, current dimensions, and perspectives for the 21st Century*. Windhoek: Macmillan Education Namibia, 2014. In the same volume, André du Pisani wrote on 'Namibia's foreign relations and security policy: Exploration of a critical nexus', pp. 367-392, and published an earlier chapter specifically on 'Peacemaking in southern and central Africa: Namibia's role', published in Clive Cowley (ed.), *Namibia Yearbook No. 8 – 2001/2*. Windhoek: Guidebook Press.

Advanced academic research on Namibia's foreign policy and relations, was undertaken by Samuel Abraham Peyavali Mushelenga, until recently the country's Deputy Minister of International Relations and Cooperation. The two key academic studies are: 'Foreign Policy – Making in Namibia: The Dynamics of the Smallness of a State', unpublished Master of Arts Thesis (International Relations), Pretoria: UNISA, November 2008, and by the same author 'The Economic Diplomacy of a Small State, the Case of Namibia', a thesis for the degree of Doctor of Literature and Philosophy at University of South Africa, Pretoria, 2015.

More recently, Peya Mushelenga, at the time the country's Deputy Minister of International Relations and Cooperation, published two useful academic articles on the topic of the country's foreign relations, namely: 'A new states' debut in regional diplomacy: Namibia and the Southern Africa Development Community (SADC)' (co-authored with Jo-Ansie van Wyk), *Africa Review*, 9(1),

	2017, pp. 58-70, https://doi.org/10.1080/09744053.2016.1239933, and 'The Role of the Academia in Foreign Policymaking: International Practices and Perspectives as Lessons for Namibia', *India Quarterly*, 74(2), 2018, pp. 1-19, https://doi.org/10.1177/0974928418766734
3	Paul Gore-Booth, *With Great Truth and Respect*, London: Constable, 1974, p. 15. For a useful overview of public diplomacy, see J. Melissen (ed.), *The new public diplomacy, soft power in international relations*. New York: Palgrave Macmillan, 2005, https://doi.org/10.1057/9780230554931
4	For a most useful overview of diplomacy in its different dimensions, see Leon P. Poullada, 'Diplomacy: The Missing Link in the Study of International Politics', in D.S. McLellan, W.C. Olson, & F.A. Sondermann (eds.), *The Theory and Practice of International Relations*, 4th edition. Englewood Cliffs, NJ: Prentice-Hall, 1974, pp. 194-202. For a more recent introduction to the topic of diplomacy in a globalised world, see David Armstrong, 'The Evolution of International Society', in John Baylis, Steve Smith & Patricia Owens, *The Globalization of World Politics An introduction to international relations*, 5th edition. Oxford: Oxford University Press, 2011, pp. 36-38.
5	Theo-Ben Gurirab (first Foreign Minister of Namibia after independence), *Debates of the National Assembly*, 1990, p. 203.
6	Colin Leys & John Saul, *Namibia's liberation struggle: The two-edged sword*. London: James Currey, 1995, p. 172.
7	Sam Nujoma, *Where Others Wavered: My Life in SWAPO and my participation in the Liberation Struggle of Namibia*. London: Panaf Books, 2001, p. 189.
8	The four-volume series published by The Nordic Africa Institute in Uppsala, Sweden, provide a detailed account of the contribution the different Nordic countries made to National Liberation in Southern Africa. The titles are: Tore Linné Eriksen (ed.), *Norway and National Liberation in Southern Africa*, 2000; Tor Sellström, *Sweden and National Liberation in Southern Africa Vol. 1: Formation of a Popular Opinion (1950-1970)*, 1999; Tor Sellström (ed.), *Liberation in Southern Africa – Regional and Swedish Voices*, 1999; and Iina Soiri & Pekka Peltola, *Finland and National Liberation in Southern Africa*, 1999.
9	Sabine Neidhart, n.d., 'SWAPO and the OAU Liberation Committee, 1963-1990', unpublished research paper, University of Toronto. See also: Samuel A.P. Mushelenga, 'Foreign policy-making in Namibia: the dynamics of the smallness of a state', unpublished MA thesis, University of South Africa, 2008.
10	For a useful overview, see Chris Saunders, 'Namibian diplomacy before Independence', in Anton Bösl, André du Pisani & Dennis U. Zaire (eds.), *Namibia's Foreign Relations Historic contexts, current dimensions, and perspectives for the 21st Century*. Windhoek: Macmillan Education Namibia, 2014, pp. 27-36. See also Tilman Dedering, 'Petitioning Geneva: Transnational aspects of protest and resistance in South West Africa/Namibia after the First World War', *Journal of Southern African Studies*, 35(4), 2009, pp. 785-801, https://doi.org/10.1080/03057070903313160
11	Republic of Namibia, *White Paper on Foreign Policy and Diplomacy Management*. Windhoek: Ministry of Foreign Affairs, 2004, p. 23.
12	*Debates of the National Assembly*, June 1991, pp. 83-86.
13	Ibid., pp. 80-81.
14	For an analysis of Namibia's foreign policy posture shortly after independence, see André du Pisani, 'Namibia forges a regional role for itself', in Clive Cowley (ed.), *Namibia Yearbook No.2 – 1991/2*. Windhoek: Guidebook Press, pp. 57-61; André du Pisani, 'Namibia, impressions of independence', in P. Rich (ed.), *The dynamics of Change in Southern Africa*. Basingstoke: The Macmillan Press, 1994, pp. 199-217, https://doi.org/10.1007/978-1-349-23617-6_10, and André du Pisani, 'Namibian foreign policy: Transformation and emerging global orders (1989-1999)', in C. Keulder (ed.), *State, Society and Democracy: a reader in Namibian Politics*. Windhoek: Gamsberg Macmillan, 2000, pp. 297-311.
15	*The Constitution of the Republic of Namibia* (as amended in 2015), Article 96, Foreign Relations.

16 The Namibia Defence Force (NDF) became the first, and one of the most important, strings in the bow of the politics of 'National Reconciliation'. The particular approach of the government of Namibia to reconciliation is that it is a process that can come about through institutional design.

17 Since 1995, India (later China) has played a key role in the training of pilots for the Namibia Air Force and in providing aircraft, particularly former French-designed and built helicopters. This was done under various bilateral agreements, such as: *Agreement between India and Namibia on terms and conditions of service for Indian air force officers on deputation to Namibia*, signed in Windhoek on 20 February 1995; *Maintenance Contract between Namibia and Hindustan Aeronautics Limited*, signed in Windhoek on 22 June 1995; *Maintenance Contract between Namibia and Hindustan Aeronautics Limited*, signed in Windhoek on 26 September 1995; *Maintenance Contract between Namibia and Hindustan Aeronautics Limited*, signed in Windhoek on 27 September 1995; *Training Contract between Namibia and Hindustan Aeronautics Limited*, signed in Windhoek on 8 November 1995; *Agreement between India and Namibia on terms and conditions of service for Indian air force officers and airmen on deputation to Namibia*, signed in Windhoek on 15 March 1996; and *Maintenance Contract between Namibia and Hindustan Aeronautics Limited*, signed in Windhoek, 27 March 1996.

18 Examples of such International Bilateral Agreements include, but are not limited to: *Agreement between Namibia and Brazil on maritime cooperation*, signed in Windhoek on 4 March 1994; *Protocol between Namibia and China on provision of military assistance*, signed in Windhoek on 23 March 1995; *Protocol between Namibia and China on provision of military assistance*, signed in Beijing on 25 October 1996, *Agreement on provision of military goods by China to Namibia*, signed in Beijing on 20 April 1998, and *Protocol between Namibia and China on provision of military assistance*; and signed in Beijing on 2 July 1999.

19 See 'Chinese-funded military college inaugurated by Namibia's President', *New Era*, Friday 25 October 2019, p. 9.

20 Republic of Namibia, *Statement on Defence Policy*, presented to Parliament by the Minister of Defence, February 1993, pp. 1-13 with two Annexures.

21 Ibid., 3-4.

22 Ibid., 4.

23 Ibid.

24 Ibid.,12.

25 Ibid.

26 Ibid., 13.

27 Ibid., 1-55.

28 Republic of Namibia, Ministry of International Relations and Cooperation, *Namibia's Policy on International Relations & Cooperation*, Windhoek, January 2017, pp. 1-63.

29 Republic of Namibia, Ministry of Defence, *Defence Policy*, Windhoek, 2011, p. 2.

30 Ibid., 9-10.

31 Ibid., 11-16.

32 Ibid., 21-22.

33 Ibid., 23-25.

34 One of the few scholarly studies of Namibia's peacemaking efforts is that by Job Shipululo Kanandjembo Amupanda, titled: A Comparative Analysis of Namibia's Peacemaking Role in the Southern African Development Community Region: 'The case of the Democratic Republic of Congo and Angola (1996-2002)', unpublished MA (Political Science) thesis, Stellenbosch University, December 2012.

35 Adam Hartman, 'Indian navy shares peace with Namibia', *The Namibian*, Tuesday, 19 September 2019, p. 6; see also 'Nach Schiffsbesuch: Indien will in Namibia investeren', *Allgemeine Zeitung*, Donnerstag, 19 September 2019, p. 1.

36 Since 1993, the NDF participated in the following peace support missions: Cambodia, Angola, the Democratic Republic of Congo (DRC), Burundi, Eritrea, Liberia, Sierra Leone, Darfur (Sudan), South Sudan, Lesotho, Ivory Coast, Central African Republic and Sri Lanka. See Republic of Namibia, Office of the Prime Minister, *20 Years Independence 1990-2010 – a Visionary Nation on the move towards 2013*, Windhoek, 2010, pp. 240-250.

37 See https://bit.ly/2wzvaZc [Accessed 3 December 2018].

38 See 'Mystery shrouds military building project', report by Patience Nyangove and Marianne Nghidengwa, *Confidénte*, 29 September to 5 October 2016, p. 3. Namibia violated all UN Security Council Resolutions on the Democratic People's Republic of North Korea and against, Mansudae Overseas Projects a UN-listed company from that country. At the time of writing, December 2018, a Chinese company, Qingdao Construction (Namibia), was awarded the contract to complete the new Defence Headquarters at the Suiderfhof Military Base in Windhoek.

39 Sources: *Military Budget Organization* at http://military budget.org/Namibia and SIPRI.org. See also: Republic of Namibia, *Statement on National Defence Budget* by Hon. Penda Ya Ndakolo, Minister of Defence, Vote 08: Defence Appropriation Bill 2018/19, 13 April 2018, pp. 1-21.

40 Republic of Namibia, *Statement on National Defence Budget* by Hon. Penda Ya Ndakolo, Minister of Defence, Vote 08: Defence Appropriation Bill 2018/2019, 13 April 2018, p. 14.

References

Amupanda, J.S.K. 2012. A Comparative Analysis of Namibia's Peacemaking Role in the Southern African Development Community Region: The case of the Democratic Republic of Congo and Angola (1996-2002). Unpublished Master's thesis, Stellenbosch University.

Armstrong, D. 2011. The Evolution of International Society, in J. Baylis, S. Smith & P. Owens (eds.), *The Globalization of World Politics An introduction to international relations.* 5th edition. Oxford: Oxford University Press. pp. 36-38.

Bösl, A., Du Pisani, A. & Zaire, D.U. (eds.). 2014. *Namibia's Foreign Relations Historic contexts, current dimensions, and perspectives for the 21st Century.* Windhoek: Macmillan Education Namibia.

Dedering, T. 2009. Petitioning Geneva: Transnational aspects of protest and resistance in South West Africa/Namibia after the First World War. *Journal of Southern African Studies*, 35(4):785-801. https://doi.org/10.1080/03057070903313160

Defence Act (Act 1 of 2002).

Defence Amendment Act (Act 20 of 1990).

Du Pisani, A. 1991. Namibia forges a regional role for itself, in C. Cowley (ed.), *Namibia Yearbook No. 2 – 1991/2*. Windhoek: Guidebook Press.

Du Pisani, A. 1994. Namibia, impressions of independence, in P. Rich (ed.), *The dynamics of Change in Southern Africa*. Basingstoke: The Macmillan Press. pp. 199-217. https://doi.org/10.1007/978-1-349-23617-6_10

Du Pisani, A. 2000. Namibian foreign policy: Transformation and emerging global orders (1989-1999), in C. Keulder (ed.), *State, Society and Democracy: A reader in Namibian Politics.* Windhoek: Gamsberg Macmillan. pp. 297-311.

Du Pisani, A. 2002. Peacemaking in southern and central Africa: Namibia's role, in C. Cowley (ed.), *Namibia Yearbook No. 8 – 2001/2*. Windhoek: Guidebook Press.

Du Pisani, A. 2014. Namibia's foreign relations and security policy: Exploration of a critical nexus, in A. Bösl, A. du Pisani & D.U. Zaire (eds.), *Namibia's Foreign Relations Historic contexts, current dimensions, and perspectives for the 21st Century.* Windhoek: Macmillan Education Namibia. pp. 367-392.

Gore-Booth, P. 1974. *With Great Truth and Respect.* London: Constable.

Gurirab, T-B. 1990. *Debates of the National Assembly.* p. 203.

Kahiurika, N. 2017. 'Defence buys more weapons'. *The Namibian*, 20 January. https://bit.ly/3bZJFoz [Accessed 3 December 2018].

Leys, C. & Saul, J. 1995. *Namibia's liberation struggle: The two-edged sword.* London: James Currey.

Militarybudget.org. 2012. *Namibian Military Budget.* http://militarybudget.org/namibia/ [Accessed 1 March 2019].

Ministry of Defence (MOD). 1993. Statement on Defence Policy, presented to Parliament by the Minister of Defence, February.

Ministry of Defence (MOD). 2011. *Defence Policy*. Windhoek: Ministry of Defence.

Ministry of Defence (MOD). 2018. *Statement on National Defence Budget, Vote 08: Defence Appropriation Bill 2018/2019*. 13 April. Windhoek: Ministry of Defence.

Ministry of Foreign Affairs (MFA). 2004. *White Paper on Foreign Policy and Diplomacy Management.* Windhoek: Ministry of Foreign Affairs.

Ministry of International Relations and Cooperation (MIRC). 2017. *Namibia's Policy on International Relations & Cooperation*. Windhoek: Ministry of International Relations and Cooperation.

Mushelenga, S.A.P. 2008. Foreign Policy – Making in Namibia: The Dynamics of the Smallness of a State. Unpublished Master's Thesis. Pretoria: UNISA.

Mushelenga, S.A.P. 2015. The Economic Diplomacy of a Small State, the Case of Namibia. Unpublished Doctoral thesis. Pretoria: UNISA.

Mushelenga, S.A.P. 2018. The Role of the Academia in Foreign Policymaking: International Practices and Perspectives as Lessons for Namibia. *India Quarterly*, 74(2):1-19. https://doi.org/10.1177/0974928418766734

Mushelenga, S.A.P. & Van Wyk, J-A. 2017. A new states' debut in regional diplomacy: Namibia and the Southern Africa Development Community (SADC). *Africa Review*, 9(1):58-70. https://doi.org/10.1080/09744053.2016.1239933

National Assembly. 1991. *Debates of the National Assembly*, June.

Ndaitwah, E.D. Gen (rtd). 2017. *A Life and Views of a Soldier Author's Perspective.* Beau Bassin (Mauritius): Lambert Academic Publishing.

Neidhart, S. n.d. SWAPO and the OAU Liberation Committee, 1963-1990. Unpublished research paper. Toronto: University of Toronto.

Nujoma, S. 2001. *Where Others Wavered: My Life in SWAPO and my participation in the Liberation Struggle of Namibia.* London: Panaf Books.

Nyangove, P. & Nghidengwa, M. 2016. Mystery shrouds military building project. *Confidénte*, 29 September–05-October, p. 3.

Office of the Prime Minister. 2010. *20 Years Independence 1990-2010 – a Visionary Nation on the move towards 2013*. Windhoek: Office of the Prime Minister.

Poullada, L.P. 1974. Diplomacy: The Missing Link in the Study of International Politics, in D.S. McLellan, W.C. Olson & F.A. Sondermann (eds.), *The Theory and Practice of International Relations.* 4th edition. Englewood Cliffs, NJ: Prentice-Hall. pp. 194-202.

Saunders, C. 2014. Namibian diplomacy before Independence, in A. Bösl, A. du Pisani & D.U. Zaire (eds.), *Namibia's Foreign Relations Historic contexts, current dimensions, and perspectives for the 21st Century.* Windhoek: Macmillan Education Namibia. pp. 27-36.

Stockholm International Peace Research Institute (SIPRI). 2017. *SIPRI Military Expenditure Database*. https://www.sipri.org/databases/milex [Accessed 1 March 2019].

South African Defence Act (Act No. 44 of 1957). https://www.acts.co.za/defence_act__1957

The Constitution of the Republic of Namibia. 2015. https://www.namibiabooks.com/english-books/product/162-the-constitution-of-the-republic-of-namibia

09

The Trajectory of Zimbabwe's Foreign Policy and Defence Diplomacy

Torque Mude and Sadiki Maeresera

Introduction

Zimbabwe's pursuit of foreign policy through defence diplomacy has largely escaped scholarly attention. However, defence diplomacy has featured prominently in the country's foreign policy lexicon and practice. Like other states, Zimbabwe uses defence resources and capabilities in peacetime for the fulfilment of foreign policy and security objectives. With the diminishing likelihood of the threat or use of force in the pursuit of foreign policy goals in contemporary world politics, Zimbabwe adopted the concept of defence diplomacy and institutionalised it in pursuit of bilateral and multilateral relations. Interstate defence and security cooperation, provision of defence attachés, the conduct of joint permanent commissions on defence and security, and special force training programmes within Southern Africa and the African continent have been part of Zimbabwe's foreign policy in the 21st century.

This chapter discusses the interplay between Zimbabwe's defence diplomacy and foreign policy since the turn of the millennium. The constitutional obligations of the Zimbabwe Defence Forces (ZDF) underscore the role of the military in fulfilling the country's foreign policy objectives. Even though the term 'defence diplomacy' is not explicitly mentioned in any formal document, it falls within the wider scope of Zimbabwe's foreign policy. For instance, the Zimbabwe Defence Policy reiterates the commitment of the ZDF to the creation of common regional security architecture and the maintenance of international peace and security. To this end, the country's military engages with regional and subregional political, economic and collective security institutions, including those of the African Union (AU), the Southern African Development Community (SADC), and other African states, in realisation of defence diplomacy. Understanding Zimbabwe's pursuit of foreign policy objectives through defence diplomacy requires an explanation of the two concepts under discussion, foreign policy and defence diplomacy, and these are outlined below.

Conceptual overview of foreign policy and defence diplomacy

Foreign policy and defence diplomacy are intrinsically interrelated in so far as the latter implies activities in realisation of the former. However, it is also important to clearly grasp what the two concepts denote independently of each other, and where and how they are related.

Debating foreign policy

Foreign policy is not a new concept and is generally considered to be one of the ways in which the processes of international politics operate. The term has been influenced by a number of divergent philosophical standpoints, such as realism, which emphasises the pursuit of national interests by any means; idealism, which places emphasis on morality; and institutionalism, which values the role of institutions and cooperation. However, there is some consensus that foreign policy relates to the pursuit and projection of national interests in relation to other states as well as non-state entities.

Dominant foreign policy scholars, such as Modelski (1962:6-7), define it as activities designed to alter the behaviour of other states as well regulate a state's own actions in the international political environment, while Padelford and Lincoln (1977:197) state that it is the process through which states pursue their interests, goals and objectives. Similarly, Rodee (1967:571) views foreign policy as the pursuit of principles adopted by states to change the behaviour of other states and safeguard their national interests. From a multilateralism lens, Frankel (1968:1) conceptualises foreign policy as a collection of actions and decisions in relations between states, highlighting the terms interdependency and institutionalism which emphasise collective action and decision-making as the pillars of contemporary international politics.

While states have varying foreign relations goals, ranging from attaining selfish goals to war, the end of the Cold War saw a shift from a reliance on military force or violence for survival to military cooperation as a tool for statecraft (Winger, 2014). However, peace and security have remained the primary objectives of defence diplomacy, in much the same way as they were during the era of relying on military force for state security. Like other states, Zimbabwe has been active in defence diplomacy in pursuit of the country's foreign policy goals, which include the attainment of peace and security at home, and within the Southern African subregion, the African continent at large, and the entire international community. Thus, the chapter now turns to a discussion of the concept of defence diplomacy.

Understanding defence diplomacy

Defence diplomacy denotes the peacetime use of military forces and related infrastructure as tools of foreign and security policy (Cottey & Foster, 2004:5-6). The concept emerged at the end of the Cold War as an antithesis to the obsession with the threat or use of force as the means to achieve peace and security (Clarke, O'Connor & Ellis, 1997). As a variant of soft power, defence diplomacy is concerned with the use of armed forces in non-violent operations, including regional defence fora, personnel exchanges, aircraft visits, confidence- and security-building, as well as joint training and exercises (Chernyl, 2008). These activities aim to manage state relations, as well as consolidate collective security, and are sometimes referred to as military diplomacy. While the terms are usually conflated, the latter is an aspect of the former, referring to the role of military attachés and their related activities.

Thus, it is clear that the activities associated with defence diplomacy fall within the spectrum of foreign policy. This is partly attributable to the fact that the security of a state, which is the primary objective of international relations, cannot be understood only in terms of individual interests, but must rather be viewed collectively alongside the welfare of other states. Having said that, it can be argued that Zimbabwe's practice of defence diplomacy with other African states and regional organisations is designed to enhance national, regional and international security, which are interrelated due to political, economic and security interdependence.

Zimbabwe's foreign policy and defence diplomacy: Complementary bedfellows

Even though the National Defence Policy of the ZDF does not make explicit reference to defence diplomacy, the country's military forces, in close coordination with the foreign ministry, have engaged in several defence diplomacy associated activities. The ZDF is an active participant in the SADC early warning system, which was established in 2010 to deal with anticipated security challenges stemming from conflicts. The Regional Early Warning System, which was established at the recommendation of the Interstate Defence and Security Committee (IDSC), is part of the SADC collective security infrastructure that brings together the military wings of SADC member states to safeguard peace and security in the subregion.

Furthermore, the hosting of the Regional Peacekeeping Training Centre by Zimbabwe is an example of the country's defence diplomacy in relation to SADC member states. The centre falls under the auspices of the SADC Organ on Politics, Defence and Security, and was established in 1996 to provide training for peace support activities in the subregion and continent. It aims to promote regional integration in peace and security issues and to equip SADC member states with technical peacekeeping skills. Hence, the centre operates as a regional security management institution which aligns with Zimbabwe's interests, and those it has in common with other SADC states. This is attributable to the post-Cold War discourse of military cooperation, rather than a military competition-oriented foreign policy.

Moreover, the ZDF actively participates in the SADC Brigade and African Standby Force (ASF) for regional peace operations, under the ASF Policy Framework launched in 2008. The ASF is headquartered in Zimbabwe, and its responsibilities include participating in peace support missions, interventions for peace and security maintenance at the request of a member state, and actions to manage conflicts in Southern Africa and beyond. With a mandate to manage the security of the whole of Southern Africa, the fact that the ASF is headquartered in Zimbabwe is as an example of Zimbabwe's management of its relations with Southern African countries through the defence and security apparatus.

Zimbabwe's defence diplomacy in the pursuit of its foreign policy objectives has also been seen in the country's commitment to the maintenance of peace and security in the region, through its contribution to regional forces for peace support operations. In 2014, following the attempted coup in Lesotho, the ZDF joined South Africa and Namibia to help create the conditions for national security and political stability (Vhumbunu, 2015). While the peace support efforts were geared towards peace and security in the region, they also served to promote Zimbabwe's national security, which partly depends on stability in the region. Apart from the national and collective security objectives, the ZDF's participation in the Lesotho peace process illustrates Zimbabwe's cordial defence and security relations with its Southern African counterparts.

Zimbabwe's advancement of foreign policy goals from a defence diplomacy perspective extends beyond the Southern African region. Zimbabwe is amongst the contributors to the ASF, which was previously commanded by a Zimbabwean, Major General Trust Magova (*The Sunday Mail*, 2015). The ASF is a multidisciplinary force which acts under the direction of the AU and is deployed in situations of crisis on the African continent. However, since it was declared functionally ready in 2016, the African Standby Force is yet to be deployed, due to a range of factors including the divergent strategic interests of member states, financial resources constraints, and politicisation of operations in regional mechanisms (Darkwa, 2017). However, it is not the focus of this chapter to discuss the challenges confronting the ASF, but rather to highlight Zimbabwe's commitment to African security.

While defence diplomacy focuses on the ways in which states pursue their own interests in global affairs, contributing to security on the continent goes a long way towards the preservation of interstate relations, and the mere fact of coordination and cooperation within collective security frameworks is an indication of the desire to coexist in a peaceful and secure environment. Compared to World War I, World War II and Cold War politics of military competition, aggression and ideological conflicts, the use of the armed forces as a non-violent diplomatic tool is one of the factors that explain the absence of major interstate wars in contemporary world affairs.

The establishment of joint permanent commissions on military and security issues is one of Zimbabwe's variants of soft power, enabling it to avoid military confrontation with other countries. For example, the Zimbabwe/Botswana Joint Permanent Commission on Defence and Security has gone a long way to unite the two countries, even when they had political differences. For example, Ian Khama of Botswana was critical of Robert Mugabe's dictatorship in Zimbabwe, leading to a diplomatic row between the two countries. Defence diplomacy has been crucial in dealing with security challenges in Zimbabwe-Botswana economic relations, and through the joint permanent commission, Zimbabwe has been able to boost her national security and human security through cooperation in combating transnational crimes, including human trafficking, trafficking of precious minerals, cattle rustling, and drug trafficking, amongst others (30th Session of the Zimbabwe/Botswana Joint Permanent Commission on Defence and Security, 2016).

The exchange of information and experience on military and intelligence issues has also been one of the premises of joint permanent commissions. A case in point is the South Africa/Zimbabwe Joint Permanent Commission on Defence and Security, which involves the seconding of Zimbabwean Airforce instructors to train South African Airforce pilots, aircraft technicians and other support staff (Ministerial Session of the South Africa/Zimbabwe Joint Permanent Commission on Defence and Security, 2005). As a result, South Africa and Zimbabwe have consolidated a special relationship with roots in postcolonial political and diplomatic engagement emanating from a shared history of oppression, and of cooperation during the liberation struggles of the two states.

Moreover, the exchange of intelligence between Zimbabwe and South Africa has yielded considerable results in dealing with transnational crimes and terrorism. In 2004, South African and Zimbabwean military intelligence-sharing led to the interception of a group of mercenaries who were en route to Equatorial Guinea to stage a coup. Samuel Mani and his men were arrested in accordance with universal jurisdiction, which empowers any state to arrest perpetrators of universal crimes such as terrorism, piracy, war crimes and other international crimes. The arrest of the mercenaries, which was arose from Zimbabwe's defence diplomacy, resulted in the strengthening of relations between Zimbabwe and Equatorial Guinea.

Defence diplomacy between Zimbabwe and South Africa has therefore benefited not only the two states, but others as well. In addition to the incident described above, the Zimbabwe-South Africa Joint Permanent Commission on Defence and Security has accelerated interaction between the air forces of the whole Southern African region through experience and training exchanges (Ministerial Session of the South Africa/Zimbabwe Joint Permanent Commission on Defence and Security, 2005). To this end, the security of the entire subregion is bolstered by the military engagement initiatives instigated by these two states.

Zimbabwe's defence diplomacy has also been illustrated by the country's consistency in deploying its defence forces for peacekeeping purposes in neighbouring states. In 2014, the ZDF were deployed as military observers in Mozambique to ensure post-election tensions did not escalate into violence between the two major contesting parties, Mozambican National Resistance (RENAMO) and the Mozambique Liberation Front (FRELIMO) (Channel Africa, 2014). The ZDF joined forces deployed by eight other states to maintain peace in violence hotspots in the Tete, Sofala, Nampula and Inhamabane provinces in Mozambique (All Africa, 2014). Defence- and security-related exchanges and assistance between Zimbabwe and Mozambique date to Zimbabwe's war of liberation, which was characterised by the training of freedom fighters and grooming of political leaders in Mozambique.

As a result of the strong military ties between the two, Zimbabwe aided its neighbour during the Mozambican civil war by deploying troops under the direction of the United Nations Operation in Mozambique (ONUMOZ) to monitor the peace process in the country. The mandate of ONUMOZ was to monitor the ceasefire, separation and concentration of forces, demobilisation, storage and destruction of weapons; and provide security in the major transport corridors. In the aftermath of the civil war, Zimbabwe trained 540 Mozambican military officers at a military facility in Nyanga in the eastern part of the country (ONUMOZ News, N.d), and the initiative was known as the Joint Commission for the Formation of the Mozambican Defence Forces. Since then, Zimbabwe has maintained strong military ties with Mozambique. As a result, the two countries regular conduct infantry-training exchanges and visits.

Regular joint multinational field training of military personnel has been carried out by Zimbabwe and its SADC counterparts with the aim of preparing SADC military peacekeepers. In 1997, Zimbabwe hosted the multinational joint field training code, named Exercise Blue Hungwe, in Nyanga to train SADC peacekeepers in international peacekeeping tactics and techniques (Inter Press Service News Agency, 1997). A total of 1,570 military personnel from Botswana, Tanzania, South Africa, Swaziland, Namibia, Mozambique, Lesotho, Zimbabwe and Malawi participated in the exercise (Inter Press Service News Agency, 1997). Similar exercises include Exercise Blue Crane, which was conducted in 1999 in the Indian Ocean and at a South African Battle School in the Kalahari Desert (De Coning, 1999), to which Zimbabwe sent military personnel.

In 2009, military forces from the SADC Brigade conducted joint military drills under operation Golfinho at the Angola Special Forces Centre in Cabo Ledo in northern Bengo province. Military forces from Zimbabwe joined their counterparts from Swaziland, Mozambique, Congo, Democratic Republic of Congo (DRC), Malawi, Namibia, Lesotho, Madagascar, Mauritius, Mozambique, South Africa, Botswana and Angola in the joint military exercise (South African Government News Agency, 2009). Exercise Blue Kunene was also conducted in Namibia in 2016 with Zimbabwe military forces taking part, and was designed to prepare SADC member states' air forces for rapid deployment in response to humanitarian crises in Africa and beyond (DCD Defence, 2017).

While Zimbabwe's defence diplomacy has been largely tailored to safeguard African peace and security, examples of Zimbabwe's selfish interests in some bilateral and multilateral defence and security engagements cannot be ignored. For instance, the regular and consistent deployment of military forces in Mozambique and the DRC are widely speculated to have been motivated by Zimbabwe's desire to protect the Beira corridor, through which oil is transported to Zimbabwe. Regarding military assistance to the DRC, it has been argued that the interventions were designed to protect diamond mines and other business ventures owned by Zimbabwe's political elite. If these claims are true, they support the realist assumption that the actions of states as they relate to others are driven by selfish interests (Morgenthau, 1967). They also resonate with Carr's (1964:239) assertion that morality in foreign policy is used as a scapegoat for the pursuit of national interests. Be that as it may, Zimbabwe's defence diplomacy has been crucial in the fulfilment of the country's foreign policy goals, including national security, regional security and international security. Hence, Zimbabwe's national interests have been accomplished through peaceful cooperation with other states and international organisations.

Conclusion

In the pursuit of intrinsically related national, regional and international peace and security objectives, Zimbabwe has resorted to defence diplomacy in its relations with state and non-state entities. As a soft power tool in world affairs, defence diplomacy has created, maintained and consolidated cordial relations between Zimbabwe and her neighbouring states. Furthermore, defence diplomacy has been instrumental in the country's multilateral foreign policy, through which national, regional and international peace and security have been supported by the non-violent use of the defence apparatus to advance strategic objectives through cooperation. For Zimbabwe, defence diplomacy therefore appears to be one of the most important means of statecraft.

Editors' note

Zimbabwe was ruled as an authoritarian state by Robert Gabriel Mugabe since independence in 1980. Mugabe became increasingly unpopular as a result of his personal style, the mismanagement of the economy, corrupt practices, favouritism and earlier human rights abuses. In November 2017, some sections of the Zimbabwean Defence Force (ZDF) took control of the Zimbabwe Broadcasting Corporation and key areas in Harare, the capital of Zimbabwe. The uprising took place amid tensions in the ruling party. In a heated atmosphere, First Vice-President Emmerson Mnangagwa, a favourite of the ZDF, was relieved of his duties by President Mugabe. A week later, the Chief of the ZDF, Constantino Chiwenga, strongly criticised the firing of Mnangagwa. Mugabe was removed as party leader and given a deadline for resignation. Mugabe stalled for some days but eventually resigned. Mnangagwa was sworn in as President on 24 November 2017.

Zimbabwe as an authoritarian state ruled by Mugabe and following recent developments is not yet in a period of transition from authoritarian rule to democracy. The resignation of President Mugabe under pressure from the military, the latter stopping short of a coup in November 2017, is not yet implying the achievement of a stable or sustainable democracy in the near future. What evolved in 2017 was a *change within government* and not a *regime change*. Democratic transition implies a change from an authoritarian regime to a (more) democratic regime, including a change of the previous ruling party (or incumbent political elite) to new incumbents. The notion of transition implies that civil society, following elite differences within the ruling party, moves to a significant extent into the public space at the moment of transition. During the 2017 stalemate in Zimbabwe, the civil community went to the streets but were not the main dynamo of the change. They seemed to have been merely supporting the military in their attempt to force Mugabe out of Zimbabwe's power politics. A transition to democracy under current conditions remains remote. Space for citizen politics may open up, but it remains to be seen whether the "new"/"old" elite that arose from recent internal differences will allow significant change. Possible transition to democracy was for the moment arrested. It remains to be seen whether the post-Mugabe ZANU-PF elite will become divided on a future pathway to democracy and how it will impact on foreign and defence diplomacy. Zimbabwe's future remains full of both risk and possibilities.

References

30th Session of the Zimbabwe/Botswana Joint Permanent Commission on Defence and Security. 2016. https://bit.ly/33avlq4 [Accessed 19 May 2018].

All Africa. 2014. *Mozambique: Foreign military observers arrive.* 16 September 2016. https://bit.ly/2TAMm9r [Accessed 20 May 2018].

Carr, E.H. 1964. *The twenty years' crisis, 1919-1939: An introduction to the study of international relations, 2nd edition.* New York: Harper and Row.

Channel Africa. 2014. *International military observers to deploy in Mozambique.* 22 October. https://bit.ly/3cJSIRa [Accessed 20 May 2018].

Chernyl, A. 2008. *The Candy Bombers: The untold story of the Berlin aircraft and America's finest hour.* New York: Penguin.

Clarke, D.L., Ellis, J.D. & O'Connor, D.B. 1997. *Send guns and money: Security assistance and U.S. foreign policy.* Westoir: Praeger.

Cottey, A. & Foster, A. 2004. *Reshaping defence diplomacy: New roles of military cooperation and assistance.* London: Oxford University Press.

Darkwa, L. 2017. The African Standby Force: The African Union's tool for the maintenance of peace and security. *Contemporary Security Policy*, 38(3):471-482. https://doi.org/10.1080/13523260.2017.1342478

DCD Defence. 2017. *Exercise Blue Kunene gets underway in Namibia.* 24 August. https://bit.ly/2vbJk2i [Accessed 21 May 2018].

De Coning, C. 1999. Exercise Blue Crane: A Unifying moment for SADC. *Conflict Trends*, 1:19-23.

Frankel, L. 1998. *The making of foreign policy.* London: Oxford University.

Inter Press Service News Agency. 1997. *Southern Africa-Disarmament: dead bodies, artillery and peace.* 15 April. https://bit.ly/39E31P7 [Accessed 22 May 2018].

Ministerial Session of the South Africa/Zimbabwe Joint Permanent Commission on Defence and Security. 2005. https://bit.ly/2TC37kF [Accessed 21 May 2018].

Modelski, G. 1962. *A theory of foreign policy.* London: Pall Mall Press.

Morgenthau, H.J. 1967. *Politics among nations: The struggle for power and peace.* New York: Knopf.

New Era. 2016. *SADC prepares for joint military exercise.* 9 November. https://bit.ly/2TMXrmS [Accessed 22 May 2018].

ONUMOZ News. n.d. *Regional Peacekeeping-ONUMOZ.* https://bit.ly/2lup5Qq [Accessed 19 May 2018].

Padelford, N.J. & Lincoln, G.A. 1971. *The dynamics of international politics.* London: Macmillan.

Rodee, C.C. 1967. *Introduction to foreign policy and the powers of political science.* New York: Palgrave.

South African Government News Agency. 2009. *SADC Standby Brigade conducts joint military exercise.* 23 February. https://bit.ly/38zie2M [Accessed 22 May 2018].

The Sunday Mail. 2015. 'Waging peace: Creating an African standby force'. 6 December. https://bit.ly/2Izajru [Accessed 20 May 2018].

Vhumbunu, C. 2015. Appraising the efficacy of SADC in resolving the 2014 Lesotho conflict. *Conflict Trends*, 3:3-11.

Winger, G. 2014. *The Velvet Gauntlet: A theory of defence diplomacy.* Vienna: Institute of Human Sciences.

10

China in a Global World

Ian Liebenberg and Justin van der Merwe

Abstract

This chapter provides an overview of the growth of China as a political, military and economic power since its emergence as an independent communist state in 1949. China became a notable political force during the era of decolonisation (1950-1980) and one of the leading states within the Non-Aligned Movement (NAM). Due to its relative economic development and substantial population, China became well-known for posing alternatives to Western domination. During the era of decolonisation, China's external involvement increased through its use of soft power and as a result of its support for liberation movements in Africa. The end of the Cold War saw the demise of the bipolar world and resulted in unipolarity. More recently, however, multipolarity has taken root through the rise or resurgence of non-Western emerging powers. Since 1990, and especially since 2000, China has moved from being a regional hegemon to a global power. This chapter describes the rise of China and its current status as an aspiring global hegemon. Although the chapter is mainly descriptive, it also provides some reflective and analytical notes on China's current and conceivable future role on the international stage.

Background

The Washington Conference of 1921/1922 recognised China's sovereignty and independence. From 1922, the area now known as China experienced violent Western colonial interventions, civil war, and contesting "Republics", before the emergence of the communist People's Republic of China in 1949, which became a notable power in the Global South. China grew in stature in global politics between the 1960s and 1990s, growth which accelerated from 2000. Today, it is one of the undisputed global political and economic powers.

The rise of modern China represents a unique historical trajectory. The Chinese civilisation went through tumultuous periods and several changes, ranging from the early rise of interactive communities (3000 BCE) and the Shang/Yin settlements (1700-112 BCE), through several dynasties such as the Chou and Ch'in period (1100-221 BCE), the Ch'in Empire (221-206 BCE), and the Han Dynasty. After the demise of the Han Empire, the Wei, Shu Han and Wu dynasties were overtaken by the Sui and T'ang dynasties (circa 500-756 CE). The *Sturm und Drang* that led to the creation of today's geographical region of China foreshadowed what was to come.

Over these periods of new orders supplanting or surpassing old ones, unique forms of writing, bureaucracy, legislation, and military organisation (including conscription) evolved. From 1211, periods of Mongol rule were interspersed with the growth of a gradually unifying China. Systems of administration developed, trade flourished, and literature and culture bloomed through both long-term internal developments and some infusion from outside, until the Mongols were driven out around 1400. The centralised rule and extensive (centralised) bureaucracies that have become key features in modern China began to develop in this period. The Ming dynasty brought further developments and unification, and the aims of foreign policy at the time were for the centralised state to maintain the security of a (presumably) uniting China, prevent further Mongol interference, and to retain and expand trade channels.

Gavin Menzies suggests that, following the expulsion of the last of the Mongols, Emperor Zhu Di built up an army of nearly a million and brought Japan and Korea under Chinese influence, and some would argue that this already augured well for a greater China. Zhu Di also dispatched a large armada of merchant and battleships, initiating a maritime tradition that was to grow significantly in the years to come (Menzies, 2003). Regarding grey diplomacy, these ambitious maritime ventures certainly brought China into the international picture as far back as the middle of the 1400s, if only briefly. The Ch'in dynasty marked further cultural growth.

In his work, *Africa in History*, Basil Davidson points out that trade between Africa, China and India developed between 900 and 1300 CE (Davidson, 2001:114, 193). The rise of Islamic expansion also played a role here (Davidson, 2001:72, 193). By the 1400s, trade between the East Coast of Africa and the Far East was well-established, though it was soon to be interrupted and violently taken over by the Portuguese (Davidson, 2001:194). The decline of the dynasties in China introduced the 'Western Challenge' or Western intervention from 1839 onwards.

As mentioned, the Washington Conference of 1921/1922 signalled the West's formal recognition of China's status. Despite international recognition, the country was to experience leadership and military rivalries, Japanese aggression, internal and external strife, and a civil war that lasted from 1945 to 1949. In 1949, a Chinese communist government came to power under Mao Zedong. The Nationalist forces withdrew to Taiwan and declared a republic, despite mainland China viewing it as merely a belligerent province. This remains a contentious international issue to this day.

In Beijing, a red star rises

Following the establishment of the People's Republic in mainland China in 1949, development and socio-economic transformation were both expected and demanded by the Chinese people, and the political leadership that created these expectations had to address the pressing questions of modernisation, industrialisation and large-scale land reform. The decades 1949 to 1979 saw many developments, as the country experienced (sometimes contradictory) political developments, experiments in policy, intense leadership clashes, and elements of Soviet-style five-year plans. The period was also marked by economic policies that swung from a focus on industrialisation to land reform for the peasant population. The Hundred Flowers campaign (1956-1957) opened up criticism of Mao and brought great political turmoil. However, Mao survived. The Great Leap Forward saw attempts to build a rural industry, ending more in disaster than success (Service, 2007:331ff.), but Mao's image remained largely intact despite public criticism (Service, 2007:334). The so-called Cultural Revolution that arose with Mao's tacit consent, had to be reined in by the Chairman himself by 1969 (Service, 2007:339).

Despite these upheavals, during the 1950s, together with the Soviet Union, China represented a rising 'Red Danger' for the (liberal) capitalist West or its allies. The latter formed a military alliance, the North Atlantic Treaty Organization (NATO), while a Russo-Chinese treaty signed in February 1950 brought together the People's Republic of China and the Soviet Union. Other treaties signed during the visit of Zhou Enlai (Chou En-lai) to Moscow in 1952 further cemented these ties, and China soon announced its first five-year plan along the lines of a Soviet model (Calvocoressi, 1982:54). The Korean War during the 1950s seemed to draw China and the Soviet Union closer together and created greater distance from the United States (US) and its allies (Calvocoressi, 1982:58-60). The Cold War was in full swing.

However, relations between the Soviet Union and China were strained, despite their shared commitment to international communism. Calvocoressi suggests that, by 1956/1957, the relationship was 'ruffled by suspicion and friction' due to differences in strategy on how to spread the communist ideology abroad. The issue was further complicated by personal differences between Mao and Khrushchev (Calvocoressi, 1982:64ff.). The rising influence of China, its involvement in Africa, its links with Nicolae Ceausescu of Romania within Moscow's arc of influence, its move away from industrialisation and Marxism-Leninism (as perceived by Communist leadership in Moscow), and border clashes with the Soviet Union all played a role in creating distance between Moscow and Beijing (Boggs & Boggs, 1974:72-75; Lundestad, 1991:242; Service, 2007). So too did national pride, with Lundestad (1991:239) noting that,

> ... [t]wo countries as strong and proud as the Soviet Union and China could not see eye to eye despite their commitment to the ideology of communism ... China was not a major power at the moment, but the Chinese traditionally (assumed) that they are (a centre of the world) and believed in a great future.

To complicate matters, China opened itself to a rapprochement with the US (Dallek, 2007), and the overtures made by the then president, Richard Nixon, closely advised by Henry Kissinger, contributed to more tension between the Soviet Union and China. Kissinger and Nixon succeeded in the goal of splitting the Soviet Union and China, despite these two countries sharing similar goals. China gained international stature through this exercise and proved that it was an actor on the global stage, although in the politics of the so-called 'Third World' or the 'Global South', it had already achieved this stature. The ping-pong diplomacy of Mao and the Chinese leadership's choice to do their own thing were key reasons for the split with the Soviet Union (Dallek, 2007:267-268; Lundestad, 1991:239, 241).

Meanwhile, in the West, the ruling discourse and world view defined by political and military leaders was that the world was caught up in a Cold War between 'rational' liberal capitalism and 'irrational' communism. Much of this was underpinned by the mentality of the US and its allies of being the benevolent masters of world politics – global guardianship or *Herrschaft*. The US had been the undisputed Western and global economic power since World War I, and its economy already outstripped that of Britain by 1900, further benefitting from the two World Wars (1914-1918 and 1939-1945) which brought social dislocation and havoc to Europe, but were never fought on American soil. The US enjoyed a certain privilege during this time due to its relative isolation, and status as a supplier to those at war, stimulating massive economic growth and the start of a military-industrial complex that would grow in decades to come (De Wet & Liebenberg, 2012:247-249).

Red stars in Africa

The Soviet Union became involved in anti-colonial struggles and wars of national liberation in Africa, sometimes by choice, sometimes by imposed conditions (Eidelberg, 2015:35ff.). By contrast, China mostly followed a soft approach of infrastructural development in exchange for geopolitical influence against the West and the Soviet Union. The China-constructed Tanzam railway, linking Tanzania and Zambia, bears testimony to this. A capital-intensive project, the line was surveyed in 1968, work started in October 1970, and the ambitious venture was completed by the middle of 1976. Completing a railway over 1,800 kilometres through challenging environments from rainforests to near desert was an engineering milestone, and the Tanzam enterprise raised more than an eyebrow in the West (*New York Times*, 29 January 1971; *Chinese Economic Studies*, 1977:27).

During 1970, the Peoples' Republic of China also ventured into less-soft diplomacy on the African continent, albeit tentative. One example is the case of Angola, which lapsed into civil strife in 1975 after the hasty withdrawal of the Portuguese colonisers and interference by the US, apartheid South Africa and Zaire, a chosen proxy of France, Belgium and the UK. Mozambique and Angola saw independence arriving when the authoritarian regime of Caetano fell in Portugal in 1974 and was replaced by a leftist government. The Soviets and China supported the Mozambican liberation movement FRELIMO, although Mozambique was not 'a primary Cold War battle ground' (Ciment, 1997:15). However, Angola was to become something of a test for the foreign policy of a rising China.

China chose to support one (and later two) of the three then feuding Angolan liberation movements. The Chinese sent approximately 100 advisors to Kinshasa to assist Holden Roberto's Front for the National Liberation of Angola (FNLA) movement (Ciment, 1997:46; Meredith, 2005:313). Roberto was both corrupt and close to the American Central Intelligence Agency (CIA) (Gleijesus, 2002:238-239; Shubin, 2008:45, 63), but despite him being on friendly terms with the US, he remained open to involvement from China. Roberto visited Beijing in 1973 and persuaded the Chinese to supply FNLA with arms and instructors (Meredith, 2005:313), and Shubin observes that this added to the highly complex situation in Angola as the Popular Movement for the Liberation of Angola (MPLA) had earlier also visited Beijing (2008:59-60). The matter of Chinese involvement was also discussed by Gerald Ford, Henry Kissinger, George Bush, Mao Zedong and Deng Xiaoping (Shubin, 2008:59-60). Mao Zedong and Deng Xiaoping were deeply critical of the American government's support of apartheid South Africa, and South Africa and the CIA were already part of a messy equation (Shubin, 2008:59, 60). The Chinese withdrew their advisors when, to their surprise, they discovered that the CIA and South Africa were already assisting Holden Roberto in the field. The situation in Angola was confusing due to the intermingling of colonial, neocolonial and liberation struggle interests, personalities, social ideals, and contending ideologies.

Ciment noted that, '[i]f politics make strange bedfellows, then Angolan politics positively made for bizarre ones' (1997:119). For a moment, the US and apartheid South Africa (exploiting the Cold War mythology for their benefit) seemed to work together with Communist China, with a tactical consensus on some version of anti-Sovietism. In making a rational calculus, China eventually backed out, becoming aware of the complexity of such a Kafka-esque involvement. The Chinese leadership withdrew from the engagement with the FNLA and narrowly prevented an international debacle with itself as the loser.

Angola was not the only case where China became involved. At times, it also supported the Zimbabwean African National Union (ZANU) during the liberation struggle against the minority regime of Ian Smith in then Rhodesia (Shubin, 2008:158-159).

Back home in the 1980s: Lessons learnt, future visions

A connection between lessons learnt, foresight and the will to succeed through action (or praxis) can change a political context from idealism to one of achievement. Despite human rights abuses and authoritarianism, Chinese leadership through the Communist Party managed a collective of people and made important decisions aimed to enhance the economic future of the country. While there were several challenges and human suffering from 1950 to the 1960s, China increased its influence on the international scene during the 1970s, establishing a platform for what was to come.

In 1976, Deng Xiaoping succeeded an ailing Mao. Changes were needed and as a result, he introduced the Four Modernisations, which were goals to strengthen the fields of agriculture, industry, national defence, and science and technology. The plan aimed to coordinate and integrate China's internal and external policies in complementary fashion, and if successful, would see a rejuvenation of China's economic power and stature in the global community.

The four modernisations were to change China from an actor in the Global South to a major force in international economics, and a growing actor in international politics. With significant experience on 'how not to do it', and a commitment to building a united China as a force to be reckoned with, the initiation of the four modernisations was a well thought-out strategy linking domestic challenges and the international context with China's national interests. From an outsider's perspective, this approach may be seen as linking (and perhaps intertwining) socialism and state-sponsored enterprise, and complementing this with continuous adaptations to macro- and micro-economic needs.

Some argued that the new economic approach was not capitalism as seen in Western contexts. Chinese theorists suggested that it steered clear of simplistic solutions such as 'pure' capitalism and 'pure' communism. (Pan, 1987; Yiwei, 1988; Jiatun, 1991; Congming, 1991; Wenming, 1984). Lu Congming echoed these sentiments, suggesting that a re-assessment of socialist and capitalist thought could achieve a theoretical, and hence a practical, working economy that responds to internal needs and external interests (Congming, 1988:25ff.; see also Jiatun, 1991).

Since the 1970s, and particularly since the late 1980s/early 1990s, China demonstrated a strong upward trajectory, with agricultural reforms from 1980 already adding value by midway through the decade (Wenming et al., 1984). This was also part of what its state elite had viewed as 'Greater China' (Hoogvelt, 1997:217). In the late 1980s, Lynn Pan suggested that China demonstrated a unique development trajectory in comparison to Western states, wondering 'Would China become the world's next colossus?' (Pan, 1987:238).

China, 1990-2020: Economic power and the global political economy

Samir Amin argues that, since the formation of what is commonly called the 'Washington Consensus' (a set of agreements between the International Monetary Fund (IMF), the World Bank, and US Treasury Department), the world economy has been dictated by liberal-capitalism through a Western (core-state) consensus, and alternative pathways to the dominant capitalist paradigm were not popular (Amin, 2006:168). He argues that China and Russia (and other so-called Third World countries) found themselves confronted with the dominance of capitalism, and the marginalisation of alternative economic pathways, namely socialism (Amin, 2006:168). However, Western-style capitalism faced its own problems. As the dominant system, it too did not achieve economic equality. On the contrary, it deepened class differences and increased the gap between rich and poor both globally and regionally (Amin, 2006; Chomsky, 2007; Martin & Schumann, 1997; Keulder, 1996; Hoogvelt, 1997). As neoliberal globalisation has spread across the globe, characterised by liberalising markets, trade openness, deregulation and privatisation, the situation has worsened (Amin, 2006; Chomsky, 2007; Dyer, 2006). Other alternatives were needed.

However, questions persisted over the extent to which China was actually proposing an alternative system, or whether it was merely repeating the prevailing Western-led system, albeit with Chinese characteristics. By the end of the 1990s, China acted boldly on the international stage by adopting its 'going out' policy in 1998, and shortly thereafter joining the World Trade Organization (WTO) in 2001. In contrast to its stated ambitions of providing an alternative to the dominant system, there are two initiatives intimately tied to China's global ambitions which demonstrate its acquiescence to global capitalism: BRICS, and the One Belt One Road (OBOR) Initiative, founded by Xi Jinping in 2013, who prioritised foreign affairs after becoming president earlier in the year.

The BRICS alliance is probably the strongest proponent of what today is commonly called South-South relations, the origin of which can be traced back to the NAM, and the partially China-led Bandung Conference hosted in Indonesia in 1955 between African and Asian heads of state. Building on this, the Brazil, Russia, India and China (BRIC) alliance of prominent emerging economies was founded in 2005. The term 'BRIC' was initially coined by Jim O'Neill from Goldman Sachs in 2001, by which he hoped to capture the prominent emerging economies from the non-West, whose markets had vast growth potential and substantial populations. For example, in 2013, the BRICS accounted for 42% of the global population and 40% of the global gross domestic product (GDP) (Lumumba-Kasongo, 2015:87). The BRIC states started hosting formal annual summits from 2009, and in 2010 South Africa was invited to join the group, making it 'BRICS'.

The most significant achievement of the bloc thus far was the creation of a New Development Bank (NDB) in 2014 to help finance infrastructure projects in the BRICS countries and within their respective regions. This bank, along with the China-controlled Asian Infrastructure Investment Bank and the Silk Road Fund, supposedly heralded a challenge to the prevailing Washington Consensus. Proponents of this argument suggest that the emerging powers, led by China, are attempting to challenge Western capitalism by replacing it with a Chinese model of development, or 'Beijing Consensus'. The goal is also to challenge the hegemony of the dollar with the renminbi.

However, despite this goal, the NDB (at least initially) chose the US dollar as its preferred trading currency (Johnson, 2015:209), as did the Contingent Reserve Arrangement (CRA). The CRA is a framework which assists the BRICS states to manage their short-term balance of payments problems. However, it too resulted in a further strengthening of the IMF, as if a country seeks a loan in excess of 30% of its borrowing quota, it would be required to take out a structural adjustment loan and subject itself to conditionality (Bond, 2016:613). Some have also questioned the viability of the NDB with regards to its ambitions and extent of required infrastructure, as it possessed a total strength of $100 billion against the World Bank's $250 billion (Bertelsmann-Scott et al., 2016). Although the increased use of local currencies (not the US dollar) in trade and financial deals is cause for some optimism, in short, the creation of an alternative financial system to substantively challenge the prevailing Western-led one seemed unlikely.

China's OBOR initiative was devised to recycle some of China's accumulated capital and to repurpose the construction materials based in its state-owned enterprises (SOEs), and it was hoped that this would increase exports and further globalise the renminbi. OBOR is therefore an amplified version of China's 'going out' policy that was launched in the late 90s to increase capital outflow whilst seeking to further expand the reach of Chinese companies (Rolland, 2017:130).

OBOR's land and maritime routes (spanning East, Middle and West Asia, the Middle East, Europe and Africa) comprise a series of parallel and interlinked features, including intercontinental railway routes, freeways, ports, and energy pipelines. OBOR comprises over 60 countries, including 4 billion people and a market share of approximately one-third of global GDP (Ferdinand, 2016:950). OBOR presents an opportunity for Chinese companies to invest in developing industrial, manufacturing, and special economic zones and parks (Du, 2016:31), and as centres for manufacturing, these parks will serve as distribution nodes along the many transport corridors of OBOR. Public Private Partnerships (PPPs) will be the dominant modus operandi of OBOR, and Chinese credit will be extended to Chinese contractors to carry out the work of OBOR in these countries (Hayes, 2017:1). China-employed financial instruments (issued by the Silk Road Fund, Asian Infrastructure Investment Bank, and NDB) will fund Chinese projects in these territories, stimulating their markets, and even creating new ones.

However, OBOR faces several difficulties, not least of which are the significant security challenges. OBOR traverses areas where the Islamic State (IS) has been involved, and passes through the war-ravaged Iraq and Afghanistan. The safe passage of capital, goods and people along OBOR routes is also contingent on security in the seas around the Horn of Africa, and in states such as Somalia in East Africa and Yemen in the Middle East, where piracy poses a constant threat. On land, one has to contend with groups such as Al Shaabab.

There are mixed views on how China should deal with these security threats (Swaine, 2015:9). In certain quarters, it is believed that the Maritime Silk Road is closely linked to China's goals of transforming into a substantial maritime power. As Liang (2015, in Sidaway & Woon, 2017:596) contends, it is hoped that OBOR would turn the Peoples' Liberation Army Navy (PLAN) into 'a robust blue water naval capability dedicated to sea lines of communication defense'. Others believe that it is essential for China to establish contacts and ensure friendly ports and turnaround facilities based in other countries, as this will extend the range of possible Chinese maritime activities (Chaturvedy, 2017). The so-called String of Pearls is a strategy in which China is allegedly attempting to secure a series of compliant ports and installations which would ensure their dominance over the South China Sea and beyond. Based on this, it seems that China may be reconsidering its stance on non-interference and non-intervention (Mustafic, 2017:117).

In a similar vein to the BRICS alliance, many have argued that OBOR is a bold attempt to insert Chinese characteristics into broader capitalist development as a challenge to the Washington consensus. From this perspective, OBOR is calculated as a broader geopolitical gambit to challenge the Washington Consensus, similar to the way in which the Marshall Plan was a US-led reconstruction of Western Europe after World War II.

Although OBOR would signal a substantial advance by a growing global power, what is overwhelmingly more likely is that OBOR will fit into the Western-led system of accumulation, particularly when assessed against broader trends concerning the BRICS reinforcement of this system (Van der Merwe, 2018; Van der Merwe, Taylor & Arkhangelskaya, 2016). Chances are slim that OBOR will do anything other than reinforce the status quo concerning the broader systemic level and its preferred means of accumulation. The changes being rung in by OBOR are effectively style over substance, or just more of the same.

In 2018, China has assumed the role of globalisation and free trade enforcer, taking over this role from the US, whose withdrawal from international engagements is owed to President Donald Trump's trade protectionist policies and all-out trade wars with traditional allies such as Canada, the European Union, and China. The single most talked-about item at the 2018 BRICS summit in Johannesburg was trade openness, and China came out strongly against US trade protectionism.

Economic growth, defence and international status

D'Anieri, a US-based political scientist, argues that 'China's booming economy has probably brought more people out of poverty than any global development scheme, but development also contributes to the economic and military might that many fear' (2014:298). Despite some 'heat-up' (a decline in sustained growth of 10%) in 2011, China's macroeconomic policies contributed to relative global economic stability, and the country accumulated massive holdings of foreign currencies, including US$4 trillion (D'Anieri, 2014:298), in comparison to just over US$2 trillion in 2010 (D'Anieri, 2014:308). This phenomenon is expected to continue, as the Chinese central bank buys US bonds that in effect fund the massive US trade deficit, argues D'Anieri (2014:298).

Chinese expenditure during the 1970s was hard to calculate and estimates by prominent economists suggested that defence expenditure could have been US$4–5 billion, assuming that China had a 4–5% growth rate. Others suggested US$10–12 billion, while the US Arms Control and Disarmament Agency at the time estimated that the expenditure might have been as high as US$15 billion (IISS [International Institute for Strategic Studies], 1976:50), although this is likely an inflated figure or overestimation.

Between 1977 and the mid-1980s, the four modernisations were conceptualised in China. During the late 1980s, IISS reports that, despite an economic growth rate of approximately 8%, defence spending in China declined (IISS, 1989:147). At the time, the total armed forces of the People's Republic stood at 3.2 million men and women, of which the army represented 2.3 million (around a million conscripts on two-year stints). The navy staff consisted of about 300,000, and the air force had 470,000 (IISS, 1989:147ff.). IISS argues that, given the available budget and perhaps also due to doctrine, the military posture of China resulted in a territorial 'defensive force and lacked the ability, facilities and logistics capabilities for protracted, large-scale military operations outside China' (IISS, 1976:48). However, the same publication noted 'that China is gradually acquiring a greater logistic capacity' (IISS, 1976:48).

By 2012-2013, the IISS reported that China was making wide-ranging efforts to improve its military capacity, mirroring the country's economic growth, and the Chinese Defence Paper, issued in April 2013, stressed that the armed forces should be 'commensurate with China's international standing' (*The Military Balance*, 2014:206). The paper also pointed to the need to enhance maritime power. Restructuring, professionalisation, modernisation and diversification, including the armaments industry, were prioritised (*The Military Balance*, 2014:207). The PLA was to undergo a qualitative revolution in equipment, while maritime power was not to be neglected. However, there were challenges.

Following the 'overheating' of the economy in 2011, Chinese economic growth slowed to 7.8%, down from 9.3% in 2009, and monetary policy had to be tightened. The Chinese defence budget for 2013 was set at US$112 billion. When defence spending accelerated, it was carefully monitored to keep increases in line with the comparable expansion of the overall Chinese economy (*The Military Balance*, 2014:209). Simultaneously, as China became more integrated into the global economy from the late 1990s, production capacity and market-networks were extended. Since 2007, policy requirements were set by the Chinese defence industry regulator and in 2014, the active defence force (all arms of service) was set at 2.3 million (army, 1.6 million; air force, 200,000; navy, 398,000), while the number of staff in the Strategic Missile Forces was 100,000 (*The Military Balance*, 2014:209). Like elsewhere on the globe, large-scale investments were made in cyber-warfare and counter cyber-warfare capabilities.

Concerning economic engagement, defence and international status there are a further three areas discussed in this chapter. The first matter relates to the little-known entry of China into a new 'space race' between competing global powers and the associated quest for control of airspace. Involvement in space is also seen as an arena that powers can enter only once they have graduated into the league of developed or rich nations. Advanced technological and scientific development and competitiveness are also precursors for entry into space, and China scores highly in these spheres. The other two areas relate to China's growing ambitions both in its immediate region but also further afield, and the tensions and responsibilities that arise from this. China's relationship with Russia in historical perspective was covered in the discussion thus far, so its regional rivalry with the other regional power, India, will briefly be discussed. Lastly, China's involvement in Africa has grown exponentially – both as an economic power and, increasingly, as a military one as well. Therefore, we end off with China's involvement in UN peacekeeping initiatives in Africa, as this appears to be the chosen mode in which China chooses to operate militarily within Africa.

A red star in space

The space race, as it was commonly referred to at the time, started during the Cold War, and the two leading competitors were the US and the Soviet Union. Expertise for developing missile construction, existing military knowledge, and practical platforms for development were taken over from a defeated Nazi-Germany in 1945, when German rocket experts from Germany surrendered to the Allied Forces and started sharing their knowledge of rocket science. Other Germans scientists offered their services to the Soviet Union. The space race between the Soviet Union and the US became one of the defining aspects of the Cold War era and complemented the search for military power and dominance by these two superpowers (Cordesman & Kendall, 2016).

China entered the space endeavour rather late by sending a satellite into space in 1970, followed by a successful soft landing on the moon in 1976. Since 2000, China's space activities have developed at a greater speed. In 2009, the Vice-Chairman of the Chinese Commanding Council said that, 'space is a … commanding height for international strategic competition … and means control of the ground, oceans and electromagnetic space ... [thus having] a strategic initiative in one's hands'. The Chinese Defence White Paper (2015) refers to space as the 'commanding height in international competition', and the Chinese government therefore took an intense interest in preparing for fighting 'informationised wars', as well as developing an array of anti-satellite weapons (ASAT) weapons, i.e. kinetic kill, directed energy, co-orbital capabilities, and an advanced manned space programme (Cordesman & Kendall, 2016).

Current competition between China and the US has broad civil and military implications, as it relates to power projection, national status, and pride (Cordesman & Kendall, 2016), and there is no need to add that a modern and expansive space programme forms part of 'China's Space Dream' as articulated by President Xi Jinping, and acts as a crucial pillar of international prestige. In March 2003, through their Shenzhou programme, China launched the first manned mission (Shenzou 5), while Shenzou 7 saw a three-person crew launched into space and China's first spacewalk. In 2016, nine more taikonauts went into space (Cordesman & Kendall, 2016), and in 2012 the first space docking took place, with Spacelab Tiangong. By 2016, a second space lab, Tiangong 2, was launched into orbit. China also executed a second soft landing on the moon following the earlier attempt in 1976 (Cordesman & Kendall, 2016), and the landing of Mars rovers and deep space exploration are underway. China combines civilian and military objectives in their space approach, and arguably currently boasts the most robust and dynamic space programme.

Petra Ebeling (2016:16) remarks that, in being so advanced, 'China has become a world class player in the field'. Its cooperation in space with Russia is good, although USA/China cooperation is at a low ebb for various reasons. Ebeling suggests that China would be an affordable and logical partner for the European Space Agency (ESA), which became involved in the Tiangong-1 project, and could participate in the latest space technologies (Ebeling, 2016). However, Tellis argues that, at its heart, Chinese interests in space and counter-space measures are rooted in their strategic needs and not haphazard government choices (Tellis, 2007:41ff.; see also Polpeter, Anderson, Wilson & Yang, 2016).

Closer cooperation between China and ESA will most likely become a contentious matter for the US. Kulacki (2014) points out that the USA space programme, whether for (deep) space exploration, delivery of inter-continental ballistic missiles (ICBMs), ASAT or other military purposes, is becoming increasingly hamstrung by financial constraints, due to the US's immense deficit and continued indebtedness to other global actors (Cordesman & Kendall, 2016; Polpeter, Anderson, Wilson & Yang, 2016). Ebeling (2016) points out that, despite China being a latecomer to highly diversified and specialist goal-driven space projects, the Chinese influence is set to grow at the expense of the US's prestige. The reasonable result would be China-US tensions mounting as the US realises that its self-assumed world hegemony is being challenged within a context of its declining capacity.

Notes on the region

China is a significant regional power, sharing this status with India and Japan. For this discussion, we will focus on China and India, as the two regional hegemons share extensive borders. In discussion with one of the authors some years ago, Shrikant Paranjpe referred to India as an 'apologetic hegemon'. However, times are changing, and both India and China are now regional hegemons with a global presence, and no longer need to be apologetic.

In 1954, India and China signed the Tibet agreement, while an Indo-Soviet Treaty was signed in 1971 (Paranjpe, 2013:72, 74). In 1974, India became part of what is known as the Nuclear Club, and today India has a clear capacity for a weaponised nuclear programme. Since the establishment of NAM, India has always played an important and frequently leadership role, acting as a spokesperson and leading member of NAM. Simultaneously, India cooperated with the USSR regarding military agreements and the arms trade.

However, some changes took place. During the late 1990s and early 2000s some closer interaction marked the relations between the US and India (Kamdar, 2007:200). Kamdar refers to this interaction as new strategic partnership (or cooperation) between the US and India, including booming trade and, 'gave Americans the idea that India is exclusively focused on the US', but cautions that, 'Nothing could be further from the complex reality of today's geopolitics' (Kamdar, 2007:275). Kamdar goes on to note that 'India is not going to play junior partner to America's military and corporate research apparatus' (2007:278), as India holds influential soft and hard power capacities. The country may not want to seem to be leaning towards the US (Kamdar, 2007:200), and remains open to trading with anyone on the global scene.

For example, India seems to be rebuilding its relations with Russia. India participates in a multipolar world economy, with trade partners such as the European Union, especially France and Germany, Africa, the Middle East, and Latin-America (Kamdar, 2007:277). The country has extensive trade ties with the Middle East and countries in the Arabian Gulf region (Kamdar, 2007:263), and is an important political, economic, and military player on the global stage. Within the region, India and China seem to have found well-rationalised reasons for peaceful existence, and little change in this domain is foreseen in the medium- and even long-term. India is aware of the need to live in peace with its northern neighbour, and in November 2006, Chinese Premier Hu Jintao visited New Delhi, where the two countries agreed to boost bilateral trade to US$40 billion by 2010, a figure long surpassed.

Soft or smart diplomacy and new responsibilities: UN peacekeeping

With its return from relative isolation during the early years of Communist rule, and given current security developments, the Chinese started getting involved in United Nations (UN) peace deployments. By 2014, small numbers of personnel were or are deployed in Cote d'Ivoire (UN-UNOCI), Western Sahara (MINURSCO), and Cyprus (UNFICYP), while larger numbers are seen in the Democratic Republic of the Congo (MONUSCO, 220 members), Lebanon (UNIFIL, 343), Liberia (UNMIL, 564), South Sudan (UNMISS, 340) and 233 members with UNAMID Sudan (*The Military Balance*, 2014:239-240). Between 2014 and 2018 the picture changed again. From just over 2000 soldiers deployed in 2014, the figure went up to over 3000 in 2015, then saw a drop, but for 2016 to 2018 it remains over 2000. By January 2018, the numbers deployed on peace missions counted for 2,634 (ISDP Backgrounder, 2018:3). China became the third largest contributor to the UN budget, the second largest contributor to the UN peacekeeping budget, the 12th highest provider of peacekeepers and the largest contributor of troops for peacekeeping in the UN Security Council (ISDP Backgrounder, 2018:3).

China's involvement in Africa intertwines with its role as a rising global hegemon, and foreign policy, defence diplomacy, resource procurement and national interests are closely connected. China has become a major economic actor on the continent of Africa, and largely diminished the stake that the US, France and the UK held (Neethling, 2015). Neethling (2015:8) also notes that:

> China offers its African partners a mix of political and economic incentives and drives home the message of a win-win situation ... (China) increased its footprint in Africa [but] adheres to a strict policy of non-intervention (or non-interference) in the affairs of African states.

The lack of socio-political stability or absence of peace in Africa also touches China's interests. Quoting Wang, Neethling indicates that China's attitude towards UN peacekeeping changed from 'ardent opposition in the 1970s to avid support in the 2000s' (Neethling, 2015:11). However, more correctly, China had little choice in the matter. Part of this increased involvement has to do with economic reasons, as stability is good for business, while part is to demonstrate global responsibilities and diplomacy (Wang, quoted in Neethling, 2015:11). Moreover, an inescapable reason for increased involvement in these operations is to respond to global expectations and UN insistence that member states participate in peacekeeping efforts. Neethling makes some deductions about China's involvement in UN peacekeeping: (1) Beijing's emergence in the field (including Africa) stands in direct relation to China's growth and international influence; and (2) China's peacekeeping involvement on the African continent stems from the need for stability in Africa as a central trading partner of China.

China's involvement on the African continent is generally pragmatic, and its drive for influence is in the main underpinned by soft power. With the spread of China's international influence, it is likely that China will become more involved in UN peacekeeping, particularly in Africa because, from whichever perspective one views China's growing role, it will have to take part in future global multipolar governance.

Conclusion

China remains a substantial power in regional and global circles. The latest indications from the country indicate that it is preparing to play a greater role in world affairs, as suggested by its OBOR initiative, which represents its boldest global undertaking yet. However, the extent to which China has the appetite for such a role remains unknown. China's rise has also caused shifts in geopolitical contours which have led to new sites of struggle and contestation, such as outer-space and Africa, as well as growing regional tensions, and China will have to pay increasing attention to these areas if it is to manage and negotiate these challenges effectively. Implicitly, those who fear China's rise also fear its concurrent military rise, but whether its growing economic and political clout is associated with an increasingly belligerent military presence also remains to be seen. How are we to interpret this rise, and to what lengths will it go to continue on this trajectory? The comparative global experience of superpower behaviour leaves much to be admired, although whether this will be tempered by a more multipolar world is also uncertain.

References

Amin, S. 2006. *Beyond US hegemony? Assessing the Prospects for a Multipolar World.* London: Zed Books.

Ball, P. 2015. Railways in History and the TAN-ZAM/TAZARA project. *The Heritage Portal.* Pretoria: South Africa.

Bertelsmann-Scott, T., Friis, C. & Prinsloo, C. 2016. *Making sustainable development the key focus of the BRICS New Development Bank.* Pretoria: South African Institute of International Affairs.

Boggs, J. & Boggs, G.L. 1974. *Revolution and Evolution in the Twentieth Century.* New York: Monthly Review Press.

Bond, P. 2016. BRICS banking and the debate over sub-imperialism. *Third World Quarterly*, 37(4): 611-628. https://doi.org/10.1080/01436597.2015.1128816

Calvocoressi, P. 1982. *World Politics since 1945* (4th edition). London: Longman.

Chaturvedy, R.R. 2017. China's Strategic Access to Gwadar Port: Pivotal Position in Belt and Road. *RSIS Commentaries*, No. 005. Singapore: Nanyang Technological University.

Chomsky, N. 2007. *Hegemony or Survival: America's Quest for Global Dominance.* London: Penguin Books.

Ciment, J. 1997. *Angola and Mozambique: Postcolonial Wars in Southern Africa.* New York: Facts on File Inc.

Cong, L. 1991. *Basic Contradictions of Capitalism. China: Issues and Ideas.* Beijing: Beijing Review Press.

Conming, L. 1991. *Modern Capitalism Reassessed. China: Issues and Ideas.* Beijing: Beijing Review Press.

Cordesman, A.H. & Kendall, J. 2016. *Chinese Space Strategy and Developments.* London: Centre for Strategic and International Studies (CSIS).

Dallek, R. 2007. *Nixon and Kissinger: Partners in Power.* London: Allen Lane.

Davidson, B. 2001. *Africa in History: Themes and Outlines.* London: Phoenix Books.

De Wet, F. & Liebenberg, I. 2012. Conflict and Economic Consequences: Comparative notes on 'going to war', in T. Potgieter & I. Liebenberg (eds.), *Reflections on War: Preparedness and Consequences.* Stellenbosch: African Sun Media. https://doi.org/10.18820/9781920338855

Du, M. 2016. China's 'One Belt, One Road' Initiative: Context, Focus, Institutions, and Implications. *The Chinese Journal of Global Governance*, 2(1):30-43. https://doi.org/10.1163/23525207-12340014

Dye, T.R. 2002. *Power and Society: An introduction to the Social Sciences* (9th edition). New York: Harcourt College Publishers.

Dyer, G. 2006. *Future Tense: The coming World Order.* London: Serpent's Tail.

Ebeling, P. 2016. China's Space Program: How cooperation between China and Europe changes as China's space program advances. Unpublished MA thesis, Leiden University.

Eidelberg, P. 2015. Tempest in a Teacup? The Angolan War as 'Cold War' template. 1975-1989, in I. Liebenberg, G. Risquet & V. Shubin (eds.), *A Far-Away War: Angola, 1975-1989.* Stellenbosch: African Sun Media.

Ferdinand, P. 2016. Westward – the China dream and 'one belt, one road': Chinese foreign policy under Xi Jinping. *International Affairs*, 92(4):941-957. https://doi.org/10.1111/1468-2346.12660

Fuquan, T. 1990. The United States: A debtor Nation. *China Issues and Ideas* (Special edition dedicated to world debt challenges). Beijing: New Stars Publishers.

Gleijesus, P. 2002. *Conflicting Missions: Havana, Washington and Africa, 1959-1976.* Chapel Hill: University of North Carolina Press.

Hayes, N. 2017. The impact of China's one belt one road initiative on developing countries. *International Development*. 30 January. https://bit.ly/2QfH80Q [Accessed 27 July 2019].

Hoogvelt, A. 1997. *Globalisation and the postcolonial world: The New Political Economy of Development.* Hampshire: Macmillan. https://doi.org/10.1007/978-1-349-25671-6

ISDP Backgrounder. Institute for Security and Development Policy. Stockholm: ISDP. https://bit.ly/2INQ1L7

IISS (International Institute for Strategic Studies). 1976. *The Military Balance 1975-1976.* London: IISS.

IISS (International Institute for Strategic Studies). 1989. *The Military Balance 1988-1989.* London: IISS.

IISS (International Institute for Strategic Studies). 2014. *The Military Balance 2014.* London: IISS.

Japan Science and Technology Agency (JSTA)/Center for Research and Development Strategy (CRDS). 2014. *A Comparative Study on Space Technology in the World 2014.* Tokyo: JSTA/CRDS.

Jiatun, X. 1991. Reunderstanding Capitalism. *China: Issues and Ideas.* Beijing: Beijing Review Press.

Johnson, R.W. 2015. *How long will South Africa Survive? The looming crisis.* Jeppetown, Johannesburg: Jonathan Ball.

Kamdar, M. 2007. *Planet India: The Turbulent Rise of the World's Largest Democracy.* Toronto: Simon & Schuster.

Keulder, C.J. 1996. *Trends in the Modern World Economy and Democratization in Peripheral States.* Pretoria: HSRC Publishers.

Kulacki, G. 2014. *An Authoritative Source on China's Military Space Strategy.* Chicago.

Lumumba-Kasongo, T. 2015. Brazil, Russia, India, China and South Africa (BRICS) and Africa. *Africa Development*, XL(3):77-95.

Lundestad, G. 1991. *East, West, North, South: Major Developments in International Politics, 1945-1990.* Oslo: Norwegian University Press.

Martin, H-P. & Schumann, H. 1997. *The Global Trap: Globalisation and the Assault on Democracy and Prosperity.* Bangkok: White Lotus.

Menzies, G. 2003. *1421: The Year China Discovered the World.* Toronto: Bantam Books.

Meredith, M. 2005. *The State of Africa: A History of Fifty Years of Independence.* Cape Town: Jonathan Ball (with Toronto: Free Press).

Mustafic, A. 2017. China's One Belt, One Road and Energy Security Initiatives: A Plan to Conquer the World? *Inquiry*, 2(2):107-134. https://doi.org/10.21533/isjss.v2i2.87

Neethling, T. 2015. China's international peacekeeping contributions and the evolution of contemporary Chinese strategic considerations. *Strategic Review for Southern Africa*, 37(2):7-27.

Pan, L. 1987. *The New Chinese Revolution.* London: Amish Hamilton.

Paranjpe, S. 2013. *India's Strategic Culture: The Making of National Security Policy.* New Dehli: Routledge.

Pollpeter, K., Anderson, E., Wilson, J. & Yan, F. 2017. *China Dream, Space Dream: China's Progress in Space Technologies and implications for the United States.* New York.

Rolland, N. 2017. China's 'Belt and Road Initiative': Underwhelming or game-changer? *The Washington Quarterly*, 40(1):127-142. https://doi.org/10.1080/0163660X.2017.1302743

Service, R. 2007. *Comrades: Communism – A World History.* Oxford: Macmillan.

Shubin, V. 2008. *The Hot 'Cold War': The USSR in Southern Africa.* London: Pluto Press.

Sidaway, J.D. & Woon, Chih Y. 2017. Chinese Narratives on 'One Belt, One Road' in Geopolitical and Imperial Contexts. *The Professional Geographer*, 69(4):591-603. https://doi.org/10.1080/00330124.2017.1288576

Swaine, M.D. 2015. Chinese views and commentary on the 'One Belt, One Road' initiative. *China Leadership Monitor*, 47(2):3.

Tellis, A.J. 2007. China's Military Space Strategy. *Survival*, 49(3). Washington: Carnegie Endowment. https://doi.org/10.1080/00396330701564752

Van der Merwe, J. 2018. Reintegrating Africa and the Middle East into China's system of accumulation, in X. Li (ed.), *Mapping China's One Belt One Road Initiative.* London: Palgrave Macmillan. https://doi.org/10.1007/978-3-319-92201-0_8

Van der Merwe, J., Taylor, I. & Arkhangelskaya, A. 2016. *Emerging powers in Africa: A new wave in the relationship.* London: Palgrave Macmillan. https://doi.org/10.1007/978-3-319-40736-4

Wenming, S. 1984. *On rolls the Green Revolution.* Beijing: Guoji Shudian.

Yiwei, J. 1988. *From Enterprise-based Economy to Economic Democracy.* Beijing: Beijing Review Press.

11

India's Military Diplomacy

Rahul Anand Maslekar

Abstract

Independent India has utilised its armed forces to progress its international relations predominantly by rendering assistance for disaster relief, peacekeeping, and capacity-building through professional military training. The Indian Ministry of Defence considers improving defence cooperation with other countries essential for the nation's security, promoting mutual trust, and conflict prevention and resolution. India's defence cooperation is decided at the highest level involving the Cabinet Committee for Security and National Security Council. The scale and scope of India's defence diplomacy has steadily expanded since the end of the Cold War, but a number of factors, both organisational and political, continue to constrain its reach and effectiveness, and the Ministries of External Affairs and of Defence do not seem to agree when it comes to defining the objectives of India's military diplomacy. The country's aim to maintain strategic autonomy tends to reduce the intensity of its military partnerships, while the political and bureaucratic leadership continues to recoil at the idea of power projection and developing expeditionary capabilities for the Indian armed forces. The national aspiration of becoming a dominant regional power remains somewhat unrealised.

Introduction

India occupies an important geo-strategic location in the Indian Ocean Region (IOR), and its strategic interests extend from its immediate neighbourhood to an outer arc formed by the eastern littorals of Africa, the Persian Gulf, Central Asia and Southeast Asia. This geography provides India with an opportunity not only to define and protect its national interests but also to exert its benign influence in its extended neighbourhood (Sakhuja, 2011). India does not have any expansionist territorial aspirations and has never shown aggressive intent against any country, which has long been its outlook, instead using trade, religion and culture, what is now often termed 'Soft Power', to influence other countries (Malone, 2011). Since independence, India has also utilised its armed forces to progress its international relations, mostly by rendering disaster relief, peacekeeping, and capacity-building through professional military training. In the 21st century, Indian diplomacy has matured and learnt, albeit slowly, the importance of utilising all facets of its national power: political, diplomatic, economic, technological and military, in furtherance of the national interests.

India's military diplomacy, similar in many ways to other forms of diplomacy, includes defence-related visits, meetings, and negotiations; participation in international security conferences; defence treaties and mutual pacts; import, export or gifting of military equipment; joint exercises by armed forces; and training of personnel. All these activities would generally be undertaken in line with the general foreign and security policy guidelines set by the political leadership, but they would have strategic and military significance. Thus, effective military diplomacy, while safeguarding the state's independence, security, and integrity, also ensures the widest possible freedom of action for the state. A strong military power projection capability can dissuade potential adversaries and increase bargaining power in diplomatic negotiations through either a coercive display of force or a mere benign presence. Historically, coercion was exercised mostly through the use of navies, which led to the coining of the term 'Gun Boat Diplomacy'. Colonial powers intimidated weaker states into subjugation, or at least into accepting unequal terms for trade and concessions for exploiting natural resources or labour. In the 21st century, military intervention by major powers into another country, purportedly to prevent a humanitarian disaster arising from internal conflict, has become quite common. Such interventions normally get international approval and sanction from the UN (Dorman & Otte, 1995).

International view of military diplomacy

It is important to note the views of various countries about the conduct of military diplomacy. The Indian Ministry of Defence considers improving defence cooperation with other countries as essential for the nation's security, promoting mutual trust, and conflict prevention and resolution (Dutta, 2009), while the US government engages in defence cooperation in terms of military alliances and agreements, conducting joint operations and interoperability exercises, and facilitating access and influence. The UK sees multinational defence cooperation as an arrangement where two or more nations work together to enhance military capability, although the country ensures that its defence cooperation with other nations does not affect its relations with the US and NATO. Meanwhile, Australia uses the terms 'defence international engagement', classifying defence cooperation as a subset of international engagement and as the actions of the target country that are funded by the Australian Department of Defence through a separate Defence Cooperation Allocation. Russia defines military cooperation as the military relations of friendly states aimed at the joint solution of defence problems, which are determined by the compatibility of the respective state's interests, coherence of a political course, and mutual interest in providing international and national security. China sees defence cooperation as foreign military relations, and one of the most important aspects is to prepare its own officers for next generation military leadership (Muthanna, 2006). In a newspaper article published on 21 February 2015, C. Raja Mohan highlighted the importance given to 'Defence Diplomacy' by President Xi Jinping during his special address to all the Defence Attachés posted in Chinese embassies the world over, as well as those defence officials dealing with foreign relations.

Historical perspective of India's defence diplomacy

In ancient India, diplomacy was considered a quasi-military activity. The epics of Ramayan and Mahabharat speak of alliances between powerful kingdoms built through marriages, but occasionally coercion was utilised, backed by military power. Expanding regional influence through the conduct of 'Ashwamedha Yagna'[1] was an Indian way of exploiting military capability as an instrument of coercion for transacting interstate relations (Basham, 2004), and the last known Ashwamedha Yagna was conducted by Maharaj Jai Singh II of Amber, Jaipur in 1716 CE (Narayanan, 2015). Kautilya (also known as Chanakya),[2] the most acclaimed strategist and author of Arthashastra,[3] was aware that stratagems would work only when backed by credible military power. He maintained that the ruler of the State of Magadh, Chandragupta Maurya,[4] had a large and professionally trained standing army maintained by the State, although Kautilya recognised that there was no glory in war. In this context, he believed that negotiation was a strategic device, designed to lead to victory rather than compromise, andshould be pursued until the end. While never questioning the primacy of politics in warfare, Kautilya viewed diplomacy and foreign policy as instruments of war (Boesche, 2003).

Indian kingdoms relied not only on their armies but also their navy to project power. The peninsular kingdom of the Cholas[5] in the far south in medieval India was a notable maritime power, leading naval expeditions to Sri Lanka and the Maldives in South Asia, and a campaign to Southeast Asia in 1025 CE. Their overseas campaign against the kingdom of Shrivijaya in Southeast Asia involved both the army and the navy. The Cholas were engaged in a maritime trading relationship with China, and when Shrivijaya threatened this trade, which passed through the Straits of Malacca, the Cholas responded with a show of strength. The chief reason for their naval venture in Southeast Asia was to gain control of the strategic points along the Straits of Malacca, although they had no territorial ambitions outside South Asia (Malone, 2011). Today the Straits of Malacca, Sunda, and Lombok have gained extreme strategic importance for India, China and many other countries, as a large percentage of their trade, and particularly energy resources, pass through these choke points. India is worried for security reasons too, with Chinese nuclear submarines reportedly venturing into the Indian Ocean and passing through these channels, ostensibly on 'Anti-Piracy Mission'.

Independent India's defence engagements

After independence, India sought to insulate itself from the impact of the Cold War by adopting a deliberate strategy of military isolationism. Prime Minister Nehru explicitly rejected the use of armed forces for expeditionary operations, and also insisted that the membership of the Non-Aligned group was limited to those countries which did permit establishment of foreign military bases on their territory. India remained a member of the Common Wealth, but refused to join any of the Western military alliances, and even as it sought weapons from the Soviet Union at the turn of the 1960s, India was careful to circumscribe its military engagement with the USSR. One major exception to India's military isolationism in the Cold War period was its active participation in the international peacekeeping operations authorised by the United Nations Security Council (UNSC).

Along with this, India continued to play its role as a security provider to smaller states on the subcontinent by reviving the British protectorate arrangements with Nepal, Bhutan and Sikkim in 1949-1950 (Raja Mohan, n.d). After the 1971 Bangladesh War, India came up with its own version of the Monroe Doctrine, called the 'Indira Doctrine', aiming to assert India's primacy in South Asia. New Delhi also sought to influence its neighbours against allowing military bases and facilities from the world superpowers in their territories. Unfortunately, limited diplomatic, economic and military capacities meant that the Indira Doctrine was not very effective.

The 21st century has also seen sustained efforts by China to establish closer defence ties with nearly all of India's neighbours, with the exception of Bhutan, which has been subjected to severe Chinese military coercion over territorial claims. The Chinese focus has been on developing maritime infrastructure in these countries which can serve a dual purpose, commercial as well as naval, and subsequently taking over the assets on long-term lease. Gwadar port in Pakistan and Hambantota port in Sri Lanka are examples of China's foothold in the Indian neighbourhood, but such Chinese initiatives are certainly not conducive for India's national interests and are a setback for its regional defence cooperation (Tanham, 1992). Fortunately, the 2017 Doklam plateau stand-off between Indian and Chinese forces in the Bhutanese territory did not escalate into a border conflict, partly due to India's resolute military posture, backed by astute diplomacy (Chengappa, 2017).

After the end of the Cold War and the demise of the Soviet Union, India reconfigured its economic and foreign policies, re-assessing its policy of military isolation of the previous decades and launching its military engagement with the US. The Kickleighter proposals (initiated in the early 1990s) provided the framework for service-to-service interaction between the two armed forces (Vinod, n.d), and the framework elaborated in 2005 defines multiple missions for operational cooperation, and calls for greater defence industrial collaboration. India's defence cooperation with the US is probably the most expansive in terms of the areas covered, with the US now conducting more military exercises with India than with any other partner. India, which did not buy a single weapons platform from the US in the Cold War period, has acquired a number of systems since 2005, such as one major naval ship with considerable heli-lift and amphibious capability, and C-17 Globemaster and C-130J Super Hercules transport aircraft, which have significantly enhanced India's Out of Area capability (Rajghatta, 2007). Today, the US considers India an important partner and expects it to play a significant role in the US strategy for Asia, especially in the Indo-Pacific region. India's forward movement on defence engagement with the US has also opened the door for similar interactions with Britain, France and Russia, as well as deepening defence ties with US allies in Asia like Japan, South Korea and Australia. Today, India has bilateral defence cooperation agreements with more than 40 countries, varying greatly in their scope and intensity depending on whether the country is a major power, immediate neighbour, or a state of special interest to India along the Indian Ocean littoral and beyond (Tharoor, 2012).

India's defence diplomacy in its immediate neighbourhood

In South Asia, India's defence diplomacy with its neighbours falls into a category of its own. In the case of Pakistan, the two countries have negotiated a range of nuclear and military confidence-building measures (CBMs), but Delhi and Islamabad have struggled to institutionalise any contact between the two military establishments outside of a hotline that operates between the two headquarters, as the military CBMs between the two sides are negotiated by the Foreign Secretaries and not by military professionals (Ghosh, 2009). In a similar vein, India's military engagement with the armed forces of Bangladesh only showed improvement after the late 2000s. While the armies of the countries have not clashed, para-military forces on both sides, the Border Security Force of India and the Bangladesh Rifles, have not had happy relations. However, the broad framework agreement for cooperation signed by the two Prime Ministers, Dr Manmohan Singh and Sheikh Hasina, in 2011 has provisions for substantive military and security cooperation. Defence officers are now training in each other's institutions.

Although India has categorically refused to involve itself militarily as part of the International Security Assistance Force in Afghanistan, it signed a strategic partnership agreement with the country that includes the option of substantive Indian military support to Kabul. India has also agreed to train up to 600 Afghan army officers every year in India, with some getting specialised training in counterinsurgency, and recently gifted some attack helicopters to Afghanistan to enhance its capacity for undertaking anti-insurgency operations (Panda, 2016). After the failed intervention in the Sri Lankan civil war in the late 1980s, New Delhi has since returned to engage with the armed forces of Sri Lanka, and though opposed by Tamil Nadu, it gave substantial military aid to Sri Lanka in its fight against LTTE. A seeming change of heart, this was to keep Pakistan and China from getting too close to Sri Lanka militarily. However, India could not dissuade Sri Lanka from granting berthing facilities in Colombo harbour to Chinese submarines in 2016, an act considered blatantly Anti-India.

In the case of Nepal, the Indian army maintains a special relationship with the Nepalese army in that the Chief of Army of each country has been accorded the same honorary status in the other country, and Nepalese citizens can enrol into the Indian army's Gorkha regiments. During a visit to Nepal by the new Indian Prime Minister Narendra Modi in Nov 2014, a 'Made in India' 'Dhruv' advance light helicopter (ALH) was gifted to the Nepalese army (Press Trust of India, 2014). However, the present political dispensation in Nepal, headed by Prime Minister Oli of the Communist Party, seems to be getting under Beijing's influence, much to India's chagrin.

Bhutan also has special status with India, which maintains a military training team in Bhutan. The countries have signed an agreement to ensure that no activity inimical to the other is allowed to take place in the country, and Bhutan has agreed to consult India on all matters concerning its defence. Along with this, the present King is an alumnus of the Indian National Defence College, and is its youngest student (Special Correspondent, India Strategic, October 2010).

In 2011, India signed a new partnership agreement with Maldives that focuses on deepening maritime security cooperation. In 1988, India was quick to respond militarily to help save President Abdul Gayum's government from rebels, but since 2013, President Abdulla Yameen seemed to take an antagonistic stand against India, apparently under influence of massive Chinese economic and military aid. For example, in 2018 the Maldives navy for the first time declined to attend the biennial MILAN symposium hosted by the Indian navy. However, with change of leadership, India Maldives relations appear to be once again getting better and working towards mutual interests.

The general global impression seems to be that India, although a rising economic and military power, has been mostly reactive in its policies, rather than acting with bold and imaginative initiative with its neighbours. On the other hand, India's subcontinental neighbours have been caught off-guard by the exponential rise in China's economic and military power projection capabilities, which have undermined India's regional influence.

India's defence diplomacy with Central and East Asian nations

The politics, security and economics of Central Asia have always been important for India, and Prime Minister Modi has visited all the countries of this region, with security cooperation being discussed prominently. The spread of ethno-religious instability and terrorism in the region could have grave consequences for India's security, while a politically stable Central Asia can emerge as a major market for Indian goods, as well a key source of energy, particularly natural gas (Sajjanhar, 2016). With a rare display of futuristic vision, India established its first military base in Tajikistan, which is manned, equipped and maintained by Indian Air Force personnel (Pandit, 2013). Tajikistan straddles the access route to this region, with India planning a strategic opening through Chabahar port in Iran and then through Afghanistan. Operationalisation of the first phase of Chabahar port after its inauguration by the Iranian President in December 2017 enabled India to send the first consignment of wheat to Afghanistan, bypassing passage through Pakistan (Haidar, 2017). Economic liberalisation in 1991 also saw India initiating its 'Look East' Policy, which aimed to combine political, economic and security leverage in the Asia-Pacific. New Delhi's engagement with the Association of Southeast Asian Nations (ASEAN) reflects the increasing geo-strategic importance of the South China Sea and its littorals to India's regional status (Tharoor, 2012). In 1996, India joined the security forum of ASEAN, the ARF (ASEAN Regional Forum), in 2005 the ASEAN leaders invited India to join the East Asia Summit process that was to focus on broader political and security issues facing Asia, and in 2010 India participated in the first expanded gathering of the ASEAN Defence Ministers Meeting (Ministry of External Affairs Portal, August 2012). The stability and freedom of navigation in the South China Sea are vital interests for New Delhi, as around 55% of India's trade with Asia passes through this strategic sea route.

The Indian navy has been at the forefront of the military push in this region, with Indian naval ships making frequent visits to the countries of SE Asia. The navy has special berthing rights in Vietnam, while the Indian navy's Exercise Milan, a multinational naval exercise conducted since 1995, has now been institutionalised as a biennial event that draws in a large number of countries along the Indo-Pacific littoral. In 2008, India took another initiative by convening the Indian Ocean Naval Symposium, which brought together all the navy chiefs from the Indian Ocean area (Indian Navy, 2015). Along with this, India is developing close defence ties with Singapore and Vietnam. Singapore conducts joint training exercises with the Indian army and air force at Indian military bases (MoD Annual Report 2015-2016), while an Indian army Combat Engineers team was recently sent to Lao PDR (People's Democratic Republic) to train their cadres in de-mining and bomb disposal to clear a large number of unexploded bombs and mines from the Vietnam War era. Indian air force instructors stationed in Malaysia have trained Malaysian fighter pilots on combat tactics, and every year Defence Services Staff College training is provided to military officers from ten countries in the region. India's special and rising relations with ASEAN nations was marked by the presence of ten ASEAN top leaders, heads of government or of the state, at the 79th Republic Day celebrations on 26 January 2018 in New Delhi. Maritime security, anti-terrorism measures and cyber security issues encouraged all the leaders of ASEAN and India to join on one platform (Jacob, 2018).

India's defence engagements with African nations

Today, Africa looms large in the security and geo-strategic considerations of many nations, and the continent is fast emerging as one of the most sought-after destinations for bilateral engagements. India's relations with Africa are conditioned and energised by historical linkages and strong political foundations of the past. Indian troops had fought as part of British forces during Robert Napier's expedition to Abyssinia in April 1868, and in both the World Wars in North and East Africa. Sacrifice and valour of Indian soldiers is part of African history. One Indian army division had played a crucial role in Ethiopia regaining its independence by overthrowing Italy's military control. As an acknowledgement of the sacrifices of Indian soldiers, in 1941 Sudan had gifted £100,000 to India, and that money went into making the majestic Administrative and Academic Block of National Defence Academy in Khadakwasla. This building has been named 'Sudan Block' in gratitude.

New Delhi's approach to the African continent reflects a balance between national values and interests, taking into account the diversity of Africa as well as the policies of other key players. Training and enhancing military leadership capacities has been the focus, with Indian military training teams working in many African countries, and many African military personnel being trained in various Indian defence institutions. India played a central role in the establishment of the Botswana Command and Staff College, Harar Military Academy of Ethiopia, and the Nigerian Military Academy, and the first Commandant of the Nigerian Academy was an Indian army officer. IAF personnel man the aviation wing of the Mauritian police force, while naval personnel do the same for Mauritius and Seychelles coast guards, and an IAF helicopter training team has been in Namibia for over two decades.

When parts of Africa have been afflicted by rebellions and conflicts, and restoring peace became a priority, India joined UN peacekeeping missions in a number of African countries, including Burundi, Ethiopia and Eritrea, Liberia, Sierra Leone, Somalia, Sudan and South Sudan, and Zaire (now DR Congo), and the fairness, professional conduct and valour of Indian soldiers on these missions was acknowledged by the UN, as well as the host countries (UN News, n.d). The year 2018 marked 75 years of Indian troops presence on African soil, mostly to liberate countries from foreign occupation or to restore peace, as mandated by UN Peacekeeping Missions. India also assisted Mozambique in providing coastal security by deploying two naval ships during the 2003 African Union Summit in Maputo, and in 2004 during the World Economic Forum summit attended by many heads of state (Beri, 2014). India is also steadily expanding its military engagement footprint with the countries of the North and South American continents.

Humanitarian activities by Indian armed forces

The 21st century has seen an exponential spread of terrorism through the seas of the IOR. 80% of the world's oil and gas is transported through the choke point of the Gulf of Aden and along the Somali coast, which has faced the scourge of piracy. India has joined the international effort to combat this threat by deploying a naval ship since the year 2008, and Indian naval warships have safely escorted more than 3000 merchant vessels through the area. On a few occasions, punitive action has also been taken against the pirates, and these efforts are sure to raise India's image as a responsible military power (Indian Navy, 2015). Over the years, India has been steadily enhancing its Out of Area Contingency and military intervention capabilities and has demonstrated them in recent times. During the 1991 Gulf War, India airlifted more than 100,000 civilian workers who were forced to leave Iraq, the largest airlift since the Berlin airlift at the end of World War II (Fabian, 2011). During the Southeast Asian tsunami in 2004, the Indian armed forces were at the forefront of rescue and relief operations, with over 30 Indian navy ships setting sail with rescue teams and relief material, even while engaged in relief and rescue on the Indian eastern seaboard (Sakhuja, 2005). Indian naval ships have evacuated stranded Indians and citizens of other countries from war zones, such as Lebanon in 2006, Libya in 2011, and Yemen in 2015. Along with this, India has been regularly exercising its armed forces with every major country in the world including China, displaying its strategic reach capability. These exercises are not only conducted bilaterally but also in multinational scenarios. The Indian navy conducts IBSAMAR exercises with the navies of Brazil and South Africa, as well as participating in trilateral exercises with the navies of the US and Japan. The Indian air force regularly participates in Exercise Red Flag, a multinational aerial combat exercise organised by the US air force, and also exercises with the air forces of the UK, France and Russia. Such exercises contribute to greater understanding of each other's capabilities and capacities. Indian air force aerobatic teams, Surya Kiran and Sarang, have thrilled audiences the world over with their daredevil precision flying.

Indian response to expanding Chinese footprint in IOR

The 21st century has seen a dramatic rise of China in economic and military terms. This has given rise to its quest to become a superpower. Steadfastly China has sought to spread its footprint in the Indian Ocean Region by building maritime infrastructure along many of the littorals, which is ostensibly intended to provide security to its energy trade passing through these waters. India considers the Chinese action as detrimental to its influence in the IOR and a potential security threat. But this should naturally be expected of a rising power, and Chanakya even espoused it in his 'Mandala Theory'[6] on foreign policy in the treatise Arthashastra (Kangle, 1965). In fact, without an overt display of aggressive diplomacy; India, too, has attempted to do the same by establishing defence cooperation relations with most of the countries sharing common borders with China and in its immediate neighbourhood. South Korea has been a significant defence systems supplier to India, including providing Offshore Patrol Vessels (OPVs) to the Indian navy. In 2015, India and Japan agreed to deepen their strategic relations, with mention made of the possible acquisition of long-range amphibious aircraft 'Shinmaywa US-2' in the near future, giving India an extended capacity to patrol the further reaches of the Indian Ocean (Duchatel et al., 2015). In the same year, India and Mongolia agreed to elevate their relationship to the strategic level, and the Indian navy increased the frequency of its ships showing the flag in the South-China Sea, even paying a goodwill visit to Chinese ports.

India's decision-making apparatus

India's defence cooperation gets decided at the highest level, involving the Cabinet Committee for Security (CCS) and National Security Council (NSC), assisted by the NSC Secretariat (NSCS) and Strategic Planning Group (SPG), Ministry of External Affairs, Ministry of Defence and individual Service Headquarters. At apex level, decision-making rests with the NSC, which comprises the Prime Minister as Chairman, the Ministers of Home Affairs, Defence, External Affairs, and Finance, and the Chairman of Niti Ayog[7] (National Integrated Transformation Institute) as members (Kanwal, 2016). However, defence cooperation and defence diplomacy are still considered subsidiary to the political and economic initiatives conducted by the Ministry of External Affairs (MEA) to build relations with other nations. Compared to the importance given by other nations to military engagements to ensure their national interests, India's focus on leveraging its military capacities, experience and prowess for similar purpose seems to be minimalistic, and at times lethargic. This is not to say that the Indian defence forces have shied away from such tasks, but their participation has been controlled and cleared by the MEA, and is also largely impacted by the enthusiasm and energy displayed by the political dispensation of the day towards building bilateral and multilateral relations in pursuit of national interests.

Challenges to Indian defence diplomacy

The scale and scope of India's defence diplomacy has steadily expanded since the end of the Cold War. Nevertheless, a number of factors, organisational and political, continue to constrain its reach and effectiveness. At the organisational level, a shortage of staff in the headquarters of the Ministry of External Affairs (MEA) and the Ministry of Defence (MoD) remains a major impediment. Very few Indian Embassies and High Commissions have Defence Attachés posted to look after military and security interests or to render advice to civilian diplomats, and the MEA and the MoD do not appear to agree when it comes to defining the objectives of India's military diplomacy. As of 2018, India had just four Defence Attaches posted amongst its twenty-nine diplomatic missions in Africa.

While the leadership of the Foreign Office has come to value the possibilities of military diplomacy, the MoD remains deeply conservative and has been reluctant to follow suit.

Connected to this is an issue that is rooted in the peculiar structure of India's civil-military relations. Few democracies have the kind of overwhelming dominance by the political setup and civilian bureaucracy over the military service as is seen in India (Limaye, 2007). This has led to a suboptimal engagement of defence personnel in diplomatic activities. While training to defence officers on the basics of international relations and diplomacy is carried out during various in-service courses, the professional diplomats are not regularly exposed to defence-related issues, hence the general lack of enthusiasm to pursue defence diplomacy as part of the nation's overall diplomatic efforts. It is still rare to find senior military officers accompanying the Prime Minister or the External Affairs Minister on their official visits.

India also needs to resolve a number of political and strategic ambiguities to strengthen its military diplomacy. The need to maintain strategic autonomy tends to reduce the intensity of military partnerships, especially with the world superpowers, as India's political establishment is apprehensive of the danger of becoming militarily subordinate. The second conflict is between the traditional imperative of territorial defence and the new need of securing India's growing interests far from its shores. The Indian political and bureaucratic leadership continues to recoil at the idea of power projection and developing expeditionary capabilities for the Indian armed forces, yet they frequently call upon the security forces to manage emergencies in the immediate and extended neighbourhood. India has even attempted coercive diplomacy, using its military might against Sri Lanka when the air force air-dropped humanitarian aid over Jaffna in 1987, leading to the signing of the Indo-Sri Lanka Accord.

The Indian security debate tends to be reticent about acquiring and deploying the military instruments of power projection, although steps have been taken to build the requisite capabilities by acquiring strategic transport aircraft and naval ships. The Indian establishment is traditionally opposed to forward military presence through foreign military bases, but its growing aspirations as a regional power cannot be met unless it is able to protect its national interests, including beyond its shores. Similarly, to be able to operate in distant waters, the Indian navy will need victual facilities around the Indo-Pacific littorals. A beginning has been made through an agreement signed during Indian Prime Minister Modi's visit to Oman in February 2018, to utilise the Duqm Port facilities for logistic and maintenance requirements of the Indian navy (Panda, 2018). Similar facilities would also be essential for its air force, and while Indian military aircraft and ships have been given temporary transit facilities by many friendly countries, India will have to develop a range of special political relationships and military partnerships to acquire larger basing facilities.

Conclusion

In the future, India may have to confront growing security challenges in its immediate neighbourhood, as well as in other regions important for its expanding national interests. It is expected that there will be greater regional and international demand for India's military services, support and cooperation, and the country will need to take a more pragmatic and practical approach to utilising its military capacities. As part of overall diplomatic efforts, its defence diplomacy would be vital to build confidence amongst nations, decrease the risk of conflicts, and encourage peaceful dispute resolution. Like other types of national engagements, defence cooperation is an investment for building capacities and relationships. It, therefore, means that mainstreaming defence diplomacy along with other facets of national power projection is essential for the country in its quest for a position at the international high table.

Notes

1. Ashwamedha Yagnais a Sanskrit term referring to a horse sacrifice ritual of Vedic times in ancient India. It was used by ancient Indian kings to prove their imperial sovereignty. The process involved releasing a horse to wander for a period of one year, and the horse would be followed by the king's warriors. In the territory traversed by the horse, any rival could dispute the king's authority by challenging the warriors accompanying it. After one year, if no adversary had managed to kill or capture the horse, the animal would be guided back to the king's capital. It would be then sacrificed, and the king would be declared an undisputed sovereign.

2. Kautilya (Chanakya) was an Indian teacher, philosopher, economist, jurist and royal advisor. He is traditionally identified as Kautilya or Vishnugupta, who authored the ancient Indian political treatise, the Arthashastra. He mentored Chandragupta Maurya, the first ruler of Maurya dynasty to build a large empire by bringing smaller fiefdoms under one control

3. Arthashastra is an ancient treatise on statecraft, economic policy and military strategy, incorporating Hindu philosophy. Kautilya is credited as the author, although there is a possibility of the book being a compilation of works by many authors of the time. After being lost for many centuries, one original copy written on palm leaves was discovered in South India in 1905. One principle tenet of statecraft was the pursuit of power through realpolitik.

4. Maurya Empire was founded in 322 BCE by Chandragupta Maurya, a pupil of Chanakya, by taking over the kingdom of Magadh after overthrowing the Nanda rulers. The Maurya empire spread its rule over a large territory, extending from present-day Afghanistan to Bangladesh, covering the entire peninsular India except for a small territory at the southern tip. Emperor Ashok was the third ruler of the Mauryan dynasty. The Mauryan empire had well-established trade relations with the Egyptians, Greeks and Syrians, and India's national emblem is based on the Lion Capital of Emperor Ashok at Sarnath.

5. Chola Empire was the longest-ruling dynasty of southern India, from 300 BCE to 1279 CE. During the 11th century, the empire had extended its maritime influence from the Maldives to the Malaya peninsula, backed by a strong naval force. The kingdom was centrally governed, with the king being assisted by disciplined bureaucracy. The Chola kings were patrons of art and architecture. Rajaraja Chola I and Rajendra Chola I were the greatest rulers of the Chola dynasty, during the period 985 CE to 1044 CE.

6. Mandala Theory. Chankaya (Kautilya) propounded the 'Mandala Theory' which emphasises the imperatives of international relations for any nation-state. Kautilya's writings are studied in detail in major institutes for defence and strategic studies, along with Sun Tzu, Clausewitz and others.

7. Niti Ayog. The National Institution for Transforming India is the premier policy 'Think Tank' of the Government of India, providing both directional and policy inputs.

References

Basham, A.L. 2004. *The Wonder that was India – A Survey of the History and Culture of the Indian Sub-Continent before the Coming of the Muslims*, 3rd edition. London: Picador, Pan Macmillan Ltd.

Beri, Ruchita. 2014. India – Mozambique relations: Towards fresh opportunities? *Africa Trends*, October-December. New Delhi: Institute of Defence Studies and Analyses.

Boesche, R. 2003. Kautilya's Arthasastra on War and Diplomacy in Ancient India. *The Journal of Military History*, 67(1). https://doi.org/10.1353/jmh.2003.0006

Chengappa, R. 2017. 'India-China Standoff: All You Need to Know About Doklam Dispute'. *India Today*, 17 July. https://bit.ly/3cG4YfX [Accessed 24 June 2019].

Dorman, A.M. & Otte, T.G. 1995. *Military Intervention- From Gunboat Diplomacy to Humanitarian Intervention.* Aldershot, England: Dartmouth Publishing Company Limited.

Duchatel, M., Brauner, O.& Seibel, K. 2015. Japan's National Defence Policy Reforms. *Stockholm International Peace Research Institute (SIPRI) Year Book 2015*. Oxford, UK: Oxford University Press.

Dutta, A. 2009. Role of India's Defence Cooperation Initiatives in Meeting the Foreign Policy Goals. *Journal of Defence Studies*, 3(3).

Fabian, K.P. 2011. Biggest Ever Air Evacuation in History. *Indian Foreign Affairs Journal*, 7(1), January-March.

Ghosh, S. 2009. Two Decades of Indo-Pak CBMs – A Critique from India. *IPCS Issue Brief 132*. New Delhi: Institute of Peace and Conflict Studies.

Haidar, S. 2017. 'Iran Inaugurates Chabahar Port'. *The Hindu*, 3 December. https://bit.ly/3aE28Gw [Accessed 24 June 2019].

Indian Navy. 2015. *Ensuring Secure Seas: Indian Maritime Security Strategy, Naval Strategic Publication 1.2*. New Delhi: Integrated Headquarters Ministry of Defence (Navy).

Jacob, J. 2018. 'India, ASEAN to Bolster Maritime Security Ties with Eye on China'. *Hindustan Times*, 26 January. https://bit.ly/3auILj4 [Accessed 24 June 2019].

Kangle, R.P. 1965. *The Kautiliya Arthashastra Part III*. Mumbai: Bombay University Press.

Kanwal, G. 2016. *The New Arthashastra – A Security Strategy for India*. New Delhi: Harper Collins India.

Limaye, S.P. 2007. India: Confidence Amid Change, in W.M. Carpenter & D.G. Wiencek (eds.), *Asian Security Handbook*, 3rd edition. New York: ME Sharpe Inc.

Malone, D.M. 2011. *Does the Elephant Dance*. New Delhi: Oxford University Press. https://doi.org/10.1093/acprof:osobl/9780199552023.001.0001

Ministry of Defence, Government of India. 2016. Annual Report 2015-2016. https://bit.ly/2vPnJgb [Accessed 24 June 2019].

Ministry of External Affairs. 2012. *ASEAN Regional Forum (ARF)*. https://bit.ly/39yUkpl [Accessed 24 June 2019].

Muthanna, K.A. 2006. *Enabling Military to Military Cooperation as a Foreign Policy Tool: Options for India*. New Delhi: Knowledge World.

Narayanan, Y. (2015). *Religion, Heritage and the Sustainable City*. New York: Routledge. https://doi.org/10.4324/9780203750797

Panda, A. 2016. Why India Transferred Attack Helicopters to Afghanistan. *The Diplomat*, 1 February. https://bit.ly/2PXKJk0 [Accessed 24 June 2019].

Panda, Ankit. 2018. 'India Gains Access to Oman's Duqm Port, Putting the Indian Ocean Geopolitical Contest in the Spotlight'. *The Diplomat*, 14 February. https://bit.ly/2vEJW0I [Accessed 24 June 2019].

Pandit, R. 2013. 'India airlifts military hospital to Tajikistan to strengthen geostrategic footprint in Central Asia'. *Times of India*, 18 April.

Press Trust of India. 2014. 'To Boost Ties, Narendra Modi Presents Advanced Chopper to Nepal'. *The Indian Express*, 25 November.

Raja, M.C. n.d. Nehru's realism. https://bit.ly/2vEKJPd [Accessed 24 June 2019].

Raja, M.C. 2003. 'Beyond India's Monroe Doctrine'. *The Hindu*, 2 June.

Raja, M.C. 2015. 'Raja – Mandala: Between Talk and Action'. *The Indian Express*, 27 October.

Rajghatta, C. 2007. 'USS Trenton is now INS Jalashva'. *Times of India*, 19 January.

Sajjanhar, A. 2016. *India-Central Asian Relations: Expanding Vistas of Partnership*. Raisina Debates. New Delhi: Observer Research Foundation. https://bit.ly/2IRCvG5 [Accessed 24 June 2019].

Sakhuja, V. 2005. Indian Naval Diplomacy: Post Tsunami. *Navy Articles No 1640*. New Delhi: Institute of Peace and Conflict Studies.

Sakhuja, V. 2011. *Asian Maritime Power in the 21st Century*. Institute of Southeast Asian Studies, Singapore: ISEAS Publishing. https://doi.org/10.1355/9789814311106

Special Correspondent. 2010. NDC: Marking its Golden Jubilee with Pride. *India Strategic*. https://bit.ly/3azTatN [Accessed 12 June 2014].

Tanham, G. 1992. Indian Strategic Thought – An Interpretive Essay. *Rand Project – India's Future Strategic Role and Power Potential*. Santa Monica: Rand Corporation.

Tharoor, S. 2012. *Pax Indica-India and the World of the 21st Century*. New Delhi: Penguin Group.

UN News. n.d. India: A Long and Deep Tradition of Contributing to UN Peacekeeping. https://bit.ly/2VUkM8J [Accessed 24 June 2019].

Vinod, M.J. n.d. *India-United States Relations in a Changing World: Challenges and Opportunities*. https://bit.ly/3auK3KW [Accessed 4 October 2014].

12

Managing India's Strategic Resources and Reserves

Ajey Lele

Abstract

For armed forces, the capacity to secure military dominance depends on the effectiveness of military weapon systems, weapon delivery platforms, and other infrastructure. The military industrial complex is required to ensure timely and adequate supply of resources for these purposes. As such, the resources and reserves play a very important role in the overall process of nation-building. Management and ensuring self-sufficiency of strategic resources is a complex task and requires a multidisciplinary approach. It involves not only financial and technological investments but is also about formulating a policy for the import and export of such materials. This chapter undertakes a broad assessment of India.

Introduction

The aim of this book is to discuss defence diplomacy, national security strategies, and management of strategic resources and reserves. States have various instruments at their disposal, from defence to diplomacy, to ensure that their strategic interests are safeguarded. Countries develop military architectures to implement national security strategies, and one of the most important aspects in ensuring the effectiveness of military weapons systems, weapon delivery platforms and other infrastructure, is timely and adequate supply of resources for these purposes. In addition, resources and reserves play a very important role in the overall process of nation-building. This chapter examines the strategic resources and reserves in the Indian context. While there are various natural resources, from water to jungles to oil to mineral, for the purposes of this work, the major focus is to understand minerals as India's primary strategic resources and reserves.

It is important to mention that this chapter does not discuss these issues at a narrow empirical level with significant data analysis, but rather at a more conceptual level, where data has been referred to for the sake of situating the issue within larger contexts. For a subject like this, an assessment only based on specific data would suffer from the limitation of only being relevant in a specific context.

Context

The survival of a nation rests upon continued access to and use of natural resources. Access to water is essential for everything, from the maintenance of a healthy population to agricultural production and industrial development. Along with this, food, mineral deposits, forestry resources and oil deposits provide a socioeconomic basis for the development of a state. The crucial significance of various natural resources ensures that threats to their availability become much politicised, sparking controversy, and at times even leading to intrastate or interstate conflicts (Hamilton, 2003). This raises the question of whether every resource is strategic. The strategic value of these resources could vary from state to state, depending on their physical availability within geographical boundaries and the state's overall requirements. It is therefore important to first evaluate what the word 'strategic' means, and what the criteria would be from the state's point of view in order to consider the resources and reserves as strategic.

The word 'strategic' has different meanings under different circumstances, and there are various dictionary definitions, although generally it is associated with long-term planning. In the 21st century, 'strategic' is increasingly used in various sectors of life, from social to business, yet it is broadly still primarily associated with the military. For defence forces, 'strategic' is about the careful planning necessary to win battles, as and if they happen. Generally, for the armed forces, what is short-term, and what is going to happen (or is already happening) in the immediate future and for which the overall canvass is narrow, is known as 'tactical'.

In order to appreciate the intricacies of the strategic context, it is essential for any defence establishment to develop an ability to anticipate possible future crises, as this allows them to prepare for future wars. The strategic environment depends on various geostrategic and geopolitical factors, such as the cultural ethos, climate, economy, and geography of the state; locating the state in the current international environment; nature of industrial infrastructure; growth of technology; and the natural resources available within the state. The planning of any strategy also depends on the nature of the state's international dependence in terms of economy, technology, and resources. The terminology used to define mineral assets is divided into two major groups: Resources and Reserves.

Due to the finite nature of natural resources, states will generally try to ensure that enough reserves are available to handle any eventualities. Having theoretical geographic and geological understanding of the possibility of resource availability is insufficient, so information about quantity, type, quality, accessibility, and financial and technological capabilities to extract and process them is important.

On occasion, it has been observed that there is some misperception in the understanding of the terms 'resources' and 'reserve', as they get used interchangeably. According to the British Geological Survey (BGS, n.d.), mineral resources are defined as 'natural concentrations of minerals or, in the case of aggregates, bodies of rock that are, or may become, of potential economic interest due to their inherent properties'. There is also an economic aspect associated with it and resources are required to be present in sufficient quantities to make it of intrinsic economic interest. On occasion, the entire method of extraction from the earth becomes a trial and error process and the state needs to have the financial capabilities to take the risk that the entire process of resource extraction may not yield favourable results. Eventually, 'that part of a mineral resource, which has been fully evaluated and is deemed commercially viable to work, is called a mineral reserve' (BGS, n.d.). In addition, the scope to call a particular mineral extract from the earth or ocean surface is restricted to those minerals where the state or agency has a valid legal access (permitted reserves).

Broadly, a resource is a geological commodity that exists in both discovered and undiscovered deposits, while reserves are that subcategory of a resource that have been discovered, have a known size and utility, and can be extracted for a profit. For example, of the world's estimated oil resource of three trillion barrels, the world's reserves are estimated at about a third of that amount (CliffsNotes, 2016). Some reserves are important for militaries in the production of weapons systems and weapon delivery platforms, meaning there are certain resources and reserves which have specific utility in the designing and manufacturing processes of military infrastructure, and are therefore considered strategic. However, not all states will necessarily recognise the same resources and reserves as strategic.

Control over natural resources has been one of the key determinants of wars in the past. An early study of the causes of modern wars points out that 14 of the 20 major wars, from 1878 to 1918, had significant economic causes often related to conflicts over resources. The rise of industrialism has also led to a struggle for raw materials, such as the case of Chile hoping to secure a share in the nitrate trade. Chile took up arms against Bolivia and Peru for the control of guano mineral deposits in the War of the Pacific from 1879 to 1884 (Acemoglu et al., 2012). In recent times, the best example of conflicts over resources is the 1990 Gulf War. The United States (US) justified fighting this war by claiming that it was in line with the Carter Doctrine.[1]

Classifying resources and reserves

Mining has a long history. Since civilisation began, people have used different mining techniques to access minerals in the earth, and there is evidence indicating that people from ancient Egypt, Rome and Greece were engaged in mining. During the 1600s, miners used explosives to break up large rocks, while motorised mining tools, such as drills, came into existence much later. The industry witnessed a major change with the Industrial Revolution, and during the 1700s and 1800s, miners were assisted with better explosives and more advanced mining equipment, such as drills, lifts and steam-powered pumps (General Kinematics, 2013). The methodologies and technologies associated with mining have evolved over the centuries, and state and various other private agencies now have systems which are quick, accurate, energy-efficient and environmentally friendly.

It is important to note that 'materials' have been fundamental in the advancement of human society since prehistoric times, so much so that the system of describing the progression of human society is based on minerals and archaeological systems, such as Stone Age, Bronze Age, Iron Age, and Steel Age. Presently, various methods and systems are in place to classify mineral resources and some of them have been accepted globally. Developed nations have created reporting standards that can be used universally, and after almost two decades of efforts, specific guidelines have been set out by the Society for Mining, Metallurgy and Exploration (SME) in the US. This has helped to create an international accepted standard for mineral asset reporting, and in 1994, the Committee for Mineral Reserves International Reporting Standards (CRIRSCO) was formed. The committee is a group of representatives of organisations that are responsible for developing mineral reporting codes and guidelines in most parts of the world (Australia, Asia, Canada, Chile, Europe, South Africa, and the US). Interestingly, this group does not include important states like China, Russia and India, although these states are known to follow similar, and in some places more elaborate, classification schemes.

Regarding mineral resources, there are a few specific subcategories. An 'Inferred Resource' is one that is based on limited sampling, and reasonably assumed but limited information. Samples might include those from outcrops, trenches, pits or drill holes. An 'Indicated Resource' is one whose quantity, grade (quality), shape, size and continuity can be more confidently reported. A 'Measured Resource' represents the highest level of geologic knowledge and confidence in a resource. The resource characteristics are well-established through detailed and reliable exploration work, meaning that economic and technical factors can be more confidently applied. Mine and production planning can give more detailed estimates of economic viability.

In terms of mineral reserves, the subcategories are based on a feasibility study bias. A Reserve is Probable when economic extraction can be justified, while a Reserve is Proven when economic extraction is justified. This distinction is generally based on geologic knowledge and, as with resources, many projects include a hybrid classification, such as 'Proven and Probable' (Geology for Investors, n.d.).

Minerals and mining in India

With a population of about 1.4 billion, India is the second most populous country in the world after China, as well as the sixth largest economy in the world, with a nominal GDP of $2.45 trillion, and ranks third in GDP in terms of purchasing power parity at $9.49 trillion. (Caleb Silver, 2019) Compared to Western countries, India's GDP is highly dependent on agriculture (which accounts for 17%), although the services sector has started picking up and now accounts for 57% of the GDP, while industry contributes 26%. India recently surpassed China as the fastest growing large economy and is predicted to jump up to rank 4th on the list of the World's Top 10 Economies by 2022 (Bajpal, 2017). It is important to have this backdrop to appreciate the evolution and future of India's mining activities.

India is a nation well-endowed with natural mineral resources, ranking 4th amongst the mineral producer countries, behind China, the US and Russia, on the basis of volume of production, as per the (FICCI, 2013) Report on Mineral Production by the International Organizing Committee for the World Mining Congress. The country produces around 87 to 89 minerals, including four fuel minerals, ten metallic minerals, 49 non-metallic minerals, three atomic minerals, and 22 minor minerals, including building and other materials (Hazra, Chauhan, Gupta & Sharma, 2013). In 2011, the Indian mining industry contributed about 2.63% to the GDP, which is one of the lowest amongst the larger emerging economies, such as China (20%), Australia (8%) and Russia (14.7%) (US Geological Survey Report 2011-12). However, this contribution has not varied much over the years since 2011, although in some years the trend has actually been in a negative direction, with the contribution decreasing to approximately 2% to the GDP.

The largest portion of mining in India is coal, which accounts for almost 80%, while the remaining 20% is made up of numerous metals and other raw materials, such as gold, copper, iron, lead, bauxite, zinc and uranium. India is in the top position in the world in respect of mica and mica splitting; ranks 3rd in production of coal, barytes and chromite; 4th in iron-ore production; and 6th in bauxite and manganese. India is also 10th in respect of aluminium production (Rathi, 2015). Overall, India's mining industry is made up of a large number of small operational mines, and the average number of mines which report mineral production in India hovers around 2000, excluding minor minerals, petroleum (crude), natural gas and atomic minerals.

As per the 2017-18 Annual Report of the Ministry of Mines, there has been roughly an 8-12% increase in the production of minerals every year, although for financial year 2018 it was 13%, with minerals worth Rs 1.13 lakh crore produced in FY18 (Ministry of Mines, 2018). The number of small operational mines which reported mineral output in the country, excluding atomic, fuel and minor minerals, was 1,531 in 2017-18. There are around 200 mines each in Tamil Nadu, Madhya Pradesh and Gujarat, but Rajasthan is in the leading position in terms of estimated value of mineral production in the country, with a 20.26% share in the national output, followed by Odisha with 17.77% (*The Economic Times*, 2018).

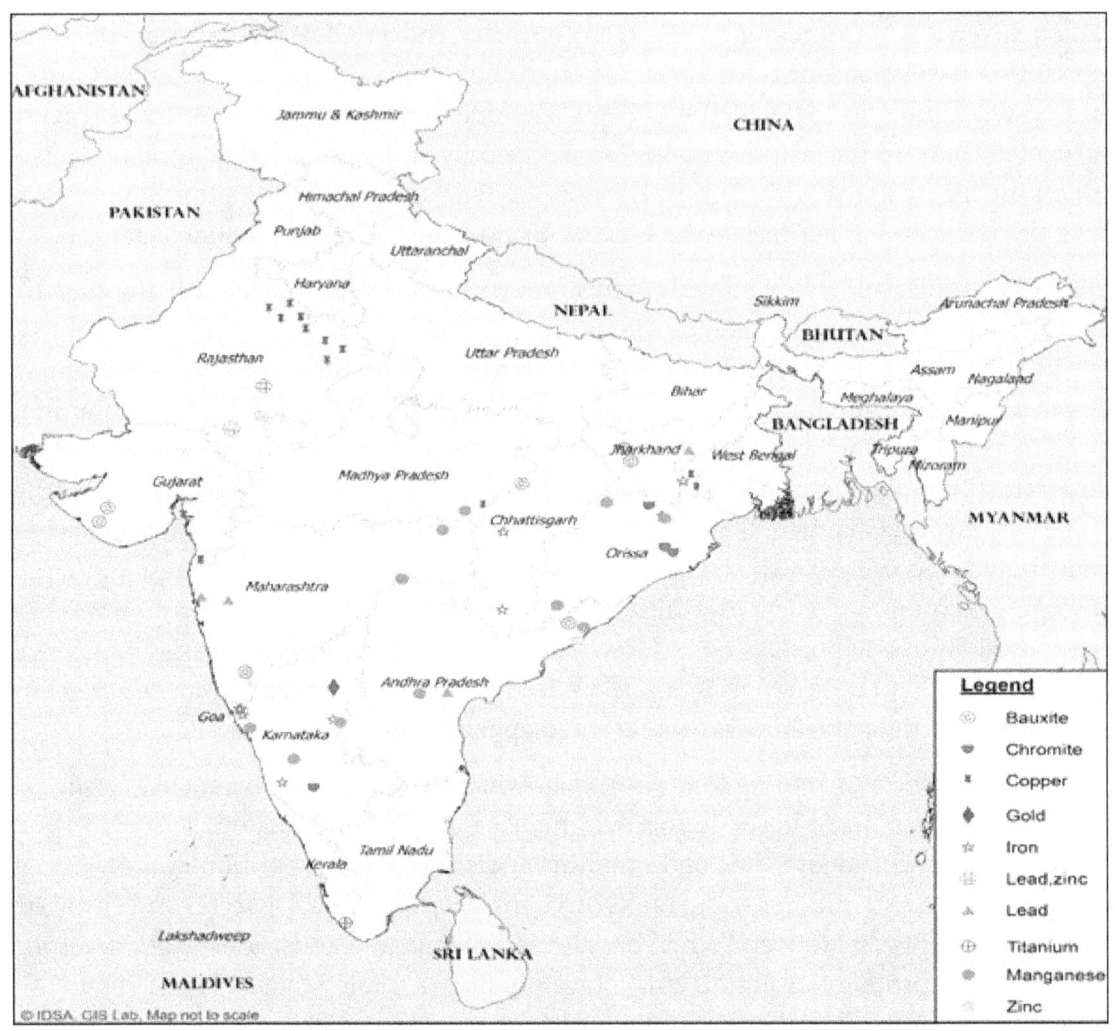

FIGURE 12.1 India's mineral resources

Strategic resources

The first attempt to define materials/minerals/resources as 'strategic' was made by the US Army and Navy Munitions Board following World War I. Two classifications were identified: strategic materials, and critical materials. Strategic materials were distinguished by their necessity for national defence, their high degree of importance in wartime, and the need for strict conservation and distribution control. Critical materials were considered less essential and more readily available domestically, requiring some degree of conservation (Kessel, 1990:13-14). However, this term is seldom used. Broadly, strategic materials could be defined as (Weston, 1984:1):

- The materials needed to supply the military, industrial and essential civilian needs of a state during a national emergency; and
- The materials not found or produced in sufficient quantities to meet such needs of the state.

It is difficult to have a universal definition of strategic resources, as what is strategic to one state may not be strategic for another, and in some instances, all the resources required for the strategic industry of a particular state may be available to them in abundance. Along with this, the strategic quotient in respect of the military hardware could vary from state to state. For example, states with nuclear weapons capabilities could have specific requirements which may not be required by other states. Similarly, the equipment used for the extraction of strategic resources from the earth or ocean beds require energy for their operations, meaning that obtaining these resources involves a dependency on other resources, like water, coal, gas, oil, etc. Thus, individual states have their own outlook regarding the necessity of strategic materials.

The defence industry requires strategic materials, and this usually caters for three aspects: weapons platforms (aircrafts, ships, submarines, tanks, etc.); weapons and ammunition (guns, bullets, bombs, missile, etc.); and equipment (radars, sonars, staircases, batteries, tents, functional food, etc.). A state equips its defence industry based on the type of warfare that their forces are envisaged to be engaged in, like mountain warfare, desert warfare, amphibious operations, etc. Some of the major sectors of the defence industry are the aerospace industry, shipbuilding industry, tank manufacturing, and the missile industry, and the resources required in the production of each of these could vary depending on the situation and necessity. Some of these could be strategic resources, and it would be the duty of the state to ensure the necessary supply of such resources.

However, it would be incorrect to consider the defence industry as the only strategic industry, as nuclear, space, civilian aircraft manufacturing, and railway equipment manufacturing could also be strategic for the state. Amongst these, the nuclear industry has significant strategic significance in terms of both the defence and energy industries, and the sources of nuclear energy are heavy metals such as uranium, thorium, radium, plutonium and lithium. Uranium is the most important of these, and its main ores are pitchblende, uranite, samarskite, and thorianite.

There are some important geographical areas of uranium deposits around the world, but the geographical distribution of thorium is much more restricted. The main ores of thorium are monazite, allanite and thorianite. Beryllium (obtained from beryl, which is found in association with feldspar and mica in pegmatites), zirnium (found in zircon in beach sands) and ilimenite (found in a concentrated form in beach sands) are other important nuclear minerals (Minerals Knowledge, 2009). All these minerals or resources have specific qualities and are not easily available and are therefore considered very important strategic resources and reserves. The nature and requirements of the nuclear industry are unique, and the associated geopolitical aspects are distinctive in nature. However, this chapter will not be discussing this further as the core focus is not on atomic elements.

India's strategic mineral resources

Geographically, India is a unique country, as it covers a wide range of terrains, including rain forests, deserts, and snow-capped mountain ridges, and is enclosed by the disaster-prone Himalayan mountain ranges to its north and northeast. The country has a land frontier of 15,200 km, a coastline of 7,516.6 km, and an exclusive economic zone of 2.2million km². Thus, the Indian defence forces have the task of guarding various types of land and sea borders, as well as a vast airspace, and are required to remain prepared to engage in both conventional and nuclear warfare. Worldwide, India currently has the 3rd largest military, is the 6th biggest defence spender, and is also one of the largest importers of conventional defence equipment, spending around 30% of its total defence budget on capital acquisitions, while 60% of defence-related requirements are currently met through imports (Make In India, 2017).

For many decades, India's premier defence research organisation has been the Defence Research and Development Organization (DRDO), which is responsible for India's entire missile programme. Defence Public Sector Units (DPSUs) are an integral part of India's defence production architecture, and account for more than 65% of the total output, with an annual production value of around US$4 billion. The private sector also plays a significant role in the defence industry as subcontractors and ancillary industry, and are often the suppliers of raw materials, semi-finished products, parts and components to DPSUs, ordnance factories, base workshops of the army, base repair depots of the air force, the dockyards of the navy, etc. Foreign companies account for the majority of procurement from the private sector in India, with approximately 60% of Indian defence procurement coming from overseas sources (based on various reports available in the public domain) (India – Defense, 2018). Thus, despite defence hardware having a significant import component, there is still an appreciable dependence on local industry, both public and private.

No country is expected to officially declare which resources it considers strategic, and while there are no direct pointers to identify what India considers strategic in terms of materials, a broad estimation could be made based on available information about the administration of minerals in the country and the technological requirements of a few strategic sectors. However, is also important to know which materials are in short supply, about the nature of the supply route of such materials, and about the level of dependence on foreign agencies.

As discussed earlier, the strategic relevance of resources could be subjective and vary from state to state. However, the general processes of weapons and platforms development remain similar, regardless of the agency, and the mineral/materials requirements of the defence industry are predominantly the same: antimony, molybdenum, borates, nickel, chromium, rare earths, cobalt, silver, copper, titanium, diamond, tungsten, germanium, vanadium, lithium and zinc.

These materials have been identified based on various references made to them in the literature, and on discussions with scientists, the academic community, military officials and policymakers. However, the list is not exhaustive, and different defence industries could have their own lists based on their requirements. Based on open-source information, it could be safe to assume that the above-mentioned minerals have strategic relevance for India. The following section presents some details about some of these in the context of India (Lele & Bhardwaj, 2014:83-88).

- **Antimony (Sb):** The antimony resources in India are reported to be inferior in quality, and the country currently does not produce antimony, with the entire demand being met through imports.

- **Borates:** Borax is not produced in India, as economically workable deposits have not been established so far, and all domestic need is met through imports of raw borax.

- **Cobalt (Co):** Associated mainly with copper, nickel and arsenic oxide, cobalt is an important strategic mineral with wide usage and unique properties. Most of the cobalt in India is recovered during copper and nickel processing as there is no production of cobalt from indigenous ores. The remaining demand for refined cobalt is met through imports.

- **Fluorite (CaF_2):** The production of fluorite is scarce in the country and mainly fulfilled as a by-product in phosphoric acid production during the processing of phosphate rock. However, the chemical and aluminium industry requires a more refined and purified form; hence, the demand is solely met by imports. The production of fluorite is limited in India, and grades of fluorite produced do not meet the specifications of the chemical industry, which is the biggest user of fluorite, meaning that India will remain dependent on imports owing to both quality and quantity issues.

- **Molybdenum (Mo):** Molybdenite (MoS2) is the principle ore of molybdenum and usually extracted as a by-product of copper mining. The principle use of molybdenum is in stainless steel and in chemicals/catalysts. The global and domestic demand is known to be high as considerable growth in super alloys and the stainless-steel sector is taking place, and molybdenum demand in India is mostly met by imports.

- **Nickel (Ni):** Nickel is one of the most important elements that enhances the properties of iron manifold and makes products hard; it is used in stainless steel production. There is no primary source of nickel production in India; however, nickel is recovered as nickel sulphate crystals, a by-product obtained during copper production. Most of the domestic demand is met by processing alloys and scraps, with the remaining demand met by imports.

- **Selenium (Se):** Selenium gets recovered as a by-product during copper, lead-zinc, gold and platinum ore processing; India does not have any primary source available for extraction.

- **Tungsten (W):** Tungsten is an important strategic mineral in India owing to its usage in high-end technology industries. India meets the demand mainly by imports and recycling of alloys and scrap. India possibly has technological constraints to extraction, and hence is known to be depending more on imports.

India's import reliance

Import dependency is not uncommon, and generally occurs for two reasons: minerals which are not physically available within the geographical area of that state; and minerals which are available in large deposits of that state but whose import is more economical than excavation and processing. For some minerals, India's import-dependence is total, while for others it is partial. Coal and oil are two resources where India has significant import-dependency, and there are a few other areas where the dependence on imports is significant, and strategic minerals is one such area. Thus, dependency management is a significant (and serious) global business for strategic decision-makers.

India primarily relies on China, Brazil, the Democratic Republic of Congo (DRC), Russia, Australia, and the US for its imports. India has had an excellent relationship with Russia for many decades, but because of India's nuclear policies, the Indo-US relationship has witnessed various ups and downs in the past. India fought a war with China in 1962, although there has been significant harmonisation in the relationship has been witnessed in recent years. Of the six states mentioned above, India is most dependent on the DRC for mineral imports, yet the DRC is the country with the most political turbulence, experiencing various civil wars. When discussing India's bilateral relations, and specifically in the case of DRC, attention must be paid to the internal situation in the country, as unsettled political conditions and an ongoing conflict would obviously impact the state's exports.

Over the years, India has signed various bilateral arrangements to purchase minerals from a number of African states, Australia, Brazil, China and the US. With some states, working groups in the fields of metallurgy and the mining sector have been established, and there are also some agreements on cooperation in the transfer of technology.

Hazards for India's mining sector

For any industry, the going cannot be always smooth and the same is true of India's mining sector, which faces various societal, political, financial, and technological hazards. While the mining sector caters to the demands of a wide range of industries, there are some peculiar needs of the defence industry which need to be satisfied. It is therefore to be expected that both industries find ways to ensure that these routine hazards do not impact the need for strategic materials by the defence industry.

The environmental impact of mining is a universal problem, to which there is no immediate direct solution. The available options are a mix of best practices accepted and implemented at global level, some of which would require local geography-based actions. Depending on the nature of the site and activity undertaken, mining operations can leave a temporary or permanent impact on the surrounding environment, including water pollution, damage to flora and fauna, adverse effects on agriculture (e.g. infertile soil), air pollution leading to respiratory diseases in humans, and impacting the survival of wildlife. The environmental challenges bring various other issues to the fore as well, such as the management, rehabilitation, and legislation on environmental protection and biodiversity conservation, issues related to human rights violations, and controls on excessive use of water in various mining activities.

All these issues are applicable in some form or another to India, which currently has a huge cache of mineral resources and a very active mining industry. There is a significant amount of private and some foreign investment into this sector, and successive Indian governments have kept the industry thriving, as the growth of the country is heavily dependent upon its performance.

India has a significant amount of open pit mining, a method in which extraction of a mineral is done near the surface, creating large open pits. The primary reason for using this mining methodology is its relatively low cost-extraction ratio. Unlike underground mining methods, opencast mining does not require costly structural supports and extraction technologies, and it is comparatively safer, meaning that companies save on the cost of expensive insurance premiums. However, it does present huge social and environmental challenges. Removal of earth contributes to soil erosion, land degradation and the destruction of natural habitats, while the chemicals used in extraction mix with water during the rainy season and end up polluting underground water reserves.

Contaminants mixed into the soil lead to land degradation, and the dust generated by the chemicals used in the mining lead to chronic human health issues, and a lasting impact on biodiversity.

Another hazard associated with mining is illegal mining, which has been a global phenomenon for many decades, and is prevalent around the world, including in India, where it mostly takes place in low-grade areas of mining sites. Normally, it is expected that the material which gets mined here cannot be strategic material, and from a defence industry point of view, such activity may not have any significant impact.

The threat from Naxalism could be considered as one of the major dangers for India's mining industry. Naxalism is a violent movement based on Maoist ideology, which since 1967 has been one of the most significant internal threats faced by the Indian State. For some years, there have been mineral-rich areas are under the control of the Naxalites, which is impacting on the growth of the mining industry in some parts of India.

The map in Figure 12.2 gives a broad indication of the regions where the problem is prevalent and shows that various deposits of strategic materials are found in Naxal-affected areas. The Indian state needs to decide their policies regarding the excavation of minerals like tungsten and manganese, factoring in the threat from Naxalism.

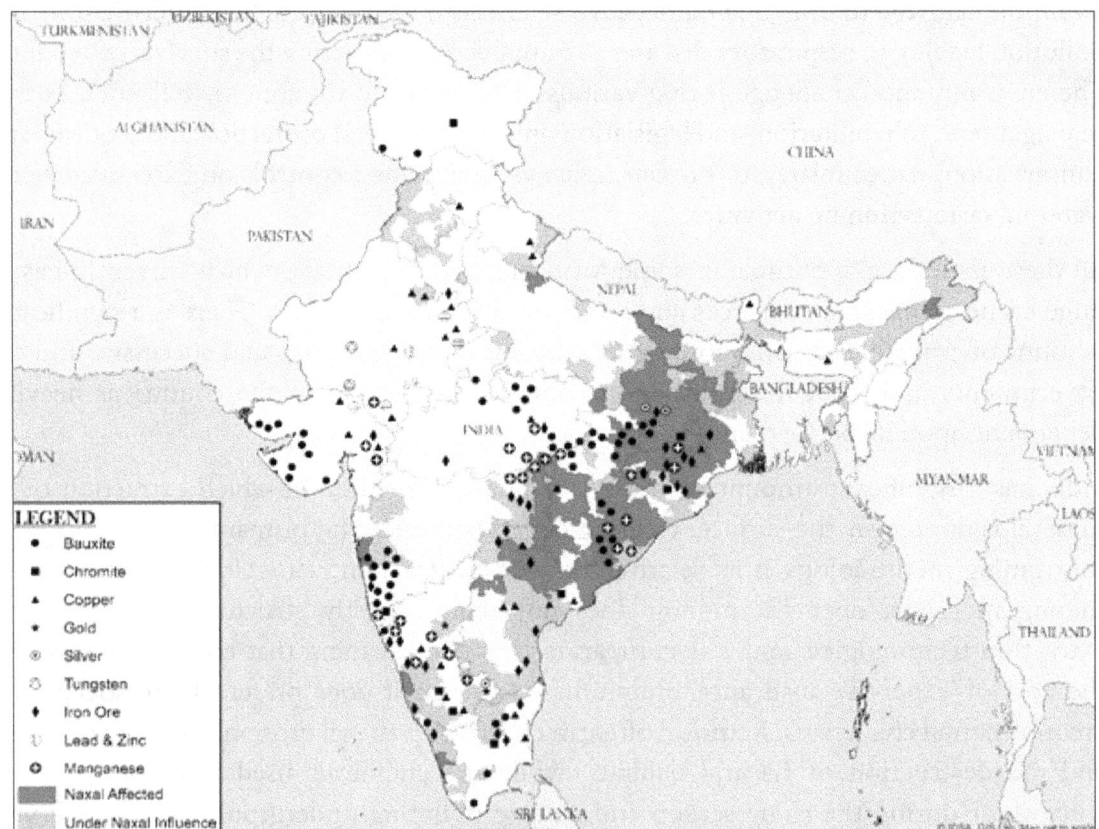

FIGURE 12.2 Naxal-prone areas, superimposed on areas with rich mineral and resource deposits

Rare Earth Elements and India

Rare Earth Elements (REEs) or Rare Earth Materials (REMs) are normally discussed as a separate category to strategic materials, owing to their specific qualities and importance for the defence industry. Rare earths are a set of 17 elements at the bottom of the periodic table used in a variety of renewable energy and defence applications, including precision-guided munitions, wind turbines, unmanned aerial vehicles, hybrid vehicles and tactical wheeled vehicles (Snow, Pelletier & Eddy, 2012). REEs exhibit a range of special properties which are used in many modern and 'green' technologies. The International Union of Pure and Applied Chemistry defines the Rare Earth Elements as the 15 lanthanides together with yttrium and scandium (Department of Natural Resources and Mines, 2014).

REEs generally fall into one of two categories: Light Rare Earth Elements (LREEs) and Heavy Rare Earth Elements (HREEs), with varying degrees of use and demand. REE mineral deposits are usually rich in either LREEs or HREEs, but rarely contain both in significant quantities. The Heavy Rare Earths are Europium (Eu), Gadolinium (Gd), Terbium (Tb), Dysprosium (Dy), Holmium (Ho), Erbium (Er), Thulium (Tm), Ytterbium (Yb), Lutetium (Lu) and Yttrium (Y). The Light Rare Earths are Lanthanum (La), Cerium (Ce), Praseodymium (Pr), Neodymium (Nd) and Samarium (Sm).

Interestingly, India was one of the early investors in the area of REE, establishing Indian Rare Earths Ltd. in 1950, immediately after independence from British colonial rule. This profit-making organisation has four production plants, but due to the limited natural availability of REEs, India has not achieved much in this field. Similarly, a cost benefit analysis indicated that it would be better to import these materials from China than to produce them, which has also been the approach of a number of other states, which found that making investments to extract these materials from the earth was very costly. This has made China the sole leader for doing business in REEs.

During the last few decades, with the increasing impact of industrialisation and the growth of the domestic defence industry, India has started realising the necessity of REEs and is making investments accordingly. However, some believe that India's policies are not favourable for doing business. Significant rare earths minerals found in India include ilmenite, sillimanite, garnet, zircon, monazite and rutile, collectively called Beach Sand Minerals (BSM), and India has almost 35% of the world's total BSM deposits. Their importance lies in their unique electronic, optical and magnetic characteristics, which cannot be matched by any other metal or synthetic substitute. From 1998 to 2006, India took these minerals off the prescribed substances list, but recently added them again. The following diagram provides details about REE deposits in India.

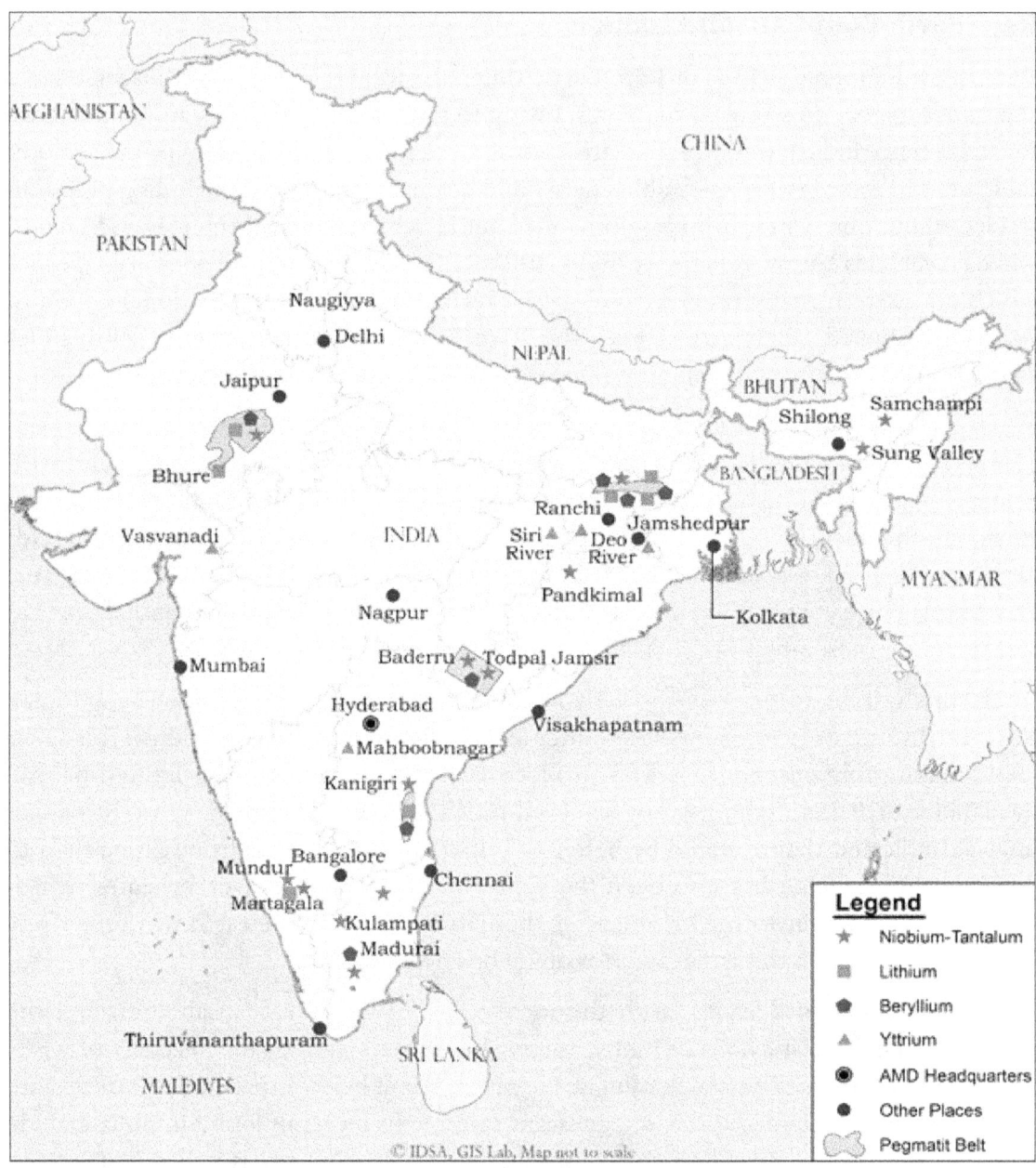

FIGURE 12.3 Rare Metal and Rare Earth deposits in India

Conclusion

India is emerging as one of the major economies of the world and sees industrialisation as key for growth. Numerous industries are included in this, one of which is the defence industry, while various scientific laboratories that operate in India require a range of resources for their activities. Apart from energy and water resources, the resources of critical importance are materials/minerals.

In recent times, India's need for strategic materials has been growing, owing to its investments in the nuclear, aerospace, and defence sectors, and various assessments indicate that cobalt, germanium, molybdenum and tungsten could be the strategic minerals in higher risk brackets for India. It is not only important for India to ensure the requisite and timely supplies of such materials, but there is also a need to look for suitable alternatives. For this purpose, studies could be undertaken to explore the possibilities of devising specific material substitution strategies.

Every Indian industry and research, development and innovation structure demand different types of minerals. With the introduction of programmes like 'Make in India', India allowing 100% foreign direct investment (FDI) in the defence sector, and foreign suppliers offering technology development as part of an 'offset' strategy, the demand for materials by the strategic industry is expected to grow significantly in the future. However, even today there is a significant import-dependence for procurement of these materials, and there is a need to find ways to reduce this dependence.

India needs to develop a mechanism to undertake improvements in existing mineral processing and extraction methods, and needs to make substantial investments for such purposes, keeping the long-term interests of the country in mind. Unfortunately, India is not able to get free access to the mineral deposits within its own country, owing to domestic factors like the Naxal issue, meaning that innovative solutions are required to ensure that deposits within the country are fully exploited. Within the country, there is a need to encourage research institutions to innovate new minerals, and to find correct and cost-effective alternatives to existing materials. It is also necessary to establish a dedicated facility for strategic mineral research, including finding efficient methods for recycling.

With nature being more favourable to them, some states are in advantageous positions with regards to ownership of strategic materials, which has led to dominance by interest groups, and some hoarding. The REE-dependency of various states on China has been one of the most hotly discussed subjects globally, and considering the on-off nature of the India-China relationship, it is important for India to find alternative strategies to decrease their dependence on China. This could be regarded as both a challenge and an opportunity. India many not be as blessed as China in terms of natural deposits of REE, but there is a possibility for India to make appropriate investments in this sector, particularly by undertaking deep sea mining.

India also needs to attract more significant private industry, and this requires a simple and transparent mechanism with clear and enforceable timelines to grant mining permissions and/or other related activities. In this, the state needs to enable the private industry to do business in various strategic fields.

Strategic materials are key components of resource geopolitics. India needs to develop a multipronged approach to cater for their requirements in terms of strategic materials, and should invest in finding correct substitutions, recycling strategic materials, researching new materials, and finding innovative solutions to reduce the dependence on specific strategic materials.

Notes

1. The Carter Doctrine was a policy proclaimed by US President Carter in his State of the Union Address on 23 January 1980, which stated that the US would use military force, if necessary, to defend its national interests in the Persian Gulf region. The doctrine was a response to the threat posed by Soviet troops in Afghanistan to the free movement of Middle East oil.

References

Akshay, K.V.L. 2016. 'India not realising potential of rare earth industry'. *The Economics Times*, 19 October.

Bajpai, P. 2017. *The World's Top 10 Economies*. 7 July. https://bit.ly/330K2vC [Accessed 5 September 2018].

British Geological Survey. n.d. *What is the difference between resources and reserves?* https://bit.ly/32Zve0p [Accessed 12 April 2018].

Caleb Silver. 2019. Top 20 Economies in the World. 7 June. https://bit.ly/3cQHHbk [Accessed 6 June 2019].

Cliffsnotes. 2016. Resources and reserves. https://bit.ly/38CPRQZ [Accessed 15 April 2018].

Department of Natural Resources and Mines (DNRM). 2014. *Heavy Rare Earth Elements (HREE) opportunities in Queensland*. Queensland: Geological Survey of Queensland.

FICCI Mines and Minerals Davison. *Non-Fuel Minerals, A report by FICCI Mines and Metals Division*. https://bit.ly/2wYRhIp, p. 9 [Accessed 5 April 2019].

General Kinematics. 2013. *A Brief History of Mining: The Advancement of Mining Techniques and Technology*. https://bit.ly/3aDW4O2 [Accessed 10 July 2018].

Geology for Investors. n.d. *Classification of Mineral Resources and Reserves*. https://bit.ly/38y67mn [Accessed 2 July 2018].

Golosov, D.A.M., Tsyvinski, A. & Yared, P. 2012. A Dynamic Theory of Resource Wars. *The Quarterly Journal of Economics*, 127(1):283-331. https://doi.org/10.1093/qje/qjr048

Hamilton, A. 2003. Resource Wars and the Politics of Abundance and Scarcity. *Dialogue*, 1(3):27-38.

Hazra, A.K., Chauhan, S.B.S., Gupta, A. & Sharma, E. 2013. *Development of Indian Mining Industry – The Way Forward*. New Delhi: Federation of Indian Chambers of Commerce & Industry (FICCI).

India – Defense. 2018. International Trade Administration. 10 October. https://bit.ly/3aAiXC4 [Accessed 6 June 2018].

Kessel, K.A. 1990. *Strategic Minerals: U.S. Alternatives*. Washington, DC: National Defence University Press. https://doi.org/10.21236/ADA229895

Lele, A. & Bhardwaj, P. 2014. *Strategic Materials: A Resource Challenge for India*. New Delhi, India: Pentagon Press.

Make In India. 2017. Defence Manufacturing Sector, Achievements Report. https://bit.ly/2wDdw6Q [Accessed 7 September 2018].

Minerals Knowledge. 2009. *Nuclear Minerals*. https://bit.ly/2TvQCal [Accessed 24 July 2018].

Ministry of Mines. 2018. *Annual Report 2017-18*. https://bit.ly/3cFWfKK [Accessed 18 February 2019].

Rathi, M. 2015. *A brief report on mining and minerals industry in India*. New Delhi: Corporate Catalyst.

Snow, J., Pelletier, P. & Eddy, S. 2012. *The value of REEs*. Canada: IAMGOLD Corporation.

Weston, R. 1984. *Strategic Materials*. New Jersey: Rowman & Allanheld.

The Economic Times. 2018. 'India produces minerals worth Rs 1.13 lakh cr in FY18'. 24 June. https://bit.ly/32Y1VLI [Accessed 6 May 2019].

13

India's Security Strategy
Beyond deliberate ambiguity?

Shrikant Paranjpe

Framework

A national security policy that seeks to protect a nation's interests presents an interplay between two sets of issues: the technical and political issues, and capability and intent issues. The technical dimension covers material sources of national power that span geopolitical, economic, technological and other aspects, including the domestic and international linkages that each of these issues would have. The political issues work at three levels: the domestic political environment, its linkage with the international scenario, and the overall international situation. The political component is based on the principle of the 'primacy of the political'. This principle suggests that: (a) political order has primacy over all other societal associations in the sense that ordered patterns of relationships between social forms depend upon the political order, and is function is therefore to preserve social order; and (b) the performance of this political function presupposes that the good which the political order aims at cannot be identified with any specific interest, but rather with the good of the whole.

The non-material sources of national power are factored into the political dimension of the state. While the technical dimensions of security would determine the capability of a state, it is the political dimension that determines intent. Policy is thus an interplay between capability and intent, a product of matching the two with a goal that seeks to address the national interests of the state. The movement from policy to strategy is from a predominantly political to an executive domain. Policy is primarily a political statement, while strategy seeks its implementation in real terms, with the most efficient use of available means to accomplish the chosen ends. Such a strategy may or may not be spelt out in detail; it is the overall policy that would provide the road map for understanding the strategy of that state. On the other hand, doctrine is the nuts and bolts of strategy, targeting specific sectors (like nuclear, space, internal security, etc.) to provide a road map for the execution of strategy.

National interest is defined within the context of the core values of a nation, as identified by the Constitution: as being a product of history (civilisation); the value systems of the polity and economy; and the society and culture. The aspects which determine the core values are the geography, geopolitics, and the political, economic and socio-cultural context.

The origins of the concept of national security can be found in the historical formulations of national interest. As Walter Lippmann put it, 'a nation has security when it does not have to sacrifice its legitimate national interests to avoid a war, and is able, if challenged to maintain them by war' (Baylis, Smith & Owens, 2008:229). Arnold Wolfers argues that 'security, in an objective sense measures the absence of threats to acquired values, in a subjective sense, the absence of fear that such values will be attacked' (Baylis, Smith & Owens, 2008:229), and this was the dominant theme of national security through most of the Cold War years. The term 'security' was deemed to belong to the armed forces, which were entrusted with protecting the national interests of a state. National interest was also closely linked to security, defined as defence of a nation's borders. As an organising concept in international relations, national security provides us with several advantages. It helps us to focus on common elements and uniformities in the external policies of all nations, and is in a sense the base on which foreign policies of nations are structured. Secondly, it helps us to focus on the underlying unity of internal and external activities of the state. It recognises that external behaviour of states is an integral part of the total behaviour of the state, and that internal and external security are essentially interlinked.

India

The Estimates Committee of the Indian Parliament, in its 19th Report on the Ministry of Defence, raised some crucial questions about India's defence policy. In its statement to the Committee, the Ministry of Defence explained that India's defence policy has essentially been to defend the territory, sovereignty, and freedom of the country, while the Estimates Committee considered this an oversimplification. It felt that India should have a national security doctrine which not only takes a long-term view of the country's security requirements but also looks into problems of internal security (Estimates Committee, 1992). Although the Indian National Security Council (NSC) was established in 1999, the Indian government has not yet presented an official document that spells out a National Security Strategy for India. Amongst the various reasons given for such a failure is a possible lack of political consensus on national security issues. It has been argued that there are differing perceptions of the threats India faces from its neighbours; ideological differences; different world views held by political parties regarding the current global situation; and equally complex and conflicting arguments about various internal security challenges.

However, the stand taken by the political establishment regarding articulation of a national security strategy has, in a sense, been consistent. In a reply to the Standing Committee on Defence (1995-96) in the Tenth Lok Sabha, the Defence Secretary argued that (Kanwal, 2017:2-3):

> ...there is a policy; the only thing is that it is not written down as a separate document and published as such ... As a matter of policy we have not published such a document and the Government has not been in favour of publishing a separate document ... Non-publication of the document does not mean in any way non-existence of policy.

Replying to the debate on the Demands for Grants of the Ministry of Defence on 10 May 1995, Prime Minister P.V. Narsimha Rao, who was also the Defence Minister, stated (Kanwal, 2017:2-3):

> We do not have a document called India's National Defence Policy. But we have got several guidelines which are followed, strictly followed and observed ... This policy is not merely rigid in the sense that it has been written down, but these are the guidelines, these are the objectives, these are the matters which are always kept in view while conducting our defence policy.

Similarly, the Ministry of External Affairs (MEA), in its Annual Report for 1998-99, stated:

> India's external relations were guided by well-established principles. These have formed the basis of our foreign policy for decades. They enjoy a broad national consensus, thus providing a strong foundation of stability and continuity. We view foreign policy as an integral part of the larger effort of building the nation's capabilities: through economic development, strengthening social well-being and the quality of life and of protecting India's sovereignty, territorial integrity and security, not only in its defence and economic aspects, but in the widest strategic sense of the term.

In April 2018, the government formed a new integrated institutional mechanism called the Defence Planning Committee (DPC), under the chairmanship of the National Security Advisor. This committee would consist of the Chairman Chiefs of Staff Committee, the three Service Chiefs, Defence Secretary, Foreign Secretary and Secretary (Expenditure) Finance Ministry. There would be subcommittees on Policy and Strategy, Plans and Capability Development, Defence Diplomacy, and Defence manufacturing Ecosystem. The integration of defence, foreign policy and finance would ensure an integrated approach to dealing with issues of national security. The DPC is expected to prepare a draft national security strategy, along with undertaking a strategic defence review (Behera, 2018).

A national security strategy for India would be based on India's core values, its principles, a clear assessment of its interests, and a determination to tackle the challenges that the country could face. An understanding of world affairs, internal security, and territorial integrity have always been over-riding priorities in India's strategic perspectives and these, along with its approach to peace and development, constitute the 'governing image' of India's policies. However, Indian security thinking has long been criticised for being abstract, rather than concrete.

Consequently, there is no spelling out of a national security strategy in terms of specific threats and possible ways to address them. It has been argued that a national security strategy normally provides a statement of objectives, an appreciation of the global, regional and domestic security environment, an assessment of the country's capabilities, and the approach to be taken at various levels to address these issues. It is true that there has been a distinct reluctance by India to present a clear-cut strategic doctrine and articulate the same in terms of policy. However, as was argued by the then Prime Minister, India has several guidelines which are followed and observed.

These goals and objectives have been clearly spelt out in the Indian Constitution.[1] Various statements made by the government at different times, as well as the annual reports of the concerned ministries, provide an appreciation of the security environment, an assessment of capabilities, and the approaches to be taken to address any issues. This article argues that the distinct reluctance on the part of India to present a clear-cut strategic doctrine and articulate the same in terms of policy stems from a belief in the utility of a deliberate ambiguity, and not from a lack of strategic culture, as George Tanham would have us believe (1992).

It is in this context that this article seeks to present an understanding of India's security strategy as it has evolved over the years, the challenges and issues faced, and the methods applied to address them.

Goals

To understand Indian security strategy, it is necessary to examine the sources that contributed to the evolution of India's strategic culture. India started its focus on history in the age of Indian nationalism in the 19th century. It was the first systematic effort to identify the concept of 'India' and seek historical references to present the country as an entity. One can flag three periods of history in which India was an entity with relatively defined territories within the geopolitical frontiers of modern-day South Asia. The first was the period of Ashoka (273-232 BCE), the second was the Mughal Empire during the reign of Akbar (1556-1605 CE) and the third the Maratha Peshwa empire (1798 CE). This South Asia lies between Afghanistan in the west and Myanmar in the east, south of the

Himalayas, covering the Indo-Gangetic plains in the north and the Deccan plateau of Central India with a peninsular coastline.

The Peace dimension of Hinduism was presented in the tenets of *Kshma* (forbearance) and *Vasudhaiva Kutumbakam* (the world is but one family), while Indian nationalists accept both Ashoka and Akbar as symbols of tolerance and as 'Indian'. Alongside this comes another Hindu tenet: *Sarva Dharma Samabhava* (peaceful coexistence amongst all religions).[2] The ancient Indian cultural legacy has been used as a base for a peace discourse in India.

The vision that the freedom struggle and post-independence India sought to project through the Nehru years (1947-1964) rested on ideological precepts such as anti-imperialism, liberal internationalism, and Gandhism (Power, 1969:22). At a theoretical level, the Indian stand was closer to the liberal institutionalists who accepted the key assumptions of realism, like the utility of military power, but at the same time insisted upon the utility of institutions as a framework for cooperation (Baylis, 1997:200-202). The anti-imperialist stance was a direct product of the colonial experience and the need to formulate an independent world view, while liberal internationalism drew from those who were at the core of the freedom struggle. In the Cold War years, neutralism represented India's desire to build a peaceful and prosperous society that was based on justice and equality and fostered all-round development. During the colonial period, it manifested itself in the desire to keep away from extra-regional hegemonic aspirations.

The fundamental question which India asks herself is not how to maintain security in a state of anarchy in international relations. Rather, the question is: how is peace maintained in a society of nation-states? The Indian approach, therefore, takes a global/international perspective of security, instead of a national perspective focusing on the problem of survival of the nation-state. It revolves around two fundamental principles/dimensions: one, the recognition that in any conflict situation, the roots of conflict need to be tackled; and two, conflict needs to be resolved without recourse to violence (Appadorai, 1969:111-117). The first is a long-term perspective and includes the social, political, and economic aspects of any conflict. It presumes that conflicts are the product of tensions arising from social, political, and economic issues that ultimately escalate into military and armed conflict. The latter is a more short-term view that looks at the pacific settlement of disputes.

The trend of revisionism emanates from a strong cultural tradition that called for a better world order and the innate ability of the Indian civilisation to bring about this change in society. The belief that the current world order is hegemonic and needs to change to provide welfare for the masses lead India to take a revisionist position in world affairs. This position has manifested itself in a variety of ways in terms of political policy in independent India.

A study of India's security strategy would have to focus on the following areas:

1. Military-security and strategic compulsions, looking at conventional and new security threats to India emanating from a changing strategic environment;
2. Politico-diplomatic issues;
3. Changes in science and technology the use of nuclear, space, and electronics technologies;
4. The economics of defence; and
5. Internal security, as the balance between external and internal security concerns is key to a national security policy.

The Cold War years

During the early years of Independence, India's security strategy followed two main trends: the first represented India's urge to retain newly won independence while upholding its peace policy; the second reflected the application of these principles in the context of building regional solidarity and the spread of regionalism. However, regionalism never became a fundamental concern of Asian states. Rather, interstate conflicts caused by unsettled boundaries, the existence of large groups of minorities, clashes between elites, and the onset of the Cold War in Asia with the Korean War (1950-1953) were some of the more serious obstacles.

From the Bandung Conference (1955) onwards, there was a slow shift towards a development of a neutralist policy that addressed the global concerns of the Cold War conflict, and the fundamental tenets of peace and independence were to become the foundations of the new non-aligned policy. The security dimensions of the non-aligned approach drew on these basic tenets and ensured that countries focused on the fundamentals of national interest, as defined by the notions of peace and independence, thereby structuring security strategies to achieve these goals. Such a perspective of non-alignment viewed the Cold War as the context within which definitions of interest had to be articulated (Subrahmanyam, 1988:250), ensuring the continued validity of non-alignment as a security strategy in the days of the Cold War and the period of détente. However, the post-Soviet scenario has raised new questions about this approach that need to be discussed further.

Until the India-China border war in 1962, there was very little debate on a national security strategy in India. This was mainly because of an apparent lack of expertise, and the success of Nehru's non-aligned policy. However, unlike during the Nehru phase, the post-Nehru debates appeared to focus more on power approaches to security policy. These debates were to remain within the broad parameters of international relations, except when they discussed defence matters in a technical sense or reflected on the experiences of the 1962 and 1965 wars (Rana & Subrahmanyam, 1988; Kavic, 1960; Khera; 1968; Thomas, 1978; Rao, 1970; Smith, 1994). It must be noted, however, that the focus of most of the debates remained issue-based or sectoral in nature, and rarely covered overall security policy. Rana describes the discussion on security policy in India as mainly 'debating literature' (1988:31). However, it is necessary to note some diverse perspectives on defence policy. Unlike Thomas (1978), who identifies political factors as determinants of policy, Kavic (1960) tends to include the armed forces as a strong influence on policymaking.

One can identify five distinct phases in the development of Indian strategic thinking on its security policies (see also Table 13.1). The first is the period from independence until the 1962 conflict with China, when the dominant trend was 'defence through diplomacy'. The second began with a re-armament programme and the recognition that defence through military preparedness would be necessary for national security. This phase saw the eventual crystallisation of a South Asian-centric perception of India's power status, as well as a shift towards problems of internal security. The third phase began with the disintegration of the Soviet Union, and it was in this period that the overt ideological rationale of revisionism started to give way, leading to a more realist frame of reference with a willingness to strike up a security dialogue with the United States (US). The fourth phase was a continuation of the post-1991 framework that saw further application of the 'realist' posture that had come to dominate India's understanding of its national interest. This manifested in the decision to begin developing nuclear weapons capability in 1998, and the signing of the Indo-US Civil Nuclear Cooperation Agreement (2008). The fifth phase also saw efforts at diversifying and expanding India's security footprint.

Indian security strategy during the Nehru years rested on his model of development, and the policy of defence through development. In essence, this approach accepted the logic of defence through diplomacy, and developed a security framework that had its roots in politico-diplomatic activities and the process of modernisation through industrial development. Thus, the key to security was seen as a long-term strategy of self-reliance through development. However, it was the 1962 war that brought about a change in these perceptions, with a direct linkage being sought between defence capability and politics. The post-1962 Reports of the Ministry of Defence reflected this change, acknowledging the need for a long-term view of defence planning to tackle tensions across the border, although the Indian commitment to peace and non-aggression was affirmed, along with the objective of building a social order by democratic means in which social, economic, and political justice would permeate all institutions of national life (Ministry of Defence, 1964:2).

The late 1960s brought about several changes. The first was that Pakistan sought to reassert itself, both by moving closer to China, and through conflict with India, first in the Rann of Kutch and later in Kashmir in 1965. The late 1960s also saw several initiatives taken by the

US and the Soviet Union that were of significance to India. Richard Nixon's 'Guam doctrine' and Henry Kissinger's 'Four Power Balance doctrine' spelt out the American position vis-à-vis India, while the Soviet Union developed the Brezhnev Plan for Collective Security in Asia, the Kosygin Plan for Economic Co-operation, and a series of treaty initiatives, one of which culminated in the Indo-Soviet treaty of Peace, Friendship and Co-operation of 1971. While the 'Four Power Balance Doctrine included the United States, the Soviet Union, China and Japan as the four powers that would be responsible for order in Asia, implicitly excluding India; the Brezhnev Plan sought to exclude China from the proposed security cooperation thus creating an impression that it sought to encircle China.

This period also saw the beginning of Soviet arms aid to India. Traditionally, India had depended on the West, particularly the United Kingdom (UK), for armaments, but this changed with the signing of the MiG deal with the Soviet Union in 1962 (Chari, 1979). The deal included provision for production, although MiGs were only delivered after the Chinese war was over. This was followed by the purchase of Petya class frigates and submarines in the mid-1960s (Thakur & Thayer, 1993), and Su-7B fighters, DT-76 and T-54 main battle tanks, and other equipment in later years (Smith, 1994). Over the years, Indian dependence on the Soviet Union grew, and it became the most important defence supplier to India.

The post-Bangladesh era (from 1971) saw a growing level of credibility about India's position in South Asia, with some serious efforts being made to develop Indian military capability, as both consolidation and modernisation of the armed forces were undertaken. India conducted its first nuclear test in 1974, demonstrating its ability to produce a nuclear weapon. This was also the phase that saw India seeking to assert itself as a regional power in South Asia. The 'Indira Doctrine', as it has been called, represented a tough and uncompromising approach towards other South Asian countries (Cohen, 2001:137).

The 1979 Soviet intervention in Afghanistan was a significant year for India, and it saw a renewed US military interest in South Asia, with arms pouring into Pakistan in support of the Afghanistan Mujahedeen. The 1980s also saw a significant shift in patterns of conflict, as conventional border-type wars ceased to be major threats, and the focus shifted more to problems of internal security. Low-intensity conflicts, militancy, and insurgency emerged as key concerns of the decade, and these called for new approaches and strategies, resulting in the growth of paramilitary forces and changes in strategic doctrines. Nuclear and space science received increasing focus, and enhanced nuclear capability and the development of missile systems were the other marked features of this period.

The 1980s saw a more active security strategy being pursued by India, as it started to intervene in the Sri Lankan crisis to provide support to the Tamil minority population in the North and North Eastern regions of the country. This support eventually led to the 1987 Indo-Sri Lanka accord, which provided for the entry of Indian peacekeeping forces into the conflict zone. Along with this, India undertook a military operation in the Maldives to defeat a coup attempt in 1988, which was the first such operation that India was involved in outside of the South Asian region.

India also undertook a massive military exercise along the IndoPakistan border, 'Operation Brass-tacks', that led to a rise in bilateral tensions, as well as 'Operation Checkerboard' in the North East, to tackle covert Chinese intervention in Indian territory (Cohen, 2001:146). However, it was during the Kargil Crisis of 1999 that India was able to match its diplomacy with military strategy to ensure that Pakistan withdrew from the territory it had occupied across the Line of Control in the Kargil sector of Jammu and Kashmir. Pakistan's covert support to Jihadi activities across the border was exposed, and the US put pressure on Pakistan to withdraw back across the Indian border (Riedel, 2002).

In stark contrast to the importance that the Indian army has been given in the planning for defence, Indian maritime forces were given a low priority until the 1970s. Pleas for an active maritime policy, as articulated by K.M. Pannikar (1945), went unheard in a land-bound defence perspective, as India's security strategy has long been dominated by considerations of the defence of land frontiers. This is partly a product of the long history of aggression and migration along land routes, either from the North West or from the North and North Eastern regions of India. It is also a product of the equally long history of a 'secure' Indian Ocean, due to the British presence and the relatively small coastal navy of Indian rulers. Consequently, much of the work on Indian security strategy has focused on its land forces.

The unique geopolitical position of India in terms of its peninsular presence, along with its growing military capability, present an opportunity for the country to emerge as a key player in maintaining order in the Indian Ocean region. The Indian navy's first Maritime Vision was expressed in the Naval Plans Paper of 1948Indian navy was to consist of cruisers and destroyers, structured around small aircraft carriers, with the objective of protecting India's sea lanes of communication (Ministry of Defence, 2007). Although the first conflict with Pakistan over Kashmir in 1947-48 did not see any naval activity, the rationale was one of 'territorial defence', a view that continued to dominate Indian strategic perspectives for over two decades. During the 1965 conflict, the role of the navy was restricted to the protection of trade. It was only in the 1971 conflict that the navy played a significant role, where the primary tactical success came from the use of missile attacks in the Arabian Sea.

The detonation of the Chinese nuclear device in 1964 set the Indian nuclear agenda in motion, and Indian nuclear policy in the early years revolved around two principles: the promotion of research and development for harnessing nuclear energy for peaceful purposes, and the attainment of self-sufficiency in the nuclear programme. Prime Minister

Shastri admitted to parliament that he was willing to consider the use of nuclear blasts for peaceful purposes (Lok Sabha, 1964), and is reported to have authorised the Indian Atomic Energy Commission (AEC) to go ahead with designing a nuclear device and preparation of the non-nuclear component so that the lead-time required to build an explosive could be reduced from 18 to six months (Wholstetter, 1977:109). However, these decisions were followed by a protracted debate on the Nuclear Non-proliferation Treaty (NPT). The early years of Indira Gandhi as prime minister saw much political uncertainty in India, but it was the rejection of the NPT that confirmed the end of the uncertainty of the 1960s. By the early 1970s, the Indian nuclear agenda began to take a definitive direction.

At the Fourth Atoms for Peace Conference in September 1971, the Chairman of the Indian AEC announced that India had been working in the field of nuclear explosive engineering for peaceful purposes on a top-priority basis (Chandrashekar Rao, 1974:210). In her replies to Parliament in November 1972 and again in November 1973, Prime Minister Mrs. Indira Gandhi made it clear that the AEC was constantly reviewing the progress of underground nuclear explosion technology from both the theoretical and experimental angle. However, she denied that there was any schedule fixed for a nuclear explosion (Lok Sabha, 1972; Rajya Sabha, 1973).

It was after the nuclear implosion in 1974 that India finally developed a coherent nuclear doctrine to suit the changed circumstances. The test demonstrated that India was capable of producing a nuclear explosion, but what remained in question was its intent. At the policy level, the earlier Shastri position of peaceful use of nuclear energy with a focus on research in Peaceful Nuclear Explosion (PNE) was now further expanded, although the new approach was based on the same geopolitical constructs of national security that had governed the earlier line. However, the test did not alter India's nuclear disarmament and peace policy. In her statement to the Indian parliament, Gandhi went to great lengths to stress that the test was part of the research and development work that the AEC had been carrying out in line with the national objective of harnessing nuclear energy for peaceful purposes (Lok Sabha, 1974). At the diplomatic level, the effort to create a deterrent capability threatened to translate into weapons intent, which helped India to retain the diplomatic advantage of being a non-nuclear power and continue its disarmament and peace agenda, and this deliberately ambiguous nuclear posture was to remain the basis of Indian nuclear policy for a long time.

On 11 and 13 May 1998, 24 years after having detonated its first nuclear device at Pokharan in 1974, India conducted a series of nuclear tests. Prime Minister Vajpayee announced that the tests were conducted with a fission device, a low-yield device and a thermonuclear device, adding that the measured yields were in line with the expected values (*The Times of India*, 1998). Expanding on the statement, the Principal Secretary to the Prime Minister stated that the tests had established India's capability for a weaponised nuclear programme.

The dichotomy between defence and development has been a recurrent theme in debates on India's security strategy and is interrelated with the debate on arms production. One important impact of the 1962 war was the attention it generated on planning for defence. The following tasks were identified: (i) expansion and modernisation of the army; (ii) modernisation of the air force; (iii) creation of an adequate production base; (iv) improvement and expansion of the means of communication and transport; and (v) replacement of old ships so as to make the navy a balanced force (Ministry of Defence, 1964:2-3). The Defence Plan prepared in 1964 identified as its main objective the need to build up adequate defences to safeguard the country's territorial integrity (Ministry of Defence, 1968:4).

Internal security threats have become significant since the 1980s, resulting in a rise in paramilitary and related expenditures, and this was reflected in the budget allocation made for paramilitary and police in the Home Ministry budget. The Internal Security Division of the Ministry of Home Affairs deals with matters relating to internal security and law, order, including anti-national and subversive activities of various groups/extremist organisations, terrorist financing, policy and operational issues on terrorism, security clearances, monitoring of ISI activities, etc. The Annual Report 2015-16 of the Ministry includes the following as areas of concern in the context of internal security: terrorism in the hinterland of the country, cross-border terrorism in Jammu and Kashmir, insurgency in the North Eastern States, and left wing extremism in certain areas (Ministry of Home Affairs, 2017:4).

Post-Soviet era

The global order began to change with the Gorbachev initiatives of Perestroika and Glasnost, and his 'New Thinking' in foreign policy was followed by the East European transformation of 1989, the Kuwait crisis and the first Iraq war, and the disintegration of the Soviet Union. It was in the aftermath of the Soviet Union collapse that economics and technology started to displace the military as the key determinants of power, and terrorism started to take a new form as it moved away from a state-centric phenomenon to one based on abstract religious ideology. Transnational issues, like human rights and environmentalism, started to gain ascendancy, while social networking grew as a new tool of communication.

The post-Cold War era saw four transformative events in India's strategic perspective that had far-reaching implications:

1. The economic watershed in 1991 when India launched an economic liberalisation and reform process because of its economically parlous situation;
2. The enunciation of the 'Look East' policy in 1993, followed by the 'Act East' policy in 2014, which indicated a shift from a West-Asian focus to one on the Indo-Pacific region;

3. The foreign and security policy watershed when India conducted a series of tests at Pokhran in 1998 and declared itself a nuclear weapon power; and
4. The transformation in India's world view when Indo-US relations moved from estrangement to engagement and, in the post-9/11 context, towards a mutually beneficial strategic partnership. The Indo-US nuclear deal for cooperation in civilian nuclear technology in 2005 symbolised this shift.

The Indian economic reform programme led to a sustained average annual growth of 8%, meaning that India was able to ride through the recession that hit the Western world in the early part of the 1990s decade. India emerged as an attractive 'strategic partner' to countries in the European Union (EU), the Association of Southeast Asian Nations (ASEAN), and the US. From a country dependent on the Aid India Consortium and food aid from the US, India today gives financial and technical assistance to a large number of developing countries, and its food self-sufficiency has made it a major interlocutor on issues of food security. Economic diplomacy has now emerged as an important tool in the Indian armoury vis-à-vis both the developed and the developing world, while a stable and growing economy at home enabled India to play an active role in global negotiations at the World Trade Organization (WTO), BRICS and G-20 meetings.

India's Look East Policy evolved during the early 1990s, primarily in the areas of economics and trade, and was targeted towards Southeast and East Asia (Ministry of External Affairs, 2007:ii, v). The Indian economic reform process generated a new-found confidence that encouraged the growth of India's economic engagement with East Asia, and India became a Sectoral Dialogue Partner (1992) and then a Full Dialogue Partner of ASEAN (1995). In 1996, India joined the ASEAN Regional Forum.

Parallel to its ASEAN linkages, the Bay of Bengal Initiative for Multi-sectoral Technical and Economic Cooperation (BIMSTEC) was created in 1997 to include countries in South and Southeast Asia. The aim was to create an enabling environment for rapid economic development, accelerate social progress in the subregion, and promote active collaboration and mutual assistance on matters of common interest. In 2014, India went a step further to shift from a Look East to an Act East policy, and India's relationship with ASEAN was the foundation of this. The policy, which was originally conceived as an economic initiative, has gained political, strategic and cultural dimensions, including establishment of institutional mechanisms for dialogue and cooperation (Ministry of External Affairs, 2017).

The NPT regime, with its multifarious components such as the Nuclear Suppliers group, Missile Technology Control Regime (MTCR), and Fissile Material Cut-off Treaty (FMCT), amongst others, had sought to place the P-5 (the five nuclear powers – China, Russia, the US, the UK, and France) in a monopolistic managerial framework. This caused tension with other countries, which was compounded by the restraints placed on dual use technologies. The first symbolic defiance of this restraint came in the form of the 1974 nuclear test at Pokhran. The 1974 test had a limited agenda, an act of revisionist defiance highlighting the technological competence of a Third World country. However, the May 1998 nuclear tests represented this defiance at a time when the nuclear regime had become more stringent. It is against the backdrop of this nuclear non-proliferation and technology-denial regime that one must assess the India-US Civilian Nuclear Cooperation Agreement signed in 2008.

India has argued that it is a responsible nuclear weapon state, conscious of its obligations to the international community on the control of weapons of mass destruction (WMDs). India also reiterated its commitment to global nuclear disarmament and argued that it has always been critical of clandestine activities with respect to WMDs, seeking to be a partner and not a target for the global nuclear disarmament (Saran, 2005). The passing of this deal through the International Atomic Energy Agency (IAEA) and the Nuclear Suppliers Group (NSG), as well as acceptance by the US Congress, symbolise the success of India in breaking through the denial regime and gaining legitimacy for its stand as a nuclear-capable power. Today, India has become a member of the Wassenar Agreement and the Australia Group and the Missile Technology Control Regime and is seeking to join the NSG. These efforts would help to strengthen India's position as a member of the international community and enhance its credibility as a supplier of military products (Grevatt, 2018).

The Draft outline of the Indian Nuclear Doctrine, released on 17 August 1999, argued for autonomy in decision-making about security for India (National Security Advisory Board, 1999). The key features of the nuclear doctrine, as announced by the Cabinet Committee on Security, are (Basrur, 2006):

i. Building and maintaining a credible minimum deterrent;
ii. A policy of 'No First Use', where nuclear weapons will only be used in retaliation against a nuclear attack on Indian territory or on Indian forces anywhere;
iii. Nuclear retaliation to a first strike will be massive and designed to inflict unacceptable damage;
iv. Nuclear retaliatory attacks can only be authorised by the civilian political leadership through the Nuclear Command Authority;
v. Non-use of nuclear weapons against non-nuclear weapon states;
vi. In the event of a major attack against India, or Indian forces anywhere, by biological or chemical weapons, India will retain the option of retaliating with nuclear weapons;

vii. A continuance of strict controls on export of nuclear and missile related materials and technologies, participation in the Fissile Material Cutoff Treaty negotiations, and continued observance of the moratorium on nuclear tests;

viii. Continued commitment to the goal of a nuclear weapon free world, through global, verifiable and non-discriminatory nuclear disarmament.

The elaborate nuclear decision-making apparatus formalised by the government revolved around the National Security Council, as well as a nuclear command and control system and the National Command Authority. The Strategic Forces Command was established to control, deploy and use nuclear weapons, to structure strategic nuclear forces, and to plan for nuclear operations and nuclear contingencies. The Strategic Policy group in the Bhabha Atomic Research Centre (BARC) was set up to liaise with the government and the military and contribute to overall policy and plans. The Strategic Forces Command drew up a strategic targeting list, identified appropriate sites for storing nuclear cores and weapons systems and the emplacement of vectors, and worked on nuclear weapon use plans to respond to certain scenarios.

Bharat Karnad concludes that India's nuclear policy has given up the baggage of self-abnegation and denial, in that the Indian nuclear deterrent is finding its strategic bearings, while Strategic Forces Command finds its feet and the conventional military establishment outlines a role for nuclear weapons as a shield against limited conventional wars (2008:97-106). The changes in the Indian position could lead one to question whether India has moved away from its 'revisionist' position to one more aligned with the status quo.

The Defence Production Policy announced by the Ministry of Defence in January 2011 reiterated the vision of self-sufficiency (Ministry of Defence, 2011). Initially, the defence manufacturing sector was reserved for the public sector only but in 2011, the Central Government opened it to participation by the private sector, too. The government also planned to involve academia, research and development institutions, and technical and scientific organisations to achieve self-sufficiency. The government announced increases in defence exports and industry licences, promoted defence partnerships, introduced a defence innovation fund for the promotion of indigenous technologies, and introduced a technology-funding scheme for the private sector (Grevatt, 2017a, b, c).

However, it has been pointed out that financial constraints, bureaucratic delays and internal organisational shortcomings have delayed the modernisation of the armed forces in India, and these problems extend to limitations of the Defence Research and Development Organization and the Ordinance Factories to deliver the necessary services (Bedi, 2018). A Committee of Experts (CoE) was constituted by the Ministry of Defence to recommend measures to enhance combat capability and rebalance the defence expenditure of the armed forces. The committee submitted its report in December 2016, and the government informed parliament that the report was taken up by the Ministry of Defence to frame key action points and establish a roadmap for implementation (Ministry of Defence, 2018a).

In the Technology Perspective and Capability Roadmap 2018, Defence Ministry seeks to guide the private sector industry in planning or initiating technology development, partnerships and production arrangements, with an emphasis on 'Made in India' (Ministry of Defence, 2018b).

The Indian navy's Maritime Strategy today speaks of the need to project power as a means of supporting foreign policy objectives (Ministry of Defence, 2007). The areas of primary interest that have been identified as needing attention include: (a) The Arabian Sea and the Bay of Bengal, which largely encompass India's Exclusive Economic Zone, Island Territories, and their littoral reaches; (b) The choke points leading to and from the Indian Ocean, i.e. the Strait of Malacca, Strait of Hormuz, Strait of Bab-el-Mandeb, and the Cape of Good Hope; (c) the island countries; (d) the Persian Gulf as a source of oil supply; and (e) principal international sea lanes that cross the Indian Ocean Region. The secondary areas of interest include: (a) The Southern Indian Ocean Region; (b) The Red Sea; (c) The South China Sea; and (d) The East Pacific Region. The likely scenarios in a use of military force by the Indian Navy have been outlined in the Indian Maritime Doctrine as follows (Ministry of Defence, 2007):

1. Conflict with a state in our immediate neighbourhood, or clash of interest with an extra-regional power;
2. Operations in the extended and or strategic neighbourhood in response to a request for assistance from a friendly nation;
3. Anti-terrorist operations conducted multilaterally or unilaterally;
4. Actions to fulfil international bilateral strategic partnership obligations;
5. Ensure good order at sea, which includes Low Intensity Maritime Operations (LIMO) to combat asymmetric warfare, poaching, piracy, and trafficking in arms/drugs;
6. Ensuring safety and security of International Sea Lanes through the Indian Ocean;
7. Actions to assist the Indian Diaspora and Indian interests abroad; and
8. Peacekeeping operations under the aegis of the United Nations, independently or as part of a multinational force.

South Asia is central to Indian strategic thinking. The 1970s saw a distinct stress on India's role as a regional power in the South Asian region, and the implicit aspect of a hegemonic position was sought to be softened by subsequent governments. The Janata Party government suggested 'mutually-beneficial bilateralism', while the Gujral doctrine talked of non-reciprocity with small powers, non-intervention, and peaceful bilateral negotiations for resolution of disputes (Gujral, 1997).

India has long maintained that it plays a key role in any consideration on the issue of peace, stability, order and security in the South Asian regional state system, which has recently seen a re-emergence of traditional sources of conflict along with non-traditional threats. Some of the traditional issues that South Asia is confronted with include the spill-over of the Afghan conflict, imperfect borders with China and Pakistan that have seen border skirmishes and tensions, growing competition in the Indian Ocean area, and a re-assertive China with its initiation of the China Pakistan Economic Corridor and the One Belt One Road proposal.

Along with this, the changing nature of terrorism is now visible in its impact on South Asia. Earlier forms of terrorism were state-centric in that the agenda of the terrorist was located in a particular people in a particular geopolitical region, but the terrorism that is taking shape in the post-9/11 era is not located in any state-centric formulation. It is a clash of ideas, often religious, which the terrorists fight through the use of force or violence if necessary. The tensions with Pakistan have the added dimension of terrorism from non-state actors.

In October 2000, President Putin visited India and the countries signed the Declaration of Strategic Partnership (2000), which declared that relations would be 'based on mutual understanding and long-term confidence in each other, this envisages the elevation of their multifaceted ties to an even higher and qualitatively new level'. The strategic partnership entailed cooperation in the following areas: Political, Trade and Economic, Defence, Science and Technology, and Culture. The provision in the first agreement of regular summit-level meetings between the two countries has helped to continue the mutual dialogue. Military-technical cooperation between the two countries includes joint research, development, and the production of advanced defence technologies and systems, such as the development of the BrahMos Missile System, and the production of SU-30 aircraft and T-90 tanks in India. The two countries also hold annual training exercises between their armed forces (Embassy of India in Moscow, 2018).

The post-Cold War years have altered the security considerations between India and the US. There had already been a serious effort to evolve a strategic dialogue with the US, with the first attempt to structure approaches to defence cooperation between the two countries was made in the 1990s by reciprocal exchange of information and personnel under what became known as the Kickleighter Proposals (Kumar, 1997:783). In 1995, the two countries signed the Agreed Minute on Defence Cooperation, covering service-to service and civilian-to-civilian cooperation, as well as cooperation in defence production and research (Sboto, 2008). However, the Indian nuclear tests of 1998 broke the early momentum of the bilateral relationship and were followed by a prolonged dialogue between the Indian Foreign Minister Jaswant Singh and the American Under Secretary of State Strobe Talbott, seeking to re-establish the broken links between the two countries.

From an Indian perspective, it was an attempt to get the US to understand the Indian decision to strive for nuclear weapons capability, but it was only after September 2001 that Indo-US security ties gained real momentum, as both countries came to acknowledge a desire for greater bilateral interaction on security issues. The Defence Policy Group was revived, and the new key word was 'inter-operability' (Embassy of the United States of America, 2005). It signified the mutual desire of the countries to work more closely in the area of military cooperation, and highlighted the possibility of sharing strategic doctrines and operations in the future to tackle new challenges.

Bilateral interactions continued to gather momentum through the early 2000s. In January 2004, the two countries agreed to expand their cooperation in three specific areas: civilian nuclear activities, civilian space programmes, and high-technology trade, as well as expand their dialogue on missile defence. These areas of cooperation were designed to progress through a series of reciprocal steps that built on each other and were the first phase of the Next Steps in Strategic Partnership between the US and India (NSSP) (Embassy of India, 2008). In July 2005, the US State Department announced the successful completion of the NSSP, providing for expanded bilateral commercial satellite cooperation and removal or revision of some US export licenses for certain dual-use technologies (Embassy of India, 2008).

This Joint Statement, along with the June 2005 US India Defence Framework Agreement, constituted a step forward on all four issues of the NSSP. It was also the first step towards a far more ambitious agreement on Civilian Nuclear Cooperation that came to be signed in July 2005 eventually put into place in 2008. In 2009, President Obama reaffirmed the global strategic partnership between India and the US (Embassy of India, 2010), while Secretary of State Hillary Clinton and the Indian External Affairs Minister established a 'Strategic Dialogue' during Clinton's visit to India in July 2009 (Embassy of India, 2010). The countries also signed the Logistics Exchange Memorandum of Agreement under which the militaries of India and the US share each other's military assets and facilities for repair, maintenance and supplies (Annual Defence Report, 2016).

Over the past few years, the present government of Narendra Modi has sought to expand security cooperation with other countries, including through reaffirming its close relations with the US and Russia, and efforts to build a dialogue with China. Other such efforts include the inter-governmental agreement with France for Dassult Rafale fighters, defence collaboration with Japan with terms of purchase and production in India, co-development of defence products with Israel, and participation in aerospace operational and naval exercises with Australia. Indian efforts at expanding its security footprint began with the establishment of the Fakhor Air Base in Tajikistan, and it now plans to build its first naval base in the Indian Ocean region as a joint project with the Seychelles government on Assumption Island (*The Hindu*, 2016).

Along with this, in 2018 Prime Minister Modi took several concrete security steps in Southeast Asia. These included an agreement with Indonesia to develop a port in the city of Sabang that would overlook the western entrance to the Strait of Malacca; a pact with Singapore on logistical support for naval ships, submarines and military aircraft during visits; a visit to Malaysia; and a promise to ASEAN to promote a rules-based order in the Indo-Pacific region (*The New Indian Express*, 2018).

TABLE 13.1   Survey of security perceptions and strategies

Year	Security perceptions	Security strategies and the context of power
1947-1962	- Conventional threat from neighbours. - Focus is on Pakistan.	1. Defence through diplomacy. 2. Strategy evolved as an alternative to the bipolar military options of the Cold War. 3. Regionalism is key outlook (Asian and Afro-Asian). 4. The context of power is primarily military. 5. Revisionist agenda.
1962-1972	- Conventional threat manifests itself. - Focus is on Pakistan and China.	1. Limits of diplomacy exposed in 1962. 2. Development of military capability is accepted as the means of achieving national security. 3. Bilateralism in the context of South Asia emerges as the key focus. 4. The context of power is primarily military and economic. 5. Revisionist agenda continues.
1972-1991	- Conventional threat continues. - Internal security problems start to manifest in the latter period in the context of low-intensity conflict and insurgency (Kashmir).	1. Military capability continues to be the focus. 2. Defence through a politico-military strategy. 3. Dual use technology emerges as important factor. 4. India evolves a South Asia-centric approach. Considers itself a regional power. 5. The context of power is mainly economic and technological capabilities. 6. Revisionist agenda continues.
1991-1998	- Threats now more global. - Issues like economic and trade, technology start to be raised.	1. The economic liberalisation (1991) and nuclear tests (1998) are watersheds. 2. Economic and political stability, technological growth in face of sanctions makes India demand space in the decision-making circles of the world. 3. Defence through an Economic technological – military strategy. 4. Global world view, not South Asia centric. 5. Look East policy. 6. Technology is seen as main source of power. 7. Moving away from revisionism?
1998 to date	Focus on threats in areas of technology and trade; growing concern about assertive China	1. Indian nuclear test of 1998. 2. Indo-US Nuclear Deal. 3. Act East Policy. 4. Use of public diplomacy. 5. Stress on defence modernisation along with indigenous production. 6. Moving away from revisionism?

SOURCE: Prepared by the author

Security strategy

Rodney Jones labels Indian strategic culture as 'omniscient patrician', arguing that philosophical and mythological factors form the foundation of this culture (Jones, 2006). He identifies the origins of Indian-ness that give mythological and metaphysical significance to the subcontinent as a territorial expression, and argues that the Indian thought process is ahistorical and generally resists being event-driven or trapped in deadlines, such that India is perceived as an ageless civilisation having a natural claim to greatness. Writings on India's foreign and security policy have traditionally sought to locate history and culture as a key component to an unwritten ethos, such as the *Mahabharata* and the *Bhagwat Gita*, which present a picture of the necessity of the use of force and at the same time the need for peace. The primary duty of the government was to enforce social order, and its coercive authority was recognised as it alone made life, property, morality or virtue possible (Prasad, 1968; Appadorai, 1992). If the fundamental task of any strategy is the efficient use of the available means to accomplish policy goals, then any debate on India's security strategy would have to balance its available soft- and hard-power resources. It is these aspects that enable one to understand the Indian reluctance to spell out a concrete strategic doctrine, retaining a deliberate ambiguity about national security strategy.

The first aspect relates to the geopolitical context that impinges on India's strategic mindset. The second is the contrast between the identity of India as it has been presented through the ages, versus the historical realities. The second flows from the first in that it focuses on the conceptual debate about the legitimacy of the use of force in international relations. In the context of nuclear weapons capability, this has a direct bearing on the position on minimal nuclear deterrence in a nuclear doctrine that also asserts the need for global nuclear disarmament. The debate regarding India being a revisionist power as opposed to one supporting the status quo is also a part of this debate on security strategy.

The geopolitics of South Asia resulted in the military orientation of ancient Indian civilisations being more defensive and non-expansionist in nature. India battled several incursions from the North West frontier areas, yet the strategic perspectives of Indian rulers in the subcontinent remained defensive. One important reason was the natural geopolitical isolation of the subcontinent. The Indian subcontinent lies along the southern fringe of the Eurasian landmass and is virtually cut off from the rest of the world by the Himalayas, which constitute a formidable northern boundary against the Tibetan plateau. Towards the western end lie the Karakoram and the Hindukush ranges that, along with the Sulaiman and the Kirthar ranges, eventually meet the sea. The traditional passes to enter the subcontinent were through the Hindukush along the Kabul valley into the northern part of the Indus valley, or from central Afghanistan into western Punjab. In the east, the southern Himalayas eventually branch off to become Naga Hills and the Manipur plateau, and various hill lines follow south demarcating the border with Myanmar. There have been very few invasions from the east. It is noteworthy that none of the Indian empires, including those of Ashoka, the Mughals or the Marathas (Peshwa), whether indigenous or created by outsiders, expanded beyond these geopolitical boundaries.

Indian identity in terms of its strategic perceptions were spelt out in the initial years of independence, focusing around the concepts of independence and peace. The former had an external dimension of 'staying away from politics of groups aligned against one another' (Nehru, 1971:2) and an internal dimension of self-reliance. The source of the peace tradition was the assimilative cultural tradition and came to be articulated as an approach seeking conflict resolution. This is a product of India's history and culture spanning over several centuries, and it is this image that clashes with the question of whether the use of force is legitimate.

The debates in India about its strategic policy are state-centric, maintaining a belief that the post-Soviet era has not altered the hierarchal structure of the world order. These debates therefore tend to be located around the following issues: The first debate has a politico-military frame of reference. Given the tradition of peace that was central to India's world view, the newly independent country had to address the issue of military power in its strategic perspectives. Referring to the influence of Gandhi on what Nehru called a Cold War mentality, Nehru spelt out his views on the utility of force in terms of state policy (Singh, 1994). He understood the need of a country to maintain its military strength to avoid or conduct a war if necessary. However, there is always a need for keeping the option for compromise open, not necessarily on fundamentals but on areas where dialogue is possible. It was therefore necessary to make a distinction between appeasement and weakness. Nehru did not expect a person to be a pacifist, arguing that each one must maintain his strength, but also asked, 'why shout it out? Why talk about it? Why threaten the other at all the time' (Mende, 1958:126).

India has since moved away from the Nehruvian position of underplaying the use of force. The first time that India gave any indication that it was willing to seek options other than those within the peace approach was in 1971, when prime minister Indira Gandhi talked of 'other solutions to this problem' in response to Pakistan's actions in East Pakistan and the resultant influx of almost 10 million refugees into India (Kak, 2012:91). Today, there is a willingness to accept the utility of force as an option, even if done with restraint. India had also conducted a putative strike against Pakistan, shelling Pakistani installations across the Line of Control in Kashmir after the terrorist strike on the Jammu and Kashmir State Legislature in 2001 (Ladwig, 2010:1168).

In 2015, India conducted surgical strikes against terrorist camps along the Indo-Myanmar border, and in 2016, against terrorist launch pads in Pakistan-occupied Kashmir (Indiatimes, 2015; MEA & MoD, 2016). The Defence Minister stated that the armed forces in Kashmir had been given full authority to conduct operations against Pakistan's attempts to abet cross-border terrorism, as well as dealing with militancy in the Valley. He added that in war-like zones, military solutions were to be provided by military officers, not through the comments of politicians (In the case of China, the Doklam crisis that erupted in 2017, where the Chinese attempted to reshape the boundary and the security matrix with India at the India-China-Bhutan trijunction, was resolved to Indian satisfaction. India was able to achieve three tasks: hold the Chinese road-building efforts and prepare for a military retaliation by China; maintain Bhutan's interests and territorial integrity; and brave the inevitable Chinese pressure (Bagchi, 2017).

Revisionism has been a dominant theme in the Indian approach to international issues. The debate on revisionism has for a long time centred on the hegemonic status quo dominance that was the feature of the hierarchal world order. However, during the 70s, there was a subtle shift in the revisionist posture. India's own emergence as a hegemonic power in South Asia led it to take a different perspective towards South Asia on the one hand, and towards the world at large. The Indian position in the region came to be viewed in terms of its role in the regional state system of South Asia as a hegemonic power, and hence a power that had to take on the responsibility of maintaining peace and order in the region.

The traditional anti-status quo posture that India had espoused through the Cold War years has undergone a change, and the challenges that were posed to the nuclear club through the 1974 test had become obsolete by 1998. While India may continue to argue in favour of its role in global decision-making circles through a demonstration of its technological capability via the nuclear and space route, thus seeking a 'revisionist' position, the crossing of the nuclear threshold has blunted India's demands. This is especially so because of the ambiguity in the Indian position about the nuclear status of Pakistan and Iran, as India refuses to grant the same revisionist logic to either of these countries. Similarly, the rhetoric of the New International Economic Order of the 70s now has to confront Indian economic diplomacy at the WTO, BRICS and the G-20 forums, where India is emerging as one of the key actors. Thus, the dilemma is whether revisionism, as one of the key ingredients of an Indian world view, is more rhetoric than a critical component of policy.

India appears to have quietly abandoned the classical form of non-alignment that put it in the bracket of the Afro-Asian developing world. Today, while India may still identify itself as a Third World developing country, it considers itself a prominent actor seeking to lead the region in the global economic and other forums, and the limitations of revisionism are being recognised. The old ideological rhetoric of non-alignment has come to be replaced with a far more realist world view that seeks to remove the ideological blinkers. The exploration into the possibility of a strategic partnership with the US, France, Japan and Australia is a product of this new-found realism in foreign policy.

India's new security strategy, with a geopolitical focus on India's strategic concerns, can be spelt out as follows.

Basic principles

At the domestic level, there is an emphasis on the Indian success at establishing a pluralist representative system of governance based on the framework of unity in diversity. Meanwhile, At the international level, the focus is on India's principled commitment to peace policy and independent understanding of world affairs. India asserts its commitment to national security, and hence the legitimacy of the use of force and need for nuclear weapons capability, and at the same time reiterates its commitment to non-proliferation of nuclear weapons and pursuit of global nuclear disarmament. In this context, there is an emphasis on developing a peaceful uses programme in the nuclear area, and the use of advance technology for peaceful (developmental) purposes. This is especially applicable to technologies relating to nuclear, space, and electronics, which are dual use technologies.

Regional level

The utility of nuclear deterrence between India and Pakistan remains unclear. In the short term, one would have to make a distinction between security considerations, which include border conflicts and internal security, and nuclear strategies. Conceivably, one can argue for a 'no first use' agreement and to not attack one another's nuclear installations. India can also argue that the critical Indian security concerns stem from China, not Pakistan. Here, Indian nuclear preparedness gains a different meaning, as the country can use its nuclear capability to strike up a new level of dialogue with China on politico-security issues. The Indian army ended their 71-day August to September 2017 stand-off over a Chinese road-building project in Doklam, and it is likely that this was possible because the PLA simply lacked the military ability to push the Indians out. Chinese resolve to 'take all measures to uphold its territorial integrity' is likely to be a product of this stalemate, but Doklam also provided a clear template for other countries to use in the face of incessant small-scale land grabbing (Joshi, 2017).

Global level

India faces a hard choice at the global level. International interaction has moved away from traditional methodologies of formal or informal negotiation to tacit bargaining (Agrawal, 1996:46), in which one state attempts to influence the policy decisions of the other through 'countervailing actions', rather than negotiation. These actions consist of threats, postures, deliberate delays, and building allies both within and outside of the countries. Tacit bargaining is likely to work on economic and technology transfer issues in the context of India, as the issue of modern technologies is a central security concern today. Here, the bargain may hinge on the degree to which the nuclear weapon powers accept India's emergent status. Advanced technologies of the day may continue to be under denial regimes or be so costly as to make them unaffordable, while other technologies may either be of no real use or be created indigenously. It is here that Indian reluctance to present a clear-cut statement of its strategic doctrine has its utility, as it would give India the space to negotiate and take care of its national interests.

Notes

1. Directive Principles of India's Constitution, Art. 51 of the Indian Constitution, calls for the promotion of international peace and security, maintaining just and honourable relations between nations, fostering respect for international law and treaty obligations, etc.
2. Ashoka's conversion to Buddhism and his preference for cooperative practices in relations with other states is the core of India's Panchsheel philosophy. Ashoka's Empire lasted from 273 to 232 BCE. Two concepts of Akbar (Mughal Empire [Akbar] 1556-1605) need to be mentioned: Deen-e-Ilahi (Divine Faith) and Suleh Kul (Peace to All). The former was an attempt to create a new religious world view that attempted a synthesis of the then contemporary religions; the latter became a policy that sought to integrate the Hindu society in governance.

References

Agrawal, S. 1996. 'New Rules of the Game'. *Outlook*, 14 August.

Annual Defence Report. 2016. *Janes Defence Weekly*. 14 December.

Appadorai, A. 1969. On Understanding Indian Foreign Policy, in K.P. Misra (ed.), *Studies in Indian Foreign Policy*. New Delhi: Vikas Publishers.

Appadorai, A. 1992. *Indian Political Thinking: Through the Ages*. New Delhi: Khama Publishers.

Bagchi, I. 2017. 'How India refused to play Chinese Checkers and Won'. *The Times of India*, 29 August. https://bit.ly/3336vbq [Accessed 30 May 2018].

Basrur, R. 2006. Minimum Deterrence and Indian Pakistan Nuclear Dialogue: Case Study on India. *LNCV South Asia Security Project Case Study 2/2006*. https://bit.ly/2Q0LCs5 [Accessed 2 August 2011].

Baylis, J. 1997. International Security in the Post-Cold War Era, in J. Baylis & S. Smith (eds.), *The Globalisation of World Politics*. Oxford: Oxford University Press.

Baylis, J., Smith, S. & Owens, P. 2008. *The Globalisation of World Politics*. Oxford: Oxford University Press.

Bedi, R. 2018. 'Growing pains'. *Janes Defence Weekly*, 21 February.

Behera, L.K. 2018. 'Creation of Defence Planning Committee: A Step towards Credible Defence Preparedness'. IDSA Comment, 19 April. https://bit.ly/3btL8Mk9 [Accessed 26 March 2020].

Chari, P.R. 1979. Indo-Soviet Military Co-operation: A Review. *Asian Survey*, XIX(3):230-244. https://doi.org/10.1525/as.1979.19.3.01p0028w

Cohen, S. 2001. *India: Emerging Power*. New Delhi: Oxford University Press.

Embassy of India. 2008. *India-US Relations: A general overview*. https://bit.ly/3cLBmxw [Accessed 26 February 2008].

Embassy of India. 2010. *General Overview of India-US Relations*. https://bit.ly/2TB0Tlz [Accessed 28 August 2010].

Embassy of India in Moscow. 2018. *Bilateral Relations: India and Russia*. https://bit.ly/39C3X6K [Accessed 11 March 2018].

Embassy of the United States of America. 2005. *People, Progress, Partnership: The Transformation of US-India Relations*. New Delhi: Embassy of the USA.

Estimates Committee. 1992. 10 Lok Sabha, 19 Report, Ministry of Defence: Defence Force levels, manpower management and policy, 1992-93. New Delhi.

Grevatt, J. 2017a. 'India announces increases in exports and industry licences'. *Janes Defence Weekly*, 4 January:23.

Grevatt, J. 2017b. 'India MoD formalises technology funding scheme for private sector'. *Janes Defence Weekly*, 15 February:20.

Grevatt, J. 2017c. 'India introduces Defence Innovation Fund'. *Janes Defence Weekly*, 19 April:20.

Grevatt, J. 2018. 'India Joins the Australia Group export control regime'. *Janes Defence Weekly*, 31 January.

Gujral, I.K. 1997. *Speech at the United Service Institute of India*. 23 January. New Delhi: EPD.

Indiatimes. 2015. https://bit.ly/3cLNLBF [Accessed 12 March 2018].

Indian Defence News. 2017. https://bit.ly/2Tys00L [Accessed 12 March 2018].

Jones, R. 2006. *India's Strategic Culture*. Defense Threat Reduction Agency, Advanced Systems and Concept Office.

Joshi, M. 2017. Xi's new PLA strategy: Implications for India. Observer Research Foundation, 7 November. https://bit.ly/2Q1ejoP [Accessed 23 March 2018].

Kak, K. 2012. India's Grand Strategy for the 1971 war. *Indian Defence Review*. https://bit.ly/331mPJG [Accessed 17 March 2018].

Kanwal, G. 2017. *Imperative Need for a Comprehensive National Security Strategy*, Vivekananda International Foundation, 20 April. https://bit.ly/39B1I3F [Accessed 1 March 2018].

Karnad, B. 2008. *India's Nuclear Policy*. Westport, CT: Praeger Security International.

Kavic, L.J. 1967. *India's Quest for Security: Defence Policies, 1947-65*. Berkley: University of California Press.

Khera, S.S. 1968. *India's Defence Problem*. Bombay: Longmans.

Kumar, D. 1997 Defence in Indo-US Relations. *Strategic Analysis*, XX(5):783.

Ladwig III, W.C. 2010. India and Military Power Projection: Will the Land of Gandhi become a Conventional Great Power? *Asian Survey*, 50(6):1168. https://doi.org/10.1525/as.2010.50.6.1162

Lok Sabha. 1964. *Debates*, Series 3, Vol. XXXV(10), Session 10, 27 November, Col. 2287.

Lok Sabha. 1972. *Debates*, Series 5, Vol. XX(3), Session 6, 15 November, Col. 49.

Lok Sabha. 1974. *Debates*, Series 5, Vol. XLI(1), Session 2, 22 July, Cols. 264-269.

MEA & MoD. 2016. Transcript of Joint Briefing. 29 September. https://bit.ly/2PZLCc6 [Accessed 12 March 2018].

Mende, T. 1958. *Conversations with Nehru*. Bombay: Wilco Publishing House.

Ministry of Defence. 1964. *Annual Report, 1963-64*. New Delhi: Government of India.

Ministry of Defence. 1968. *Annual Report, 1967-68*. New Delhi: Government of India.

Ministry of Defence. 2007. *Freedom to use the seas: India's Maritime Military Strategy*. New Delhi Integrated HQ.

Ministry of Defence. 2011. *Defence Production Policy*. 1 January. https://ddpmod.gov.in/sites/default/files/1400562644.pdf [Accessed 2 May 2019].

Ministry of Defence. 2018a. Press Information Bureau. https://bit.ly/2PW0pUY [Accessed 7 March 2018].

Ministry of Defence. 2018b. Technology Perspective and Capability Roadmap (TPCR). https://bit.ly/3cln40G [Accessed 27 June 2018].

Ministry of External Affairs. 1999. *Annual Report, 1998-99*. New Delhi: Government of India. https://bit.ly/2PXYv6r [Accessed 27 April 2018].

Ministry of External Affairs. 2007. *Annual Report, 2006-07*. New Delhi: Government of India.

Ministry of External Affairs. 2017. *ASEAN-India Relations*. New Delhi: Government of India. https://bit.ly/38woWX3 [Accessed 23 May 2018].

Ministry of Home Affairs. 2017. *Annual Report 2016-17*. New Delhi: Government of India.

National Security Advisory Board. 1999. Draft Report on Indian Nuclear Doctrine. https://bit.ly/39Bo2Kf [Accessed 27 June 2019].

Nehru, J. 1971. *India's Foreign Policy*. New Delhi: Publications Division.

Pannikar, K.M. 1945. India and the Indian Ocean. London: George Allen and Unwin.

Power, P.F. 1969. Ideological Current in India's Foreign Policies, in K.P. Misra (ed.), *Studies in Indian Foreign Policy*. New Delhi: Vikas publishers.

Prasad, B. 1968. *Theory of Government in Ancient India*. Allahabad: Central Book Depot.

Rajya Sabha. 1973. *Debates*, Vol. XXXVI(4), 15 November, Cols. 138-139. https://doi.org/10.1108/eb016279

Rana, A.P. 1979. *Imperative on Nonalignment: A Conceptual Study of India's Foreign Policy Strategy in the Nehru Period*. New Delhi: Macmillan.

Rana, A.P. 1988. International Relations, in A.P. Rana & K. Subrahmanyam (eds.), *A Survey of Research in Political Science, Vol. 5: International Relations*. New Delhi: ICSSR, p. 31.

Rana, A.P. & Subrahmanyam, K. 1988. *A Survey of Research in Political Science, Vol. 5: International Relations*. New Delhi: ICSSR.

Rao, P.V.R. 1970. *Defence Without Drift*. Bombay: Popular Prakashan.

Rao, P.V.R. 1974. Proliferation and the Indian Test: A View from India. *Survival*, XVI(5), September-October. https://doi.org/10.1080/00396337408441497

Riedel, B. 2002. American Diplomacy and the 1999 Kargil Summit at Blair House. *CASI Policy Paper Series*. http://www.sas.upenn.edu/casi [Accessed 24 April 2011].

Saran, S. 2005. Nuclear Non-Proliferation and International Security. *Institute for Defence Studies and Analysis Key Speeches*. https://bit.ly/331gKwW [Accessed 8 December 2005].

Sboto, S. 2008. Indo-US Military Cooperation – Taking Stock. Foreign Area Military Association. https://bit.ly/2xipJOs [Accessed 26 February 2008].

Singh, J. 1994. Affordable Credible Defence of India. *Strategic Analysis*, XVI(11):125-156.

Smith, C. 1994. *India's Ad hoc Arsenal: Direction or Drift in Defence Policy?* Oxford: SIPRI.

Subrahmanyam, K. 1988. Defence Policy and Analysis, in A.P. Rana & K. Subrahmanyam (eds.), *A Survey of Research in Political Science, Vol. 5: International Relations*. New Delhi: ICSSR.

Tanham, G. 1992. *Indian Strategic Thought: An Interpretative Essay*. New York: RAND. https://doi.org/10.1080/01636609209550082

Thakur, R. & Thayer, C. 1993. *Soviet Relations with India and Vietnam*. Delhi: Oxford University Press. https://doi.org/10.1007/978-1-349-09373-1

The Hindu. 2016. 'Seychelles committed to Indian naval base', 24 March. https://bit.ly/2v5SXzo [Accessed 26 June 2019].

The New Indian Express. 2018. 'With ports, ships and promises, India asserts role in Southeast Asia', 3 June. https://bit.ly/2UlZZtS [Accessed 26 March 2020].

The Times of India. 1998. 'India conducts 3 underground N-tests', 12 May. https://bit.ly/2JfTbaD [Accessed 26 March 2020].

Thomas, R.G.C. 1978. *The Defence of India: A Budgetary Perspective of Strategy and Politics*. New Delhi: Thomas Macmillan.

Wholstetter, R. 1977. The Buddha Smiles: Absentminded Peaceful Aid and the Indian Bomb. *ERDA Monograph* 3, 30 April.

Epilogue

Introduction

An astute observer of international politics, in following global events unfolding over the past 50 years, remarked not so much tongue-in-cheek that the fallacy of a unipolar world was evident for decades including during the Cold War, and the phenomenon is becoming more evident day by day. He suggests that 'the process of globalisation to the extent that it exists ... has been proven to be far from linear. Some general trends may be observed by some, but there are visible signs of deglobalisation in various areas such as political-military and economic spheres'.[1] His statement reminds one of an argument once posed by the sociologist, Anthony Giddens, cautioning theorists that the globalisation of (social) life also implies fragmentation and alienation on various socio- and political levels, which is likely to invite conflict rather than peaceful existence.

This collected volume through various contributions touches on how the post-1945, post-decolonisation and post-Cold War era transformed power, diplomatic and strategic relations and defence diplomacy in the "Global South". As the assassination of an Iranian general in Iraq by a US drone attack in January 2020 illustrates, the space of global politics remains tense, if not explosive. If not for Iranian restraint, this thoughtless act of aggression outside the parameters of international law could have led to some conflict of magnitude.

One may argue that the then Cold War divide made conflict more containable and perhaps predictable. The consequences of the Cold War conflicts in the "Third World", however, were enormous in human and material terms be it through so-called proxy wars or direct intervention by powers that perceived themselves as Gladiator-World Saviours (for example, the US involvement in Vietnam and US involvement in enforced regime changes in Latin-America). Despite a brief moment of (perhaps delusional) optimism following the end of the Cold War, the present context remains one of tension, increasing fragmentation and fragile relations that can change in a moment through one single un-reflected-upon military act.

The United Nations and the Security Council

On 1 January 2020, the estimated total of the world population was 7,763,035,303 persons. About 36 percent of these live in China and India. Twelve countries, the United States, Indonesia, Brazil, Pakistan, Nigeria, Bangladesh, the Russian Federation, Mexico, Japan, Ethiopia, The Philippines, and Egypt in descending order have each more than 100 million inhabitants.[2] Only three of these 14 countries have a permanent seat in the UN Security

Council. By far the most strategic institution of the United Nations, it does not reflect the real economic, political, economic, military, demographic and the power potential of its member states. Especially, the permanent seat of Great Britain and that of France are remarkable, given the fact that India, Indonesia, Brazil, Nigeria, the entire Middle East and the entire Latin America and Caribbean region are not represented. Of the block of the five BRICS countries, Brazil, Russia, India, China and South Africa, only three have a permanent seat. To manage global conflict, it is perhaps fitting to mention that large scale reform around the UN Security Council in terms of representation is necessary. For example, should Brexit become a reality, one can rightly ask whether the UK should still have a seat in the Security Council? This would even be more pertinent if Scotland in their next referendum choose to break away from the UK. The Security Council should also be extended to include other influential states from the South. Such a step would allow for a more inclusive balance of power and broader consultation on conflict and defence matters in the Security Council.

Latin America and the Caribbean

In Latin America, the Cold War represented a period in which military coups became institutionalised. The first institutional coup was that of 1962 in Peru. Brazil followed in 1964; a coup planned after explicit consultation with both the national elites and US government representatives. The Brazilian example gave rise to a succession of Latin American dictatorships, subsequently known as 'national security regimes', established by right-wing military leaders, in which the appointment of cabinet members in the successive military or civil-military governments went hand in glove with internal promotions in one or other branch of the armed forces. In almost all of Latin America, Peru as exception (1968-1980), national security or ultra-right repressive regimes came to power. Even in the first years of the democratic transitions at the end of the Cold War, there were countries with military-approved governments or co-governments, for instance in Brazil, El Salvador, Honduras and Guatemala. The late 1980s and 1990s saw transition to democracy, notably in Argentina and Chile. The era of transition from authoritarian rule to democracy was not to last forever in all Latin-American states. In Honduras (2009) and Bolivia (2019), the armed forces were 'invited' or 'co-invited' to stage coups. Are we potentially seeing a regression of democratic politics in Latin America? This is a question worth contemplation.

In post-Cold War Latin America, dictatorial military regimes had been succeeded by elected civilian governments. Democratic transitions considerably diminished the political influence of the armed forces. Sometimes outgoing military governments arranged their own transition pacts with the incoming civilian government implying a kind of co-governance in the shadows of power. Arguably, however, military influence in civil politics has been substantially diminished.

Whatever efforts the outgoing military could mobilise, the final outcome was a significant reduction of political influence, accompanied with sharp cutback of budget, personnel and equipment which occurred in most Latin American countries. This generic transition to democracy implied significant change for the once powerful and centralised authoritarian regimes, the loss of the de facto monopoly on intelligence matters and direct influence of, or control of government. In general, it was a process of gradual but controlled conversion. Especially after the Central American peace agreements in the 1990s and the electoral defeat of the Sandinista government in Nicaragua, the reduction in military spending was dramatic: in cases standing armies of 55,000 to 280,000 officers and troops became "miniature" armies of 10,000 to 15,000.

Over the entire region, the armed forces decreased: at present, the armed forces in the largest countries and with the largest population, are relatively small: 334,000 in Brazil whose population is 212 million; 268,000 in Colombia with a population of nearly 50 million; 265,000 in Mexico with a much larger population of 128 million; and 195,000 in Venezuela with a population of 31 million. The exception seems to be Colombia. The bloated armed force of Colombia is partially explained by its warfare against two guerrilla movements (the ERP and until 2016 the FARC) and more than 50 organised private armies of criminal gangs, not counting local militias along the entire Pacific coast.

Predictably, military expenditure is the highest in Brazil. Brazil spends nearly 45 percent of all Latin American and Caribbean national defence spending. Second, third and fourth places are held by Colombia, Mexico and Venezuela. The long-term percentage of the military budget of the GDP between 2006 and 2017 is around three percent in the case of Colombia and 1,5 percent in the case of Brazil and Honduras. All other countries spent considerably less.[3]

Only Brazil has a significant military industrial complex and a space programme. Chile's military budget until 2020 was guaranteed by the ten percent of the copper revenues. This new 'strategic contingence fund' fuelling the military budget will be administered by the Central Bank in Chile, the erstwhile dictatorship of the Pinochet brutal military rule.

There was always suspicion about the establishment of American territorial bases in the years of the Pink Tide of nationalist-leftists government (c.2000–c.2015). But in May 2017, it was announced that American forces will lead an unprecedented joint exercise with the armies of Brazil, Colombia and Peru. The returning military influence in the region goes together with an enormous commercial, economic and development assistance programme by China. It seems that some balance between East and West is maintained in terms of cooperation, with Chinese investment and commercial cooperation likely to increase in the region.

The once important ALBA-country system is diminishing in political influence due to falling oil revenues of Venezuela and the withdrawal of Ecuador (2018) and Bolivia (2019).

In the three remaining larger countries, namely Cuba, Nicaragua and Venezuela, the armed forces maintain an "osmosis type" of relation with the political system and the economy.

During the last two decades of civilian rule, problems of persistent inequality, corruption, institutional fragility and high levels of violence (not so much political as criminal) and insecurity continued and may open a leeway to military institutions to once again expand their influence if not well managed. Brazil's new civilian government with a retired army captain as president who with nostalgia speaks of the good years of dictatorship as does his vice-president, a retired general, is an example.

Relations between Latin American countries and the USA remain hovering between acceptance and hostility and in cases are contradictory or opaque. The Trump fundamentalism and xenophobia against people entering the USA via Mexico remains a bone of contention and most likely tensions will rise in magnitude as the US (apartheid-like) Wall is erected.

Future developments in the economy play a large role. Any decline in the economy of the USA may impact on Latin America and there seem to be indications that an economic decline in the USA will not be easily arrested. Capitalism on a credit card has become expensive – even untenable. Then there is the uneasy truth to be kept in mind: Major or hegemonic powers in (economic) decline, frequently tend to become more aggressive in military posture as their own feelings of insecurity increase. The US is no exception here. Developments here are to be carefully monitored and analysed as there is no crystal ball to read the future in the region.

Africa

Africa's history ever since Muslim expansion and Western colonialism has seen many torturous events and historical permutations. From an era of liberation struggles, some of them extremely brutal and dislocating such as Algeria and Zimbabwe, many African states after independence became autocracies or one party states. Some were more successfully run than others. Compare the stable rule of Tanzania under Julius Nyerere and Zambia under Kenneth Kaunda with brutal rule in Uganda and Somalia. Africa became vulnerable to the coup syndrome with Nigeria, Ethiopia, Ghana, and Burkina Faso as examples. Some military regimes were stable and reflected a fairly good human rights record such as Burkina Faso under Thomas Sankara, a visionary leader. Sankara, however, was not pliant to the West (especially France). His outspoken dream of a Burkina Faso detached from French neocolonial economic rule led to a coup d'état and his death, bringing a more pliable leader to power who remained in the French sphere of neocolonial influence. In Uganda, under the brutal rule of the dictator Idi Amin Dada thousands perished until Amin was overthrown through the intervention of Julius Nyerere (Mwalimu) of Tanzania.

In many states, corruption became endemic after independence with Zaire under Mobutu and the Central African Republic under Bokassa as examples. There were some success stories too. Zambia became independent from Britain without an armed struggle but rather a "negotiated independence" after civil resistance and labour strikes. In Botswana, under Sir Seretse Khama, the same occurred. Botswana reflects a constitutional state with stable rule, little corruption and a good economic growth rate. That corruption on the continent is far from defeated can be seen in Nigeria and in southern Africa, South Africa under the rule of Jacob Zuma is an example.

The case studies on Africa included in this volume are all from southern Africa. After an anti-colonial struggle that started in 1894 against the German colonisers, Namibia's struggle for liberation continued during the rule of the Union of South Africa (1915-1947). Sporadic revolts such in northern Namibia by Herero and Ovambo people as well as the Bondelswarts rebellion of 1921 in the south of Namibia were supressed, amongst others by using the newly established South African Air Force. When the South West African People's Organization (SWAPO) started their armed struggle in earnest in 1966, conflict escalated in the region. The Cold War myopia played no small role in this. South Africa, now under minority apartheid rule, was feverishly anti-communist and viewed itself as a Western ally. The "black danger" (Afrikaans: *swart gevaar*) and a deep dislike for communism, the "red danger" (Afrikaans: *Rooi Gevaar*), conflated into an ideology-driven South Africa mobilised to uphold the white state. The struggle by SWAPO and its People's Liberation Army of Namibia (PLAN) was interpreted as part of the red danger and total communist onslaught (Afrikaans: *Totale Aanslag*). Others interpreted it as a proxy war. The Cold War mania came as manna from heaven for the apartheid government that declared itself as an ally of the West fighting a communist/Marxist-Leninist threat spearheaded by Moscow.

South Africa's invasion in Angola (1975), with the knowledge of the USA, was to set the scene for further bloodletting. The Republic of Cuba became involved to support the Angolan government. In Angola, the Popular Movement for the Liberation of Angola (MPLA) came to power in November 1975 following the hasty departure of the colonialist Portuguese forces after a bloodless coup against the dictatorship of Caetano. South Africa's alliance with anti-Luanda forces with covert support by the West for Jonas Savimbi's rebel movement increased the turmoil in Angola. The Soviet Union was forced largely through Castro's commitment to Africa to support the government in Luanda. The military support for the MPLA heightened tensions. South African forces claimed that their fight against SWAPO guerrillas necessitated strong action. In countering the SWAPO threat, South Africa's involvement was to escalate. SWAPO in turn infiltrated northern Namibia relentlessly. South African involvement with covert Western support (i.e. Reagan's policy of "constructive engagement") led to economic instability and large scale social dislocation in Angola, the consequences still lasting today. The South African military had a more or less permanent presence in Angola through some large-scale operations and perhaps hundreds of smaller ones. Savimbi's Union for the Total Independence of Angola (Unita) became a favourite proxy of South Africa and apartheid's tacit supporters.

Between 1966 and 1988 South African forces embarked on numerous large scale (semi-) conventional operations against SWAPO that also led to military conflicts with MPLA's armed forces (or FAPLA). Especially with Botha in power, the war in Angola gained in importance and the State Security Council decided that Pretoria will take all measures, diplomatic, economic and especially military to dislodge Swapo and weaken the MPLA government. Post 1979, numerous large-scale operations that were undertaken included, amongst others, Operation Sceptic ("Smokeshell"), Operation Protea (hundreds of Swapo and Fapla soldiers killed), Operation Daisy (1981), Operations Super, Meebos, Phoenix and Boswilger (between 1982 and 1985). The battles at Cuito Cuanavale, Lomba and Tumpo of 1987 and 1988 finally brought about a stalemate, perhaps describable as a technical defeat to apartheid forces, though at high costs to the Angolan forces. Namibia finally became independent after a century of struggle against colonialism. In accordance with the UN General Assembly Resolution 435, Namibia became independent in March 1990 having seen its first free elections in 1989. Peace could have been achieved earlier, but the USA's policy of constructive engagement was to lengthen the suffering.

One of the historic ironies (if not a tragedy) of the Namibian struggle for independence is that if apartheid had relinquished their hold on the mandate for South West Africa in die 1970s as demanded by the United Nations General Assembly (UNGA), the debilitating conflict that spilled over numerous borders could have been terminated. Instead, against the wishes of the Namibian people themselves, the United Nations and the Non-Aligned Movement, Pretoria virtually colonised Namibia as a perceived "fifth province". The UN Security Council remained divided, which prolonged an unnecessary war. In the end, Pretoria made a fatal strategic misjudgement. The South African state was not fighting "terrorists", "Marxists" or dupes of Moscow, but a determined Namibian people intent on independence after nearly a century of struggle. Ironically, the authoritarian government and the security establishment of South Africa became proxies for the US during this period.

Today, Namibia like Botswana, its neighbouring country, is a stable constitutional state. It is a dominant party system with SWAPO holding on to power that seems to be slowly eroding. In terms of foreign and defence diplomacy, Namibia is following an independent pathway. Managing foreign relations tends to be pragmatic rather than ideological. The country maintains relations and exchanges with countries in the EU (especially Germany), Russia, China and even North Korea setting an example of independent thinking on the continent. Despite challenges such as poverty, economic growth, and some corruption (not comparable with its neighbouring state South Africa), Namibia seems to hold. The

Namibian Defence Force (NDF) is small and the purpose is national defence. The country faces no external enemies and forms part of the Southern African Security architecture.

The next case study, South Africa, as one of the so-called large states in Africa, followed a somewhat different trajectory. Colonial conquest first by the Dutch and then British determined its future political development. Indigenous black resistance was subdued by military force, whether it came from the Zulu, Xhosa or other people. Even the Boer Republics that stubbornly held onto their independence became a target after the discovery of gold in the Transvaal (today Gauteng Province). The Anglo-Boer War (South African War) broke out in October 1899 and lasted three torturous years until 1902. The extended guerrilla face of the war was marked by a scorched earth policy by the British with thousands of white and black people dying in concentration camps. What some termed the last of the gentleman's wars and others the first of the total wars (but was in fact a resource war) again had a major influence on the future. Peace was concluded in 1902. The end of the Anglo-Boer War saw a country marked by struggle between white indigenous people (Afrikaners) and the British. The "land of Boer against Brit" now became the land of Boer and Brit (even if the relationships between the two races were strained and somewhat uneasy). The Union of South Africa came into being in 1910.

Despite protest and initially liberal resistance by black people against lack of citizenship, the white controlled government of Smuts and later the National Party with its policy of racial segregation (apartheid) was not to give way. This was not made easier by the rise of Afrikaner Nationalism that led to the creation of a state where apartheid as a comprehensive project of social engineering was implemented from 1948 onwards. The rights and land of black people were whittled away with the comprehensive and notorious land acts of 1913 and 1936. Despite black people taking part as contingents in both the First and Second World Wars together with South African soldiers, no compromise was made and right to equal citizenship did not materialise. Passive resistance that marked the 1950s was to turn into an armed struggle and underground mobilisation by the 1960s.

Further, despite dozens of UNGA Resolutions, Pretoria doggedly clung to the apartheid-ideology and Namibia. The armed struggle, mass mobilisation and underground organisation of the African National Congress (ANC) and Pan Africanist Congress were repressed through a barrage of security laws frequently justified as necessary to suppress "terrorists", Marxist/Leninist types and dupes of Moscow. The rising Black Consciousness Movement (BCM) from 1976 onwards, was likewise severely repressed. Under the motto of Total Onslaught and a total national security strategy, the white state moved from resemblances of a police state to a highly militarised state ensconced in a garrison mentality between 1963 and 1989. Only in 1990 after decades of struggle, international pressure (a lot of it initially spearheaded by African countries and the Non-Aligned Movement) led to the mould being broken. Thousands of detentions, the torture and killing of prisoners, and covert operations by shady security forces against activists could not beat the combination of international sanctions, an arms embargo, and boycotts of South African products, diplomatic isolation, disinvestment, mass protest and a limited armed struggle. Things were falling apart; the centre could not hold.

Under manifold pressures and a declining economy in South Africa, the liberation movements were unbanned in 1990 and a lengthy, tension ridden (and sometimes violence filled) period started. The ANC committed itself to negotiations. South Africa saw a negotiated transition to a constitutional state between 1992 and 1996 when the new constitution was accepted. South Africa was finally "free" from colonialism and apartheid, the latter sometimes described as colonialism of a special type. The legacy in terms of human development and education was horrendous and social challenges abounded. The dominant party, the African National Congress, was in government, now facing immense challenges on numerous levels. Thanks to a statesman like President Nelson Mandela, South Africa returned and was welcomed into the international community. Likewise held for Africa, though some states (such as Nigeria and Angola) had some reservations about the new kid on the block.

As pointed out in the chapter on South Africa, various experiments with the economy on a spectrum from (radical) social democratic and liberal capitalism were undertaken. The role and posture of the security and military forces changed to that of a force in a democracy and some levels of civil control over the military were instituted. Whereas under President Mandela's foreign policy was aimed at re-entering the global world and gaining recognition in Africa, foreign policy under President Thabo Mbeki became more directed towards Africa. Mbeki's ideal of an African Renaissance and an African Peer Review Mechanism was welcomed by some and viewed with scepticism by others on the continent. Under the disastrous rule of Zuma, foreign policy got less attention because of internal squabbles, protest against service delivery and expanding corruption; the latter phenomenon to such an extent that some talk about state capture. After the fall of Zuma, President Cyril Ramaphosa indeed inherited a precarious state and society.

South Africa's defence diplomacy remains mainly value driven (conflict resolution and re-construction oriented), favouring negotiation and diplomacy before military force.

The South African Constitution, the White Paper on Defence and the Defence Review mandate stemming from the 1990s direct the functions of the Department of Defence and Military Veterans (DDMV) and the South African National Defence Force (SANDF). Promoting security includes regional security through defence cooperation with the Southern African Development Community (SADC) and to provide capacity for regional and international peace-support operations.

As much as foreign policy and defence diplomacy are closely intertwined, so is the notion of creating conditions for peace. Peace diplomacy is not a common concept but related to defence diplomacy. Peace diplomacy can be seen as the activities associated with peacemaking, peacekeeping and peacebuilding. Arguably, South Africa's current military diplomatic approaches fall within the ambit of peace diplomacy.

Keeping the above in mind, bi- and multilateral involvement by South Africa in peacemaking, governance, development and post-conflict reconstruction processes is taking place in at least 18 countries on the continent. Since 2010, South Africa has participated in several peace-support operations while the philosophy is to maintain a mission-based force. Operational commitments outside the country reflect international and regional cooperation aims and peace support operations.

In discussing South Africa, the African Standby Force (ASF) needs to be mentioned. The greatest obstacle in establishing and maintaining such a force remains finances, followed by coordination and leadership. Streamlining coordination between the militaries of states, regional organisations and the African Union (AU) in terms of dedicated mission-orientated operations will need continuous attention. The challenge is to deliver effectively on expectations without overstretch. This means a long-term national security strategy for South Africa and continuous close alignment with its defence diplomacy to facilitate interaction with partner states. Simultaneously, time frames need to be planned, closely coordinated and adhered to in efforts undertaken in, or by, SADC and the AU/ASF. Within the financial and budgetary constraints and aware of the asymmetric nature of contributing states, a block-by-block approach is necessary, together with a commonly accepted strategy derived from an agreed-upon vision. The military leadership of forces to be deployed for peace missions and/or socio-economic reconstruction or policing need more say on entrée/exit dates and strategies.

Since 2000, Africa has seen roughly 50 peacekeeping operations in 18 countries. Partnership peacekeeping rose in prominence. Peace operations took place both as attempts at conflict resolution and retro-actively after conflict broke out or escalated.

These peace operations were conducted by the UN, AU, EU and the Economic Community of West Africa States (ECOWAS), with the UN as the dominant player. Since the AU increased its involvement in 2003, it has deployed 40,000 peacekeepers in multipartnership or hybrid peacekeeping missions. At any given stage, South Africa contributed close to 3,000 members to peace operations on the continent, thus around ten percent. The reality is that future success will depend on: well-coordinated, planned and executed operations that are cost effective within a definite time frame; to what degree asymmetrical states can contribute to each mission; the effectiveness of civil oversight; and to what extent military leaders have input in deployment strategies, time frames (both 'in' and 'out') versus available funding, material capacity and skilled resources. Most importantly, success will depend on future multistate cooperation within the current budgetary constraints.

To conclude: the transition to a constitutional democracy allowed South Africa to re-enter African and world politics. Between 1990 and 2020 South Africa transformed from a hegemon to benevolent partner on the continent. This new diplomatic posture resulted in a context where the defence diplomacy of South Africa in following foreign policy complemented the country's role as peacemaker and potential agent for change. South Africa's involvement in the region and Africa has carved out a role for the country as a potential peace multiplier.

In terms of the military, the defence posture changed from one of apartheid aggression to a peaceful defence posture. Defence in a democracy was the guideline for the re-professionalisation and reform of the military. Previous liberation movements (non-statutory forces), the militaries from the "independent" homelands and the South African Defence Force (SADF) were integrated while simultaneously demobilisation and rationalisation took place. A Defence Review Process (DRP) was undertaken during 1997/1998 which included civil participation. Since then a second defence review process was undertaken during 2014/2015. Unfortunately, little of the latter review's recommendations were implemented. The arms deal that took place to replace obsolete arms between 1994 and 1999 (navy and air force especially) was controversial. Some suggested that the new arms were far too expensive and more suitable for a military that was threatened by conventional foreign aggression and South Africa had no enemies and hence faced no immediate or conventional threat. The arms deal was also marked by corruption, which marred the process and the image of the military.

It has to be mentioned though that despite severe budget cuts in defence spending, the South African government delivers on its obligations to peacekeeping on the continent. In this sense, as well as involvement with regular military operations with neighbouring states and naval exercises with navies from Western countries, Latin-America and China, South Africa maintains an outward peace-orientated military diplomacy and forms a noticeable part of the southern African and African security architecture.

In terms of foreign diplomacy, South Africa seems to have a balanced approach in keeping bi- and multilateral relations with both East and West as well as African states. Trade relations include the UK, Germany, The Netherlands, France, and Spain as well as India, China and numerous other states in the East. In BRICS, South Africa keeps its contacts including bilateral agreements with Latin-America. In terms of previous "comrades in arms", South Africa maintains strong relations with Cuba and fully supports the Palestinian people's right to self-determination and attaining its freedom from Israeli repression and domination.

The third case study on southern Africa remains both interesting and complex, if not somewhat tragic. Zimbabwe (previously Rhodesia) gained independence in 1980 after a long and brutal liberation struggle (*Chimurenga*) against the minority government of Ian Smith. The country had much potential regarding agriculture and the economy, though small in measure of scale when compared to South Africa. The first Prime Minister, Robert Gabriel Mugabe, was well educated and committed to socialism and preached reconciliation. However, when Mugabe became President he ruled increasingly as a dictator, despite initial promises of reconciliation with former enemies. Josiah Nkomo, an erstwhile partner, was sidelined and eventually ousted in a process that included the killing of thousands of people in western Zimbabwe. Opposition parties were severely restricted. Mugabe's brutal rule received much criticism from the West as well as some African states. Mugabe craved and clung to power until he was removed and replaced by a new ruler, a previous military ally, now turned president. It is clear, however, that the coup-like removal of Mugabe did not open much space for democracy. For the people of Zimbabwe it remains a case of democracy deferred. Some argue that it was not such much Mugabe's economic policy (a mixed economy complemented with socialist jargon) but Mugabe's disastrous personal style, corruption and blatant cronyism that led to the implosion of the Zimbabwean economy. Belated land-reform was implemented without planning and education/training of the incumbent farmers. Land reform was also marked by corruption and cronyism. Senile and intolerant, Mugabe's rule undermined governance and social equality as well as economic growth while he doggedly centralised power and eventually even alienated the military, his strongest support base. Zimbabwe's struggle may have been won for independence, but it is clear the end of a liberation struggle did not mean entrenching democracy. Zimbabwe still faces huge challenges, which some say will hardly be corrected by a new president, an ex-military general who is facing sporadic protest. In terms of our case studies, Zimbabwe remains the "weakest link".

Zimbabwe after the fall of President Mugabe is not yet in a period of transition from authoritarian rule to democracy. The "resignation" of President Mugabe under pressure from the military, the latter stopping short of a coup, does not imply the achievement of a stable or sustainable democracy in the near future. What evolved was a *change-within-government* and not a *regime change*. Democratic transition implies a change from an authoritarian regime to a (more) democratic regime including a change of the previous ruling party (or incumbent political elite) to new incumbents. The notion of transition implies that civil society, following elite-differences within the ruling party, moves with a significant extent into the public space at the moment of transition. In the political stalemate in Zimbabwe, civil society/the public/the civil community went to the streets but were not the main dynamo of the change. The civil community seemed to have been merely supporting the military in their attempt to force Mugabe out of Zimbabwe's power politics. A transition to democracy under current conditions remains remote.

To achieve economic sustainability and democracy remains a major challenge; in short, democracy has been deferred. Space for citizen politics may open up, but it remains to be seen whether the "new"/"old" elite that arose from recent internal differences will allow significant change. Any possible transition to democracy was clearly arrested. The advent of real political transition is marked by deep differences between and within the ruling elite and a relatively ineffectual opposition. Zimbabwe's future is full of both risks and possibilities. Unfortunately, the role of the military which in training and competence is quite professional has been tarnished by Mugabe's rule. In terms of peace operations and the Security Organ for Peace in southern Africa, Zimbabwe remains a factor, albeit not strong.

It seems that southern Africa does however reflect a certain level of stability. One trusts that this will remain so and spread to other African regions less fortunate and plagued by conflict.

In terms of the future, a lot remains to be done in enhancing the African Union's ideals and in arresting intra-state wars. Some of these conflicts are worsened by wars of greed, wars for scarce resources and interstate rivalry. In some cases, foreign intervention worsens the situation, such as France in West-Africa and US attacks through drones in Somalia. Other states have seen more stability and this will hopefully increase. Much will depend on how political leadership deals with these tensions and takes ownership of peacemaking and peacebuilding on the continent while distancing themselves from those core countries that intervene in African affairs (in the case of France, numerous examples exist over the past decades).

"The East"

There are some continuing regional and global issues that are likely to dominate the politics of Asia in the years to come. The election of American President Donald Trump forced Asia to confront a new reality. The 'America First' doctrine along with Trump's policies towards Iran and North Korea, his efforts to redefine America's role in NATO and the Indo-Pacific region and the trade war with China brought in new uncertainties. America's role in Syria and Iran has had spillover effects on the order in the West Asian region. Secondly, several of the large Asian economies have felt the impact of the global slowdown. This slowdown has been compounded with the US-China trade war. In some cases, like India, it would have an adverse impact on the process of government's reform agenda.

Third, is the increasingly assertive posture that China has started to take in the South China Sea and the Indian Ocean region. It is making efforts to create a footprint in the littoral states of the Indian Ocean with the Belt and Road initiative and close ties with Pakistan in the form of China Pakistan Economic Corridor. On one hand, the Chinese investments in infrastructure development have been welcomed; however, on the other hand, the Asian countries have started to realise the implications of their inability to repay the loans. In the case of Sri Lanka, for example, the agreement with state-owned China Merchants Port Holdings to lease 70 percent stake of the strategically-located Hambantota port may plunge Sri Lanka further into the Chinese debt trap with Colombo turning to Beijing for fresh loans. In Myanmar, opposition to Chinese-backed projects is mounting due to a feeling that China is only interested in exploiting their natural resources. Myanmar has already suspended the Myitsone dam development in northern Myanmar.

Terrorism continues to dominate the discourse on peace and stability. The dimension of Islamic State in its various manifestations, especially the intrusive cross-border nature of Islamic terror continues to be a source of concern. This is seen in the context of Pakistan's policies in Kashmir and India's refusal to negotiate with the separatist elements in the state. The complex battles in Syria that has witnessed several countries participating in the struggle, either for or against the Assad government or fight against the Islamic State are a part of this complexity. In Afghanistan, the Taliban continues to dominate the discourse on approach to peace and stability in the war-torn country.

While climate change has been on the global agenda, there is little sympathy for the Western activists who have promoted this agenda. These Asian economies are still in the process of industrialisation and need the use of natural resources like coal and oil. In terms of the BRICS forum, BRICS is growing slowly and has seen some radical changes in Brazil and India and much depends on how these modes of cooperation will evolve. There is little doubt that a growing BRICS can contribute to a better future for many on the globe. However, managing broader BRICS cooperation and increasing its influence will require wise and prudent leadership in the years to come. One may speculate that with Russia taking over the Chairmanship, more activity may arise and it will depend on how such interaction evolves.

What would be the drivers that dominate the regional scene in Asia in the years to come? At the regional level, the ongoing conflict in the Middle East is likely to dominate the security agenda in the years to come. The aspirations of Iran to be recognised as a major actor in the region have brought it in direct confrontation with the traditional balance of forces dominated by Saudi Arabia. Iran's skirmishes through its non-state allies in Lebanon, Yemen and Iraq and the counter moves by the US and Saudi Arabia are likely to continue over a period of time. In South Asia, India's concerns regarding cross-border terrorism from Pakistan are now being tackled by it in a more aggressive military posture. The continuing dominance of the military establishment in the new government of Pakistan means that this issue will fester in the coming years. This Indian assertive policy is also seen against Chinese intrusions along the border. Sri Lankan politics is yet to settle down.

The elections in Sri Lanka have thrown up new challenges of reconciliation between the Sinhalese majority and the Tamil minority. The Rohingya issue in Myanmar has seen a clash between the idea of national interest as interpreted by Myanmar's establishment and the proponents of human rights. American reluctance to play a dominant role in the Indo-Pacific region and a growing concern about China means that the regional powers are likely to enter into new security arrangements. Japan and Australia, actors that previously avoided active participation in the politics of Asia, are now shifting their priorities. The years to come promise a turbulent time for Asia.

Conclusion

Current global developments are interconnected. Some powers rise while others decline. During the last three American presidential terms, especially that of Trump, relations within the NATO military treaty seem to have become one of increasingly strange bedfellows ('global partners'), one may argue. Is Trump's defence policy altering the entire world system of alignments, treaties and military and diplomatic conventions? Some would argue that under Trump the US is becoming more predictable, namely one can foresee an increasingly aggressive posture willing to export violence thousands of kilometres outside the US. Others may argue that the US has become more unpredictable. The same may, however, apply to a host of other international actors.

Will other NATO countries continue to tolerate Trump's one-sided actions and his paternalistic approach to the "smaller" NATO partners? Future developments here may be interesting as it is clear that relations are growing rather tense as different interests and views of a peaceful world amongst NATO members seem to diverge. An increasing aggressive policy by the USA, partly driven by the insecurities around its economic decline, may alienate other European partners that more and more seem to work on other constructive means to temper international conflicts.

Other powers are rising, some alliances slip away and new ones are formed. What will evolve on the global defence terrain with increasingly important international actors such as Brasilia, India, China, North Korea, Turkey and Iran? While one hegemon declines, other states may play a role in a multipolar world or a new hegemon may arise.

Is this the end of the beginning or the beginning of the end? Indeed, we face a tense future and a problematic if not potentially dangerous/disastrous changing world order as globalisation and de-globalisation seem to become intertwined phenomena. Only time can tell as historical and contemporary political and military permutations evolve.

The Editors

Notes

1. Skype interview with Professor Vladimir Shubin, 24 January 2020.
2. https://countrymeters.info/en/World [Accessed 6 January 2020].
3. Gerardo Hernández and Carlos-Alfonso Romero-Arias, 'La Guardia Nacional y la militarización de la seguridad pública en México', *URVIO Revista Latinoamericana de Estudios de Seguridad 25*, July-December 2019. https://doi.org/10.17141/urvio.25.2019.3995 [Accessed 8 January 2020].

Index

A

African National Congress (ANC) 101, 118, 119, 271, 272
African Union (AU) 8, 14, 101-103, 107, 109, 112, 113, 116-120, 122, 139, 140, 148, 155, 158, 160, 166-168, 172, 179, 182, 214, 273, 276
African Union's Peace and Security Council 120, 167
aggression 27, 69, 106, 131, 135, 136, 139, 182, 190, 245, 247, 265, 274, 278
alienation 8, 12, 128, 141, 142, 145, 146, 265
Anglo-Boer War 271
Angola 10, 72, 76, 79, 101, 102, 106, 112, 115, 116, 151, 155, 157, 159, 160, 166, 168, 174, 175, 184, 192, 193, 269, 270, 272
anti-colonialism 4, 192, 269
apartheid 4, 7, 8, 12, 101-107, 109, 118, 127, 131, 142, 143, 145-147, 159, 192, 193, 268-272, 274
Argentina 6, 7, 21, 23, 25, 35-37, 39-43, 74, 81, 94, 172, 266
armed struggle 105, 269, 271, 272
asymmetric warfare 7, 8, 253
Australia 5, 157, 208, 211, 224, 225, 230, 231, 251, 255, 259, 278
authoritarianism 145, 194
authoritarian rule 118, 145, 186, 266, 275
authoritarian state 7, 185, 186

B

balance of forces 277
balance of power 35, 266
Beijing 174, 190, 191, 193, 196, 202, 212, 277
bipolarity 4, 106, 189, 256
Boer Republics 271
border disputes 43
Botha, P.W. 270
Botswana 114, 115, 155, 157, 166, 167, 169, 172, 183, 184, 214, 269, 270
Brazil 6, 11, 13, 15-30, 35-37, 39, 40, 43, 55, 59, 60, 74, 78, 81, 91, 92, 94, 108, 155, 157, 159, 162, 170, 172, 174, 195, 215, 230, 231, 265-268, 277
BRICS 10, 195-197, 250, 259, 266, 274, 277
Britain 1, 2, 4, 6, 35-37, 74, 107, 155, 192, 210, 211, 214, 223, 233, 247, 266, 269, 271
British empire 2

C

Canada 59, 73, 76, 81, 105, 155, 159, 197, 224
capitalism 3, 6, 128, 192, 194, 195, 268, 272
Castro, Fidel 69, 70, 72-75, 78, 79, 81, 87, 269
Castro, Raúl 70, 76-78, 81
Central Intelligence Agency (CIA) 57, 71, 75, 106, 193
Che Guevara 69, 74, 75
Chile 6, 7, 23, 25, 33, 35-46, 57, 60, 61, 73, 81, 94, 223, 224, 266, 267
China (People's Republic of China [PRC]) 2-5, 7, 10, 11, 14, 44, 60, 87, 91, 93, 104, 107, 108, 131, 145, 147, 155, 157, 158, 162, 163, 170, 172, 174, 175, 189-203, 208-210, 212, 213, 215, 216, 224, 225, 230, 231, 233, 235, 244-247, 250, 253-256, 259, 260, 265-267, 270, 274, 276-278
Christianity 9, 88, 103, 145
citizens 11, 18, 78, 88, 90, 103, 128, 132, 134, 135, 140, 144, 145, 163, 210, 213, 269
civilian population 7, 90
civil war 2, 75, 82, 131, 159, 184, 189, 190, 211, 230
climate change 3, 38, 45, 129, 141, 277
Cold War 4, 6, 7, 14, 43, 57, 68, 69, 76, 106-108, 127, 128, 147, 158, 160, 180-182, 189, 191-193, 199, 207, 210, 211, 216, 240, 243, 244, 249, 254, 256, 258, 259, 265, 266, 269
Colombia 6, 21, 23-25, 36, 49-64, 74, 79, 80, 91, 94, 267
colonialism 2, 4, 6, 159, 268, 270, 272

communism 3, 4, 6, 30, 52, 70, 75, 102-104, 106, 189-194, 201, 212, 269
communist 2, 131
compromise 209, 258, 271
conflict 1, 2, 4, 5, 8, 9, 11-15, 29, 34-39, 41, 43-45, 49, 50, 54, 61, 62, 75, 91, 93, 101-103, 106-109, 111, 112, 114, 115, 120, 121, 128, 132, 135, 137, 141, 142, 146, 156, 160, 164, 166-168, 181, 182, 207, 208, 210, 214, 217, 218, 222, 223, 230, 243-247, 253-256, 258, 260, 265, 266, 269, 270, 272, 273, 276-278
conflict resolution 34, 37, 108, 109, 112, 114, 121, 167, 258, 272, 273
constitutional state 131, 137-139, 269, 270, 272
constructive engagement (USA) 269, 270
counterinsurgency 49-51, 54, 56-62, 64, 70, 79, 167, 211
covert operations 272
Cuba 3, 6, 40, 64, 67-82, 87-89, 91-93, 97, 101, 107, 108, 157, 268, 269, 274
Cuban diplomacy 68, 73
Cuban Revolution 6, 64, 68

D

deployment of forces 118
detention 105, 271
development 3, 4, 6, 12-15, 20-22, 26-29, 40-44, 67, 68, 71, 76, 78, 89, 101-103, 105-109, 111, 112, 123, 128, 130, 134, 136, 138, 140, 142, 143, 149, 155, 159, 161, 163-166, 171, 172, 174, 177, 184, 187-190, 192-197, 199, 220, 226, 227, 233, 239-248, 250-254, 265, 266, 269-271, 275, 276
diplomacy 1, 2, 4, 8-16, 20, 22, 24, 25, 29, 38, 67, 69, 70, 72-74, 76, 77, 80, 81, 87, 91, 92, 101-104, 108, 109, 111-114, 117-123, 127, 131, 135, 137-139, 155-157, 160, 163-168, 171-173, 179-186, 190, 192, 201, 202, 207-212, 215-218, 221, 241, 245, 247, 250, 256, 259, 265, 270, 272-274
diplomacy of isolation (South Africa) 104

E

economic decline 268, 278
economic interest 118, 22

economy 4, 67, 71, 76, 77, 81, 87-90, 93, 96-98, 102, 121, 122, 143, 163, 165, 166, 170, 172, 185, 192, 194, 197-201, 222, 225, 240, 250, 268, 272, 275
Egypt 1, 7, 55, 120, 157, 169, 170, 218, 223, 265
Euro-socialism 3

F

FARC (Revolutionary Armed Forces of Colombia) 21, 25, 55, 80, 267
force projection 7, 111
foreign policy 2-4, 8-16, 19, 20, 24, 33, 40, 41, 69, 72, 92, 101, 102, 106-111, 115, 118-123, 146, 147, 155-160, 172, 173, 179-182, 185, 190, 193, 202, 209, 210, 215, 240, 241, 249, 253, 259, 272-274
fragmentation 8, 12, 128, 265
France 1, 2, 6-9, 14, 59, 61, 64, 74, 91, 105, 119, 121, 157, 159, 174, 192, 201, 202, 211, 215, 251, 255, 259, 266, 268, 274, 276
frontline states (FLS) 101, 106, 158

G

genocide 117, 119
German West Africa 104
Giap 3
globalisation 3, 6, 8, 12, 33, 38, 128, 195, 197, 265, 278
global order 22, 108, 110, 249
global policeman 11
global security 41
Global South 4, 6, 9, 10, 12, 67, 78, 189, 192, 194, 265
gold 94, 95, 225, 230, 271
guerrilla warfare 52, 77

H

hegemonic
    aspirations 243
    enterprise 107
    interests 7
    powers 11, 115, 259, 268
    states 9, 12
    struggles 12
    terrorism 12
hegemons 8, 11, 101, 102, 107, 110, 121, 123, 189, 201, 202, 274, 278

hegemons (regional) 110, 189, 201
hegemony 6, 8, 11, 12, 15, 106, 196, 200
Hindu 218, 243, 255, 261
human rights 3, 7, 40, 63, 109, 120, 121, 166, 185, 194, 231, 249, 268, 278

I

independence 2, 4, 5, 34, 35, 68, 74, 89, 96, 104, 105, 110, 128, 155, 157-160, 165, 170, 172, 173, 175, 185, 189, 193, 207, 208, 210, 214, 233, 243-245, 258, 268-271, 275
independence wars 89
India 2-5, 10, 11, 14, 104, 107, 145, 147, 155, 157, 169, 170, 172-174, 184, 190, 195, 199, 201, 207-218, 221, 224-226, 228-236, 239-261, 265, 266, 274, 276-278
insurgency 58, 60, 70, 80, 246, 249, 256
interstate wars 127, 182
intra-state wars 276
Iran 5, 9, 107, 108, 157, 213, 259, 265, 276-278
Iraq 5, 7, 148, 196, 215, 249, 265, 277
Islam 9, 190, 196, 277
Islamic State (IS) 196, 277
Israel 5, 7, 12, 55, 60, 72, 81, 107, 147, 255, 274
(apartheid) Israel 12
Italy 1, 3, 155, 214

J

Japan 2, 5, 6, 11, 44, 131, 190, 201, 211, 215, 216, 246, 255, 259, 265, 278

K

Kashmir 2, 245, 247, 249, 256, 258, 259, 277
Kenya 120, 158, 169
Korea 51, 54, 63, 103, 190
Korean War 5, 51, 191, 244

L

Lesotho 113-115, 151, 169, 175, 182, 184
liberation movements 4, 67, 72, 75, 80, 106, 157, 158, 189, 193, 272, 274
liberation struggles 5, 68, 155-158, 173, 183, 193, 268, 275
Liberia 79, 104, 105, 175, 202, 214
Libya 7, 8, 107, 108, 148, 157, 215

M

Malaysia 5, 213, 256
Mandela, Nelson 101, 102, 107-109, 114, 115, 121, 149, 272
Mao Zedong 3, 190, 193
maritime patrol 27, 152
maritime power 197, 198, 209
military power 1, 9, 11, 14, 106, 110, 140, 146, 197, 206, 207, 210, 213, 241, 256
Marxism 3, 4, 73, 191
Marxism-Leninism 3, 4, 191
media 9, 119, 142, 145, 161
Middle East 5, 7, 8, 12, 44, 68, 78, 145, 196, 197, 201, 236, 266, 277
military operations 52, 54, 55, 59, 77, 133, 135, 198, 247, 274
military posture 155, 165, 198, 210, 268, 277
military power 1, 9, 11, 14, 106, 110, 140, 146, 199, 208, 209, 212, 215, 243, 258
military reform 55
military rule 267
modernisation 4, 6, 59, 111, 113, 139, 171, 191, 194, 198, 245, 246, 249, 252, 256
Moscow 4, 69, 71, 191, 254, 269-271
Mozambique 72, 79, 116, 151, 169, 170, 184, 185, 193, 214
multipolarity 7, 11, 127, 189, 201-203, 278
Myanmar 242, 257, 258, 277, 278

N

Namibia 4, 79, 101, 102, 104-106, 112, 115, 116, 155-175, 182, 184, 185, 214, 269-271
negotiated settlement 8, 115, 121, 131
neo-colonialism 4
neo-imperialism 4
Nigeria 10, 120, 157, 158, 169, 170, 214, 265, 266, 268, 269, 272
Non-Aligned Movement (NAM) 3, 4, 104, 105, 107, 108, 158-160, 189, 195, 201, 270, 271
North Africa 7
North Atlantic Treaty Organization (NATO) 11, 14, 191, 208, 276, 278

North Korea (Democratic People's Republic of Korea [DPRK]) 3, 5, 44, 147, 157, 170, 175, 270, 276, 278
nuclear arms 147
nuclear war 147
nuclear weapons 147, 246, 250-252, 260

P

peace agreements 25, 80, 267
peace deployments 201
peace diplomacy 80, 102, 108, 273
peacekeeping 39, 60, 102, 103, 111, 112, 114, 116, 127, 139, 140, 147, 150, 155, 168, 169, 181, 184, 199, 201, 202, 207, 210, 214, 247, 253, 273, 274
peacemaking 102, 108, 109, 111, 115, 139, 172, 174, 273, 274, 276
peace operations 22, 41, 114, 120, 133, 148, 182, 273, 276
peace-support operations 121, 272, 273
Peru 6, 23-25, 35-37, 41, 43, 57, 59, 60, 64, 73, 81, 89, 94, 223, 266, 267
political Christianity 9
Portugal 1, 3, 15, 17, 18, 20-23, 26-28, 57, 106, 158, 190, 192, 193, 269
poverty 9, 10, 89, 92-94, 129, 140, 142, 143, 197, 270
power balance 246
Pretoria 4, 7, 101, 103-105, 270, 271
proxy wars 265, 269

R

Reagan, Ronald 73, 269
reconstruction 71, 76, 78, 102, 103, 109, 111, 112, 197, 273
revolution 3, 6, 9, 64, 68, 74, 81, 90, 191, 198, 224
Rhodesia 191, 275
right-wing extremism 145
right-wing military leaders 266
Russia 3, 7, 8, 11, 21, 77, 87, 91, 93, 108, 145, 147, 170, 195, 199-201, 208, 211, 215, 224, 225, 230, 250, 255, 265, 266, 270, 277

S

sanctions 68, 73, 104, 105, 256, 272
scarce resources 8-10, 76, 141, 146-148, 229, 276
Scotland 266
Security Council (United Nations) 39, 104, 105, 110, 115-117, 158, 170, 175, 202, 210, 265, 266, 270
security forces 106, 133, 217, 272
security interest 118, 164, 166, 216
security policy 128, 164, 172, 180, 208, 239, 244, 245, 250, 257
silent diplomacy 76
social engineering 271
Socialist bloc 76, 77, 80
soft diplomacy 192
South Africa 3, 7, 10, 79, 101-123, 127-149, 151, 152, 155, 159, 160, 162, 166, 168-170, 172, 173, 182-184, 192, 193, 195, 215, 224, 266, 269-275
South African Defence Force (SADF) 101, 106, 168, 274
South African National Defence Force (SANDF) 109-114, 116-118, 122, 128, 130-139, 148-152, 272
South African War 271
South America 13, 15, 16, 20-25, 28, 29, 33-38, 42, 43, 60, 81, 92, 214
Southern Africa 72, 109, 128, 133, 138, 139, 164, 172, 173, 179, 182
South Korea 211, 216
South West Africa 104, 105, 162, 173, 270
Soviet Union 4, 5, 67-69, 71, 76, 77, 80, 191, 192, 199, 210, 245, 246, 249, 269
space programmes 200, 255, 267
Spain 1, 6, 49, 55-57, 60, 63, 64, 68, 79, 90, 91, 94, 95, 146, 274
Sri Lanka 175, 209-212, 217, 246, 277, 278
state security 97, 180
state terror 9, 12
state terrorism 7
Syria 72, 218, 276, 277

T

Tanzania 4, 151, 156, 157, 166, 167, 169, 172, 184, 192, 268

terrorism 7, 12, 13, 63, 73, 129, 145, 146, 148, 166, 183, 213, 215, 249, 254, 259, 277

torture 52, 271

transition 1, 7, 101-103, 106, 108, 110, 121, 136, 138, 143-145, 155, 160, 186, 266, 267, 272, 274-276

transition through negotiation 121

transition to democracy 101, 110, 143, 160, 186, 266, 267, 275, 276

U

Uganda 7, 78, 158, 169, 268

Union of South Africa 269, 271

Union of Soviet Socialist Republics (USSR) 4, 157, 201, 210

United Kingdom (UK) 7, 8, 14, 21, 36, 60, 61, 64, 105, 108, 121, 148, 157, 159, 172, 193, 202, 208, 215, 246, 251, 266, 274

United Nations 39, 73, 101, 102, 117, 139, 155, 157, 158, 166-170, 184, 201, 210, 253, 265, 266, 270

United Nations General Assembly (UNGA) 81, 158, 270, 271

United States of America (US/USA) 4-9, 11, 12, 14, 15, 20-25, 29, 33-42, 46, 51-62, 64, 67-70, 73-82, 88, 89, 91, 92, 94, 97, 105-108, 121, 127, 145, 146, 148, 149, 155, 159, 169, 172, 191-194, 196-202, 208, 210, 211, 214-216, 223-226, 230, 231, 236, 245-247, 250, 251, 254-256, 259, 265-270, 276-278

uranium 225, 227

V

Venezuela 21, 23-25, 29, 41, 64, 70, 73, 76, 78-82, 87-98, 267, 268

Vietnam 3, 213, 265

W

West Africa 8, 9, 79, 104, 105, 156, 162, 173, 269, 270, 273

Western colonialism 6, 268

Windhoek 163, 170, 172-175

Z

Zambia 4, 151, 155, 157, 166, 169, 192, 268, 269

Zimbabwe 112, 115, 116, 121, 151, 155, 157, 166, 168, 169, 179-186, 193, 268, 275, 276

Contributing Authors

TOBIE BEUKES holds a PhD in Political Science from Stellenbosch University (SU), South Africa. He is a senior researcher at the Centre for Military Studies (CEMIS), Faculty of Military Science, Stellenbosch University. His research interests are numerous and he published amongst others on private military/security companies and corruption in state and society. The Faculty of Military Science is associated with the South African Military Academy (SAMA), an all-forces tertiary institution of the South African National Defence Force (SANDF) based at Saldanha, South Africa.

ANDRÉ DU PISANI is Emeritus Professor of Politics at the University of Namibia (UNAM). He has published widely on security, democratic theory, Namibian politics and the political economy of the South African Development Community (SADC). He has been engaged in the work of the Southern African Defence and Security Network (SADSEM) since its founding in 2001. André is a published poet, photographer and researcher in rock art in Namibia.

RAYMOND STEENKAMP FONSECA (PhD) is a senior lecturer in the Department of Political Science, Faculty of Military Science, Stellenbosch University, and former editor of *Scientia Militaria*. He regularly lectures on international security, geopolitics and international political economy at the South African National Defence College, Military Academy, and Naval Staff College. [orcid: 0000-0002-9834-8528]

DIRK KRUIJT is Professor Emeritus of Development Studies at the Faculty of Social Sciences, Utrecht University; Research Fellow at the Centre for Military Studies (CEMIS), Faculty of Military Science, Stellenbosch University, and Investigador Integrado Centro de Estudos Internacionais (CEI), Instituto Universitário de Lisboa (ISCTE – IUL). He has conducted extensive fieldwork in Latin America and the Caribbean. His research interests are civil-military relations, guerrilla movements, ethnic and class conflicts, urban violence, social exclusion and informality. He recently published the book *Cuba and Revolutionary Latin America. An Oral History* (2017) and was co-editor (with Kees Koonings and Dennis Rodgers) of *Ethnography as Risky Business: Field Research in Violent and Sensitive Contexts* (2019). [orcid: 0000-0001-8488-965X]

AJEY LELE is a senior fellow at the Manohar Parrikar Institute for Defence Studies and Analyses (IDSA), New Delhi. He has obtained a Master's in Physics and a Master's and MPhil in Defence and Strategic Studies. He completed his doctorate at the School of International Studies, Jawaharlal Nehru University (JNU), New Delhi. His specific areas of research include issues related to weapons of mass destruction (WMD), space security, and strategic technologies. He publishes widely and authored various works. [orcid: 0000-0003-4152-572X]

IAN LIEBENBERG is an Associate Professor and Director of the Centre for Military Studies (CEMIS) at the Faculty of Military Science, Stellenbosch University. He previously worked at the Institute for Democracy in South Africa (IDASA) as Director Research, the Human Sciences Research Council of South Africa (HSRC) as senior analyst and lectured in sociology at the University of South Africa (Unisa). He edited and co-edited fifteen works and wrote more than a 100 articles some translated in Russian, German and Dutch. He contributed to numerous reports between 1998 and 2018 and is editor of *A Far-Away War: Angola, 1976-1988*. His research interests include auto-ethnography, the Angolan War, Southern African politics and liberation struggles. [orcid: 0000-0003-0351-9476]

SADIKI MAERESERA holds a PhD in Political Science from the University of KwaZulu-Natal in South Africa. He is a research fellow at the Institute of Strategic Research and Analysis, Zimbabwe National Defense University. He is also a visiting lecturer in National Security and Geopolitics at the School of Military Science, University of Namibia, and the Department of Politics and Public Management at Midlands State University in Zimbabwe. [orcid: 0000-0001-8000-2062]

ADRIANA A. MARQUES holds a PhD in Political Science from University of São Paulo (Brazil). She was a graduate research fellow at Brown University and at Getulio Vargas Foundation and was former Executive Secretary (2012-2014) and Vice-President (2014-2016) of the Brazilian Defense Studies Association. She is an assistant professor at Federal University of Rio de Janeiro teaching in Defense and International Strategic Management. She is associated with the Laboratory of Security and Defense Studies. Her areas of research are defence studies, civil-military relations and strategic culture. [orcid: 0000-0002-3794-3358]

RAHUL ANAND MASLEKAR served in the Indian Air Force as a helicopter pilot. He was part of the Indian Peacekeeping Force in Sri Lanka and the United Nations Peacekeeping Mission in the Democratic Republic of Congo. He formed part of the Senior Directing Staff at the Indian Defence Services Staff College and Army War College. He holds a PhD from the University of Mumbai with his thesis on the role of *Indian Military Diplomacy in African Nation Building Processes*. He has published widely in international and professional journals.

TORQUE MUDE holds a PhD in International Politics from the University of South Africa. He is a senior lecturer of international relations in the Department of Politics and Public Management at Midlands State University in Zimbabwe, and a visiting lecturer in Security and Strategic Studies at the School of Military Science, University of Namibia. His specific areas of research include international relations theory, peace and security, international law and global political economy. [orcid: 0000-0002-9885-6637]

JACINTHO MAIA NETO holds a PhD in Administration from Getulio Vargas Foundation (Rio de Janeiro, Brazil). He was a career officer in the Brazilian Army and Attaché of Defense and Army in the Kingdoms of Spain and Morocco (2012-2014) as well as Head of the Army Center for Strategic Studies. He is currently an assistant professor at the Brazilian War College and research associate at the Laboratory of Security and Defense Studies from the Federal University of Rio de Janeiro. His work relates to Defence Management and Strategic Studies, with the main foci on military transformation, hybrid warfare and the impact of security and defence agendas on Strategic Defence Management. [orcid: 0000-0001-5694-448X]

SHRIKANT PARANJPE is currently Honorary Adjunct Professor in the Department of Defence and Strategic Studies, Savitribai Phule Pune University, Pune, India. He was a Jawaharlal Nehru National Fellow (ICSSR) and Professor in the Department of Defence and Strategic Studies, and

Director Yashwantrao Chavan National Centre of International Security and Defence Analysis (YCNISDA), Savitribai Phule Pune University. He was a Fulbright Fellow (postdoctoral, Research) at the George Washington University, Washington, DC, and a visiting professor at Colorado College, Colorado Springs. He published several books and articles in the area of security studies and international relations. [orcid: 0000-0001-8899-4262]

SHADRACK B. RAMOKGADI is a researcher at the Centre for Military Studies (CEMIS), the research wing of the Faculty of Military Science, Stellenbosch University. Ramokgadi has conducted research in the field of defence administration with a focus on complex emergencies and humanitarian response capabilities in Southern Africa. His research has been presented at international and national conferences and was published in conference proceedings and accredited international and national journals and chapters to books. [orcid: 0000-0002-8791-6809]

FRANCISCO ROJAS holds a PhD in Political Science from the University of Utrecht. He is currently Rector of the University for Peace and former Secretary General of Flacso (2012-2014). [orcid: 0000-0002-0328-8156]

JUSTIN VAN DER MERWE is a senior researcher with a DPhil Geography and the Environment (Oxon), an MPhil Political Management (SU), and a BA Political Science and Sociology (SU). Justin is a seasoned researcher with specific interests in International Political Economy and Geography. His recent publications focus on the political economy of underdevelopment in the Global South, emerging powers in Africa, the One Belt One Road initiative, and BRICS and social resistance in Africa. Connect with him via Linkedin or Academia.edu.

MANUELA TRINDADE VIANA is an Adjunct Professor in the Institute of International Relations (IRI) at the Pontifical Catholic University of Rio de Janeiro (PUC Rio), where she coordinates the Undergraduate Programme in International Relations. She holds a PhD in International Politics from IRI PUC Rio, Brazil. She is senior researcher at the BRICS Policy Center where she coordinates with Professor Isabel Rocha a research project on the security-development nexus in Latin America. She is a Research Fellow in the Centre for Military Studies (CEMIS), Stellenbosch, South Africa, and a senior researcher in the Global South Unit for Mediation. [orcid: 0000-0003-2243-358X]

ANDRÉS VILLAR holds a PhD in Politics and International Studies from the University of Cambridge. Currently he lectures at the Political Science Department, School of Social Sciences and History, Universidad Diego Portales. [orcid: 0000-0002-9511-9017]

www.ingramcontent.com/pod-product-compliance
Lightning Source LLC
Chambersburg PA
CBHW080223170426
43192CB00015B/2726